Old English
An Introduction ———————————————————

Old English
An Introduction —————

Robert J. Kispert
*University of Illinois
at Chicago Circle*

HOLT, RINEHART AND WINSTON, INC.
*New York   Chicago   San Francisco   Atlanta
Dallas   Montreal   Toronto   London   Sydney*

Grateful acknowledgement is made to:

Penguin Books Ltd., for use of extracts from
    *Bede: A History of the English Church and
    People,* translated by Leo Sherley-Price.
The University of Chicago and Collins Publishers,
    for use of extracts from *Alfred the Great*
    by Eleanor Shipley Duckett. Copyright © 1956
    by The University of Chicago.

Preface

    This book is intended as a text for an introductory course in Old English, either on the advanced undergraduate or graduate level. I have, accordingly, endeavored to set forth the grammar of Old English as comprehensively as possible within the scope of such a book, to provide reading selections, along with preliminary remarks, that reveal something of Anglo-Saxon history and society, and, in later chapters, to present a modicum of correlative material that will, I hope, enhance the student's appreciation of his subject by extending his knowledge of it in various directions.

    A commentator on the national language of Anglo-Saxon England is obliged, by the nature of the surviving documents, to confine himself almost exclusively to late West Saxon, and the emphasis here is therefore upon that variety of Old English. Apart from the substitution of *w* for the Anglo-Saxon letter *wynn*, the use of the macron to indicate long vowels, the use of *ċ* and *ġ* as guides to pronunciation, and the imposition of modern punctuational devices in the reading selections and illustrative examples, no attempts at normalization have been made. To recast late West Saxon texts into some standardized form, the basis for which has often been the dialect of King Alfred, does indeed have the pleasing result of suppressing orthographical irregularities, but it leaves the student who has mastered the essentials of Old English by means of normalized paradigms and texts with the problem of adjusting his concept of the language to the configuration of it which he may later encounter in an edition like Klaeber's *Beowulf* or *The Anglo-Saxon Poetic Records* by Krapp and Dobbie. Surely the burden of learning to recognize the identity, for example, of *hīe, hȳ,* and *hī* is never very great in context even when the acquisition of Old English is in progress and partial. The reading selections in this grammar are, consequently, derived from a collocation of standard editions, with all permitted fidelity to what was originally written being considered a desideratum. Variant forms are cross-listed in the Glossary, where, incidentally, pertinent etymological data will also be found.

My approach to the grammar of late West Saxon is not innovative; traditional categories have been retained, as well as long established terminology. I have rather consistently viewed Old English as one subsequent development of Indo-European and Proto-Germanic, and, on occasion, as the precursor of Modern English. Although I have recommended the memorization of several key paradigms, I have not advocated any specific technique for teaching the grammar; any instructor will know well enough how he wishes to proceed.

As noted above, the reading selections are intended to illumine a historical period about which a beginning student of Old English may not be very closely informed. In Chapters 5 through 14 the readings, from the standpoint of their content, have been arranged in chronological order, and, for that reason, the relatively easy biographical sketch of William the Conqueror appears after the less simple prose of Wulfstan, instead of earlier in the book.

It is a genuine pleasure to thank Harriette Blechman and Priscilla VanHaverbeke of Holt, Rinehart and Winston for their most efficient and congenial assistance in the preparation of this book. My debt to previous grammarians is manifestly so great that footnotes alone cannot be an adequate recompense. In particular, I should like to acknowledge my constant reliance upon A. Campbell, *Old English Grammar;* S. Moore and T. Knott, *The Elements of Old English;* E. Prokosch, *A Comparative Germanic Grammar;* R. Quirk and C. L. Wrenn, *An Old English Grammar;* and J. Wright, *Old English Grammar.* If I have erred in my explication of Old English, the fault does not reside in any source consulted.

Chicago, Illinois   **R.J.K.**
October 1970

Contents

Chapter 4   32

Chapter 5   39

Chapter 6   47

Chapter 7   57

Chapter 8   68

Chapter 9   78

Chapter 1

Introduction

1.1   *Old English*   As a general term of linguistic denotation, *Old English* applies to several Low Germanic (West Ingvaeonic) dialects that were brought to the British Isles in the century between c.450–c.550 AD by three groups of Continental invaders: Angles, Saxons, and Jutes. The European homelands from which they migrated are not known precisely, but it is quite probable that the Angles came from what is now Schleswig-Holstein (Germany), and the Saxons from a region to the south and west, between the Elbe and the Ems. A somewhat shadowy people until their arrival in Britain, the Jutes may have come from an area on the Danish peninsula of Jutland, north of the Angles, or from the country east of the lower Rhine; in some particulars, Jutish culture does seem to have been influenced by an exposure to that of the Rhenish Franks. The degree of linguistic differentiation among the three peoples cannot have been very great; to judge by later records, any limitation on mutual intelligibility was doubtless insignificant. Not attested by manuscript or inscription until about 700 AD, Old English had somewhat earlier achieved the status of a vernacular throughout an area roughly equivalent to modern England and southeastern Scotland; it is, therefore, convenient to use the qualifying designation *Proto-Old English* (abbreviated POE) when reference is made to what can be determined about the nature of Old English during the period (450–700) before the appearance of written evidence. POE forms are conventionally cited with an asterisk (e.g., POE *hēarjan* 'to hear', but OE *hīeran* 'to hear') to indicate their hypothetical validity; this is a device traditional in historical linguistics for all recon-

1

structions. Like every language and dialect Old English was a human institution, a form of social behavior, and, as such, susceptible to modification by its speakers; it is, consequently, no surprise to discover phonological, morphological, and syntactical changes manifested in documents that derive from a span of some four hundred years (700–1100). The word *hȳran,* for example, is a later form of *hīeran,* and, to select another, *lēoht,* the noun 'light', is likewise a later form of *līoht;* in view of many similar shifts in pronunciation and spelling, the terms *Early Old English* (eOE) and *Late Old English* (lOE) serve to distinguish the periods 700–900 and 900–1100 respectively. Linguistic alteration is inexorable, and a given language may, as a result of considerable "revision," be accorded a different appellation for the purpose of more accurate description. By 1100 the dialects of the Germanic invaders had undergone internal modifications so radical that *Middle English* is used to mark the second major phase in the development of what was to become contemporary British and American English. Middle English lasted until approximately 1500, when a further accumulation of changes compels the historian of English to speak of the language as *Early Modern English;* from 1700 to the present the language is known as *Recent Modern English.*

1.2   *West Saxon* In this grammar *Old English* will have sole reference to the principal dialect of Anglo-Saxon England, namely West Saxon, which owes its supremacy not to any intrinsic merit, but, rather, to extra-linguistic circumstances that raised the kingdom of Wessex to a position of considerable political and cultural importance. On the authority of the *Anglo-Saxon Chronicle,* 787 was the year in which Vikings, primarily Danes, initiated their plundering raids upon Britain; ninety years later, and by virtue of conquest, they controlled the major portion of eastern England. They were prevented, however, from annexing even more territory by Alfred the Great, king of the West Saxons (871–899). who, in 878, after a series of indecisive battles with the Danes, mustered a force strong enough to defeat the enemy at Ethandrum (now Edington, in Wiltshire) by means of a sudden attack. Having capitulated, the Danish leader, Guthrum, concluded the Treaty of Wedmore (near Glastonbury) with Alfred, in which the former agreed not only to become a Christian, but also to withdraw from Alfred's kingdom (Wessex) to an area east of a line running northward from London through Hertford and Bedford and thence along Watling Street to Chester, an area that became known as the Danelaw. In the period of comparative peace that followed, Alfred was relatively free to "turn from the defending of his people and country, from the fear of their capture and destruction, to the thought and care of their domestic life and well-being, and spiritual health."[1] Thus, as a paternal ruler and a patron of learning, Alfred was ultimately responsible, either by himself or in collaboration with various scholars at his court, for the (rather free) translation into West Saxon of such post-Classical Latin prose works as the *Regulae Pastoralis Liber* (*Book of Pastoral Rule*) by Pope Gregory I, the Great (c.590); the *Historia Ecclesiastica Gentis Anglorum* (*History of the English Church and People*) by the Northumbrian monk, Bede (731); the *Historia aduersum Paganos* (*History against the Pagans*) by the early fifth-century Hispanic priest, Paulus Orosius (418); and the *De Consolatione Philosophiae* (*On the Consolation of Philosophy*) by the Roman philosopher and statesman, Boethius (d.524). Of these works, incidentally, only the *Book of Pastoral Rule* is extant in a manuscript which dates from the time of Alfred himself; the other translations are known only in later redactions. Finally, historians conjecture that the *Anglo-Saxon Chronicle*, essentially a national history, originated in Winchester, the capital of Wessex, under the impetus of Alfred; in any event, a chronicle extending to the year 891 was made in Alfred's reign and sent out to various centers of learning. In such a manner, then, it came about that West Saxon, unlike the other contemporaneous Old English dialects, achieved a scribal tradition of sorts and came to enjoy the prestige of something approaching a literary standard. It is no accident that the four codices (the *Exeter Book,* the *Vercelli Book,* the *Junius Manuscript,* and the *Beowulf Manuscript*), which contain the primary surviving corpus of Old English poetry, are all basically in West Saxon, though in a configuration of the language later than that spoken by Alfred. In fact, Alfredian West Saxon is commonly known as *Early West Saxon* (eWS), and is regarded as terminating in the initial years of the tenth century.

1.3 *Late West Saxon* An introductory grammar of Old English, however, must devote principal consideration to *Late West Saxon* (lWS) (c.900–c.1040), simply because the majority of significant literary monuments reflect the dialect in that stage. The heroic lay, *Beowulf,* ranks foremost among them, but celebrated shorter poems like *The Seafarer, The Wanderer,* the *Battle of Brunanburh* (937), the *Battle of Maldon* (991), and the *Dream of the Rood* are also lWS compositions. Even the poetry (e.g., *Elene*) of Cynewulf, very likely a West Mercian, or Northumbrian, who was active during the first half of the ninth century, is preserved only in a lWS "translation." An anonymous version of the Four Gospels, based upon a manuscript of Saint Jerome's *Vulgate,* is written in lWS, as are the homilies, some one hundred and sixty, of a Benedictine cleric named Ælfric (c.955–c.1025), the preeminent writer of the second period of West Saxon. In addition to the *Homilies,* Ælfric produced (995) an adaptation in his own language of Priscian's sixth-century Latin grammar, a work widely relied upon in the Middle Ages.

His other writings include a *Colloquium* (the *Colloquy on the Occupations*), the *Lives of the Saints* (996), and translations of portions of the Old Testament (997–998). Another very important writer is Wulfstan, archbishop of York (d.1023) who was the author of a famous homily often referred to by its Latin title, *Sermo Lupi ad Anglos* (the *Address of Wolf to the English*) (1014). Further examples of lWS are the anonymous *Blickling Homilies* (c.971), the poems *Judith, Deor, Widsith,* and *Genesis B;* the best known remaining fragment of prose fiction, *Apollonius of Tyre;* and, for the reason mentioned above, the Alfredian translations of Bede, Boethius, and Orosius. In sum, it appears that, around 1000, a variety of West Saxon, though rather consistently displaying non-West Saxon elements of orthography and inflection, had become a sort of cultural language that was in use throughout the whole of England, and that was employed for the copying of literary works, regardless of their original dialect; *Beowulf,* for example, was certainly composed in a dialect (Anglian) other than West Saxon. Perhaps enough has been said to indicate the desirability of beginning an acquaintance with Old English by the study of Late West Saxon, and the concomitant necessity for acquiring some familiarity with its earlier forms as well.

1.4   *Kentish*   The three other attested dialects of Old English are Kentish (spoken by the Jutes), Northumbrian and Mercian (both spoken by the Angles). Mercian is actually a general term that designates all Anglian dialects except Northumbrian. No one of the three is abundantly documented, the case, indeed, with West Saxon itself until the time of Alfred. Before the ninth century, Kentish can be recovered only from names occurring in a few Latin charters; in the ninth century, however, the dialect proper was used for a series of charters. After 900 its appearance is, in effect, confined to the *Kentish Glosses,* the *Kentish Psalm,* and the *Kentish Hymn,* all of which date from before 1100. (A gloss, incidentally, is an interlinear or marginal translation in the vernacular, and consists for the most part of a single word or a short phrase.) Every surviving Kentish text is characterized by a dialectal admixture, the earlier ones evincing features of Mercian and the later ones features of West Saxon.

1.5   *Northumbrian and Mercian*   More fully represented than Kentish are Northumbrian and Mercian. A runic inscription (c.700) on the Ruthwell [rivl] Cross in Dumfriesshire is the earliest attestation of Northumbrian; this inscription is, interestingly, a parallel version of the *Dream of the Rood* found in the *Vercelli Book* and suggests the likelihood of an original common to both. Another runic inscription, on the Franks Casket, is also Northumbrian, as are the earliest manuscripts of *Cæd-*

mon's Hymn, *Bede's Death Song*, and the *Leiden Riddle* (solution: a coat of mail); all may be assigned to the eighth century. The glosses to the *Lindisfarne Gospels*, the *Rushworth Gospels* (some of these glosses are Mercian), and to the *Durham Ritual* are tenth-century sources of the dialect. Mercian is known primarily from eighth- and ninth-century charters, from the glosses to the *Blickling Psalter* (eighth century), and to the *Vespasian Psalter* (c.850), and from those glosses to the *Rushworth Gospels* which are Mercian rather than Northumbrian.

1.6   *The Geographical Location of Old English Dialects*   Dialect boundaries are never sharply defined; as H. A. Gleason points out, the isogloss (a line drawn on a map to show the geographical limit of some particular linguistic feature) is merely "a representation of statistical probabilities."[2] Nevertheless, by combining linguistic data with historical data, it is possible to make a relatively accurate statement about the distribution of Old English dialects, after setting aside the unrealistic goal of specifying borders of exact demarcation between them. The Anglian dialects occupied by far the most extensive territory. Mercian was spoken in the Midlands between the Thames and the Humber, its western boundary being roughly a north-south line from present-day Chester to Cardiff (Wales) on the other side of which were located speakers of Keltic, driven west from their previous settlements as a consequence of the Germanic incursions. Northumbrian, as the name implies, extended north from the Humber into the Lowlands of Scotland where another group of Kelts were restless neighbors. Kentish was spoken principally in Kent and on the Isle of Wight. The remainder of England south of the Thames, excluding Cornwall, also a refuge for displaced Kelts, was West Saxon in speech.

1.7   *English*   As the French were to select the name of one Germanic tribe, the Alemanni, to stand for the whole nation (*cf.* French *Allemagne* 'Germany', *allemand* adj. 'German'), so did Latin writers choose *Angli* 'Angles' as their customary term for all the Germanic groups in Britain; in 601, to cite a well-known example, Pope Gregory referred to Æthelbert of Kent by the words *rex Anglorum* 'king of the Angles'. This practice was, however, not only confined to Latin, but also occurred in the vernacular. Until about 1000, *Angelcynn* (in Latin *gens Anglorum*) 'nation of the Angles' was current; thereafter, *Englaland* 'land of the Angles' was usual. The four dialects seem to have always been termed *Englisc* (the OE adjective *englisc* 'pertaining to the Angles' used as a noun), and, for that reason, *Old English* is to be preferred over *Anglo-Saxon* which has, furthermore, the disadvantage of many nonlinguistic connotations.

1.8   *Standard Modern English*   Standard Modern English is
not derived from West Saxon, but from the Middle English dialect of
London, of which Mercian is the Old English antecedent. Although the
dialectal situation between 1100 and 1500 is complex, scholars are generally agreed in recognizing four principal dialects of Middle English:
Northern, East Midland, West Midland, and Southern. Briefly, Northumbrian became the Northern dialect, Mercian split into East and West
Midland, and West Saxon coalesced with Kentish to form the Southern
dialect. It was inevitable that the East Midlandish speech of London, the
capital and most important city from an economic, political, and cultural
point of view, should achieve a linguistic value exceeding that accorded the
speech of the countryside and of lesser towns; the same thing happened, of
course, in France and Spain, where Parisian French and Castilian Spanish
were similarly elevated to the status of national tongues. Standard
Modern English, then, is not descended from the language of King Alfred,
but from the dialect employed by one of the very greatest of English
writers, the Londoner, Geoffrey Chaucer.

1.9   *Germanic*   With respect to its generic classification, Old
English belongs to *West Germanic* (WGmc), one of the three major subdivisions of the Germanic speaking community; the other two subdivisions are *East Germanic* (EGmc) and *North Germanic* (NGmc). Prior to
the last centuries before the Christian Era, Germanic tribes appear to
have been fairly uniform in language and culture; about 2000 BC they
had settled along the shores of the Baltic Sea (i.e., in northern Germany
and southern Scandinavia) and there had developed a homogeneous
society, devoid of linguistic separatism. They did not, however, acquire
a writing system, the runic alphabet, until c.250–c.150 BC at the earliest,
and their common speech, termed *Proto-Germanic* (PGmc), is recovered
by reconstruction only. Around the third century BC dialectal variations
began to emerge, a consequence, in part, of renewed migration, and by
100 AD a threefold division of the Germanic languages had evolved.

1.10   *North Germanic*   North Germanic encompasses the
Scandinavian languages, now principally Swedish and Danish (East
Norse), and Norwegian and its derivative, Icelandic (West Norse). Runic
inscriptions in Scandinavia date from the late third century AD, and, until
the beginning of the Viking Age (800–1050) when dialectal peculiarities
become noticeable, they indicate the existence of an undifferentiated
Scandinavian idiom, *Proto-Old Norse* (PON) (200–800). Having discovered Iceland about 860, Norwegian Vikings promptly established settlements there which eventually (900–1400) produced an impressive liter-

ature in the language variously known as *Old Icelandic* (OI) or *Old Norse* (ON). Surviving manuscripts contain many prose stories, originally part of an oral tradition, which deal with heroic conduct and represent a *genre* called the *saga* (*cf.* OI *saga* 'story', *segja* 'to say'); one of them, the *Grettis Saga* (the story of an historical outlaw named Grettir, 996–1031), records an Icelandic analogue to Beowulf's fight with the monster, Grendel. Another tale with an episode reminiscent of Beowulf's adventure in Denmark is the *Hrólfs Saga Kraka* (the *Saga of Rolf Kraki*), composed in the second half of the fourteenth century. A considerable portion of ancient Norwegian and Icelandic poetry is found in a famous compilation of mythological and heroic lays that was made about 1270, the *Elder Edda* (the word *edda* is perhaps connected with OI *óðr* 'poetry'); much other verse is also preserved. The thirteenth century is regarded as the culmination of Icelandic creativity, outstandingly exemplified by the *Brennu-Njáls Saga* (*The Saga of Burnt Njál*) (c.1250–1275) in which a noble and sensitive man, Njál, is ultimately compelled to suffer death by being burned alive together with his sons because of having become innocently involved in a blood feud through them. East Norse, it should be noted, also developed a literature in the Middle Ages, but on a far more modest scale than West Norse.

1.11   *East Germanic* For any practical purpose, East Germanic is synonymous with the language of those Goths who, having migrated (c.200 AD) from Scandinavia (*cf.* the Baltic island *Gotland,* two districts in Sweden bearing the name *Götland,* and the Swedish seaport *Göteborg*) and the region of the Lower Vistula to the plains north of the Black Sea, crossed the Danube in 348 and settled in the Roman province of Moesia (now Bulgaria); the Goths in Moesia were Visigoths (West Goths), the distinction between Visigoths and Ostrogoths (East Goths) having arisen earlier when part of the Gothic community was located west of the Dniepr River and part east of it. About 350, a translation of the Bible, from a Greek text, was made for the Moesogoths by their Cappadocian bishop, Wulfila (c.311–c.383), whose name is Gothic for 'little wolf'; like Wulfila the Goths were adherents of Arianism, a leading heresy of the early Church, which asserted that the substance of Christ was inferior to that of God, His necessary begetter. Using Germanic runes and Greek letters, Wulfila devised an alphabet for Gothic that eventually came to be employed in some monasteries of northern Italy during the Ostrogothic domination of that country under Theodoric the Great (c.455–526). One such monastery is quite likely the place where, around 500, the splendid *Codex Argenteus* was created. The *Codex Argenteus,* or 'book decorated with silver', contains the Four Gospels in the translation and alphabet of Wulfila; the manuscript is so named because of the large initial silver (and gold) letters that ornament the purple parchment upon which the text is written. Now housed in the University Library in Upsala, Sweden, the *Codex Argenteus* constitutes almost the entire corpus of Gothic; apart from it, only a short commentary, the *Skeireins* (Gothic for 'explanation'), on the Gospel of St. John, is of much importance. Gothic, the first Germanic language to be attested in a literary prose, has been extinct since well before the eighteenth century. Nothing whatsoever remains of any other East Germanic dialect.

1.12   *West Germanic*   The profusion of West Germanic dialects is the direct result of an "expansion of the continental stock between the Elbe and the Oder to the west and southwest."[3] As linguistic entities, North and East Germanic were far less affected than West Germanic by those migrations of the Germanic peoples (*die Völkerwanderung*), which took place from c.200 BC to c.500 AD; Norse and Gothic had already become independent groups at a time when the West Germanic languages were still in the process of formation.[4] The terms *Low German(ic)* and *High German(ic)* reflect the spread of West Germanic tribes into areas of relatively lower or higher altitudes above sea level; thus, the Germanic dialects of northern Europe are *low*, those of central and southern Germany, Switzerland, and Austria *high*. *Old High German* (OHG) (750–1050) dialects include Alemannic, Bavarian, East Franconian, Rhenish Franconian, and South Rhenish Franconian, all of which are represented by literary endeavor. The only example of heroic poetry in Old High German, however, is the incomplete eighth-century *Hildebrandslied*, which tells the story, common in folklore, of a combat between a father and his unrecognized son. The best known works of early German literature date from the *Middle High German* (MHG) period (1050–1500) when the court poets, or *Minnesänger*, Hartmann von Aue (c.1165–c.1215), Walther von der Vogelweide (c.1170–1230), Wolfram von Eschenbach (c.1170–c.1220), and Gottfried von Strassburg (*fl.* c.1210) were active, and the anonymous heroic epic, *Das Nibelungenlied*, was composed (c.1200–1205). High German speech is rather strikingly characterized by the Second Germanic Consonant Shift (*die zweite germanische Lautverschiebung*) in which the voiceless stop consonants [p, t, and k] were, under certain conditions, shifted to affricated stops or to fricatives, and their voiced counterparts [b, d, and g] were frequently unvoiced: *cf.* OE *heorte*, OHG *herza* 'heart'; OE *slæpan*, OHG *slāfan* 'to sleep'; and OE *fæder*, OHG *fater* 'father'. Among the medieval dialects of Low Germanic are Low Franconian, from which modern Dutch and Flemish (the Germanic language of Belgium) are descended, and Old Saxon (to 1100), spoken by those Saxons who remained on the Continent and did not venture across the Channel to Britain. By 300, however, some Saxons had moved westward to the region of the Ijsselmeer (the Zuider Zee), and by 400 to the northern coast of France (the *litus Saxonicus*) from where the initial landings in Britain were probably made in 477. Though showing the influence of Old High German, the *Hēliand* ('Saviour'; *cf.* OE *hǣlan* 'to save'; *Hǣlend* 'Saviour'), a poem of some six thousand lines about the life of Christ, is generally taken to be Old Saxon in origin; it was composed c.830. A twenty-six line fragment of an Old Saxon poem, *Genesis*, was discovered as recently as 1894 in the Library of the Vatican; dating from the first half of the ninth century, this fragment represents part of an original Old Saxon work from which the Old English *Genesis B*, interpolated in the longer *Genesis A*, was translated. The twenty-six lines of *Genesis* correspond exactly to lines 791–817 of the Old English poem. After 1100, and until the Reformation (1517), Old Saxon becomes *Middle Low German*, which, in the modern period, is simply *Low German* or *Plattdeutsch*.[5] The Saxon coastal settlements were near those of the Frisians, who had also expanded westward from their older homeland. Of all Germanic dialects, Frisian, not attested until the thirteenth century, is the one most closely allied to English; indeed, some scholars have posited Anglo-Frisian as a justifiable subgroup of West Germanic. Frisian survives as a modern language, but the number of its speakers has continued to decline.

1.13   *Indo-European*   As North, East, and West Germanic are later and separate developments of Proto-Germanic, so is Proto-Germanic itself a specialized development of still another prehistoric linguistic unity, the delineation and reconstruction of which has engaged the attention of comparative philologists since the late eighteenth century, when the existence of a common source for many ancient and modern languages was widely assumed but not yet proven. It was the achievement of nineteenth-century scholarship to demonstrate convincingly that diversity had indeed replaced uniformity, and that the structural similarities of languages like Sanskrit, Greek, Latin, Persian, and Gothic were by no means the result of independent or accidental invention, but were, instead, the vestiges of a parent speech, eventually termed *Indo-European*, or *Proto-Indo-European*. Gradually the phonological and morphological features of Indo-European were deduced from the oldest extant dialects, and, as an adjunct to that undertaking, a family of languages was established. It is now accepted that Indo-European contains the following major divisions: Indo-Iranian, including Sanskrit and Persian; Balto-Slavic, including Lithuanian, Polish, and Russian; Hellenic, consisting of the various Greek dialects; Italic, including Oscan, Umbrian, Latin and the Romance languages; Keltic, including Irish and Welsh; and the single languages Albanian, Armenian, Hittite, and Tocharian, the last two of which have long been extinct. Thus, *Indo-European* refers broadly to the eastern (India) and western (Europe) limits, maintained for many centuries, within which the original speech was first distributed and became diversified. The period of Indo-European unity is generally ascribed to the third millenium BC, but the location of an ancestral homeland, the subject of extensive discussion, has continued to elude positive identification by linguists and by archaeologists. On the circumstantial evidence of cognate words in the Indo-European languages, however, an inland region enjoying a temperate climate seems most likely; present in the inventory of genuine cognates are such critical words as *birch, snow, bee, salmon,* and *wolf,* whereas words for *ocean, olive, wine,* and for any specifically tropical or Asiatic animal or plant are conspicuously absent. At the moment, "scholarly opinion . . . is in favor of a European center of dispersion—an opinion which implies that the earliest migrations were in a southeasterly direction."[6] Cognate terms also point to a late neolithic culture and a patriarchal family organization; nothing is known about the race, or races, to which speakers of Indo-European belonged. Nevertheless, there can be no serious doubt that (later) Indo-European was a highly inflected form of speech; no fewer than eight cases (nominative, genitive, dative, accusative, ablative, instrumental, locative, and vocative) must be assumed for the declension of nouns and adjectives, whereas verbs required two distinct sets of personal endings that were variously distributed among the different tenses and moods. Some knowledge of Indo-European conditions, then, is indispensable for a clear understanding of the grammar of an idiom like Old English, which, in final analysis, is simply one more modification of the parent language.

References

1. Eleanor Shipley Duckett, *Alfred the Great* (Chicago, 1956), p. 86.
2. *An Introduction to Descriptive Linguistics,* revised edition (New York, 1961), p. 400.
3. Eduard Prokosch, *A Comparative Germanic Grammar* (Philadelphia, 1939), p. 30.
4. Prokosch, p. 34.
5. R. Priebsch and W. E. Collinson, *The German Language,* 6th ed. revised (London, 1966), p. 44.
6. Thomas Pyles, *The Origins and Development of the English Language* (New York, 1964), p. 79.

Chapter 2

The Pronunciation of Old English

2.1 *Establishing a Pronunciation for Old English* As Dr. Johnson correctly observed in the *Preface* to his *Dictionary* (1755), "language was at its beginning merely oral, [and] all words of necessary or common use were spoken before they were written"; language in short, is *sound*, and even alphabetic writing provides only a partial record of linguistic habits that originated in speech. Because language is an oral phenomenon, the task of establishing a pronunciation for an idiom no longer spoken is one that must be accomplished without the most obviously desirable source of information: a living informant. Although there is no impediment to a qualified success, scholars of Old English are obliged, in the nature of things, to construct a system of pronunciation without, for example, the illuminating details of stress and intonation that only a native speaker could supply. Relying, however, upon such tangible guides as spelling, dialectal and conservative usage, and what is known about the pronunciation of Latin in the seventh century when the Roman alphabet was adapted, with few changes, to the writing of Old English, philologists have been able to reach a consensus about the sounds of Kentish, Anglian, and West Saxon.[1] The speaker of Modern English will find that achieving a satisfactory pronunciation of any Old English dialect does not involve the labored production of exotic vowels and consonants; instead, it simply requires an understanding of a spelling system which, for the most part, represents very "comfortable" and familiar sounds.

2.2   *The Vowels of Old English*   The position of the tongue in the oral cavity is often a convenient means by which to classify the vowels of a language, especially one belonging to the Indo-European group, and the vowels of West Saxon are traditionally described on the basis of tongue height (high, middle, low) as opposed to tongue position (front, central, back). Vowels are normally *voiced* sounds, which means that the vocal cords, or bands, are brought together and then made to vibrate (open and close) when air from the lungs and trachea is forced outward through them; a sound is *voiceless* if the vocal cords are partially open when the breath is expelled. Old English vowels had both short (lax) and long (tense) values, and vocalic quantity sometimes functioned as the sole distinguishing (phonemic) feature by which ambiguity was avoided, e.g., *god* 'god', but *gōd* 'good', *þe* relative particle 'who, which', but *þē* 'to you' (singular). While the significant (phonemic) difference between short vowels and their long counterparts was one of quantity only, there was, possibly, an occasional (phonetic) difference of quality as well; thus, the long vowels *ī, ē*, and *ō*, pronounced with a greater tenseness of the tongue, probably manifested shifts beyond that of quantity alone. The long vowels of Old English were not diphthongs, but, as their closest equivalents in Modern English frequently are, it is desirable to minimize the semi-vowel, or off-glide, ([w] or [y]) that often characterizes the illustration drawn from contemporary English. Vowel length, incidentally, is not marked in Old English manuscripts. The letters employed in this grammar for writing the vowels of West Saxon are listed below, together with their suggested phonetic values; the system of transcription followed here is the one employed by H. A. Gleason in *An Introduction to Descriptive Linguistics* (New York, 1961). Please note that those symbols in square brackets have phonetic, and not orthographic, reference.

2.2.1   *y* (short, high front, lip-rounded) represents a sound not present in Modern English; it was phonetically [ü], and pronounced like the *ü* in German *füllen* 'to fill'; *cf.* Old English *fyllan* 'to fill'. The letter *y* always stands for a vowel in Old English texts.

2.2.2   *ȳ* (long, high front, lip-rounded) represents a sound not present in Modern English; it was phonetically [ü:], merely a prolonged variety of Old English *y*. The *ü* in German *grün* is customarily suggested as an approximate pronunciation; *cf.* Old English *lȳtel* 'little'.

2.2.3   *i* (short, high front, unrounded) represents the sound of *i* in Modern English *limb*, phonetically [i]; *cf.* Old English *lim* 'limb'.

2.2.4   *ī* (long, high front, unrounded) represents, strictly speaking, merely a prolonged variety of Old English *i*, and is phonetically [i:]; the contrast between *i* and *ī* in Old English was probably similar to that of the vowels in Modern English *bit* and *bid* respectively. In practice, Old English *ī* is generally accorded the value of *i* in Modern English *machine*; *cf.* Old English *tīr* 'glory'.

2.2.5   *e* (short, middle front, unrounded) represents the sound of *e* in Modern English *help*, phonetically [e]; *cf.* Old English *helpan* 'to help'.

2.2.6   *ē* (long, middle-front, unrounded) represents a prolonged variety of Old English *e*, and is phonetically [e:]; the *ey* of modern English *they* stands for a diphthong [*ey*] which is a reasonable approximation of Old English *ē*; *cf.* Old English *mēd* 'reward'.

2.2.7   *æ* (short, low front-central, unrounded) is a digraph (two letters indicating one sound), a ligature of Latin *ae*, the Classical value of which "had long before shifted to a vowel sound roughly similar to that which the English ascribed to it. The *æ* was called *æsc* 'ash,' the name of the runic symbol which represented the same sound, though it in no way resembled the Latin-English digraph."[2] *æ* represents the *a* of Modern English *at*, phonetically [æ]; *cf.* Old English *æt* 'at'.

2.2.8   *ǣ* (long, low front-central, unrounded) represents a prolonged variety of Old English *æ*, and was probably similar to the *a* of Modern English *add*, phonetically [æ:]; *cf.* Old English *ǣrest* 'first'.

2.2.9   *a* (short, low central-back, unrounded) represents the *a* of German *Mann* 'man', phonetically [a]; although the vowel of *not* is similar, there is no exact equivalent in Modern English; *cf.* Old English *bana* 'murderer'. When Old English *a* occurred before the nasal consonants [m, n, and ŋ] the vowel seems to have been somewhat nasalized and partially rounded; those modifications are apparently reflected in the frequent spelling of [a] before nasals as *o*; e.g., *nama/noma* 'name', *hand/hond* 'hand'.

2.2.10   *ā* (long, low central-back, unrounded) represents the *a* of Modern English *father*, phonetically [a:]; *cf.* Old English *bāt* 'boat'.

2.2.11   *o* (short, middle-back, rounded) when not standing for [a] before a nasal, represents the sound of *ou* in Modern English *ought*, phonetically [ɔ]; *cf.* Old English *holm* 'wave, sea'.

2.2.12   *ō* (long, middle-back, rounded) represents a prolonged variety of Old English *o*, approximated in Modern English by the diphthong [ow] in *note*. The Old English sound seems to have been phonetically closer to [o:] than to [ɔ:]; *cf.* Old English *wōd* 'enraged'.

2.2.13   *u* (short, high-back, rounded) represents the sound of *u* in Modern English *full*, phonetically [u]; *cf.* Old English *full* 'full'.

2.2.14   *ū* (long, high-back, rounded) represents a prolonged variety of Old English *u*, phonetically [u:]; the sound is approximated in Modern English by the diphthong [uw] in the word *flute*; *cf.* Old English *ūle* 'owl'.

2.3   *The Diphthongs of Old English*   There were eight diphthongs in Early West Saxon—four short and four long; they are spelled *ie, ea, eo, io* and *īe, ēa, ēo, īo*. By Late West Saxon, *ie* and *īe* had become *i* and *ī* respectively; these in turn tended to be rounded to *y* and *ȳ*, while *io* and *īo* had coalesced with *eo* and *ēo* respectively; *cf.* eWS *ierre*, lWS *irre, yrre* 'anger' and eWS *līode*, lWS *lēode* 'people'. A diphthong may, of course, be stressed on either element, but, as the second element of every Old English diphthong was to be lost in one way or another during the Middle English period, the first vowel of Old English diphthongs was doubtless the more emphatically accented. Indeed, the distinctive vocalic quality of the second vowel seems to have been very much obscured in pronunciation, with the result that *e, a,* and *o* all sounded like the short, middle-central vowel of Modern English *but*, phonetically [ə]. The first vowel of a given Old English diphthong retained the same quality that it had as an independent entity; thus, *ie* was [iə], *īe* [i:ə], *ea* [eə], *ēa* [e:ə], and so forth. Like all diphthongs, those of Old English constituted the nuclei of syllables and should be pronounced as such, without suggestion of any hiatus between the two elements.

2.4   *The Consonants of Old English*   The classification of consonants relates to the breath stream and the degree to which it is impeded by various parts of the vocal tract from the larynx to the lips. If the breath stream is completely blocked somewhere for a moment and then released, the resulting sound is a *stop*; if there is only a partial closure at some point along the vocal tract, but a closure sufficient for the production of some friction, the resulting sound is a *fricative* or *spirant*; if the vocal tract is everywhere open, to the extent that the breath stream escapes without causing any friction, the resulting sound is a *resonant*. The place along the vocal tract where maximum constriction, or closure, occurs is called the *point* of articulation. Points of articulation are functions of movable articulators (lips, tongue, velum or soft palate) and non-movable articulators (teeth, alveolar ridge, hard palate) and are named for the articulator or articulators most prominently involved; thus, for example, if both lips are brought together to impede the breath stream, the point of articulation is *bilabial*. Other common points of articulation are *dental* (tongue on teeth), *labio-dental* (lip on teeth), *alveolar* (tongue on alveolar ridge), *palatal* (tongue on hard palate), and *velar* (tongue on velum). Whatever the *manner* of articulation—stop, fricative, or resonant, a consonant may be either voiced or voiceless, though voiceless resonants are rare; strictly regarded, vowels are median oral resonants, thus named because the oral cavity is open at the mid-line. The following letters had the same consonantal values in West Saxon that they have in Modern English: *b, d, k* (rare), *l, m, n, p, t* and *w*; for a further note on *n* see 2.4.8. In word-initial position the letter *r* probably stood for a tongue-trilled [r]; before consonants and in word-final position it was very likely identical with the retroflex [r] of standard American English. The remaining consonantal symbols require a more extensive elucidation.

2.4.1   The letter *c* represented two sounds: the voiceless velar stop [k] as in Modern English *cat*, and (when palatalized) the voiceless alveopalatal affricated stop [č] which is expressed in Modern English by the digraph *ch*, e.g., *chin*. The pronunciation accorded *c* depended upon contiguous sounds. "If these were back vowels, the letter indicated the velar stop [k] (*camp* 'battle', *corn* 'corn', *cūð* 'known', *lūcan* 'to lock', *acan* 'to ache', *bōc* 'book'); if they were front (or had been in early Old English), the sound indicated was the affricate [č] (*cild* 'child', *cēosan* 'to choose', *ic* 'I', *lǣce* 'physician', *rīce* 'kingdom', *mēce* 'sword')."[3] Sometimes, however, *c* stood for [k] even in the presence of a front vowel; such apparent exceptions to the general formulation may be explained as the result of a phonetic phenomenon called *umlaut* or *mutation*, by which back vowels in root syllables were fronted in Proto-Old English by a following *i, ī* or *j*. Thus, POE *cunning* becomes Old English *cyning* 'king', but the sound of the initial consonant, now preceding a front vowel, remains [k]. To obviate the etymological considerations occasionally necessary for determining a correct pronunciation of *c*, a dotted *ċ* is used in this grammar to indicate [č] whenever it occurs.

2.4.2.   The interpretation of *g* is also a somewhat complicated matter, as this letter represents four distinct sounds. Before "consonants (*gnēað* 'niggardly', *glæd* 'glad, gracious'), initially before back vowels (*galan* 'to sing', *gōs* 'goose', *gūð* 'war'), and initially before front vowels that had resulted from the mutation of back vowels (*gēs* 'geese' from pre-historic Old English **gōsi*, *gæst* 'goest' from **gais*)"[4] *g* stood for the voiced velar stop [g] as in Modern English *get*. In most cases, *g* also had that value when it followed *n* in medial or final position (e.g., *bringan* 'to bring', *hring* 'ring', *englisc* 'English', *lang* 'long'), but, in a very limited number of words, and, commonly, when *n* is preceded by the umlauted vowel *e*, *g* appears to have been pronounced as the voiced alveopalatal fricative [ǰ], the initial sound of Modern English *gin*; that sound is here marked by the symbol *ǵ* (e.g. *lenǵu* 'length', *strenǵan* 'to strengthen'). In certain contexts the letter *g* expresses the voiced palatal [y], the initial sound of Modern English *yet*. It has that value: a) initially before *i*, *ī*, *y*, *ȳ*, *e*, and *ē* (when *ē* is not the result of umlaut) and before all diphthongs, e.g., *gīsel* 'hostage', *gē* 'you' (plural), *gēotan* 'to pour (forth)', *giefan* 'to give'; b) at the end of a word or a syllable when preceded by a front vowel, e.g., *dæg* 'day', *stigrap* 'stirrup', *hālig* 'holy', *sægde* '(he) said'; c) medially between front vowels, e.g., *slægen* 'slain', *weges* 'way' (genitive singular); and d) when originally followed in Proto-Old English by *i*, *ī* or *j*, e.g., *ege* 'terror' from POE **agi*. A dotted *ġ* is used in this grammar to represent the palatalized *g* whenever it occurs. In all other environments (e.g. *āgan* 'to own', *dragan* 'to drag, draw', *lagu* 'law', *sorgian* 'to sorrow') *g* is the voiced velar fricative [ɣ], a sound completely foreign to the consonantal repertory of standard Modern British and American English; at no risk to an acceptable pronunciation, the substitution of [g] is recommended.

2.4.3   The letter *h* is yet another example of an Old English symbol that possesses a dual phonetic value. In word-initial position before vowels, it is simply the voiceless glottal fricative [h], the first sound of Modern English *house*; *cf*. Old English *hūs* 'house'. Before consonants and after vowels, its point of articulation is farther forward, and it becomes a voiceless velar or palatal fricative [χ], identical with the final consonants of German *ach* 'alas' and *ich* 'I'; *cf*. Old English *fah* 'foe' and *niht* 'night'.

2.4.4   When the letter *s* occurs initially, finally, or before voiceless consonants, it has the sound of *s* in Modern English *sea*, a voiceless alveolar fricative, phonetically [s]; *cf*. Old English *sæ* 'sea'. When the letter occurs between voiced sounds, vowels or consonants, it is itself voiced, and pronounced like *s* in Modern English *reason*, a voiced alveolar fricative, phonetically [z]; *cf.* Old English *īsen* 'iron', *clænsian* 'to cleanse'. The letter *z* is not in the Old English alphabet. When doubled, *s* is always voiceless; *cf.* Old English *mæsse* 'mass'.

2.4.5   The rules governing the pronunciation of *f* are identical with those for *s*. Initially, finally, or before voiceless consonants, *f* represents the voiceless labio-dental fricative [f] of Modern English *false; cf.* Old English *fals* 'false'. In voiced environments it becomes the voiced labio-dental fricative [v] of Modern English *give; cf.* Old English *ġiefan* 'to give'. The letter *v* is not in the Old English alphabet. When doubled, *f* is always voiceless; *cf.* Old English *pyffan* 'to puff'.

2.4.6   Two letters peculiar to Old English texts are *þ* (thorn), originally a runic character, and *ð* (eth), a modification of the Roman lower case *d*. They did not occur in mutually exclusive environments, although in the late Old English period scribes tended to restrict *þ* to word-initial position. Both *þ* and *ð* have the same two phonetic values; each may represent the sound of the Modern English digraph *th* in *thin* and *then*, that is, the voiceless dental fricative [θ] or its voiced counterpart [ð]. Like *s* and *f*, *þ* and *ð* are voiceless initially, finally, and before voiceless consonants; *cf.* Old English *þearf/ðearf* 'need', *āþ/āð* 'oath'. Between voiced sounds, vowels or consonants, *þ* and *ð* are voiced; *cf.* Old English *ōþer/ōðer* 'other', *rēþlīċ/rēðlīċ* 'fierce'. When doubled, *þ* and *ð* are always voiceless; *cf.* Old English *siþþan/siððan* 'since'. The upper case forms are *þ* and *Đ*.

2.4.7   Besides the vocalic digraph *æ*, the Old English orthographical system contains the digraphs *cg* and *sc*, each of which represents a *single* consonant. The phonetic value of *cg* is equivalent to that of *dg* in Modern English *edge*, in other words the voiced alveopalatal affricate [ǰ]; *cf.* Old English *ecg* 'edge'. The value of *sc* is that of *sh* in Modern English *ship;* it is the voiceless alveopalatal fricative [š]; *cf.* Old English *scip* 'ship'. In two positions, however, *sc* retains its original (Proto-Germanic) value of [sk]: medially before back vowels, if the preceding vowel was not umlauted (see 6.2), and finally after back vowels; hence, *fisc* [fiš] 'fish', but *fiscas* [fiskas] 'fishes', and *tusc* [tusk] 'tooth'. In Modern English derivations, *cg* and *sc* have been replaced by *dg* and *sh* respectively.

2.4.8   When *n* precedes *g* or *c* it stands for the velar nasal [ŋ] (called *eng*), which is spelled *ng* (sing) or *n* (sink) in Modern English. While *ng* is sometimes pronounced [ŋ] in Modern English (*singer*) and sometimes [ŋg] (*linger*), it is *always* [ŋg] in Old English; *both* consonants are sounded. The combination *nc* is, in the same manner, phonetically [ŋk]; *cf.* Old English *hungor* 'hunger', *singan* 'to sing', *þanc* 'thought'. In the combination -nġ-, and everywhere else, *n* is [n] as in *sin*.

2.4.9   The letter *x* merely indicates the occurrence of Old English *h* before *s*, and is, therefore, the equivalent of [χs]; *cf.* Old English *weaxan* 'to grow'; see 2.4.3 for the interpretation of preconsonantal *h*.

2.4.10   *Double Consonants*   When consonantal symbols are doubled between vowels, a lengthened consonant is signified. The medial [m] of *fremman* 'to make', for example, should be somewhat prolonged; if the consonant is a stop, the release should be delayed. In such a manner, words like *racca* 'part of a ship's rigging' and *raca* 'rake' are distinguished from one another.[5]

2.5   *The Accentuation of Old English*   The rules of accentuation are not complicated. While the primary stress could fall on various syllables (initial, medial, or final) in Indo-European, it was fixed on the root syllable in Proto-Germanic; this innovation is reflected in Old English. As a consequence, the first syllable of an Old English word (simple or compound) receives the primary stress, unless that syllable is *be-, ġe-, for-*, in which case the second (root) syllable is stressed, or unless the word is a verbal compound, in which case the second (root) syllable is also stressed: thus, *mṓdor* 'mother', *mṓdorlēas* 'motherless', but *ġesúngen* 'sung', *forspíld* 'destruction', *wiðsprécan* 'to contradict', *āŕisan* 'to arise'.

2.6   *A Summary of the Letters and Digraphs Used in This Text To Spell the Vowels of Old English.*

Letter	Phonetic Value
y	[ü] as in German *füllen*
ȳ	[ü:] as in German *grün*
i	[i] as in *limb*
ī	[i:] as in *machine*
e	[e] as in *help*
ē	[e:] as in *they*
æ	[æ] as in *at*
ǣ	[æ:] as in *add*
a	[a] as in German *Mann;* see 2.2.9
ā	[a:] as in *father*
o	[ɔ] as in *ought*
ō	[o:] as in *note*
u	[u] as in *full*
ū	[u:] as in *flute*

For the pronunciation of Old English diphthongs see 2.3.

2.7   *A Summary of the Letters and Digraphs Used in This Text To Spell the Consonants of Old English*

Letter	Phonetic Value
p	[p] as in *pin*
t	[t] as in *tin*
k	[k] as in *kin*
c	[k] as in *kin;* see 2.4.1
ċ	[č] as in *chin;* see 2.4.1
b	[b] as in *bin*
d	[d] as in *din*
g	[g] as in *gun;* see 2.4.2
ġ	[y] as in *yet;* see 2.4.2
ġ	[ǰ] as in *gin;* see 2.4.2
f	[f] as in *fine,* or [v] as in *vine;* see 2.4.5
þ	[θ] as in *thin,* or [ð] as in *then;* see 2.4.6
ð	[θ] as in *thin,* or [ð] as in *then;* see 2.4.6
h	[h] as in *house,* or [χ] as in German *ich/ach;* see 2.4.3
s	[s] as in *sea,* or [z] as in *reason;* see 2.4.4
l	[l] as in *low*
m	[m] as in *mow*
n	[n] as in *sin,* or [ŋ] as in *sing;* see 2.4.8
r	[r] as in *run,* or tongue-trilled; see 2.4
cg	[ǰ] as in *gin;* see 2.4.7
sc	[s] as in *shin;* see 2.4.7
x	[χs] no Modern English equivalent;

2.8   *A Selection for Practice in Pronunciation*   The following selection is a Late West Saxon translation of the Lord's Prayer, as contained in a manuscript of the Gospels dating from about 1000 AD.

Fæder ūre,
þū þe eart on heofonum,
sī þīn nama ġehālgod.
Tōbecume þīn rīċe.
5   Gewurþe ðīn willa on eorðan swā swā on heofonum.
Urne ġedæġhwāmlīcan hlāf syle ūs tō dæġ.
And forġyf ūs ūre gyltas, swā swā wē forġyfað ūrum gyltendum.
And ne ġelæd þū ūs on costnunge,
ac ālȳs ūs of yfele. Sōþlīċe.

References

1. Stuart Robinson, *The Development of Modern English,* 2nd ed., revised by Frederic G. Cassidy (Englewood Cliffs, New Jersey, 1954), pp. 88–89.
2. Thomas Pyles, *The Origins and Development of the English Language* (New York, 1964), pp. 28–29.
3. Pyles, p. 109.
4. Pyles, p. 110.
5. Pyles, p. 109.

Chapter 3

3.1   *A Major Difference between Old and Modern English*   Perhaps the most striking difference between Old English and Modern English is the large number of inflectional endings characteristic of the language in its earliest period. Whereas Modern English does preserve some inflections, notably in the personal pronouns (*he-him, she-her, they-them*), the morphological system of Old English was so radically altered during the Middle English period that Old English now presents many aspects of a genuinely foreign language, even to the person who claims English as his vernacular.

3.2   *Gender and Number*   Old English nouns and adjectives are inflected for gender, number, and case, and classified according to declensions. With obvious exceptions, such as the personal pronouns, gender was not natural, but grammatical. The concept of a masculine, feminine, or neuter gender for nouns is derived from certain linguistic speculations of the Greek philosophers; the fifth-century Sophist, Protagoras, is credited with having been the first to consider the nominal category of gender in Greek, a matter actually discussed by Aristotle (384–322) in his *De Sophisticis Elenchis* (*On Sophistical Refutation*). Taken over by Roman grammarians, the categorization of nouns (and adjectives) according to one of three genders became a standard feature of later treatises on Indo-European languages. In Old English it is often necessary (especially in poetry) to recognize the gender of a noun in order to use, for example, the proper adjective(s) or antecedent(s). The gender of an adjective is governed by that of the noun that it modifies. Words like *wer* 'man', *eorl* 'warrior', and *mōdor* 'mother' almost always have the appropriate gender, but, since gender was essentially a grammatical device, some nouns happen to have an unexpected classification: *bearn* 'child, son', *mǣ̇den* 'maiden', and *wīf* 'woman, lady' are, for instance, all neuter. The gender of nouns with a nonhuman reference is completely unpredictable; *mōna* 'moon' is masculine, but *sunne* 'sun' is feminine, a reversal, incidentally, of the situation in Latin and the Romance languages. Gender, then, when critical for accurate translation, must be determined on an individual basis. The number of nouns and adjectives was either singular or plural.

3.3   *Case*   Case is a term that identifies the different (phonemic) forms, or shapes, that a noun may assume as its function and number vary. If, to illustrate, a noun such as *faru* 'journey' (feminine) is the singular subject of a sentence then its form is *faru;* if it is the singular indirect object then the form is *fare;* if it is a plural direct object, then the form is *fara.* The ability to recognize the different cases, then, is often essential for the correct interpretation of the function of a noun. The same holds true for adjectives and pronouns since all three parts of speech are declined in a similar manner. It is customary to distinguish five cases in Old English, although two of them have, without exception, a coincident form in nouns. The five cases are the *nominative,* the *genitive,* the *dative,* the *accusative,* and the *instrumental.* In brief, the nominative case form indicates that a noun is functioning as either the subject or predicate nominative, the genitive case that possession is attributed, the dative case that the noun is the indirect object of the verb, the accusative case that the noun is the direct object, and the instrumental that agency is attributed; nouns in the dative, accusative, and instrumental cases may also all be the objects of certain prepositions that require those forms. The dative and instrumental cases, singular and plural, are identical for all nouns, and one might just as well speak of a dative-instrumental case for nouns. On occasion, other case forms are also the same, frequently the nominative and accusative singular, and the genitive and dative singular; it may even happen that genitive, dative, accusative, and instrumental are all the same. Confusion is not, however, the unavoidable result as the definite article, the demonstrative adjective, and, to a lesser extent, the plain adjective have distinctive forms that can facilitate correct identification of the case in question.

3.4   *Declensions*   The total number of forms that a noun, adjective, or pronoun may assume as its function in a sentence varies constitutes the *paradigm* of its *declension.* The fact that the paradigms of

Old English nouns do not all display the same pattern will be no surprise to anyone already acquainted with an inflected language such as German or Latin; Indo-European had a multiplicity of nominal declensions, and Old English, like Old Icelandic and Gothic, preserves some of them. The Indo-European noun consisted, in general, of three elements: root, thematic or stem vowel, and ending, for example, *legh-o-s* 'bed'; *cf.* Greek *lechos* and Latin *lectus* 'bed', related to Old English *lecgan* 'to lay, set'. The root plus the thematic vowel comprise the *stem* (*legh-o-*), and nouns in the various Indo-European languages are assigned to different declensions on the basis of the stem termination. Thus, in Old English it is customary to distinguish, among others, an *a*(stem)-declension, an *ō*-declension, an *i*-declension, and a *u*-declension; some stems, however, ended in a consonant, and they make up still another series of declensions. Whenever nouns exhibit dissimilar inflectional endings for the same case, it is generally because they do not belong to the same declension. Though it is useful for an orderly classification of nouns, a knowledge of the particular declension to which a noun belongs is dispensable in translation; in fact, the thematic vowel is so frequently lost or obscured in Old English that the various declensions are not readily identifiable without recourse to the original situation in Indo-European or Proto-Germanic. In translating Old English, it is far more important to recognize the traditional case endings and to know their semantic equivalent or equivalents.

3.5   *The a-declension*   The following two paradigms should be memorized as they are representative of the Old English *a*-declension, which contains both masculine and neuter nouns; because Indo-European *o* invariably become *a* in Germanic, this declension corresponds to the *o*-declension, or second declension, of Greek and Latin; *cf.* Greek *luk-o-s*, Latin *lup-u-s* 'wolf'. Forty-five percent of Old English nouns are masculine, and nearly four-fifths of those nouns are declined on the pattern of the *a*-declension; twenty-five percent of Old English nouns are neuter, and nearly all of them are also declined on the pattern of the *a*-declension.[1]

3.5.1   *eorl* 'nobleman, warrior, chief' (masculine)

	Singuar	**Plural**
N	eorl	eorl-as
G	eorl-es	eorl-a
D	eorl-e	eorl-um
A	eorl	eorl-as
I	eorl-e	eorl-um

3.5.2   *mōd* 'mind, courage, spirit' (neuter)

	Singular	Plural
N	mōd	mōd
G	mōd-es	mōd-a
D	mōd-e	mōd-um
A	mōd	mōd
I	mōd-e	mōd-um

3.5.3   As may be expected, there are some (apparent) irregularities within the declension itself. Occasionally a neuter noun will have a nominative and accusative ending in -*u* (e.g., *scipu* 'ships'), or there may be some alternation in the shape of the root of a particular noun. For instance, two important nouns, *day* and *kinsman*, have one vowel in the singular (*dæġ-*, *mæġ-*) and another in the plural (*dag-*, *mag-*), while *tungol* 'star' is *tungl-* in all cases except the nominative singular, and sometimes the nominative plural. These minor variations are the result of several causes. A useful distinction is made between long and short nominal and adjectival roots; a root is short if it contains a short vowel (or diphthong) followed by a single consonant; it is long if it contains either a long vowel (or diphthong) or a short vowel (or diphthong) followed by two or more consonants. Monosyllabic neuter nouns of the *a*-declension retain -*u* (from Proto-Germanic -*ō*) in the plural if the stem is short, but lose it if the stem is long. The difference between *dæġ-* and *dag-* is due to conditions in Proto-Old English that favored the shift of Proto-Germanic *a* to *æ* and the palatalization of [ɡ] to [y]; see 14.3.1 and 15.3. The contrast between *tungol* and *tungl-* results from syncopation (loss) of a medial vowel, caused by placement of the primary stress upon the word-initial syllable.

3.5.4   *ja-stem Nouns*   In Indo-European some masculine and neuter nouns had stems ending not in *-o-* but in *-yo-*; cf. Latin *consil-iu-m* 'a consultation'. Those nouns became the *-ja-stems* of Germanic, a minor subdivision of the *a*-declension. They are declined like nouns of the *a*-declension, and show the same slight variations. Common *ja*-stem nouns in Old English are the masculines *ende* 'end', *here* 'army', *mēċe* 'sword', *secg* 'man'; and the neuters *cyn(n)* 'race', *ġeþēode* 'language', *rīċe* 'kingdom'.

3.5.5   *wa-stem Nouns*   Another group of Indo-European masculine and neuter nouns had stems ending in *-wo-*; as *wa*-stems in Germanic, they are also a subcategory of the *a*-declension. In the Old English nominative singular of such nouns the *-wa-* is reduced to -*u* or -*o;*

in the other cases -*w*- is retained before the endings that are identical with those of the *a*-declension. When -*w* does appear in the nominative singular, it has been restored by analogy. Common *wa*-stems in Old English are the masculines *bearu,-o* 'grove' (genitive singular *bearwes*) *lāreōw* 'teacher', *þēaw* 'custom', *þēo(w)* 'servant'; and the neuters *bealu,-o* 'evil', *cnēo(w)* 'knee', *trēo(w)* 'tree'.

3.6   *The Subsequent Leveling of Old English Nominal Endings* In Middle English the five distinctive endings of *a*-declension nouns (-*es, -e, -as, -a, -um*) were reduced to two (-*es* [əs], -*e* [ə]). As early as the tenth century, vowels in final syllables began to lose their individual qualities and began to be pronounced [ə], a direct consequence of the heavy stress placed on the root syllable of Old English words. This had the effect of obscuring the difference between -*es* and -*as,* and between -*e* and -*a.* The loss of final nasals was also a part of the process, and -*um,* which had become [əm], then fell together with [ə], from -*e* and -*a.* Although -*es* (from Old English -*as*) was extended by analogy to the genitive and dative plural, the noun at that point had no more than two actual endings ([ə] and [əs]). In a further development, the pronunciation of the final [ə], a mark of the dative singular, was discontinued by 1400, and then only the termination [əs] remained, although with diverse functions. The nominative (and accusative) singular, which never had any ending, and that form of the noun inflected with [əs] have survived without change in Modern English where, because of its dual origin (genitive singular, and nominative and accusative plural), the inflection spelled -(*e*)*s* still indicates both possession (*boy's, boys'*) and plurality (*boys*); use of the apostrophe to prevent ambiguity is an orthographical device of Modern English. Since there were other nominal paradigms besides the *a*-declension in Old English, not all forms of the Modern English noun can be explained in terms of the foregoing derivation. However, the exceptions constitute only a small minority. As formal case endings diminished in number, prepositions and a stable word order increased in importance for the expression of those meanings previously conveyed by inflection alone.

3.7   *The Definite Article*   The forms of the Old English definite article are reflexes of an Indo-European demonstrative pronoun (*to-), which had a "relatively weak demonstrative meaning," and was "therefore well adapted to be used as definite article."[2] Standing alone or followed by the indeclinable relative particle *þe* 'who, which', the Old English definite article still retains a demonstrative capacity: *þā sē þēowa ūt ēode, hē ġemētte his efenþēowan sē him sceolde ān hund peninga* 'when the servant went out, he met his fellow-servant, that one (who) owed him one hundred pennies'. The definite article was fully declined in Old

English. Since it had to agree with any following noun in gender, number, and case, and since the forms of the singular definite article are fairly distinctive, it is very often a good indicator for the resolution of ambiguities about the case or gender of a noun; *bāt* 'boat', for example, may be either nominative or accusative singular, but *sē bāt* can be only nominative singular masculine (and hence probably the subject), and *þone bāt* only accusative singular masculine (and hence probably the direct object). In the plural the definite article gives somewhat less exact information than in the singular since the plural forms are the same for all three genders. The following two paradigms should be memorized.

3.7.1   *sē* 'the' (masculine)

	Singular	**Plural**
N	sĕ	þā
G	þæs	þāra
D	þǣm, þām	þǣm, þām
A	þone	þā
I	þȳ, þon, þē	þǣm, þām

In an unaccented position, the nominative singular form has a short *-e*; the unaccented form is not indicated in this grammar.

3.7.2   *þæt* 'the' (neuter)

	Singular	**Plural**
N	þæt	þā
G	þæs	þāra
D	þǣm, þām	þǣm, þām
A	þæt	þā
I	þȳ, þon, þē	þǣm, þām

3.7.3   Late in the Old English period an analogical variant to *sĕ* developed; because all forms of the definite article except *sĕ* and its feminine equivalent *sēo* began with *þ-* it is readily understandable that *þĕ* should have arisen as a common alternate. With the radical leveling of inflections that took place during the Middle English period, the five cases, three genders, and two numbers of the definite article were reduced to the neologism *þe*, Modern English *the*. The neuter article *þæt*, however, survives as the Modern English demonstrative *that*.

3.7.4   Old English did not have an indefinite article; instead, the words *ān* 'one' and *sum* 'a certain' were used to express indefinite reference: *sum monn him plantode wīngeard and betȳnde hine ond dealf ānne*

Figure 1. SUTTON HOO PURSE LID. Courtesy British Museum.

sēað ond ġetimbrode ānne stīpel 'a certain man planted a vineyard for himself, and enclosed it and dug a winevat and built a tower'.

3.8   *The Infinitive*   A frequently encountered verbal form is the infinitive; it is always uninflected. In origin the Germanic infinitive is the neuter accusative singular of a verbal noun, which in the dative case becomes the source of the West Germanic gerund (see 10.2). With very few exceptions *-an* marks the Old English infinitive, which in many cases may have either an active or (less often) a passive meaning, depending upon the context; for example, *sē cyning hāt his þēow þone helm feċċan*, 'The king commanded his servant *to bring* (fetch) the helmet'; *sē cyning hāt þone helm feċċan*, 'The king commanded the helmet *to be brought*'. The following are some common infinitives that do not end in *-an*: *bēon* 'to be'; *dōn* 'to do'; *fēon* 'to rejoice'; *flēon* 'to flee'; *fōn* 'to seize'; *gān* 'to go'; *sēon* 'to see'; *tēon* 'to pull'; *ðēon* 'to thrive, prosper'.

3.9   *Old English Maxims*   From before 1072 to the present day, the Chapter Library at Exeter Cathedral has possessed "the largest and probably the best known of the four great miscellanies of Anglo-Saxon poetry,"[3] the *Exeter Book*; the manuscript, probably written in the period 970–990, was given to the cathedral by Leofric, the first Bishop of Exeter (1050–1072). Although later augmented by eight additional folios, Leofric's gift, the *Exeter Book* proper, consists of 123 parchment leaves upon which is recorded the only source for such poems as the *Phoenix, Juliana, The Wanderer, The Seafarer, Widsith, Deor, Wulf and Eadwacer,* the *Wife's Lament,* and the *Husband's Message*; the poems are not titled in the manuscript, which is also devoid of illustration. Also included in the collection is a set of maxims (*Maxims I*), or gnomic verses, one of several that have survived from the Anglo-Saxon period; another noteworthy compilation, the *Cotton Gnomes* (*Maxims II*), consists of sixty-six lines, and appears to serve as part of an introduction to the *Abingdon Chronicle*, or C version of the *Anglo-Saxon Chronicle*, the manuscript of which was once owned by the antiquarian, Sir Robert Cotton (1571–1631). Another source of maxims is the Anglo-Saxon *Rune Poem*, perhaps composed about 775. A medium for the statement of ancient and contemporary lore, Old English maxims were reflections on the natural properties of creatures and objects or moral guides, both social and religious, for human endeavor.[4] Consequently a formal distinction exists between the *biþ-gnome* and the *sceal-gnome; biþ-gnomes* tell about things as they *are* whereas *sceal-gnomes* suggest how things *should* or *ought* to be. Not distinguished for their literary quality, the Old English maxims, nevertheless, do "afford glimpses of the life of the people—of the hunter, of the warrior, of the gamester at the chess-board and the dice, of the felon to be hanged, of the clouds in the sky and of the wild hawk swooping down from them. These glimpses are of the briefest, and kaleidoscopic in nature; the net impression left is that of sudden vistas almost at once obscured. The general coloring of even these often quite pagan apothegms is, however, mainly Christian, as would be expected of any considerable amount of Old English verses from about the ninth century."[5] Not confined solely to specific collections, gnomic wisdom is also a stylistic feature of some Old English poetry; *The Wanderer, The Seafarer,* and, in particular, *Beowulf,* are all poems in which the maxim is interpolated. The following maxims have been excerpted from the collection in the *Exeter Book*; presented below as separate statements, they are integral parts of a poem that is two hundred and four lines in length and divided into three major sections in the original. The dialect is Late West Saxon, slightly modified here for the purpose of an initial exercise.

3.10   *Some Maxims from the* Exeter Book
(Translate into literal but idiomatic English.)

1. Forst sceal frēosan.
2. Fӯr sceal wudu meltan.
3. Lida biþ longe on sīþe.
4. God sceal man herian.
5. Snotre men sāwlum beorgað.
6. Cyning biþ anwealdes ġeorn.
7. Mæġen man sceal mid mete fēdan.
8. Stӯran sceal man mid strangum mōde.
9. Mæġ God syllan ēadigum æhte, and eft niman.
10. Boga sceal stræle, sceal bām ġelīċ mon tō ġemæċċan.
11. Scamiande man sceal in sceade hwēorfan, scīr in lēohte ġerīseð.
12. Swā moniġe bēoþ men ofer eorþan, swā bēoþ mōdġeþancas; ælċ him hafað sundorsefan.
13. Earm biþ sē þe sceal āna libban, winelēas wunian.
14. Ēadiġ bið sē þe in his ēþle ġeðīhþ; earm sē him his frӯnd ġeswīcaþ.
15. Storm oft holm ġebringeþ, ġeofen in grimmum sælum.
16. Winelēas, wansǣliġ man ġenimeð him wulfas tō ġefērum, felafǣcne dēor.
17. Cyning sceal mid ċēape cwēne gebicgan, bunum and bēagum.
18. God ūs ēċe biþ, ne wendaþ hine wyrda, ne hine wiht dreċeþ, ādl ne yldo ælmihtiġne.
19. Scyld sceal cempan, sceaft rēafere, sceal brӯde bēag, bēċ leornere, hūsl hālgum men, hæþnum synne.

20.   Ġearo sceal gūðbord, gār on sceafte, ecg on sweorde, ond
ord spere, hyġe heardum men. Helm sceal cēnum, ond ā
þæs hēanan hyġe hord unġinnost.

3.11   *Notes*   (Please note that all numbers in "Notes" sections
refer to line numbers.)

1.   *forst* for *frost* is an example of the phonetic phenomenon called
metathesis in which two successive sounds, one of which is frequently [r] or [l], are
transposed. Modern English *bird* and *third* are metathesized forms of Old English
bridd and *þridda* respectively. *sceal*: third person singular, present indicative of
sculan.

3.   *biþ*: third person singular, present indicative of *bēon; longe* is an adverb.
4.   The word order is inverted.
5.   *sāwlum* is the direct object; direct objects of *beorgan* are in the dative
case rather than in the accusative.
6.   *ġeorn* usually requires the genitive case.
7.   *mæġen* is the direct object.
8.   In adjectives, *-um* is a mark of the masculine and neuter dative singular as well as the dative plural.
9.   *ēadigum* is an adjective used as a noun; the ending *-um* shows that it
is an indirect object, here probably in the singular.
10.   *sceal* [be]; *bām* 'to both'; *tō* 'as'.
11.   *scamiande man* 'a man in shame, a shameful man'; *ġerīseð* is third
person singular, present indicative.
12.   *bēoþ* is third person plural, present indicative; *him* 'for himself'.
13.   *sē* is often combined with the indeclinable relative particle *þe* to express 'the one who', 'that one who', 'he who'.
14.   *sē* by itself may also mean 'the one who', 'he who'; *ġeswīcaþ* is third
person plural, present indicative.
15.   *ġebringeþ* is third person singular, present indicative.
16.   *ġenimeð* is third person singular, present indicative; *him* is a reflexive,
'for himself'.
17.   *mid bunum and bēagum.*
18.   *ūs* 'for us'. *wendaþ* is third person plural, present indicative; *dreċeþ* is
third person singular, present indicative. *hine* and *ælmihtiġne* are direct objects in the
accusative.
19.   *sceal* [be for].
20.   *sceal* [be].

References

1. Randolph Quirk and C. L. Wrenn, *An Old English Grammar*, 2nd ed. (London, 1958), p. 20.
2. Eduard Prokosch, *A Comparative Germanic Grammar* (Philadelphia, 1939), p. 267.
3. George Philip Krapp and Elliott van Kirk Dobbie, eds., *The Exeter Book* (New York, 1936), *The Anglo-Saxon Poetic Records*, III, p. xi.
4. Stanley B. Greenfield, *A Critical History of Old English Literature* (New York, 1965), p. 196.
5. George K. Anderson, *The Literature of the Anglo-Saxons* (Princeton, New Jersey, 1949), p. 171.

Chapter 4 ———————————

4.1   *The ō-declension*   The third major nominal declension contains feminine nouns only. That is the ō-declension, which corresponds to the ā-declension, or first declension, in Greek and Latin; *cf.* Greek *chōr-ā* 'country', Latin *ui-a* 'street, road'. Indo-European *ā* invariably becomes *ō* in Germanic, and, along with the shift of *o* to *a* (see 3.5), this change is uniquely characteristic of the Germanic languages. Thirty percent of Old English nouns are feminine, and five-sixths of these nouns are declined on the pattern of the ō-declension.[1] The following paradigm should be memorized, as it is representative of the ō-declension.

4.1.1   *talu* 'tale, number' (feminine)

	Singular	**Plural**
N	tal-u, -o	tal-a
G	tal-e	tal-a
D	tal-e	tal-um
A	tal-e	tal-a
I	tal-e	tal-um

4.1.2   Some nouns of the ō-declension have no ending in the nominative singular (e.g., *ār* 'honor', *glōf* 'glove', *þēod* 'people, nation'), while *-e* is a frequent alternative for the nominative plural, and *-(e)na* for the genitive plural. The presence or absence of a final vowel in the nominative singular is determined by the length of the root (see 3.5.3). The etymologically correct ending for the nominative-accusative plural is actually *-e*; the ending *-a* may be from the feminine *u*-declension (see 10.4.1) by analogy.

4.1.3   *jō-stem and wō-stem Nouns*   Like the *a*-declension, which encompasses two subgroups, *ja-stems* and *wa-stems* (see 3.5.4 and 3.5.5), the *ō*-declension also includes nouns for which the stem termination was not a single vowel (*-ō*), but *-jō-* or *-wō-*, derived from Indo-European *-yā-* and *-wā-*. Such nouns are feminine only, and do not differ in their declension from the "pure" *ō*-stems. Some common *jō*-stem nouns are *ecg* 'edge', *secg* 'sword', *sibb* 'relationship', and *wynn* 'joy'; common *wō*-stems are *beadu,-o* 'battle', *frætwa,-e* (plural) 'ornaments', *ġeatwa,-e* (plural) 'armaments, armor', and *mǣd* 'meadow'.

4.2   *sēo*   The feminine definite article *sēo,* which should be learned, is declined as follows:

	Singular	**Plural**
N	sēo	þā
G	þǣre	þāra
D	þǣre	þǣm, þām
A	þā	þā
I	þǣre	þǣm, þām

4.2.1   In Late Old English *þēo* developed as an analogical variant to *sēo.*

4.3   *Strong and Weak Adjectives*   In Indo-European nouns and adjectives were declined with the same set of inflectional endings (*cf.* Latin *bonus amicus* 'good friend'), and the Germanic languages preserve remnants of that system in the so-called strong declension of adjectives. One specific innovation of Germanic, however, was the development of a second, or weak, adjectival declension. The German philologist Jacob Grimm (1785–1863) was the first to apply the terms strong and weak (*stark* and *schwach*) not only to adjectives but also to the two basic schemes for verbal conjugation (see 5.1.4). For the source of the weak adjective see 4.4. Characterized by the presence of *-n-* in the case endings, the weak declension is used: a) when the adjective is preceded by a modifying word (the definite article *sē,* the demonstrative *þēs* 'this', or a possessive pronoun); b) when it modifies a noun in direct address (e.g., *lēofe dohtor* 'beloved daughter'); and c) regularly in the comparative degree and frequently in the superlative degree. In all other instances the strong declension is used. For the purpose of translation, it is not necessary to distinguish between strong and weak, but a certain familiarity with the two sets of adjectival endings is desirable. The following is a paradigm of the weak declension; see 5.2 for the strong declension.

4.3.1   *gōd* 'good' (weak declension)

	Singular			Plural
	Masculine	*Feminine*	*Neuter*	*All Genders*
N	gōd-a	gōd-e	gōd-e	gōd-an
G	gōd-an	gōd-an	gōd-an	gōd-ena, gōd-ra
D	gōd-an	gōd-an	gōd-an	gōd-um
A	gōd-an	gōd-an	gōd-e	gōd-an
I	gōd-an	gōd-an	gōd-an	gōd-um

4.3.2   Without a following noun the weak adjective is construed in a quasi-nominal capacity: *ġespræc þā sē gōda ġylpworda sum* 'then the good (one, man) spoke certain boasting words'.

4.4   *The Weak Nominal Declension*   The weak adjective declension discussed in 4.3 is, in fact, a Germanic adaptation of an Indo-European nominal declension originally devised to form agent and attributive nouns. Nouns of that declension were characterized by the suffix *-en-* or *-on-*; cf. in Latin *edō* (nominative), *ed-ōn-is* (genitive) 'glutton', and the adjective *catus* 'sly, cunning' beside *Catō* (nominative), *Cat-ōn-is* (genitive) literally 'the sly one', or *rūfus* 'red, red-haired' beside *Rūfō* (nominative), *Rūf-ōn-is* (genitive) literally 'the red-haired man'. That Indo-European declension was not lost in Old English and a relatively large number of nouns are declined according to it. Termed the weak (nominal) declension, or the *n*-stem declension, it contains nouns of all three genders; in almost every instance the inflectional endings are identical to those of the weak adjective. The following paradigms of the weak nominal declension should be learned.

4.4.1   *guma* 'man' (masculine)

	Singular	Plural
N	gum-a	gum-an
G	gum-an	gum-ena
D	gum-an	gum-um
A	gum-an	gum-an
I	gum-an	gum-um

4.4.2   *folde* 'earth' (feminine)

	Singular	Plural
N	fold-e	fold-an
G	fold-an	fold-ena
D	fold-an	fold-um
A	fold-an	fold-an
I	fold-an	fold-um

4.4.3   *ēage* 'eye' (neuter)

	Singular	Plural
N	ēag-e	ēag-an
G	ēag-an	ēag-ena
D	ēag-an	ēag-um
A	ēag-e	ēag-an
I	ēag-an	ēag-um

In Indo-European, neuter nouns of this declension invariably named a part of the body; others in Old English are *ēare* 'ear' and *wange* 'cheek'.

4.4.4   Only a small group of feminine nouns do not conform to the standard paradigm. They all end in either *-o* (*bēo* 'bee') or *-ā* (*tā* 'toe') in the nominative singular, and have *-on* (instead of *-an*) in all the oblique cases except the genitive plural and the dative-instrumental plural, which end in *-ona* (instead of *-ena*) and *-om* (instead of *-um*) respectively.

4.5   *Old English Riddles*   In addition to maxims, the *Exeter Book* contains over ninety riddles both popular and learned. Like the maxim, riddles are an ancient and widespread device for the expression of everyday wisdom; parallels to the Old English maxims are found in the Biblical Book of *Proverbs,* the Sanskrit *Vedas,* and the Arabic *Koran.* The riddle of the Sphinx is well known from the tragic story of King Œdipus, and, according to the Herodotean *Life of Homer,* the blind poet is supposed to have expired from chagrin at being unable to solve a riddle put to him by some boys. In Anglo-Saxon England riddles originated with the one hundred Latin *Ænigmata* of the scholarly Aldhelm (c.640–709), bishop of Sherborne; included in a long letter (695) addressed to Aldfrith, king of Northumbria, the *Ænigmata,* written in hexameters, were intended to glorify God's creation. "They begin with Earth, Wind, Cloud, and other natural phenomena, and end fittingly with the longest, *Creatura,* or Creation. They are unlike riddles in that they do not pose a problem and ask for an answer, but are each headed by self-explanatory titles."[2] Aldhelm's example was followed by two other churchmen whose Latin riddles have also survived: Tatwine (d.734), archbishop of Canterbury; and Eusebius, or Hwætberht (c.680–c.747), abbot of Monkwearmouth and a friend of the Venerable Bede. The Old English riddles from the *Exeter Book* are "related to the Latin tradition, but they are in the vernacular, handled in the customary alliterative verse with great freshness of treatment."[3] Each riddle is, then, a short poem, yet composed without benefit of rhyme, which was never a feature of Anglo-Saxon prosody; the poetical line is divided by a caesura into two parts, both of which have at least one alliterative element in common. Almost certainly of multiple authorship, the *Exeter Book* riddles deal with a range of topics that include natural phenomena, music, birds, weapons, fighting, and various aspects of Christianity; eight riddles, scattered throughout the collection, are moderately clever exercises in obscenity. The dialect is Late West Saxon.

4.6   *Three Riddles from the* Exeter Book   (Translate into literal but idiomatic English.)

A (no. 7 in the *Exeter Book*)
Hræġl mīn swīgað,   þonne iċ hrūsan trede
oþþe þā wīċ būge,   oþþe wado drēfe.
Hwīlum mec āhebbað   ofer hæleþa byht
hyrste mīne,   ond þēos hēa lyft,
5   ond mec þonne wīde   wolcna strenġu
ofer folc byreð.   Frætwe mīne
swōgað hlūde   ond swinsiað,
torhte singað,   þonne iċ ġetenġe ne bēom
flōde ond foldan,   fērende ġǣst.

B (no. 50 in the *Exeter Book*)
Wiga is on eorþan   wundrum ācenned
dryhtum tō nytte,   of dumbum twām
torht ātyhted,   þone on tēon wīġeð
fēond his fēonde.   Forstrangne oft
5   wīf hine wrīð;   hē him wel hēreð,
þēowaþ him ġeþwǣre,   ġif him þeġniað
mæġeð ond mæcgas   mid ġemete ryhte
fēdað hine fæġre;   hē him fremum stēpeð
līfe on lissum.   Lēanað grimme
10   þām þe hine wloncne   weorþan lǣteð.

C (no. 66 in the *Exeter Book*)
Iċ eom māre   þonne þēs middanġeard,
lǣsse þonne hondwyrm,   lēohtre þonne mōna,
swiftre þonne sunne.   Sǣs mē sind ealle
flōdas on fæðmum   ond þēs foldan bearm,
5   grēne wongas.   Grundum iċ hrīne,
helle underhnīġe,   heofonas oferstīġe,
wuldres ēþel,   wīde rǣċe
ofer engla eard,   eorþan ġefylle,
ealne middanġeard   ond merestrēamas
10   sīde mid mē sylfum.   Saga hwæt iċ hātte.

4.7   Notes

A   The solution is *swan*. A clue to the answer is perhaps provided by a symbol standing at the close of the riddle which resembles the runic letter ᚲ; having the phonetic value [k], the rune, if that it is, may be intended to suggest Latin *cygnus* 'swan'.

1.   *swīgað* is third person singular, present indicative.

2.   *wado* 'waters, sea'; the nominative singular is *wæd*, a neuter a-declension noun (see 3.5.3). The word occurs only in poetry, the standard Old English word for 'water' being *wæter*.

3.   *mec* is a direct object.

4.   *āhebbað* is the third person plural, present indicative; the subject is *hyrste* (1.4).

5.   *mec* is a direct object.

6.   Both *lyft* (1.4) and *strengu* (1.5) are subjects of *byreð* (1.6), third person singular, present indicative.

7.   *swōgað, swinsiað,* and *singað* (1.8) are all third person plural, present indicative.

8.   *ġetenġe* 'resting upon'.
     bēom is an alternate form of *bēo* 'am'.

9.   *ferende* 'moving, traveling'; *-(e)nde* is the mark of the present participle; *cf. -ent-* in Latin, *regentis* (genitive singular) 'ruling'.

B   The solution is *fire*.

1.   *wundrum* 'wondrously', the dative-instrumental plural used adverbially.

     ācenned 'born', past participle of *ācennan* 'to bring forth'.

2.   *dryhtum* 'for people'.
     tō nytte 'as a use'.
     of dumbum twām 'by two dumb things', flint and steel.

3.   *torht atȳhted* 'bright(ly) extracted'.
     þone 'which'.

3.   *wīġeð* third singular, present indicative of *wīgan;* all the finite verbs in this riddle are the same number and mood.

4.   *fēond* [against] *his fēonde*.
     forstrangne modifies *hine*.

5.   *wrīð* 'binds', by covering with ashes.
     him 'them' direct object of *hēreð; him* (1.6a) 'them' direct object of *þēowaþ; him* (1.6b) 'him' direct object of *þeġniað*.

7.   *mid ġemete ryhte* (1.7) 'with due propriety'.

8.   *him* 'them'.
     fremum 'advantageously, with advantages'; *cf. wundrum* (1.1).

9.   [*hē*] *lēanað*.

10. *þām þe* 'the one who', with *lǣteð*.

C   The solution is *Creation*. This riddle is a condensed version of a much longer one, over one hundred lines, for which the solution is also Creation (*Exeter Book*, no. 40).

1.   *eom* is first person singular, present indicative of *bēon*.

middanġeard (1.1) 'world, earth', literally 'middle-yard'; in Germanic cosmology the earth, a flat plain surrounded by water, was located between the home of the gods (above) and the home of the giants, their enemies, (below); the descriptive term *middanġeard* was readily adaptable to the Christian concept of earth as a region lying between heaven and hell. Note the purely Christian denotation of *middanġeard* in line seven of Cædmon's *Hymn* (6.9).

2.   *hondwyrm* 'handworm'; according to the *Oxford English Dictionary* "an acarid, the itch-insect (*Sarcoptes scabiei*) which burrows in the hands."

3.   *mē* dative singular, 'for me, with respect to me'.

ealle modifies both *sæs* and *flōdas,* the subjects of *sind* (1.3), third person plural, present indicative of *bēon.*

4.   *þēs foldan bearm* literally 'this of the earth bosom; a common construction.

5.   *wongas* for *wangas.*

hrīne first person singular, present indicative of *hrīnan,* which takes the dative case (*grundum*).

10.   *mid mē sylfum* 'by myself'.

saga second person singular, imperative of *secgan.*

References

1.   Randolph Quirk and C. L. Wrenn, *An Old English Grammar,* 2nd ed. (London, 1958), p. 20.

2.   Paull F. Baum, trans., *Anglo-Saxon Riddles of the Exeter Book* (Durham, North Carolina, 1963), p. xi.

3.   George K. Anderson, *The Literature of the Anglo-Saxons* (Princeton, New Jersey, 1949), p. 172.

Chapter 5

5.1   *The Verb*   The declension of nouns and adjectives makes up only one of the two major inflectional systems of Old English; the other is, of course, the conjugation of verbs. In Indo-European, verbal conjugation, though not systematic, was a relatively complex matter, as it is, for example, in Sanskrit and Greek, but as Proto-Germanic developed, considerable simplification was introduced. Moods (indicative, subjunctive, optative, imperative), numbers (singular, dual, plural), voices (active and medio-passive), and participles were either eliminated or reduced. In Old English, then, the verb has the following distinct *forms:* one voice (active); two numbers (singular and plural); two tenses (present and past, or preterite); two moods in both the present and preterite (indicative and subjunctive); one mood in the present only (imperative); an infinitive (see 3.8); a present participle (see 8.3), a past participle (see 9.2) prefixed or not by the particle *ġe-;* and a gerund (see 10.2). Duality was occasionally expressed in the first and second persons by means of the appropriate personal pronouns (*wit* 'we two', *ġit* 'you two') but the accompanying verb was plural.

5.1.1   Future time was indicated by present tense *forms,* as it still is in Modern English where, for example, 'I leave' or 'I am leaving' may mean at the moment of utterance or some time later depending upon the context. Indo-European itself appears not to have had a distinctive future tense.

5.1.2   Certain periphrastic, or compound, constructions did, however, exist in Old English, and they signified: a) the passive voice, which was formed by a combination of *bēon, wesan* 'to be', and *weorþan* 'to become' with the past participle, thus *he wæs ġecweald* 'he was killed'; b) two perfect tenses, present and past, which were formed by the combination of *wesan* and *habban* 'to have' with the past participle; and c) the simple future, which was formed by the combination of *willan* 'will' plus the infinitive when there was a sense of desire or intent, and by *sculan* 'shall' plus the infinitive when there was a sense of obligation. All these compound constructions quite closely parallel their Modern English derivatives and pose no difficulties in translation.

5.1.3   *Strong and Weak Verbs*   A comparison of two verbs in Modern English like *sing* and *dance* is sufficient to make apparent the two major categories of verbal conjugation, strong (irregular) and weak (regular) respectively. Strong verbs show internal vocalic change in their principal parts (s*i*ng, s*a*ng, s*u*ng), while weak verbs do not, but, instead, suffix the dental, or alveolar, stop consonants [t] or [d] in the second and third principal parts (dance, danced [dæns*t*], danced [dæns*t*]). Principal parts are simply those forms of a verb which must be known in order to generate its complete conjugation. The strong and weak dichotomy is yet another inheritance from Old English, where almost seventy-five percent of the verbs encountered in the best known literary works are weak and twenty-five percent are strong. In terms of the two predominant conjugational systems of Old English, the very small remaining percentage of verbs may be classified as "irregular"; that balance comprises the anomalous verbs (see 6.5) and the preterite-presents (see 11.3). Numerically disproportionate as the three groups (strong, weak, irregular) may be, they are nevertheless approximately equal in importance from the standpoint of *frequency*, since strong verbs occur very often and irregular verbs include some of the most common in the language, for instance *bēon, willan, dōn,* 'to do', *gān* 'to go', *magan* 'to be able', and *witan* 'to know'.[1] The strong verbs of Old English are subdivided into seven classes, and the weak verbs into three; a sound reading knowledge of Old English is not dependent upon an ability to identify these ten classes with precision, but a passing familiarity with their fundamental nature will be an occasional aid.

5.1.3.1   *Ablaut*   The systematic alternation of vowels in etymologically related words is an Indo-European phenomenon, often referred to in linguistics by the German word *Ablaut*, literally 'away from the sound', or by the phrase *vowel gradation*. There were two kinds of ablaut in Indo-European *qualitative* and *quantitative*. The result of a varying pitch accent, qualitative ablaut was the alternation of different vowels, most frequently *e* and *o: cf.* Greek *leg-ō* 'I speak', *log-os* 'speech';

Latin *teg-ō* 'I cover', *tog-a* 'a covering'. A front vowel (*e*) seems to have implied present 'action', and a back vowel (*o*) 'condition'. Resulting from shifts in the stress accent, quantitative ablaut involved four possible varieties, or grades, of the same vowel: e.g., lengthened [e:], normal [e], reduced [ə], and zero [Ø]; *cf.* Latin *ed-ō* 'I eat' (normal grade), *d-ēns* 'tooth' (zero-grade). In the principal parts of Germanic strong verbs qualitative and quantitative ablaut were combined to produce a systematic series of vocalic sounds and it is on the basis of a particular and distinctive series that the class of any strong verb is determined; for example, the ablaut series of Old English Class I verbs is *ī-ā-i-i* in which the first two vowels reflect qualitative gradation and the last two quantitative gradation. Through the intermediate stage of Proto-Germanic *ī-ai-i-i*, the ablaut series of Class I goes back to *ei-oi-i-i* in Indo-European where the qualitative alternation of *e* and *o* is clearly seen; in the zero-grade of an Indo-European diphthong, as here for instance *ei*, the first element is lost and the second element remains, a type of quantitative alternation manifested by the root vowel of the third and fourth principal parts. It is worth noting that the second element of an Indo-European diphthong was, in effect, a semi-vowel, the specific quality of which was regulated by the phonetic context. Before an immediately following consonant the second element was vocalic, but before a vowel it was consonantal; in reconstructions, the letters *y* (or *i̯*) and *w* (or *u̯*) are used to indicate the consonantal values of *i* and *u* respectively. Thus, *ei* and *ey* both represent the same diphthong, but in different contexts: *cf.* **eis-* 'ice' and *treyes 'three'. If a distinction is not important or necessary, the "vocalic" form is cited.

5.1.4   Although strong verbs in Modern English have three principal parts, those in Old English had four: infinitive, preterite singular, preterite plural, and past participle; the original distinction between preterite singular and preterite plural was lost during the Middle English period. The four principal parts of strong verbs in Old English are based upon the three verbal stems of Indo-European: the *present* stem, for continuing (durative) action; the *aorist* stem, for momentary (punctual) action; and the *perfect* stem, for action completed. In Germanic the three verbal stems, which had primarily signaled verbal *aspect* in Indo-European, were refashioned into a conjugational system that was primarily directed toward the expression of *time*. The present stem developed into the present tense, and an Indo-European verbal adjective formed by ablaut of the present stem plus a special ending became the Germanic past participle (see 9.2). The perfect stem appears in the first and third persons of the preterite singular, and an aorist stem supplies the remaining forms of the preterite. This coalescence of two different stems in the preterite accounts for the additional principal part required for generating the full conjugation of any strong verb.

5.1.5   From an etymological point of view, the first five classes of the Old English strong verb are closely related; they all have an underlying pattern of vocalic gradation that in Indo-European was essentially e:o:ə (present: preterite singular: preterite plural, past participle). Classes VI and VII, for which the ablauting vowels were different, are discussed separately below (see 11.1). The following verbs provide standard examples of those vocalic alternations displayed by all seven classes; memorization of their principal parts is recommended.

Class	Infinitive	Pret. Sg.	Pret. Pl.	Past Part.	
I	rīdan	rād	ridon	riden	'ride'
II	bēodan	bēad	budon	boden	'command'
III	singan	sang	sungon	sungen	'sing'
IV	beran	bær	bǣron	boren	'bear'
V	sprecan	spræc	sprǣcon	sprecen	'speak'
VI	faran	fōr	fōron	faren	'go'
VII	hātan	hēt	hēton	hāten	'be called'

5.1.6   The indicative mood in Old English was used for statements of objective fact and for questions. The following paradigm of *singan* in the present and preterite indicative is representative of all strong verbs, and should be memorized along with the accompanying personal pronouns.

Present Indicative

Singular	*Plural*
1 iċ (I) sing-e	wē (we) sing-aþ
2 þū (you) sing-est	ġē (you) sing-aþ
3 hē (he) sing-eþ	hīe (they) sing-aþ

Preterite Indicative

Singular	*Plural*
1 iċ sang	wē sung-on
2 þū sung-e	ġē sung-on
3 hē sang	hīe sung-on

There is only one inflected form in the plural for all verbs, regardless of tense or mood. The second person singular pronoun *þū* is simply 'you' in translation, and not 'thou'; a translation of *þū* as 'thou' imparts a suggestion of politesse that the word did not have in Old English.

5.2   *The Strong Adjective*   The inflectional endings of the strong adjective (see 4.3) display a close resemblance to those of the *a*-declension (masculine and neuter) and the *ō*-declension (feminine) of nouns; the strong adjectives of Germanic, as previously noted, are vestiges of the Indo-European method of declining both nouns and adjectives by suffixation of the same endings to each group. The following is a paradigm of the strong declension.

5.2.1   *gōd* 'good' (strong declension)

Singular

	Masculine	*Feminine*	*Neuter*
N	gōd	gōd	gōd
G	gōd-es	gōd-re	gōd-es
D	gōd-um	gōd-re	gōd-um
A	gōd-ne	gōd-e	gōd
I	gōd-e	gōd-re	gōd-e

Plural

	Masculine	*Feminine*	*Neuter*
N	gōd-e	gōd-a, -e	gōd, -e
G	gōd-ra	gōd-ra	gōd-ra
D	gōd-um	gōd-um	gōd-um
A	gōd-e	gōd-a, -e	gōd, -e
I	gōd-um	gōd-um	gōd-um

5.2.2   Some strong adjectives have *-u* or *-o* as an ending in the feminine nominative singular and in the neuter nominative and accusative plural; these differences are identical to those among neuter nouns of the *a*-declension (see 3.5.2 and 3.5.3) and feminine nouns of the *ō*-declension (see 4.1.2 and 4.1.3). Note that *-um*, an invariant mark of the dative-instrumental *plural* in nouns, also marks the dative-instrumental *singular* of strong adjectives in the masculine and neuter; in lWS *-um* is sometimes written *-an(-on)*. *gōd-e* in the nominative and accusative plural (feminine and neuter) is also a later writing. If a strong adjective ends in *-e* (eg. *clæne* 'clean') it retains that ending in the nominative singular masculine and the nominative and accusative singular neuter.

5.2.3   A strong adjective standing alone may acquire the status of a noun: *ac sē wonna hrefn fūs ofer fǣgum [sceal] fela reordian* 'but, rather, the dark raven, eager for the dead, will speak much'; *fǣge* is an adjective, normally translated 'doomed to die, fated'.

5.3   *The Venerable Bede*   One of the most learned figures of the early Middle Ages was the Northumbrian monk Bede (Baeda), who, according to tradition, was born at Monkton near Durham in 673. Perhaps best known for his *History of the English Church and People* (731), the culmination of his literary endeavor, he produced numerous other works of a scientific, theological, and historical nature; *The Lives of the Holy Abbots,* completed in 720, is especially notable. From 682 until his death in 735 Bede lived, wrote, and taught at the Benedictine monastery of Saint Paul at Jarrow, gaining a widespread reputation during his own lifetime for scholarship, both sacred and profane, and for piety; he is, indeed, the only Englishman placed in Paradise by Dante, who wrote his *Divina Commedia* no less than six centuries later. According to Bede's own testimony, he took much pleasure in the monastic routine and the opportunity it afforded him for study and composition. Just eighteen when he began his writing career, Bede seems only occasionally to have used the vernacular for prose, having preferred instead to express himself in Latin; the Old English version of his *History* is, of course, entirely from another, later hand. A creation of Bede's maturity, the *History* is a most exceptional document, for he was "not content to compile a bare chronicle of events and dates, or to restrict himself to hagiography as his predecessors had done. He set himself to examine all available records, to secure verbal or written accounts from reliable living authorities, to record local traditions and stories, to interpret significant events, and, in short, to compile as complete and continuous a history of the English Church and people as lay within his power. He was the first to conceive or attempt such a formidable project, and posterity acknowledges his pioneer work as a remarkably successful achievement."[2] The West Saxon translation has, likewise, a claim to merit, containing as it does some of the very finest passages of Old English prose, in spite of the fact that the translator was to a certain extent bound stylistically by the Latin original before him. Bede commences his *History* with the following selection, a description of the island of Britain; three manuscripts of the *Anglo-Saxon Chronicle* were later begun with a paraphrase of it. The dialect is Late West Saxon.

5.4   *The Opening Passage of Bede's* Ecclesiastical History

Breoton is gārsecges ēalond, ðæt wæs iū ġeara Albion hāten; is ġeseted betwyh norðdæle and westdæle, Germanie and Gallie and Hispanie. þām mæstum dælum Europe, myccle fæce onġeġen. þæt is norð ehta hund mīla lang, and tū hund hund mīla brād. Hit hafað
5   fram sūðdæle þā mæġþe onġēan, þe mon hāteþ Gallia Bellica. Hit is weliġ, þis ēalond, on wæstmum and on trēowum misenlīcra cynna. And hit is ġescræpe on læswe sċēapa and nēata, and on sumum stōwum wīnġeardas grōwaþ. Swylċe ēac þēos eorðe is berende missenlīcra fugela and sæwihta, and fiscwyllum wæterum
10   and wyllġesprynġum, and hēr bēoð oft fangene sēolas and hronas

and mereswȳn; and hēr bēoþ oft numene missenlīcra cynna
weolcscylle and musclan, and on þām bēoð oft ġemētte þā betstan
meregrotan ǣlċes hīwes. And hēr bēoð swȳþe ġenihtsume weolocas,
of þām bið ġeweorht sē weolocrēada tælhġ, þone ne mæġ sunne
15 blǣċan nē ne reġn wyrdan; ac swā hē bið yldra, swā hē fæġerra
bið. Hit hafað ēac þis land sealtsēaðas; and hit hafaþ hāt wæter
and hāt baðo ǣlċere yldo and hāde þurh tōdǣlede stōwe ġescrǣpe.
Swylċe hit is ēac berende on wecga ōrum āres and īsernes, lēades
and seolfres. Hēr bið ēac ġemēted gagātes: Sē stān bið blǣc ġym;
20 ġif mon hine on fȳr dēð, þonne flēoð þǣr nēddran onweġ. Wæs
þis ēalond ēac ġēo ġewurðad mid þām æðelestum ċeastrum, ānes
wana þrīttigum, ðā þe wǣron mid weallum and torrum and ġeatum
and þām trumestum locum ġetimbrade, būtan ōðrum lǣssan unrīm
ċeastra.

5.5   Notes

1. *iū ġeara*, an idiom, 'long ago'.

2. *ġested*, the past participle of *settan* 'to set'; past participles may or
may not be prefixed with the (perfective) particle *ġe-*.

2. . . . *and westdǣle, myccle fæce onġeġen Germanie and Gallie* . . .;
myccle fæce '(at) a great distance' is a measure of space in the instrumental case.

3. *Europe*, genitive singular.

4. *mīla*, genitive plural, 'of miles'; the so-called partitive genitive that
indicates portion; *cf.* in Modern English 'a cup of coffee', 'a glass of beer'.

5. *onġēan*, here an adverb.

5. *Gallia Bellica* 'Belgic Gaul'.

7. *on lǣswe* 'in pasturage'.

7. *sċēapa* and *nēata* are genitive plurals, but translate as 'for sheep and
cattle'.

8. *swylċe ēac* 'in like manner also', 'likewise'.

9. *berende*, the present participle of *beran* 'to bear'; *is berende* expresses
durative aspect.

9. *fugela* and *sǣwihta*, though genitive plurals, function as direct objects of *is berende*.

9–10. *wæterum* and *wyllġespryngum* are locative datives, i.e. datives of 'place
where'. The awkward syntax is occasioned by the Latin original.

10. *bēoð*, third person plural, present indicative of *bēon*; *bēoð*. . . . *fangene*
'are caught'; *fangene* is the past participle of *fōn* 'to seize, catch', here combined
with *bēoð* to express the passive. It has the (strong) ending *-e* because of its adjectival
nature.

11. *numene*, the past participle of *niman* 'to take, seize'.

12. *weolcscylle* and *musclan* are the subjects of *bēoð numene*.

12. *on þām* 'from them'.

12. *ġemētte*, the past participle of *mētan* 'to obtain'.

14. *ġeweorht*, the past participle of *wyrċan* 'to make, produce'.

14. *þone* 'the one which'.

14–15. *ne . . . ne* 'neither . . . nor'.

15. *ac* 'but' often has the force of 'but rather', 'but instead'.

15. *swā . . . swā* 'as . . . so'.

15. *hē*, i.e., *sē tælhġ*.

17. *baðo*, accusative plural; the singular root is *bæð-*.

17. *tōdǣlede* 'separated', the past participle of *tōdǣlan* 'to separate', used as an adjective before *stōwe*.

19. *ġemēted*, the past participle of *mētan*. Some weak verbs with roots ending in [t] or [d] have two forms for the past participle, hence *ġemēted* and *ġemētt*.

19. *gagātes*, nominative singular, a Latin loanword.

20. *dēð*, third singular, present indicative of *dōn* 'to do, put'.

20. *flēoð*, third person plural, present indicative of *flēon* 'to flee'.

20. *neddran* 'snakes'; in later English *neddre* (*nædre*) becomes *adder*, just as Old French *naperon* 'a large cloth' became *apron* when the initial [n] was "captured" by the indefinite article 'a'.

21–22. *ānes wana þrīttigum* 'twenty-nine', literally 'of one lacking in (or for) thirty'.

22. *ðā þe* 'which'.

23–24. *unrīm ċeastra* in apposition to *ōðrum lǣssan*, i.e., 'including others smaller, a countless number of towns'.

References

1. Randolph Quirk and C. L. Wrenn, *An Old English Grammar*, 2nd ed. (London, 1958), pp. 40–41.
2. Leo Sherley-Price, trans., *A History of The English Church and People* by Bede (Baltimore, Maryland, 1955), p. 25.

Chapter 6

6.1   *Verner's Law*   At certain places in their conjugation, some strong verbs of Classes I, II, III, and V exhibit a slight, but nevertheless regular, variation in the consonant that terminates the root; this particular variation is frequently called "grammatical change." The infinitive, the present, and the preterite singular of such verbs have a root-final consonant that differs from the root-final consonant of the preterite plural and the past participle; an example from Class III is *weorþan* 'to become', the principal parts of which are *weorþ-an, wearþ, wurd-on, word-en*. In addition to the alternation of *þ* (*ð*) and *d,* alternations between *f/v, h/g,* and *s/r* also occur in Old English. The reason for contrasting verbal roots like *wearþ* and *wo/urd-* was explained by the Danish philologist, Karl Verner (1846–1896), in an article entitled "Eine Ausnahme der ersten Lautverschiebung" ("An Exception to the First Sound Shift"), which he published in 1876; Verner was, of course, addressing himself to certain consonantal problems of Germanic as a whole. According to Grimm's Law (the first Germanic consonant shift), Indo-European [t] should normally appear in Germanic as the voiceless fricative [θ], and so it does in *wearþ,* derived from a root ending in [t]; *cf.* the Latin cognate *uert-ere* 'to turn'. (The fact that [θ] is voiced in *weorþan* has only to do with its being in intervocalic position in Old English, and not with its derivation from Indo-European.) For over fifty years after Grimm codified the Proto-Germanic shifting of Indo-European stop consonants (1822), forms such as *wurdon* and *worden,* however, could not be satisfactorily accounted for; the presence of [d] for [θ] seemed patently quixotic. From his knowledge of accentuation in Sanskrit, Verner correctly deduced that the movable stress accent of Indo-European was the direct cause of the several exceptions to Grimm's formulation. In brief, he stated that if the Indo-European stress accent did not immediately *precede* the particular consonant in question, its Proto-Germanic development would be different from what Grimm had predicted; instead of the expected *voiceless* consonant, its *voiced* counterpart would occur. Thus, Indo-European [p, t, k, and also s], the four consonants involved, might become either [f, θ, χ, and s] *or* [v, ð, ɡ, and z], depending upon the position of the stress accent in the Indo-European etymon concerned. In Old English, as it happened, the Proto-Germanic voiced consonants [ð, ɡ, and z] underwent a secondary development to [d, g, and r], hence the opposition of *wearþ* and *word-en*, of *frēas* 'froze' and *fror-en* 'frozen', and so forth; the preterite plural and the past participle, then, go back to ancient Indo-European forms bearing the stress accent in post-consonantal position. Proto-Germanic [v] remains [v] in Old English, always spelled *f*. Though much leveling of diverse verbal roots has taken place since the Old English period, Modern English *was* and *were* preserve one of the contrasts that Verner successfully explicated. The "Law" also applies to Germanic nouns in which the four Indo-European consonants may appear; for example, Indo-European **patḗr*, Latin *pater*, but Old English *fæder* 'father' with [d] and not [θ].

6.2   *Umlaut in Proto-Old English*   In the prehistoric period of Old English, the root vowel of certain words was affected by *i* [i], *ī* [i:], or *j* [y] in a following syllable. If the root vowel was a back vowel (*ă, ŏ, ŭ*) it was fronted, and if it was a front vowel (*æ, e*) it was raised; this phenomenon is known as *i-umlaut* or *i-mutation*. The cause of such vocalic shifting is disputed, but it may be that the speaker, in anticipating a frontal *i, ī*, or *j*, unconsciously modified the root vowel in such a way that it was brought *phonetically* closer to the sound that was to follow, the consequent result being a kind of vocalic harmony. In any event, the following changes occurred.

Proto-Old English	Old English
a	became æ, later *e* before the nasals *m* and *n*, as in OE *menn* 'men' from POE **manni*
ā	became ǣ, as in OE *lǣran* 'to teach' from POE **lārjan*
o	became e, as in OE *mergen* 'morning' from POE **morġin*
ō	became ē, as in OE *wēnan* 'to believe, think' from POE **wōnjan*
u	became y, as in OE *fyllan* 'to fill' from POE **fulljan*

ū	became ȳ, as in OE *brȳde* 'brides' from POE *brūdi*
æ	became e, as in OE *hefiġ* 'heavy' from POE *hæfiġ*
e	became i, as in OE *sittan* 'to sit' from PGmc *setjanan*

The raising of *e* to *i* actually took place in Proto-Germanic and was not, therefore, confined to prehistoric Old English alone. Like ablaut, *i*-mutation was at first a purely phonological phenomenon to which semantic value was only later attached, e.g., *fōt, fēt* (from *fōti*) 'feet'. The Proto-Old English diphthongs *ēa* and *īo* were also subject to *i*-umlaut; in early Old English they all became the diphthong *īe*, which, in later Old English was monothongized to *ȳ* (or *ī*). Thus: POE *ealdra*, eOE *ieldra*, lOE *yldra* 'older'; POE *hēarjan*, eOE *hīeran*, lOE *hȳran* 'to hear'; POE *hiordi*, eOE *hierde*, lOE *hyrde* 'shepherd'; POE *cīoseþ*, eOE *cīest*, lOE *cȳst* '(he) chooses'. As *i*-mutation operated with only sporadic (and explainable) exceptions, a fairly large number of Proto-Old English words was ultimately affected; a sound-causing umlaut was frequently present in the nominative plural and the dative singular ending of nouns, and regularly present in the ending of adjectives in the comparative and superlative degrees, in the ending of the second and third person singular, present indicative of strong verbs, in all personal endings of the present and preterite indicative of certain weak verbs, and in the suffix for the infinitive of those verbs. In most instances, the umlauting *i*, *ī*, or *j* was lost (syncopated) before 700, and hence rarely appears in the attested forms of West Saxon or any other dialect; *i*-umlaut is a feature of West and North Germanic only.

6.3 *Umlaut in Strong Verbs* The present indicative of strong verbs with a low or back vowel in the root syllable has two umlauted forms: the second person singular and the third person singular, the PGmc endings for which were *-is* and *-iþ* respectively; after causing umlaut the *i* changed to *e* or was lost. Consequently, a verb like *faran* 'to go, travel' is in the singular *iċ fare*, but *þū færst* (or *fœrst*) and *hē færeþ* (or *fœrþ*). If the verbal root ended in *d* [d], *t* [t], *þ* [θ], or *s* [s], consonantal assimilation usually took place after the *e* of the third singular was lost, thereby producing double forms like *hielteþ* and *hielt* from *healdan* 'to hold', *iteþ* and *itt* from *etan* 'to eat', *wierþeþ* and *wierþþ* from *weorþan* 'to become' and *cīseþ* and *cīest* from *cēosan* 'to choose'; sometimes the final consonantal cluster *-tt* and *-þþ* were simplified to *-t* and *-þ*. Syncopation and assimilation also occur in nonmutated strong verbs; e.g. *hē bīdeþ* or *hē bītt* (*bīt*) 'he awaits'. Like the sound shifts encompassed by Verner's Law, those resulting from *i*-umlaut also disturb what might otherwise be regarded as the pristine conjugation of any strong verb, and it is a good idea to keep these possible variations in mind.

6.4   *The Verb 'to be' (I)*   As in Greek and Latin, the verb 'to be' is suppletive in Germanic; in other words, more than one IE verbal root was used to supply the forms for its full conjugation. In addition to IE **es-/s-* 'be' (*cf.* Latin *esse* 'to be') and **bheu-* 'come into being, become' (*cf.* the Sanskrit root *bhū* 'be') Germanic also employed IE **wes-* 'remain, abide, dwell' with its meaning, like that of **bheu-* generalized to 'be'. An interesting cognate of **wes-*, incidentally, is the Latin name *Vesta* 'goddess of the hearth'. Old English forms beginning with a vowel or *s* are derived from **es-/s-*, those beginning with *b* are derived from **bheu-*, and those beginning with *w* are derived from **wes-*. There are two infinitives, *bēon* and (lWS) *wesan,* and two present participles, *bēonde* and (lWS) *wesende.* There is no past participle; for the gerund see 10.2.1. Because of its composite nature and irregular conjugation the substantive verb is classed with the anomalous verbs of Old English. The paradigm of *bēon/ wesan* in the present and preterite indicative should be learned.

Present Indicative

	Singular	Plural
1	iċ eom, bēo	wē sindon, bēoþ
2	þū eart, bist	ġē sindon, bēoþ
3	hē is, biþ	hīe sindon, bēoþ

Preterite Indicative

	Singular	Plural
1	iċ wæs	wē wǣron
2	þū wǣre	ġē wǣron
3	hē wæs	hīe wǣron

6.4.1   Some Indo-European verbs did not have a thematic vowel (*e/o*) inserted between the root and the personal endings. In the present stem of those "athematic" verbs, the inflection **-mi,* rather than **-ō,* signaled the first person singular; *cf. ei-mi* 'I am' and *tithē-mi* 'I put, place', which belong to the so-called *mi*-conjugation of Greek. Distributed among all branches of Germanic, a reflex of **-mi* appears in the first person singular, present indicative of the substantive verb; *cf.* Gothic *im,* Old Norse *em,* and Old English *eom* 'I am'.

6.4.2   *sind* and *sint* are alternatives for *sindon.* Late West Saxon texts show the development of *weseþ* for the third person singular present indicative, and of *wesaþ* for the plural; those forms are not particularly common, however, and neither appears even once in *Beowulf.*

6.4.3   The verb 'to be' combines with the adverb *ne* 'not' to produce contracted negatives, of which the following are some examples: *nis* (*ne is*), *nœs* (*ne wœs*), *nǣron* (*ne wǣron*), *nǣre* (*ne wǣre*).

6.4.4   In the present indicative (only) a distinction in meaning was maintained between *bēo, bist, biþ, bēoþ* and *eom, eart, is, sindon*. The former expresses "(a) an invariable fact, e.g., *ne biǒ swylċ cwēnliċ þeaw* 'such is not a queenly custom', or (b) the future, e.g., *ne biǒ þē wilna gad* 'you will have no lack of pleasures', or (c) iterative extension into the future, e.g., *biþ storma ġehwylċ āswefed* 'every storm is always allayed',"[1] while the latter expresses "a present state provided its continuance is not especially regarded, e.g., *wlitiġ is sē wong* 'the plain is beautiful'."[2]

6.5   *The Anomalous Verbs dōn, gān, willan*   In addition to *bēon,* the anomalous verbs of Old English include *dōn* 'to do', *gān* 'to go,' and *willan* to wish, to be willing'. Like *bēon* they are of especially frequent occurrence, but "have not quite adapted themselves to the system of the 'regular' verbs."[3] By definition irregular, they all have conjugational patterns so diverse that it is not possible to account for them historically within the scope of this grammar; note that the verb *gān* is suppletive. Memorization of the following paradigms is recommended.

Present Indicative

	Singular	Plural
1	iċ dō, gā, wille	wē dōþ, gāþ, willaþ
2	þū dēst gǣst, wilt	ġē dōþ, gāþ, willaþ
3	hē dēþ, gǣþ, wil(l)e	hīe dōþ, gāþ, willaþ

Preterite Indicative

	Singular	Plural
1	iċ dyde, ēode, wolde	wē dydon, ēodon, woldon
2	þū dydest, ēodest, woldest	ġē dydon, ēodon, woldon
3	hē dyde, ēode, wolde	hīe dydon, ēodon, woldon

6.5.1   There is no past participle for *willan;* the past participles of *dōn* and *gān* are *ġedōn* and *ġegān*. The present participles are *dōnde, gānde,* and *willende*. The gerund of *willan* is regular; for the gerunds of *dōn* and *gān* see 10.2.1. The subjunctive formations are listed in 7.4.1.2, and the imperatives in 8.2.

6.5.2   Like *bēon* (see 6.4.3), the anomalous verb *willan* (*wyllan*) also combines with the adverb *ne* 'not' to form contracted negatives. Some examples are: *nelle* or *nylle* (*ne wille*), *nele* (*ne wile*), *nylla* (*ne willa*), and *noldon* (*ne woldon*). The adverbial expression *willy-nilly* 'be I (you, he) willing, be I (you, he) unwilling', in other words 'helplessly', derives from the (subjunctive) phrase *will I nill I; cf.* the (indicative) compound *shilly-shally* from *shall I shall I.*

6.6   *The Personal Pronoun* (*I*)   Much subject to analogical change and other modifications, the Indo-European antecedents of the personal pronoun are a complex of reconstructed forms; nevertheless, it is not difficult to detect a fundamental relationship, for example, among Greek *egō* 'I', Latin *ego*, Gothic *ik,* and Old English *iċ*, or among Latin *tū* 'you (singular)', Old High German *dū*, and Old English *þū*. In the first and second persons the pronoun is not inflected for gender as such; depending upon the context, *iċ* and *þū* are either masculine or feminine, while *wē*, *wit* 'we-two', *ġē*, and *ġit* 'you-two' have varying references to gender. Only the third person singular is actually inflected for gender: *hē* 'he', *hēo* 'she', *hit* 'it'. The declension of the personal pronoun in the first and second persons is really a collection of disparate forms; *mīn* 'of me' is not derived from *iċ* any more than *ūs* 'to us' is derived from *wē*. One case is not necessarily predictable from another.

6.7   *The Personal Pronoun in the First and Second Persons* The following paradigms of the personal pronoun in the first and second persons should be memorized.

First Person

	Singular	*Dual*	*Plural*
N	iċ 'I'	wit 'we-two'	wē 'we'
G	mīn	uncer	ūser, ūre
D	mē	unc	ūs
A	mec, mē	uncit, unc	ūsiċ, ūs
I	mē	unc	ūs

Second Person

	Singular	*Dual*	*Plural*
N	þū 'you'	ġit 'you-two'	ġē 'you'
G	þīn	incer	ēower, īower
D	þē	inc	ēow, īow
A	þec, þē	incit, inc	ēowiċ, ēow, īow
I	þē	inc	ēow, īow

6.7.1   The dual pronouns *wit* and *ġit* agree with plural forms of the verb. A feature of Early West Saxon and Late West Saxon, the dual was completely lost by the fourteenth century.[4] Apart from the dual, Modern English has by and large retained all cases of the personal pronoun except the original accusatives: *I* (*iċ*), *mine* (*mīn*), *me* (*mē*); *we* (*wē*), *our* (*ūre*), *us* (*ūs*); *he* (*hē*), *his* (*his*), *him* (*him*). Scandinavian influence and analogical change are responsible for *they, their,* and *them,* which were *hie, hiere,* and *him* in Old English.

6.7.2   There was no reflexive pronoun in Old English, and the function of a reflexive, when required, was assumed by the personal pronoun in the dative or accusative case; e.g., *ġewāt him* (dative) *þā tō waroðe* 'he went (i.e., betook himself) then to the shore', *wit unc* (accusative) *wið hronfixas werian þōhton* 'we-two intended to defend ourselves against whales'.

Figure 2.   SUTTON HOO GOLD BELT BUCKLE.   Courtesy British Museum.

6.8   *The Story of Cædmon*   The history of English poetry begins with the name Cædmon and with the legend surrounding that name.
In Book Four, chapter twenty-four, of his *History,* Bede tells the engaging
story of a humble cowherd who fell asleep and was transformed by divine
inspiration into a religious poet, and who subsequently versified themes
of sacred history until the time of his serene death. Unfortunately, the
story is burdened with folkloristic elements, which, charming as they are,
obscure whatever factual details may lie behind them. Since there is no
other authority, nothing absolutely certain is known about Cædmon
beyond the etymology of his name, a Keltic word meaning 'soldier' or
'warrior'. There is no necessity, however, to dismiss the report of a careful
annalist like Bede as a complete fiction, or to question his intended ve-
racity; from his sources he believed himself to be writing about a person
who had actually existed, and that alone may well argue for the presence
of some historical truth in his frankly miraculous tale. If the recorded
year of Cædmon's inspiration, 680, is in any way reliable, the poet was
in fact an early contemporary of Bede (who was then seven years old);
furthermore, if Cædmon spent his life in Whitby (Northumbria), he
dwelled within a twenty-five-mile radius of Bede's monastery at Jarrow.
Thus, neither time nor distance may be invoked as plausible excuses for
error on Bede's part; the appealing distortions in his account must have
arisen through other causes, assuming always that even a small part of
what he says does correspond to a previous reality.

In any event, the only surviving work which may possibly be credited
to Cædmon is a hymn of creation; essentially an example of the dream
vision poem so popular later during the Middle English period. Bede relates that Cædmon's vision occurred one night in the stable of the monastery at Whitby where he was laboring as a cowherd, and that upon awakening from his exceptional dream Cædmon informed his superior, the
reeve, about the gift of composition that he had received; the reeve then
conducted him to the abbess of the monastery, its renowned founder, the
pious Hild (614–680). A historical figure, Hild (or Hilda) was the grand-
niece of King Edwin of Northumbria, with whom she was converted to
Christianity in 627; twenty years later she became a nun, and eventually
established a double monastery, for both men and women, at Whitby
where she died in the year of Cædmon's visitation. Much praised by Bede
for her holy ways, Hild encouraged Cædmon to abandon his secular life
and to become a brother of her Community. Having done so, the illiterate
herdsman was orally tutored in the events of sacred history and then
proceeded to create a series of poems on those subjects about which he
had learned. "He sang of Israel's departure from Egypt, their entry into
the land of promise, and many other events of scriptural history. He

sang of the Lord's Incarnation, Passion, Resurrection, and Ascension into heaven, the coming of the Holy Spirit, and the teaching of the Apostles. He also made many poems on the terrors of the Last Judgement, the horrible pains of Hell, and the joys of the kingdom of heaven. In addition to these, he composed several others on the blessings and judgements of God, by which he sought to turn his hearers from delight in wickedness, and to inspire them to love and do good. For Cædmon was a deeply religious man, who humbly submitted to regular discipline, and firmly resisted all who tried to do evil, thus winning a happy death."[5] Scholars have spoken of some poems in the *Junius Manuscript,* in particular *Genesis, Exodus* and *Daniel,* as belonging to a "Cædmonian Cycle," but the attribution is based entirely upon subject matter rather than upon demonstrated authorship.

6.9   *The Account by Bede of Cædmon's Inspiration*   The following selection recounts the circumstances of Cædmon's initial attempt at poetic composition; with the possible exception of the incomplete inscription on the Ruthwell Cross in Dumfriesshire (c.670–750), the nine lines of Cædmon's *Hymn* are the earliest attested examples of English poetry. The dialect here is Late West Saxon.

Wæs hē, sē mon, in weoruldhāde ġeseted oð þā tīde þe hē wæs
ġelȳfdre ylde, ond næfre næniġ lēoð ġeleornade. Ond hē for þon
oft in ġebēorscipe, þonne þær wæs blisse intinga ġedēmed, þæt hēo
ealle sceolden þurh endebyrdnesse be hearpan singan, þonne hē
5   ġeseah þā hearpan him nēalēċan, þonne ārās hē for scome from
þǣm symble, ond hām ēode tō his hūse. Þā hē þæt þā sumre tīde
dyde, þæt hē forlēt þæt hūs þæs ġebēorscipes, ond ūt wæs gongende
tō nēata scipene, þāra heord him wæs þǣre neahte beboden; þā
hē ðā þær in ġelimplīċe tīde his leomu on ræste ġesette ond
10   onslēpte, þā stōd him sum mon æt þurh swefn, ond hine hālette
ond grētte, ond hine be his noman nemnde, "Cædmon, sing mē
hwæthwugu." Þā ondswarede hē, ond cwæð, "Ne con iċ nōht
singan; ond iċ for þon of þeossum ġebēorscipe ūt ēode ond hider
ġewāt, for þon iċ nāht singan ne cūðe." Eft hē cwæð, sē ðe wið hine
15   sprecende wæs, "Hwæðre þū mē meaht singan." Þā cwæð hē,
"Hwæt sceal iċ singan?" Cwæð hē, "Sing mē frumsceaft." Þā hē
ðā þās andsware onfēng, þā ongon hē sōna singan, in herenesse
Godes Scyppendes, þā fers ond þā word þe hē næfre ġehȳrde, þāra
endebyrdnesse þis is:

20   "Nu sculon heriġean   heofonrīċes Weord,
         Meotodes meahte   ond his mōdġeþanc,

> weorc Wuldorfæder,   swā hē wundra ġehwæs,
> ēċe Drihten,   ōr onstealde.
> Hē ærest scēop   eorðan bearnum
> 25   hēofon tō hrōfe,   hāliġ Scyppend;
> þā middanġeard   monncynnes Weard,
> ēċe Drihten,   æfter tēode
> fīrum foldan.   Frēa ælmihtiġ."

þā ārās hē from þǣm slǣpe, ond eal þā hē slǣpende song fæste in
30 ġemynde hæfde; ond þǣm wordum sōna moniġ word in þæt ilċe
ġemet Gode wyrðes songes tōġeþēodde.

6.10   *Notes*

  1. *hē*, Cædmon.

  2. *ġelȳfdre*, 'of infirm age', therefore 'of advanced age'.

  2. *nǣfre nǣniġ lēoð ġeleornade*, the double negative is common in Old English; *cf.* below, *ne con iċ nōht singan*.

  4. *sceolden*, third person plural, preterite subjunctive of *sculan*.

 10. *þā stōd sum mon æt him*.

 15. *meaht*, second person singular, present indicative of *magan*.

20–28. Cædmon's Hymn: A Northumbria version of the *Hymn* appears in a manuscript of about 737, and is perhaps the same version that Bede had before him when he rendered the poem into Latin. The (anonymous) West Saxon "translation" inserted into the *History* is not a reconstruction from Bede's Latin, but stems directly from the vernacular, in which, to judge by manuscript copies, the *Hymn* seems to have achieved an early popularity. A repeated phrase like *ēċe Drihten*, also found in *Beowulf*, attests to the formulaic nature of the *Hymn* and suggests that Cædmon composed "against the background of a developed tradition."[6]

 20. *nu sculon [wē] heriġean*.

 22. *Wuldorfæder*, genitive singular.

 30. *moniġ word*, direct object of *[hē] tōġeþēodde*.

References

1. A. Campbell, *Old English Grammar* (Oxford, 1959), p. 350.

2. Campbell, p. 351.

3. Eduard Prokosch, *A Comparative Germanic Grammar* (Philadelphia, 1939), p. 219.

4. Stuart Robinson, *The Development of Modern English,* 2nd ed., revised by Frederic G. Cassidy (Englewood Cliffs, New Jersey, 1954), p. 124.

5. Leo Sherley–Price, trans., *A History of The English Church and People* by Bede (Baltimore, 1955), p. 247.

6. Francis P. Magoun, Jr., "The Oral-Formulaic Character of Anglo-Saxon Narrative Poetry," *Speculum*, XXVIII (1953), p. 455.

Chapter 7

7.1   *The Weak Verb*   Like the weak-adjective declension, the weak verb is a specifically Germanic innovation; there was no weak conjugation in Indo-European. The primary distinguishing characteristic of a weak verb is the dental suffix [t] or [d] in the preterite. The origin of that suffix is not entirely clear and linguists have advanced a number of theories in endeavoring to account for it. One frequently stated view traces the suffix back to some tense of Indo-European *dhē-* 'do'; hence a form like *acted* would be a combination of *act* and *did*. Another explanation identifies the dental suffix with the Indo-European determinative *-tā-*, which occurs in Latin intensive verbs, e.g., *clāmāre* 'to cry' but *clāmitāre* 'to cry loudly'. Although that determinative was used to express verbal aspect, E. Prokosch points out that "it would be well in keeping with the general trend of the Gmc. verb system, if the -tā- suffix . . . should there assume temporal function."[1] The problem is a complicated one and no solution has yet engendered universal satisfaction. The weak verb is a feature common to all Germanic languages where its conjugation has now become the productive source for new verbs; that is, any verb coming into say, English, or German is inflected on the pattern of existing weak verbs. There are three classes of weak verbs in Old English.

7.2   *The Old English Weak Verb: Class I*   As "new" formations in Germanic, weak verbs are derived from other words, mostly nouns, adjectives, or strong verbs. Class I contains all three types, of which the following are some examples: *dēman* 'to judge' from PGmc *dōm-jan,* cf. OE *dōm* 'judgment'; *cemban* 'to comb' from PGmc *kamb-jan,* cf. OE *camb* 'comb'; *scierpan* 'to sharpen' from PGmc *skarp-jan,* cf.

OE *scearp* 'sharp'; *trymman* 'to strengthen' from PGmc **trum-jan, cf.* OE *trum* 'strong'; *drenċan* 'to ply with drink' from PGmc **drank-jan, cf.* OE *dranc,* preterite singular of *drincan* 'to drink'; *settan* 'to set' from PGmc **sat-jan, cf.* OE *sæt,* preterite singular of *sittan* 'to sit'.[2] Verbs like *dēman* and *scierpan* which are fashioned from nouns or adjectives are called *denominative;* verbs like *drenċan* and *settan* are termed *causative* as the underlying meaning is 'to cause to drink' and 'to cause to sit'.

7.2.1   In Proto-Old English every personal ending of weak verbs in Class I contained either *i* [i] or *j* [y] and those sounds regularly produced umlaut (see 6.2) when conditions permitted; thus, *fremeþ* 'he makes' is from POE **framiþ; dēmaþ* 'they judge' is from POE **dōmjaþ; trymede* 'he strengthened' is from POE **trumide,* and so forth. Whereas only some forms of the strong verb were affected by umlaut (e.g., the second and third persons singular, present indicative, but not the first person singular) *all* forms of a weak verb susceptible to mutation have an umlauted root vowel. Since the fronting and raising of root vowels took place in the prehistoric period of English and since there is no alternation between umlauted forms and non-umlauted forms in the case of a given weak verb, the presence or absence of umlaut is a matter for historical consideration only.

7.2.2   *Gemination*   Some weak verbs of Class I and some strong verbs of Classes V and VI show a geminated (doubled) root-final consonant at certain places in their conjugation. Like umlaut, gemination occurred before the earliest attestation of Old English. At a time antecedent to the differentiation of the various West Germanic languages, a single consonant (except *r*) preceded by a *short* vowel was doubled by a following *j* [y] (but not by a following *i*). Thus, PGmc **framjan* became West Germanic **frammjan,* but PGmc **dōmjan* did not change; because of subsequent mutation, the resulting Old English forms are *fremman* and *dēman.* Phonetically, the geminated consonant was a prolonged or lengthened sound. In strong verbs gemination took place only in the first person singular and in the plural of the present indicative. In weak verbs gemination affected all forms except: a) the second and third singular present indicative; b) the preterite singular and plural, both indicative and subjunctive; c) the imperative singular; and d) the past participle. In other words, almost exactly one-half of the forms of a fully conjugated weak verb may show a doubled root consonant.

7.2.3   Verbs of Class I which had a root ending in *r* [r] preceded by a short vowel were subject to umlaut, but not to gemination, by a following *j.* Moreover, the *j* was not completely lost in Old English, but survived as *i* in those very forms that were geminated in other verbs; for example, a verb like *herian* 'to praise' (from POE *hærjan*) parallels *fremman* by retaining the *i* wherever *fremman* has a doubled *m*.

7.2.4   Verbs like *fremman* and *herian* have a preterite suffix in *-ed-* and a past participle ending in *-ed*. All other verbs (like *dēman*) of Class I have a preterite suffix, in *-d-* (after voiced consonants: *dēm-d-e*) or in *-t-* (after voiceless consonants: *scierp-t-e* 'he sharpened') and a past participle ending in *-ed, -dd,* or *-tt*. These variations result from syncopation of the pre-dental *-e-*, regularly in the preterite and sometimes in the past participle.

7.3   *Fremman and Herian*   The following paradigms of *fremman* and *herian* represent two of the four conjugational patterns exhibited by Class I weak verbs in the present and preterite indicative, and should be committed to memory. See 8.2 for the paradigms of *dēman* and *scierpan* which represent the remaining two types.

		Present Indicative		
Singular	1	iċ	fremm-e	heri-e
	2	þū	frem-est	her-est
	3	hē	frem-eþ	her-eþ
Plural	1	wē	fremm-aþ	heri-aþ
	2	ġē	fremm-aþ	heri-aþ
	3	hīe	fremm-aþ	heri-aþ

		Preterite Indicative		
Singular	1	iċ	fremed-e	hered-e
	2	þū	fremed-est	hered-est
	3	hē	fremed-e	hered-e
Plural	1	wē	fremed-on	hered-on
	2	ġē	fremed-on	hered-on
	3	hīe	fremed-on	hered-on

7.3.1   The personal endings of Class I weak verbs coincide with those of the strong verbs throughout the present and in the preterite plural. The *-ia-* and *-ie-* combinations of verbs like *herian* are pronounced as one syllable [-ya-/-ye-].

7.4   *The Subjunctive Mood*   The specific uses of the subjunctive in Old English are multiple, but, as in other Indo-European languages, "the mood of subjective expression, and in general its use is confined to volitional, conjectural, or hypothetical contexts."[3] A recognition of the subjunctive when it occurs is more important than a detailed knowledge of the varied linguistic circumstances which may call forth that mood. There is no constant translation for any subjunctive form, and a phrase like *hē bere* (present subjunctive) may be 'he bear', 'he would bear', 'he should bear', or 'he may bear' depending upon the context. The preceding translations exemplify the use which Modern English often makes of auxiliary verbs for expression of the conditional, a practice that began during the Old English period itself. The four (modal) auxiliaries which combined with infinitives to produce the conditional or subjunctive in Old English are *willan, sculan, magan* 'may, may well', and *mōtan* 'may, be allowed'; e.g., *wēl biþ þæm þe mōt æfter dēaðæge Drihten sēċean* means 'Well is it for that one who may be allowed to seek God after [his] death-day'. A periphrastic subjunctive was especially common "in the preterite, perhaps because it was in the preterite that the weakening of unstressed vowels to [ə] . . . left fewer inflexional mood distinctions."[4] Some linguists favor the term *optative* instead of *subjunctive;* in Greek and Sanskrit grammar the optative is a mood distinct from the subjunctive and it functions chiefly as the mood of wishing. In Proto-Germanic, however, the Indo-European optative and subjunctive were blended into a single mood, and terminations of the resulting Germanic subjunctive were largely appropriated from the old optative.

7.4.1   Formation of the subjunctive in Old English is completely regular in strong and weak verbs, both of which take the same endings: *-e* in the singular and *-en* in the plural. The present subjunctive singular is formed by suffixing *-e* to the stem of the *first* person singular, present indicative, and the present subjunctive plural is formed by suffixing *-en* to the stem of the present indicative plural; the preterite subjunctive singular is formed by suffixing *-e* to the stem of the *second* person singular, preterite indicative, and the preterite subjunctive plural is formed by suffixing *-en* to the stem of the preterite indicative plural. The following sample paradigms illustrate the conjugation of strong and weak verbs in the subjunctive; there is but one ending for all persons in the singular and (as in the indicative) one for all persons in the plural.

	Strong				Weak	
	beran	*ċēosan*	*singan*	*dēman*	*fremman*	*herian*
	'to bear'	'to choose'	'to sing'	'to judge'	'to make'	'to praise'
Present Subjunctive						
Singular 1, 2, 3	ber-e	ċēos-e	sing-e	dēm-e	fremm-e	heri-e
Plural 1,2,3	ber-en	ċēs-en	sing-en	dēm-en	fremm-en	heri-en
Preterite Subjunctive						
Singular 1, 2, 3	bǣr-e	cur-e	sung-e	dēmd-e	fremed-e	hered-e
Plural 1,2,3,	bǣr-en	cur-en	sung-en	dēmd-en	fremed-en	hered-en

7.4.1.1   *The Verb 'to be' (II): the Subjunctive*   The present subjunctive of the verb 'to be' is either *bēo* or *sīe* in the singular, and either *bēon* or *sīen* in the plural; the preterite subjunctive is *wǣre* in the singular, and *wǣren* in the plural.

7.4.1.2   *The Subjunctive of dōn, gān, willan*   For the three other anomalous verbs the singular and plural forms of the present subjunctive are: *dō, dōn; gā, gān;* and *wille, willen.* In the preterite subjunctive they are: *dyde, dyden; ēode, ēoden;* and *wolde, wolden.*

7.4.2   *Translation of the Subjunctive*   The pleasing simplicity of subjunctive formations has a drawback in translation. Because *-e,* for example, serves for both present and preterite singular the correct tense, when important, must be determined from the verbal root rather than from the ending; likewise, the person (first, second, or third) must be deduced from the subject, as the ending by itself is ambiguous. Further- more, some indicative and some subjunctive forms coincide; *singe,* for example, may be either first person singular, present indicative or present subjunctive, and *sunge,* second singular preterite indicative or preterite subjunctive. Even *sungen,* the preterite plural subjunctive, becomes iden- tical with the past participle of *singan* when the prefix *ġe-* is omitted. Similar confusions arise in the case of the weak verbs: *dēme* may be either the first person present indicative or present subjunctive, and *dēmde* may be either first or third person preterite indicative or preterite subjunctive. In practice, the general tenor of a passage may almost invariably be relied upon to suggest the proper choice between indicative and subjunctive; nevertheless, it is occasionally difficult to decide which mood an author may have intended. Lines 2953b–2954 of *Beowulf* present just that sort of problem: *wiðres ne truwode, þæt hē sǣmannum onsacan mihte* means 'he had no faith in resistance, that he was able to fight against the sea-men' if *mihte* is taken as preterite indicative, but '. . . that he would be able to fight. . . .' if *mihte* is taken as preterite subjunctive. In Old English either version is permissible from a grammatical or semantic point of view. Yet an impression that the subjunctive is somehow more refractory than the indicative would be misleading. Its limited distribution merely delays that familiarity so readily acquired with the indicative, and one must, con- sequently, be alert for sentences whch may include those subjunctive in- flections not immediately recognizable as such.

7.5   *The Personal Pronoun (II)*   The personal pronoun in the third person is derived from an Indo-European demonstrative **ki-* 'this'; *cf.* the Latin preposition *cis* 'on this side'. The deictic force of **ki-* was weakened in Germanic, much as the Latin demonstrative pronoun *ille* 'that (one)' was weakened to *egli* 'he' in Italian and *il* 'he' in French. Unlike the pronoun of the first and second persons, the pronoun of the third person is inflected for gender in the singular. The following paradigms should be learned.

Singular

	Masculine	*Feminine*	*Neuter*
N	hē 'he'	hēo 'she'	hit 'it'
G	his	hire	his
D	him	hire	him
A	hine	hīe, hī	hit
I	him	hire	him

Plural

	All Genders
N	hīe, hī, hēo 'they'
G	hira, heora
D	him
A	hīe, hī, hēo
I	him

7.5.1   Early West Saxon often has *ie* for *i* (*hiera*) and *ĭo* for *ĕo* (*hiora*); Late West Saxon frequently has *ẏ* for *i* and *īe* in all forms (*hyt, hẏ*). Modern English *she* does not derive from *hēo* but from Middle English *sche, scho* which go back to the Old English definite article *sēo*, nominative singular feminine. At first in northern England, and then elsewhere, the Scandinavian form *þai* 'they' (Middle English *thei, thay, thai*) ultimately replaced the native Old English pronoun for the third person plural, which would have become **hi* in Modern English; *their* and *them* are also of Scandinavian origin, or by analogy with *thei*.

7.6   *The Conversion of King Edwin*   An important advance in the Christianization of England was the conversion of King Edwin of Deira (southern Northumbria) in 627, an event recounted by Bede in Book Two, chapters twelve through thirteen of his *History*. Christianity was first brought to England during the period of Roman occupation, but adherence to the faith declined after the withdrawal of the Roman legions between 410 and 442. At a time roughly coinciding with the influx of the Continental Germanic invaders, Irish missionaries made attempts to revivify the Church in southern Scotland and northern England, but their success was limited.

It was not until 597 that a Roman mission to Kent was able to establish the Christian Church as a permanent and integral part of Anglo-Saxon society. That mission was composed of forty monks and headed by a certain Augustine (later Saint Augustine—but not to be confused with *the* Saint Augustine of Hippo in North Africa, author of *The City of God*) who ultimately became archbishop of the English and located his see at Canterbury where he died c.605. Augustine and his companions went out from Pope Gregory's own monastery of Saint Andrew on the Caelian Hill in Rome, for the Pope had long nurtured a keen desire to extend Christian practices to the Germanic pagans of the British Isles. In a well-known passage of Book Two, Bede tells how Gregory's interest in the English was initially aroused, more than twenty years before he became Pope, in 590.

"I must here relate a story which shows Gregory's deep desire for the salvation of our nation. We are told that one day some merchants who had recently arrived in Rome displayed their many wares in the crowded market-place. Among other merchandise Gregory saw some boys exposed for sale. These had fair complexions, fine-cut features, and fair hair. Looking at them with interest, he enquired what country and race they came from. 'They come from Britain,' he was told, 'where all the people have this appearance.' He then asked whether the people were Christians, or whether they were still ignorant heathens. 'They are pagans,' he was informed. 'Alas!' said Gregory with a heartfelt sigh: 'how sad that such handsome folk are still in the grasp of the Author of darkness, and that faces of such beauty conceal minds ignorant of God's grace! What is the name of this race?' 'They are called Angles,' he was told. 'That is appropriate,' he said, 'for they have angelic faces, and it is right that they should become fellow-heirs with the angels in heaven. And what is the name of their Province?' 'Deira,' was the answer. 'Good. They shall indeed be *de ira*—saved from wrath—and called to the mercy of Christ. And what is the name of their king?' he asked. 'Ælla,' he was told. 'Then must *Alleluia* be sung to the praise of God our Creator in their land,' said Gregory, making play on the name.

"Approaching the Pope of the apostolic Roman see—for he was not yet Pope himself—Gregory begged him to send preachers of the word to the English people in Britain to convert them to Christ, and declared his own eagerness to attempt the task should the Pope see fit to direct it. But this permission was not forthcoming, for although the Pope himself was willing, the citizens of Rome would not allow Gregory to go so far away from the city. But directly Gregory succeeded to the Papacy himself, he put in hand this long cherished project and sent other missionaries in his place, assisting their work by his own prayers and encouragement. And I have thought it fitting to include this traditional story in the history of our Church."[5]

Ælla, by the way, was the father of King Edwin. Early in 597, then, Augustine landed in the Isle of Thanet, which was under the control of Æthelbert, king of Kent, and as Bede reports:

"After some days, the king came to the island, and sitting down in the open air, summoned Augustine and his companions to an audience. But he took precautions that they should not approach him in a house, for he held an ancient superstition that if they were practisers of magical arts, they might have opportunity to deceive and master him. But the monks were endowed with power from God, not from the Devil, and approached the king carrying a silver cross as their standard, and the likeness of our Lord and Saviour painted on a board. First of all they offered prayer to God, singing a litany for the eternal salvation both of themselves and of those for whose sake they had come. And when, at the king's command, Augustine had sat down and preached the word of life to the king and his court, the king said: 'Your words and promises are fair indeed, but they are new and strange to us, and I cannot accept them and abandon the age-old beliefs of the whole English nation. But since you have travelled far, and I can see that you are sincere in your desire to instruct us in what you believe to be true and excellent, we will not harm you. We will receive you hospitably, and take care to supply you with all that you need; nor will we forbid you to preach and win any people you can to your religion.'"[6]

Æthelberht, who must already have been somewhat familiar with the Church through his Christian queen, Berta (a daughter of the Frankish king, Haribert), was converted before the end of 597, and his nephew, the king of Essex, accepted the faith in 600. In 601 a second deputation from Rome arrived in England, among the members of which was the missionary, Paulinus (d.644), later appointed archbishop of York, who was to be instrumental in the conversion of Edwin of Northumbria (c.585–633). When Æthelburh, a Christian daughter of king Æthelberht, was betrothed to Edwin, Paulinus accompanied her to Northumbria in 625 as chaplin. Edwin had tolerantly agreed to allow his bride and her retinue freedom to practice Christianity, and even to adopt the faith himself if his councillors so recommended.

Eventual debate on the matter was preceded by two incidents that served to dispose the sympathetic but hesitant king favorably toward the new religion. In 626 he narrowly escaped assassination at the hands of a treacherous emissary sent by Cuichelm, the king of Wessex; to show his gratitude, he gave permission for the baptism of his infant daughter, Eanflæd. Next, Edwin's punitive expedition to suppress the West Saxon conspiracy was entirely successful; in return for a propitious outcome the king had promised to join the Church. Nevertheless, Paulinus was obliged to exert new pressure upon Edwin before he would convene the delayed assembly of his advisers for a discussion of the merits of Christian teachings. The consensus turned in favor of the Christian Church, and, with many nobles following his example, Edwin finally submitted to baptism at York on Holy Saturday in 627. Since Northumbria had at that time gained hegemony over the six other kingdoms of the Anglo-Saxon heptarchy (Mercia, Wessex, Essex, Sussex, East Anglia, and Kent), Edwin's conversion was an event of some consequence for the progress of the Church in northern England, in spite of the temporary apostasy which followed his death in 632.

7.7   *Two of King Edwin's Councillors Present Their Views of Christianity*   Bede's account of the debate which preceded Edwin's conversion is famous for the metaphorical view of man's existence advanced by an anonymous councillor who was urging adoption of the new faith. His remarks and those of *Cēfi* (Bede: *Coifi*), the pagan high priest who spoke just before him are excerpted below; the priest's argument is interesting for its forthright pragmatism. The dialect is basically Late West Saxon with some admixture of Anglian forms.

      Him þā ondswarode his ealdorbisceop, Cēfi wæs hāten: "Ġeseoh þū, cyning, hwelċ þēos lār sīe þe ūs nū bodad is. Iċ þē sōðlīċe andette, þæt iċ cūðlīċe ġeleornad hæbbe, þæt eallinga nāwiht mæġenes nē nyttnesse hafað sīo æfæstnes þe wē oð ðis hæfdon ond

5   beēodon. For þon næniġ þīnra þeġna nēodlīcor nē ġelustfullīcor hine sylfne underþēodde tō ūra goda bīgange þonne iċ; ond nōht þon læs moniġe syndon þā þe māran ġefe ond fremsumnesse æt þē onfēngon þonne iċ, ond on eallum þingum māran ġesynto hæfdon. Hwæt iċ wāt, ġif ūre godo æniġe mihte hæfdon, þonne

10 woldan hīe mē mā fultumian, for þon iċ him ġeornlīcor þēodde ond hȳrde. For þon mē þsynċeð wīslīċ, ġif þū ġesēo þā þing beteran ond strangran þe ūs nīwan bodad syndon, þæt wē þām onfōn."

      þæs wordum ōþer cyninges wita ond ealdormann ġeþafunge sealde, ond tō þære spræċe fēng ond þus cwæð: "þyslīċ mē is

15 gesewen, þū cyning, þis andwearde līf manna on eorðan tō wiðmetenesse þære tīde þe ūs uncūð is, swylċ swā þū æt swæsendum

sitte mid þīnum ealdormannum ond þeġnum on wintertīde, ond sīe
fȳr onǣled ond þīn heall ġewyrmed, ond hit rīne, ond snīwe, ond
styrme ūte; cume ān spearwa ond hrædlīċe þæt hūs þurhflēo, cume
20 þurh ōþre duru in, þurh ōþre ūt ġewīte. Hwæt, hē on þā tīd þe hē
inne bi›, ne bi› hrinen mid þȳ storme þæs wintres; ac þæt bi› ān
ēagan bryhtm ond þæt lǣsste fæc, ac hē sōna of wintra on þone winter eft cyme›. Swā þonne þis monna līf tō medmiclum fæce ætȳwe›;
hwæt þǣr foregange, o››e hwæt þæt æfterfyliġe, wē ne cunnun.
25 For ›on ġif þēos lār ōwiht cū›līcre ond ġerisenlīcre brenġe, þæs
weorþe is þæt wē þǣre fylġen." þeossum wordum ġelīcum ō›re
aldormen ond ›æs cyninges ġeþeahteras sprǣcan.

7.8   Notes

1. *him,* i.e., King Edwin.
2. *ġeseoh,* imperative, second singular of *ġesēon.*
2. *sīe,* third singular, present subjunctive of *bēon.*
3. *eallinga,* an adverb, 'altogether, entirely'.
4. *nyttnesse,* genitive singular.
4. *o› ›is* 'until [now]'.
6. *hine sylfne* 'himself'; *hine* is reflexive and *sylfne* intensive. *underþēodde* is third person singular, preterite indicative of *underþēodan* 'to subject to'.
8. *ġesynto* 'prosperity', accusative singular.
9. *wāt,* first person, present indicative of *witan* 'to know'.
9. *godo,* nominative plural.
10. *woldan,* third plural, preterite subjunctive of *willan.*
10. *him* 'them'; *þēodde* is third person singular, preterite indicative of *þēow(i)an* 'to serve' which takes the dative for direct objects.
11. *mē þynċe›* 'it seems to me'.
12. *onfōn,* first person plural, preterite subjunctive of *onfōn* 'to receive, accept'.
13. *þæs* 'of the former', i.e., Cēfi.
14. *tō þǣre sprǣċe fēng* 'took up the discussion'.
14–15. *þyslīċ mē is gesewen* 'it appears to me thus'.
24. *cunnun,* first person plural, present indicative of *cunnan* 'to know, understand'.
25–26. *þæs weorþe is* 'for this reason it is worthy'.
26. *þǣre, fylġan* (*folgian*) takes the dative case.
26. *wordum ġelīcum þeossum.*
27. *sprǣcan,* third person plural, preterite indicative of *sprecan.*

7.8.1   Working in part from Bede, Wordsworth used the
speech of the anonymous councillor as the subject matter for "Persua-
sion," Sonnet XVI in his *Ecclesiastical Sonnets,* Part I (published 1822):

"Man's life is like a Sparrow, mighty King!
That—while at banquet with your Chiefs you sit
Housed near a blazing fire—is seen to flit
Safe from the wintry tempest. Fluttering,
Here did it enter; there on hasty wing,
Flies out, and passes on from cold to cold;
But whence it came we know not, nor behold
Whither it goes. Even such, that transient Thing,
The human Soul; not utterly unknown
While in the Body lodged, her warm abode;
But from what world She came, what woe or weal
On her departure waits, no tongue hath shown;
This mystery if the Stranger can reveal,
His be a welcome cordially bestowed!"[7]

References

1. Eduard Prokosch. *A Comparative Germanic Grammar* (Philadelphia, 1939), p. 197.
2. Samuel Moore and Thomas A. Knott, *The Elements of Old English*, 10th ed., revised by James R. Hulbert (Ann Arbor, Michigan, 1955), pp. 71–72.
3. Randolph Quirk and C. L. Wrenn, *An Old English Grammar*, 2nd ed. (London, 1958), p. 83.
4. Quirk and Wrenn, pp. 84–85.
5. Leo Sherley-Price, trans., *A History of the English Church and People* by Bede (Baltimore, Maryland, 1955), pp. 98–99.
6. Sherley-Price, pp. 69–70.
7. E. de Selincourt and Helen Darbishire, eds., *The Poetical Works of William Wordsworth*, 2nd ed. (Oxford, 1954), III, p. 349.

Chapter 8

8.1   *The Imperative Mood*   Used for commands or exhortations, the imperative mood proper is confined in Old English to the second person singular and plural of the present tense. In the majority of verbs the imperative of the second singular is simply the (infinitive) root without any ending (e.g., *ber* from *beran, dēm* from *dēman*) and the imperative of the second plural is identical with the second person plural, present indicative (e.g., *beraþ, dēmaþ*). There is, however, some customary variation in imperative formations; verbs conjugated like *fremman* and *herian* have a singular imperative ending in *-e* (*freme, here*) while weak verbs of Classes II and III have singular imperatives ending in *-a* (*boda* from *bodian* 'to proclaim', *sealfa* from *sealfian* 'to anoint', *hafa* from *habban* 'to have', *saga* from *secgan* 'to say'). Class III verbs have an imperative singular root which is the same as the root· of the third person singular, present indicative (*hafaþ, sagaþ*). There is no umlaut or gemination in the imperative singular. Old English originally had an imperative of the first person plural which ended in *-an* (e.g., *beran* 'let us hear', *bindan* 'let us bind') but that form disappeared and was replaced by the present subjunctive plural (*beren, binden*). A fairly common construction for introducing imperative or adhortative clauses consists of *(w)uton/wutun*, a surviving first person plural subjunctive of *wītan* 'to go', plus an infinitive: *uton hraðe fēran* 'let us go quickly', *wutun āġifan ðǣm esne his wīf* 'let us return to the man his wife.' In spite of minor irregularities the imperative is easily dealt with in context.

8.1.1   *The Verb 'to be' (III): the Imperative*   The imperative singular of the verb 'to be' is either *bēo* or *wes;* the imperative plural is either *bēoþ* or *wesaþ*.

8.1.2   The imperative singular of the two anomalous verbs *dōn* and *gān* is *dō* and *gā;* the plurals are *dōð* and *gāð*. The only imperative for *willan* is a second plural, negative: *nyllað* or *nellað*.

8.2   *The Conjugation of dēman and scierpan*   The following paradigms should be memorized.

Present Indicative

Singular	1	iċ dēm-e	scierp-e
	2	þū dēm-st, dēm-est	scierp-st, scierp-est
	3	hē dēm-þ, dēm-eþ	scierpt(t), scierp-eþ
Plural	1	wē dēm-aþ	scierp-aþ
	2	ġē dēm-aþ	scierp-aþ
	3	hīe dēm-aþ	scierp-aþ

Preterite Indicative

Singular	1	iċ dēmd-e	scierpt-e
	2	þū dēmd-est	scierpt-est
	3	hē dēmd-e	scierpt-e
Plural	1	wē dēmd-on	scierpt-on
	2	ġē dēmd-on	scierpt-on
	3	hīe dēmd-on	scierpt-on

8.3   *The Present Participle*   The present participle is a verbal adjective fashioned from the infinitive root plus *-(e)nde* (e.g., *ber-ende* 'bearing', *fremm-ende* 'making', *dēm-ende* 'judging', *heri-ende* 'praising', *dō-nde* 'doing'); its formation is the same for both strong and weak verbs. In Indo-European the present participle was marked by the element *-nt-* which became *-nd-* in Proto-Germanic (Verner's Law); *cf.* IE *bhéront-*, Greek *pheront-* Latin *ferent-* 'bearing', but Gothic *baírand-s*. Although a present participle coupled with some form of *to be* gave rise to the *progressive* aspect of verbs in (early) Modern English (e.g., *I am bearing, he is doing*), it is important to remember that the force of a present participle in Old English is that of an *adjective;* the participle is more closely related to the noun or pronoun which it modifies than to verbal elements. As an adjective it may be declined according to either strong or weak patterns; a) strong: *ond wē him flēondum flyġeaþ* 'and we follow him fleeing', *ond hē ġefēonde mōde* 'and he with rejoicing heart'; b) weak: *þīos wandriende wyrd þe wē wyrd hātaþ* 'this changing (mutable) destiny which we call fate'. When declined as a strong adjective (see 5.2.1) the present participle has a masculine and neuter nominative singular ending in *-e*, a neuter accusative singular in *-e*, and a feminine nominative singular in *-u/-o*. During the Middle English period, the ending *-(e)nde* was supplanted by *-ing* which, along with *-ung*, was the productive suffix for a class of verbal nouns such as *bodung* 'preaching, sermon' from *bodian* 'to preach, announce', and *grēting* 'greeting' from *grētan* 'to greet'; for further examples see 13.1.2.

8.4   *The nd-declension*   In Germanic some participial adjectives in *-nd-* assumed the function of agent nouns; "the number of these nouns varies in the several dialects. Gothic has 12, Old Norse 4, Old English about 20, Old Saxon 11, and Old High German only 2."[1] Thus, Old English *hettend* 'enemy' is etymologically 'the one hating' (*cf. hatian* 'to hate', *hete* 'hate, malice') and *frēond* 'friend' is etymologically 'the one loving' (*cf. frēoġan* 'to love, honor'). The participial substantives of Germanic were not declined like the participial adjectives, but were, instead, inflected like Indo-European present participles in *-nt-;* as a consequence, there was umlaut in the dative singular and in the nominative and accusative plural when possible. Some Old English nouns in *-nd-*, however, do have the adjectival ending *-e* in the nominative and accusative plural and the adjectival ending *-ra* in the genitive plural. *Frēond* and *hettend* are two nouns representative of the *nd*-declension, which contains masculine nouns only.

	Singular	
N	frēond	hettend
G	frēond-es	hettend-es
D	frīend, frēond-e	hettend-e
A	frēond	hettend
I	frīend, frēond-e	hettend-e

	Plural	
N	frīend, frēond, -as	hettend, -e, -as
G	frēond	hettend-ra
D	frēond-um	hettend-um
A	frīend, frēond, -as	hettend, -e, -as
I	frēond-um	hettend-um

8.4.1   Other nouns belonging to the *nd*-declension are: *āgend* 'owner', *beswīcend* 'deceiver', *fēond* 'enemy', *hǣlend* 'Saviour', *helpend* 'helper', *līþend* 'sailor', *neriġend* 'Saviour', *rīdend* 'rider', *scyppend* 'Creator', *wealdend* 'ruler', *wīġend* 'warrior', and *wrecend* 'avenger'.

8.5   *The r-declension: Nouns of Relationship*   In Indo-European certain nouns denoting close family relationship had a root suffix in *-tĕr/-tōr*, normally a suffix which imparted agency; *cf.* Latin *dā-re* 'to give', *da-tor* 'giver'. The Germanic derivatives of those nouns are, of course, *father, mother, daughter,* and *brother*, but as their Indo-

European etymologies are much obscured it is not possible to determine whether they were originally agent nouns or not, except, perhaps, in the case of *bhrāter- 'brother' which may be related to *bher- 'bear' and hence have meant the 'protector' or 'sustainer' of sisters (?).[2] The Indo-European etymon of *sister* was *swesōr-/swesr-;* the intrusive -*t*- of Gothic *swistar,* Old Norse *systir,* Old High German *swester,* and Old English *sweostor* is a later Germanic development. Modern English *sister* is influenced by the Scandinavian form. Nouns of the *r*-declension have an umlauted dative-instrumental singular and sometimes an umlauted nominative and accusative plural.

Singular

N	fæder	mōdor	dohtor	brōþor	sweostor
G	fæder,-eres	mōdor	dohtor	brōþor	sweostor
D	fæder	mēder	dehter	brēþer	sweostor
A	fæder	mōdor	dohtor	brōþor	sweostor
I	fæder	mēder	dehter	brēþer	sweostor

Plural

N	fæderas	mōdor,-dru,-dra	dohtor,-tru,-tra, dehter
G	fædera	mōdra	dohtra
D	fæderum	mōdrum	dohtrum
A	fæderas	mōdor,-dru,-dra	dohtor,-tru,-tra, dehter
I	fæderum	mōdrum	dohtrum

Plural

N	brōþor,-þru	sweostor
G	brōþra	sweostra
D	brōþrum	sweostrum
A	brōþor,-þru	sweostor
I	brōþrum	sweostrum

8.5.1   The *r*-declension contains two other nouns, both of which are collective plurals: 'ġebrōþor,-ru 'brothers, brethren' and ġesweostor,-ru 'sisters'; *cf.* German *Gebrüder* 'brothers', and *Geschwister* formerly 'sisters' but since the sixteenth century the term for 'siblings'.

8.6   *The Comparison of Adjectives*   Although the grammatical structure of Modern English does not require the declension of adjectives, the necessity for distinguishing among three adjectival degrees (positive, comparative, superlative) by means of inflectional endings remains as much a feature of the language today as it was during the Old English period. The manner of conveying those distinctions of degree has, furthermore, changed little in one thousand years; -*r* is still a characteristic mark of the comparative and -*st* of the superlative. When juxtaposed, *heard* 'hard', *heardra* and *heardost* are surely self-evident in meaning to any speaker of Modern English. The comparative degree of most Old English adjectives was formed by the addition of *-ra* to the root for the masculine nominative singular: blind 'blind', *blind-ra; blīþe* 'joyful', *blīþ-ra*. In the feminine and neuter, nominative singular the ending was *-re: blind-re, blīþ-re*. These adjectives (masculine, feminine, and neuter) regularly took *-ost* in the superlative: *blind-ost, blīþ-ost*. Adjectives like *blind* and *blīþe* are so inflected because the Proto-Old English endings for the comparative and superlative were **-ora* and **-ōst* respectively. There was, however, another set of endings for the comparative and the superlative in Proto-Old English, **-ira* and **-ist*. Predictably, the presence of [i] caused umlaut of the root vowel when conditions permitted (see 6.2); thus, the comparative degree of adjectives like *eald* 'old' and *long* 'long', originally formed with **-ira,* was *yld-ra* (eWS *ield-ra* and *leng-ra* in the historical period. **-ist* developed into the alternative ending *-est* for the superlative: *yld-est* (eWS *ield-est*), *leng-est*. Other common adjectives with umlaut in the comparative degree and *-est* in the superlative are: *feorr* 'far', *ġeong* 'young', *hēah* 'high', *sceort* 'short', and *strang* 'strong'. Please note that all adjectives were declined weak in the comparative, and either strong or weak in the superlative (see 4.3).

8.6.1   *Irregular Comparison of Adjectives*   As in Modern English a few Old English adjectives display a root in the comparative and superlative which is altogether different from that of the positive. They are the following four: *gōd* 'good', *betera, bet(e)st* (*sēlra* 'better' and *sēlest* 'best' also occur); *yfel* 'evil', *wiersa* (or *wyrsa*), *wierrest* (or *wyrst*), *miċel* 'great', *māra, mǣst;* and *lȳtel* 'little', *lǣssa, lǣst*. Whereas the standard superlative of Germanic is traceable to the Indo-European determinative **-isto-* (in reality the comparative suffix plus **-to-*), one group of superlatives is based upon **-mo-; cf.* Latin *mini-mu-s* 'smallest'. Indo-European **-mo-* becomes **-uma-* in Proto-Germanic, thereby accounting for Old English formations like *fruma* 'beginning', *forma* 'first', *meduma* 'average', literally 'the middle-most'. By analogy with the *-est* superlatives, *-uma-* was changed to *-mest* and so it appears in a dozen or more words of which the following are representative: *æftemest* 'last', *innemest* 'inmost, most intimate', *sūþmest* 'southmost', and *ȳtemest* 'uttermost, extreme'. (In late Old English *-mest* was confused with *mǣst* 'most', hence the Modern English spellings in *-most*.) The comparative degree for these adjectives ends in *-erra: æfterra* 'second, next', *innerra* 'inner, interior', *sūperra* 'southern', *ȳterra* 'outer, exterior.' There is no positive degree, because the foregoing superlatives and comparatives, and others like them, were all derived from adverbs and prepositions; *cf. æfter* 'after', *inne* 'within', *sūþ* 'southwards' and *ūte* 'outside'.

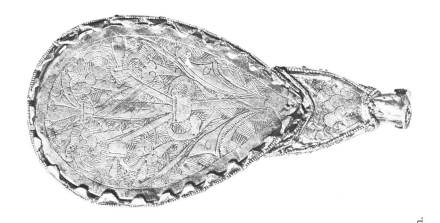

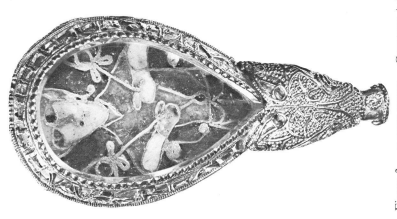

Figure 3. ALFRED JEWEL. Courtesy Ashmolean Museum.

8.7   *King Alfred's Translation of the* Cura Pastoralis *by Pope Gregory*   When Saint Augustine of Canterbury traveled to England in 597 he is thought to have carried with him a work by Pope Gregory, the *Regulae Pastoralis Liber* (*Book of Pastoral Rule*), commonly known as the *Cura Pastoralis* or *Pastoral Care;* a manual of vocational instruction for bishops, the *Pastoral Care* was written by Gregory shortly after his elevation to the papacy in 590. The book eventually acquired a considerable esteem among the learned clergy; in 734 Bede himself offered the following advice to his friend, Egbert, then bishop of York, "Study with diligence the words of the most holy Pope Gregory, his long and careful study of the life and the shortcomings of rulers of the church, so that your own words may always shine forth, seasoned with the salt of wisdom, rising above common speech, more worthy of the ears of Heaven."[3] The work which Bede was recommending deals with the motives that prompt men to accept the office of bishop, with the sort of man who should and should not be made a bishop, with the kind of life an ideal bishop should lead, with the different types of people a bishop will be called upon to help and how he should treat each, and, finally, with the necessity for a bishop to be aware of his own mortality and his appearance in the eyes of God.[4] When King Alfred was able to devote attention to the education of his people during the latter part of his reign (see 1.2), he naturally selected the *Cura Pastoralis* as a book with which English churchmen ought to be closely acquainted; Pope Gregory's didacticism was well suited to Alfred's own aims. Of those West Saxon translations labeled "Alfredian" the *Pastoral Care* seems to have been a labor of the pious king himself, or so he states in the *Preface,* which he wrote as a letter intended to accompany manuscript copies of the completed translation when they were sent out to the see of every English bishop. A versified proem to the manual contains the following excerpt which is further support for Alfred's authorship: "King Alfred translated every word of me into English and sent me to his scribes, south and north, and ordered more such to be brought to him that he might send them to his bishops, for some of them needed it who knew but little Latin."[5] Alfred had begun his re-study of a poorly acquired Latin in 887 under the direction of the Welshman, Asser (Asserius Menevensis), a scholarly priest who had agreed to divide his time between the West Saxon court and his own community of Saint David in Pembrokeshire. In 893 Asser wrote a biography of his royal student (*De Vita et Rebus Gestis Alfredi*) but mentions no West Saxon version of any Latin work save the *Dialogues* of Pope Gregory which had then been translated by Wæferth, Alfred's bishop of Worcester (873–915). On that piece of circumstantial evidence, it is, therefore, unlikely that the king commenced to render the *Pastoral Care* into

English before 894 at the earliest. Whether or not the *Pastoral Care* was his first translation is not known; on the uncertain chronology of the five major pieces of Alfredian prose, see George K. Anderson, *The Literature of the Anglo-Saxons,* (Princeton 1949), page 264. As a translator Alfred "adheres closely, even awkwardly, to the original. Face to face with the Latin language and with Gregory's training in Latin rhetoric and style, with Gregory's power of expression, either complex and elaborate, or austere and concise, the immaturity of English prose writing at this time and Alfred's lack of experience and knowledge made simplicity and short-coming inevitable. There are errors and misunderstandings of the Latin and deviations of thought, too, in this Anglo-Saxon version."[6] Yet, that the king was capable of literary endeavor at all is, in itself, remarkable; the apparently deplorable state of learning in England during the latter half of the ninth century would scarcely have provided the impetus for a less than extraordinary secular ruler to educate himself to the extent that Alfred did.

8.8   *King Alfred's Preface to the* Pastoral Care *(I)*   In the *Preface* Alfred discusses the decline of teaching and learning in his king-dom, sets forth his reasons for undertaking a translation of Pope Gregory's manual, and outlines his plans for the education of his people; the *Preface* is, of course, a piece of free composition and represents the king's own words to his bishops. The first half of the *Preface* is presented in this chapter and the second half in the next. The dialect is Early West Saxon.

     Ælfred kyning hāteð grētan Wǣrferð biscep his wordum luflīċe ond frēondlīċe; ond ðē cȳðan hāte ðæt mē cōm swīðe oft on ġemynd, hwelċe wiotan iū wǣron ġiond Angelcynn, ǣġðer ge godcundra hāda ġe woruldcundra; ond hū ġesǣliġlīca tīda ðā
5   wǣron ġiond Angelcynn; ond hū ðā kyningas ðe ðone onwald hæfdon ðæs folces Gode and his ǣrendwrecum hīersumedon; ond hū hīe ǣġðer ġe hiora sibbe ġe hiora siodu ġe hiora onweald innanbordes ġehīoldon, ond ēac ūt hiora ēðel rȳmdon; ond hū him ðā spēow ǣġðer ġe mid wīġe ge mid wīsdōme; ond ēac ða
10 godcundan hādas hū ġiorne hīe wǣron ǣġðer ġe ymb lāre ġe ymb liornunga, ġe ymb ealle ðā ðīowotdōmas ðe hīe Gode dōn scoldon; ond hū man ūtanbordes wīsdōm ond lāre hieder on lond sōhte, ond hū wē hīe nū sceoldon ūte beġietan, ġif wē hīe habbon sceoldon. Swā clǣne hīo wæs oðfeallenu on Angelcynne ðæt swīðe fēawa
15 wǣron behionan Humbre ðe hiora ðēninga cūðen understondan on Englisc oððe furðum ān ǣrendġewrit of Lǣdene on Englisc areċċean; ond iċ wēne ðætte nōht moniġe beġiondan Humbre

nǣren. Swǣ fēawa hiora ðæt iċ furðum ānne ānlēpne ne mæġ
ġeðenċean be sūðan Temese ðā ðā iċ tō rīċe fēng. Gode ælmihtegum
20 sīe ðonc ðætte wē nū æniġne onstal habbað lārēowa. For ðon iċ
ðē bebīode ðæt ðū dō swǣ iċ ġelīefe ðæt ðū wille, ðæt ðū ðē ðissa
woruldðinga tō ðǣm ġeǣmetiġe, swǣ ðū oftost mæġe, ðæt ðū ðone
wīsdōm ðe ðē God sealde ðǣr ðǣr ðū hiene befæstan mæġe, befæste.
Ġeðenċ hwelċ wītu ūs ðā becōmon for ðisse worulde, ðā ðā wē hit
25 nōhwæðer ne selfe ne lufedon, ne ēac ōðrum monnum ne lēfdon;
ðone naman ænne wē hæfdon ðætte wē crīstne wǣron, ond swīðe
fēawa ðā ðēawas.

Ðā iċ ðā ðis eall ġemunde, ðā ġemunde iċ ēac hū iċ ġeseah, ær
ðǣm ðe hit eall forhergod wǣre ond forbærned, hū ðā ċiriċean
30 ġiond eall Angelcynn stōdon māðma ond bōca ġefyldæ, ond ēac
miċel menġeo Godes ðīowa; ond ðā swīðe lȳtle fiorme ðāra bōca
wiston, for ðǣm ðe hīe hiora nānwuht onġiotan ne meahton, for
ðǣm ðe hīe nǣron on hiora āgen ġeðīode āwritene. Swelċe hīe
cwǣden: "Ūre ieldran, ðā ðe ðās stōwa ær hīoldon, hīe lufodon
35 wīsdōm, ond ðurh ðone hīe beġēaton welan ond ūs lǣfdon. Hēr mon
mæġ ġīet ġesīon hiora swæð, ac wē him ne cunnon æfter spyriġean.
For ðǣm wē habbað nū æġðer forlǣten ġe ðone welan ġe ðone
wīsdōm, for ðǣm ðe wē noldon tō ðǣm spore mid ūre mōde
onlūtan."

8.9   *Notes*

1.   *Ælfred kyning hāteð grētan,* a formal salutation; *grētan* 'to be greeted'.
2.   *Wærferð,* the Bishop of Worcester and translator into English of Pope
Gregory's *Dialogues.* Wærferth was, of course, only one of many bishops to whom a
copy of the *Pastoral Care* was sent.
2.   *hāte,* a shift from the third person to the first as the letter proper commences.
3.   *ġiond,* the diphthong *ĭo* for (later) *ĕo* is a feature of eWS.
3–4.   *æġðer ġe . . . ġe* 'both . . . and'.
8–9.   *him . . . spēow* 'they prospered', literally 'it prospered with respect to
them'.
9.   *wīsdōm,* 'scholarship, learning'.
12.   *hieder on lond,* hither in England.
15.   *behionan Humbre,* south of the Humber.
15–16.   *ðēninga,* Latin service-books; *on Englisc,* in terms of English.
17.   *beġiondan Humbre,* north of the Humber.
18.   *nǣren,* see 6.4.3.
19.   *ðā . . . ðā* 'when . . . then'; Alfred succeeded to the throne in 871.
20.   *sīe,* third person singular, present subjunctive of *bēon; cf.* the German
idiom *Gott sei Dank* 'God be thanked'.

22. *woruldðinga* 'worldly affairs'.

22. *tō ðǣm* 'to such an extent', correlative with following *ðæt;* i.e., *tō ðǣm ðæt ðū befæste ðone wīsdōm. . . .*

23. *ðǣr ðǣr* 'there where'.

24. *hwelč witu,* "Probably the Viking raids are meant; like others before and after him, Alfred regarded national calamities as divine punishment for the nation's sins."[7]

25. *ne ēac ōðrum monnum ne lēfdon, cf.* Matthew 23:13.

31. *Godes ðīowa,* monks.

35. *hēr,* in monasteries.

38. *noldon,* see 6.5.2.

References

1. Eduard Prokosch, *A Comparative Germanic Grammar* (Philadelphia, 1939), p. 259.

2. Carl Darling Buck, *A Dictionary of Selected Synonyms in the Principal Indo-European Languages* (Chicago and London, 1949), p. 107.

3. Eleanor Shipley Duckett, *Alfred the Great* (Chicago, 1956), p. 144.

4. Duckett, pp. 143–144.

5. R. H. Hodgkin, *A History of the Anglo-Saxons,* 3rd ed. (Oxford, 1952), II, p. 623.

6. Duckett, p. 148.

7. Henry Sweet, *Anglo-Saxon Reader in Prose and Verse,* 15th ed., revised by Dorothy Whitelock (Oxford, 1967), p. 224.

Chapter 9

9.1 *The Weak Verb: Class II* The weak verbs of Class II are largely denominative, and were originally derived from nouns of the (feminine) *ō*-declension (see 4.1), e.g., *ārian* 'to honor' from *ār* 'honor', *wundian* 'to wound' from *wund* 'wound'. Class II also contains a great many verbs which belonged to Class III (weak) in Proto-Germanic but shifted their conjugation to the former class in Proto-Old English. Proto-Germanic nouns of the *ō*-declension were made into verbs by addition of the suffix *-jan;* the resulting termination *-ō-jan* ultimately became Old English *-ian*, the mark of all Class II infinitives. There was no gemination of root-final consonants or umlaut of the root vowel; instead, the thematic vowel *ō* was umlauted to *ē*, and then *ēj*, through intermediate stages, became simply *i*. In the first person singular, present indicative, the ending *-ē* is a borrowing from the present subjunctive; the suffixes with *-ā-* show a common Old English development of West Germanic *-ō-* in unaccented closed syllables. The *-ia-* combination of Class II verbs is pronounced as two syllables, and thus differs phonetically from that of Class I verbs like *herian* which is pronounced as one syllable (see 7.3.1).

9.1.1 The following paradigm of *wunian* 'to dwell' is representative of a Class II weak verb.

Present Indicative

	Singular	*Plural*
1	iċ wuni-e	wē wuni-aþ
2	þū wun-ast	ġē wuni-aþ
3	hē wun-aþ	hīe wuni-aþ

Preterite Indicative

	Singular	*Plural*
1	iċ wunod-e	wē wunod-on
2	þū wunod-est	ġē wunod-on
3	hē wunod-e	hīe wunod-on

9.1.2   The past participle of Class II weak verbs ends in *-od*.

9.2   *The Past Participle*   Like the present participle, the past participle was essentially a verbal adjective, and, as such, was declined either strong (see 5.2.1 and 5.2.2) or weak (see 4.3.1): *betwux ðām nī̆ghworfenumfolce* 'among the newly-converted people' (strong); *ond wē sceolan ġehyhtan on Godes þā ġehālgodan ċyriċean* 'and we should have trust in the hallowed church of God' (weak). When used in the predicate it was sometimes uninflected: *ond him wæs myċel meneġu tō ġegaderod* 'and to him was a large multitude gathered'. Occasionally, and as in Modern English, the past participle could assume the function of a substantive: *ond fela þūsenda ofslæġenra* 'and many of thousands of slain'; *cf.* those agent nouns derived from the present participle (8.4). The past participle of strong verbs regularly ends in *-en*. The Indo-European antecedent for Old English was *-enó-; because the primary stress fell on the suffix instead of the root, the vowel of the root syllable, which in general was that of the present stem, appears in the reduced grade (ə). The perfective particle *ġe-* is usually prefixed to the past participle of any strong verb which does not already have an unaccented prefix, e.g., *numen* or *ġe-numen* 'taken' from *niman*, but *fornumen* 'destroyed' from *forniman*. Because of syncopation and assimilation (see 6.3 for examples of those two phenomena in the third singular, present indicative of strong verbs) the past participle of weak verbs may have various endings: *-ed, -od, -d(d),* or *-t(t);* weak verbs do not take the particle *ġe-*. For use of the past participle in passive-voice constructions and in the present perfect and past perfect tenses see 5.1.3.

9.3   *The Adverb*   The adverb is a modifier with a variety of discrete functions; it may qualify an adjective, a verb, or a whole sentence, and it may indicate the time or place, the manner or degree (sometimes zero: negation) of an action. The Old English adverb is regularly formed by the suffixation of *-e* [e] to an adjective; e.g., *bēohrt* 'bright' (adjective), *bēorhte* 'brightly' (adverb). This final *-e* is yet another remnant of Indo-European, where it marked the locative case (place where) of several nominal declensions; *cf.* Greek *oiko-i* 'at home', Latin *dōm-ī* 'at home'. The imposition of an adverbial function upon a previous ending for the locative was a Germanic development. When an Old English adjective already ended in *-e,* for example, *frēcne* 'daring, audacious', there was no difference between adjectival and adverbial *forms: hē under hārne stān æþelinges bearn āna ġenēðde frēcne* (adj.) *dǣde* 'he, under the gray rock, the son of a hero, alone ventured a daring deed'; *wē þæt ellenweorc ēstum miclum feohtan fremedon, frēcne* (adv.) *ġenēðdon eafoð uncūþes* 'we accomplished the courageous deed, the fight, with great good [wills, and] daringly ventured the power of the unknown'. The Modern English adverbial inflection, *-ly,* is a later reduction of *-līċe* the adverbial termination of a large group of Old English adjectives which were fashioned with *-līċ* '-like' from nouns or other adjectives; e.g., *dēofol* 'devil', *dēofollīċ* 'diabolical'; *ġēomor* 'sad', *ġēomorlīċ* 'sad'. In Middle English *-līċ* and *-līċe* became *-lich* and *-liche,* both of which were pronounced [liχ] by the end of Chaucer's lifetime; by Shakespeare's time [liχ] had changed further, to [liy], spelled *-ly* or *-lie.* Since speakers of Modern English quite naturally feel that *-ly* indicates adverbial function exclusively, a word like *friendly* (OE *frēondlīċ*), which by current usage gives the impression of being an adjective only, is sometimes gilded with an additional *-ly* by those who are excessively careful about being correct. Analogical modification has also been responsible for the presence of *-ly* in other places where it does not etymologically belong; e.g., *slow* as an adverb is now frequently *slowly,* even though the Old English form was *slāwe.* Whereas many such "reconstituted" adverbs have become a part of standard Modern English, some original forms have also been retained; anyone saying *fastly* for *fast* (OE *fæste*) would sound deservedly foolish.

9.3.1   A few adverbs end in *-a* or *-unga/-inga.* The *-a* which appears in adverbs like *sōn-a* 'soon, immediately' and *tel-a* 'well' (*cf. til* 'good'), and *fel-a* 'much', has several different sources which need not be detailed here. The ending *-unga/-inga* has already been encountered as the termination of a class of abstract nouns in the feminine, e.g., *deorc-ung* 'twilight' and *ġemilts-ung* 'pity' (see 8.3); it carries adverbial force, however, in another set of adverbs derived from nouns and adjectives; some examples are *nīed-inga* 'of necessity' from the noun *nīed* 'need, necessity', *fǣr-unga/fǣr-inga* 'quickly, suddenly' from the noun *fǣr* 'calamity, sudden danger', and *eall-unga/eall-inga* from the adjective *eall* 'all'.

9.3.2   *The Noun and Adjective as Adverb*   Frequently an oblique case-form of some noun or adjective was used adverbially. That practice, prevalent not only in Old English but also in the other Germanic languages, was simply a continuation of the process by which the standard adverbial ending *-e* had earlier been derived from the Indo-European locative (see 9.3). All *cases* except the nominative were vulnerable to adverbial adaptations, but not all *endings.* For practical purposes, only those case endings of the neuter *a*-declension (see 3.5.2) acquired a semantic duality. Those endings were ultimately extended by analogy to all declensions, here and there replacing terminations which were etymologically correct; *cf.* the adverbial genitive *niht-es* 'nightly' instead of *niht-e* for the feminine noun *niht,* and the dative-instrumental singular *lȳtl-e* 'a little' instead of *lȳtl-um* or *lȳtl-an* for the adjective *lȳtel.* Grouped by case, other nouns and adjectives employed as adverbs include the following:

a) genitive singular
   dæġes 'daily'
   ealles 'entirely'
   nealles 'not at all'
   nīedes 'of necessity'
   unġemetes 'immeasurably'
   willes 'willingly'
b) dative-instrumental singular
   ealle 'entirely'
   fācne 'deceitfully'
   sāre 'sorely'
c) accusative singular
   āwiht 'at all'
   eall 'completely'
   ġenōg 'enough'
d) genitive plural
   ġēara 'formerly'
e) dative-instrumental plural
   ġēordagum 'formerly'
   hwīlum 'at times'
   listum 'skillfully'
   miclum 'much, very'
   þrymmum 'mightily'

No accusative plural forms are recorded. A preposition was sometimes prefixed to the genitive singular of a noun or adjective to form an adverb, e.g., *in-stæpes* 'instantly, at once', *tō-ġēanes* 'towards', against', *tō-ġifes* 'freely, gratis', and *tō-middes* 'amidst, among'. With or without *tō,* the genitive singular (*ðæs*) of the neuter definite article *ðæt* could also become an adverb meaning 'to such a degree, so': . . . *wæs þæt blōd tō þæs hāt* . . . 'the blood was so hot'; *nō iċ him þæs ġeorne ætfealh* 'I did not hold him to such a degree firmly'; *tō* may similarly be coupled with *þǣm* and *þone.*

9.3.2.1   In a Modern English expression such as 'he works days' or 'he works nights' both 'days' and 'nights', are in fact relics of the Old English adverbial genitive and not, as most speakers today would construe them, plurals. The second element of the adverb *piecemeal,* ME *pecemele,* contains the modern equivalent of Old English *mǣlum,* the dative-instrumental plural of the neuter noun, *mǣl* 'measure', which is found in a number of adverbial compounds, e.g., *drop-mǣlum* 'drop by drop', *nam-mǣlum* 'by names', *stæp-mǣlum* 'gradually', *stund-mǣlum* 'at intervals', and *styċċe-mǣlum* 'here and there'. That element, or morpheme, was, incidentally, revived by the Victorian poet Gerard Manly Hopkins with the neologism *leafmeal,* 'leaf by leaf' which occurs in line eight of his poem, *Spring and Fall* (1880): "Though worlds of wanwood leafmeal lie"; Hopkins, who was acquainted with Old English, thought it "a vastly superior thing to what we have now."[1]

9.3.3   *Adverbs of 'place from which'*   A special class of adverbs with the suffix *-an* indicated movement *from* a place or a direction, e.g., *feorr* 'far' but *feorr-an* 'from afar'; in some instances, however, the *an-* form expressed both 'place at which' and 'place from which', e.g., *hind-an* could mean 'behind' or 'from behind'. Some common adverbs signifying 'place from which' are: *ēastan* 'from the east'; *heonan* 'hence'; *innan* 'from within'; *nēan* 'from nearby'; *norþan* 'from the north'; *sūþan* 'from the south'; *þanan* 'thence'; *uppan* 'from above'; *ūtan* 'from without'; and *westan* 'from the west'.

9.4   *The Comparison of Adverbs*   Like adjectives, adverbs are compared in three degrees: positive, comparative, and superlative. The regular ending for the comparative degree is *-or,* and for the superlative *-ost;* thus, *hearde* 'severely', *heardor, heardost.* Since the majority of Old English adverbs are derived from nouns and adjectives, it is not a coincidence that the several manners of comparison should closely resemble one another; both *-ra* (adjectives) and *-or* are clearly reflexes of the Proto-Old English comparative suffix **-ora,* while the adverbial *-ost* is identical with the superlative adjectival suffix *-ost* (see 8.6). An alternate Proto-Germanic suffix in **-iz* was sporadically used to form the comparative degree; that suffix, which caused umlaut of the root vowel, disappeared entirely in Old English, and, consequently, some adverbs have only an umlauted vowel as the mark of the comparative. There is also umlaut in the superlative for those adverbs if the suffix is *-est* (earlier **-ist*), but no umlaut if it is *-ost;* the following are representative: *ēaþ(e)* 'easily', *īeþ, ēaþost; feorr* 'far', *fierr, fi(e)rrest; nēah* 'near', *nȳr, nīehst;* and *sōfte* 'softly', *sēft, sōftost.* Two adverbs that were formed from adjectives having umlauted vowels are *hēa(h)* 'high', *hēar, hȳhst,* and *lange* 'long', *leng, lengest.*

9.4.1   *Irregular Comparison of Adverbs*   Corresponding to the adjectives *gōd, yfel, miċel* and *lȳtel* which form their comparative and superlative degrees from different roots (see 8.6.1) are the following ad-

verbs: *wel(l)* 'well', *bet* (or *sēl*), *bet(e)st* (or *sēlest*); *yfle* 'evilly', *wiers,*
wyrrest (or *wyrst*); *micle* 'much', *mā, mǣst;* and *lȳtle* (or *lȳt*) 'a little', *lǣs,*
lǣst (or *lǣsest*).

9.5   *Scholarship and Learning in Anglo-Saxon England*   That
King Alfred should have regarded scholarly achievement in his own reign
as lamentably remiss is readily understandable when one considers the
heights to which Anglo-Saxon erudition had progressed in the previous
century. Largely responsible for the subsequent retardation of learning,
the Danish incursions that began in 787 were, as it happened, directed
against a people who had become preeminent for education and scholarship in Western Europe. Only some five years earlier (approximately 782)
the illustrious Anglo-Saxon scholar, Alcuin (Ealhwine) had departed the
internationally renowned Cathedral School at York for the Palace School
in Aachen (Aix-la-Chapelle) where it would be his duty to administer the
educational affairs of the Frankish kingdom controlled by his royal patron
and student, Charlemagne.

The inception of native learning may be traced to those cathedral
schools established by the earliest English bishops who, following Roman
practice, were obliged to provide a training for the ministry at their sees;
in that way, instruction was first made available in "the Latin language,
the Scriptures, the computation of the Church seasons, [and] the music
necessary for the services."[2] There was, of course, a need for teachers,
and during the second half of the seventh century many Anglo-Saxons,
primarily Northumbrians, traveled to Ireland for study, and returned
to further the cause of ecclesiastical education in English church schools
and monasteries, which were just then in the process of copying and
acquiring books from Irish and Continental centers of learning. In 635
the Irish missionary Aidan (d.655) organized a monastery on the island
of Lindisfarne, off the coast of Bernicia (Northumbria); one of the most
magnificently illuminated manuscripts of the early Middle Ages, the
Lindisfarne Gospels, was created there in about the year 700.

It was from the Irish at Lindisfarne and at other Northumbrian
settlements that the Anglo-Saxons appear to have received their first
training in the Latin alphabet; "during the first half of the seventh century
the Roman missionaries in south-eastern England were so heavily engaged in their fight against deeply rooted paganism that the teaching of
letters to their converts was beyond their power."[3] The foundation of
many other religious houses soon followed that of Lindisfarne; in addition to Lindisfarne, those destined to play a significant part in the intellectual life of Anglo-Saxon England were the twin monasteries at
Monkwearmouth (674) and Jarrow (681), both established by the Northumbrian prelate, Benedict Biscop, the teacher of Bede and an inveterate

Figure 4.   PAGE FROM THE LINDISFARNE GOSPEL.   Courtesy Department of Mss., British Museum.

bibliophile who took good advantage of his five pilgrimages to Rome by returning with additional books for the two monastic libraries. The distinguished library at Jarrow was, of course, the one in which Bede labored, and from what is known about his sources the collection there must have included not only the Bible and the writings of the Church Fathers (in particular Ambrose, Jerome, Augustine, and Gregory) but also Virgil, Pliny, the historians Orosius, Cassiodorus, Gregory of Tours, and the (now forgotten) Christian poets, Juvencus, Prudentius, Sedulius, Prosper, Fortunatus, Lactantius, and Arator. "It is thought that there was a Greek text of the Acts at Jarrow in Bede's time, but it is doubtful whether the other parts of the Greek New Testament were there. Bede occasionally used Greek authorities, but he seems only to have done so in Latin translations."[4]

Libraries elsewhere in England were also well supplied. An older contemporary of Bede's, the West Saxon, Aldhelm (c.640–709), who became the first bishop of Sherborne (705) and was the first English scholar of any distinction, used the works of Lucan, Ovid, Cicero, and Sallust as well as those of Virgil and Pliny. Aldhelm had studied first at Malmesbury in Wessex under an Irish teacher, Maeldubh, and then with Adrian and Theodore (the archbishop) at Canterbury. Co-founders of the school at the Abbey of Saints Peter and Paul in Canterbury, Adrian and Theodore were both non-Keltic foreigners; Adrian (d.710) was of African origin and Theodore (c.602–690) was a Greek from Tarsus in Cilicia. Having twice declined the vacant archbishopric of Canterbury when it was offered to him by Pope Saint Vitalian, Adrian, then (668) abbot of a monastery near Monte Cassino, suggested the scholarly Greek monk, Theodore, who was at that time living in Rome, as a candidate better qualified for the position. Although Theodore was sixty-six years old and not yet even a priest, the Pope agreed to his appointment, but stipulated that Adrian should accompany him to Kent and assume the abbotcy of Saint Peter's; the two men arrived in England in 669.

Under their direction the monastery school in Canterbury was to acquire an excellent reputation; they taught their students "such art of versification, and such astronomy, arithmetic, and music, as seemed suitable for clerics, giving them not only a sound education in Latin, but also some knowledge of Greek."[5] Comfortably augmenting the influence of Keltic tradition, the force of Mediterranean learning represented by Adrian, Theodore, and their pupils (Benedict Biscop among them) was of incalculable value for the course of intellectual endeavor in eighth-century England. A detailed catalogue of the original works produced during that century is neither practical nor necessary here; it embraces a considerable number of saints' lives, poems on religious and moral themes, scriptural expositions, homilies, and at least one treatise on virginity (Aldhelm's *De Laudibus Virginitatis*); for amusement there were acrostics and learned riddles. Everything was, of course, written in Latin of a widely varying kind and quality; Bede, for example, employed a simple and direct style, while Aldhelm, who seems to have been fascinated with turgid ornamentation "often becomes a kind of Swinburne among Old English writers of prose."[6]

With the menacing appearance of Viking raiders in the last years of the eighth century, however, scholarly activity, which had already begun to decline of its own inertia, all but ceased in the north as the struggle for mere existence assumed continually increasing proportion; Lindisfarne was brutally sacked in 793 and Jarrow in 794. In the fourth decade of the following century the southern area of England also began to suffer from concentrated attacks; London was raided in 842, and again in 851 when Canterbury was stormed. The northern city of York actually capitulated to Danish forces in 867, just four years before the accession of Alfred to the throne of Wessex. When he signed the Treaty of Wedmore with the Danish chieftain Guthrum in 878, Alfred might well have been distressed at the low level to which learning had fallen; there had been over one hundred years of Viking harrassment. In spite of Alfred's efforts to rejuvenate the church and to revive learning, it was not until the middle of the tenth century that intellectual activity became once again prolific. Monastic reform was then satisfactorily accomplished; the school curriculum, still under firm church control, encompassed the standard mediaeval combination of *trivium* (grammar, rhetoric, logic) and *quadrivium* (arithmetic, music, geometry, astronomy); Latin was taught from Ælfric's grammar (995) and from others like it also produced in England; books were imported and new manuscripts produced; "before 1066 the libraries must have again become as full as ever they were in the days before the Viking ravages."[7]

9.6   *King Alfred's Preface to the* Pastoral Care *(II)*

Ðā iċ ðā ðis eall ġemunde, ðā wundrade iċ swīðe swīðe ðāra gōdena wiotena ðe ġiū wǣron ġiond Angelcynn, ond ðā bēċ ealla be fullan ġeliornod hæfdon, ðæt hīe hiora ðā nǣnne dǣl noldon on hiora āgen ġeðīode wendan. Ac iċ ðā sōna eft mē selfum
5   andwyrde, ond cwæð: "Hīe ne wēndon ðætte ǣfre menn sceolden swǣ reċċelēase weorðan ond sīo lār swǣ oðfeallan: for ðǣre wilnunga hīe hit forlēton, ond woldon ðæt hēr ðȳ māra wīsdōm on londe wǣre ðȳ wē mā ġeðēoda cūðon."

Ðā ġemunde iċ hū sīo ǣ wæs ǣrest on Ebriscġeðīode funden.
10   ond eft, ðā ðā hīe Crēacas ġeliornodon, ðā wendon hīe hīe on heora āgen ġeðīode ealle, ond ēac ealle ōðre bēċ. Ond eft Lǣdenware

swǣ same, siððan hīe hīe ġeliornodon, hīe hīe wendon ealla ðurh wīse wealhstodas on hiora āgen ġeðīode. Ond ēac ealla ōðra crīstena ðīode sumne dǣl hiora on hiora āgen ġeðīode wendon.

15 For ðȳ mē ðyncð betre, ġif īow swǣ ðyncð, ðæt wē ēac suma bēċ, ðā ðe nīedbeðearfosta sīen eallum monnum tō wiotonne, ðæt wē ðā on ðæt ġeðīode wenden ðe wē ealle ġecnāwan mæġen, ond ġedōn, swǣ wē swīðe ēaðe magon mid Godes fultume, ġif wē ðā stilnesse habbað, ðætte eall sīo ġioguð ðe nū is on Angelcynne

20 frīora monna, ðāra ðe ðā spēda hæbben ðæt hīe ðǣm befēolan mæġen, sīen tō liornunga oð fæste, ðā hwīle ðe hīe tō nānre ōðerre note ne mæġen, oð ðone first ðe hīe wel cunnen Englisc ġewrit ārǣdan. Lǣre mon siððan furður on Lǣdenġeðīode ðā ðē mon furðor lǣran wille ond tō hīerran hāde dōn wille. Ðā iċ ðā ġemunde

25 hū sīo lār Lǣdenġeðīodes ǣr ðissum āfeallen wæs ġiond Angelcynn, ond ðēah moniġe cūðon Englisc ġewrit ārǣdan, ðā ongan iċ onġemang ōðrum mislīcum ond maniġfealdum bisgum ðisses kynerīċes ðā bōc wendan on Englisc ðe is ġenemned on Lǣden *Pastoralis,* ond on Englisc 'Hierdebōc,' hwīlum word be worde,

30 hwīlum andġit of andġiete, swǣ swǣ iċ hīe ġeliornode æt Pleġmunde mīnum ærcebiscepe, ond æt Assere mīnum biscepe, ond æt Grimbolde mīnum mæsseprīoste, ond æt Iōhanne mīnum mæsseprēoste. Siððan iċ hīe ðā ġeliornod hæfde, swǣ swǣ iċ hīe forstōd, ond swǣ iċ hīe andġitfullīcost āreċċean meahte, ic hīe on

35 Englisc āwende; ond tō ǣlcum biscepstōle on mīnum rīċe wille āne onsendan; ond on ǣlcre bið ān æstel, sē bið on f īftegum mancessa. Ond iċ bebīode on Godes naman ðæt nān mon ðone æstel from ðǣre bēċ ne dō, ne ðā bōc from ðǣm mynstre—uncūð hū longe ðǣr swǣ ġelǣrede biscepas sīen, swǣ swǣ nū, Gode ðonc, welhwǣr

40 siendon. For ðȳ iċ wolde ðætte hīe ealneġ æt ðǣre stōwe wǣren, būton sē biscep hīe mid him habban wille, oððe hīo hwǣr tō lǣne sīe, oððe hwā ōðre bī wrīte.

9.7 *Notes*

4. *mē selfum* 'to myself'.

4. *on hiora āgen ġeðīode,* English.

7. *hit,* translation.

7–8. *ðȳ māra . . . ðȳ* 'the greater . . . according as'; a comparative adjective is frequently used with the instrumental case of *sē.* Modern English expressions like 'the bigger the better', 'the more the merrier', stem from just such a construction.

10. *ðā ðā* 'then when'.

12. *swǣ same* 'similarly'.

13. *on hiora āgen ġeðīode,* probably a reference to the *Vulgate* of Saint

Jerome, a retranslation of the Bible which he made in the fourth century from a previously existing Latin version.

13–14. *ōðra crīstena ðīode*, Goths and Slavs. The Scriptures, or portions thereof, were translated into Gothic about 350 AD (see 1.11); in Alfred's own lifetime Kyrillos and Methodios, the two Greek missionaries to the southern Slavs, translated much of the Bible and Christian liturgy into Old Bulgarian (Old Church Slavonic), thereby making it the earliest attested Slavic language.

14. *sumne dǣl hiora*, i.e., books of the Bible.

15. *īow*, the bishops to whom Alfred was sending copies of the *Pastoral Care*.

19. *stilnesse* 'peace and quiet'.

20. *ðǣm*, to learning.

24. *hīerran hāde*, ecclesiastical order.

27–28. *ðisses kynerīces*, Wessex.

31. *Plegmund*, a Mercian whom Alfred had invited to his court, became archbishop of Canterbury in 890; since Alfred addresses him as *ǣrcebiscep*, the *Preface* can hardly have been written before 890 (for a further indication of the time of composition see 8.7). *Asser*, a Welsh bishop who was one of Alfred's mentors and companions; later bishop of Sherborne, he wrote his biography of the king (*De Vita et Rebus Gestis Alfredi*) in 893. *Grimbold*, a Frankish scholar from the abbey of Saint-Bertin at Saint-Omer in northern France; he was attached to Alfred's court from about 886 or 887. *John* (*Iohannes*), a continental Saxon, whom Alfred made abbot of his new monastery at Athelney in Somerset.

36. *ǣstel*, the meaning is disputed, probably a 'bookmark'; *cf.* Latin *hastula* 'a small spear'.

36. *bið on fīftegum mancessa* 'is worth fifty mancuses'; a *mancus* was equal to thirty silver pence, or one-eighth of a pound.

38–39. *uncūð hū longe ðǣr* 'it is uncertain how long there [in those sees]'.

40. *æt ðǣre stōwe*, in the cathedral.

42. *bī wrītan* 'to copy'.

References

1. Louis Untermeyer, *Lives of the Poets* (New York, 1959), p. 597.

2. Dorothy Whitelock, *The Beginnings of English Society* (*The Anglo-Saxon Period*), (Baltimore, Maryland, 1952), *The Pelican History of England*, II, pp. 189–190.

3. Peter Hunter Blair, *An Introduction to Anglo-Saxon England* (Cambridge, England, 1956), pp. 312–313.

4. Blair, p. 314.

5. R. H. Hodgkin, *A History of the Anglo-Saxons*, 3rd ed. (Oxford, 1952), I, p. 309.

6. George K. Anderson, *The Literature of the Anglo-Saxons* (Princeton, New Jersey, 1949), p. 219.

7. Whitelock, *The Beginnings of English Society*, p. 203.

Chapter 10

10.1 *The Weak Verb: Class III* Unlike the weak verbs of Classes I and II, which are Germanic secondary formations (causatives and denominatives), nearly all those of Class III are etymologically primary. They derive from certain Indo-European verbs which had suffixes containing *-ē- or *ēi-; cf. *wid-ē-si, Latin uid-ē-s 'you (singular) see', *hab-ēy-ō, Latin hab-e-ō 'I have'. In North and East Germanic the long vowel *-ē- was shortened to -ĕ-, and appears as such in Class III verbs like Old Norse hef-e-r and Gothic hab-ai-s, both meaning 'you (singular) have'; the -ai- of Gothic habais is merely a spelling for [e]. High West Germanic, on the other hand, retains the long *-ē- of Indo-European; cf. Old High German hab-ē-m 'I have', hab-ē-s 'you (singular) have', and hab-ē-t 'he has'. In low West Germanic (Old English, Old Frisian, Old Saxon), however, the Indo-European diphthong *-ēi- reduced by ablaut to *-i- (*-j-) must be assumed for the original suffix of the stem; cf. Old Saxon hebb-i-u 'I have' from *hab-y-ō, with doubling of the root-final consonant caused by *-j-. The Old English cognate hæbbe shows a loss of *-j- (after gemination) and, incidentally, a substitution of -e for -u, the normal West Germanic development of Indo-European unaccented *-ō, the ending of the first person singular; no Class III verb of West Saxon preserves any direct trace of *-j-. In all subdivisions of Germanic, except Old High German, the distinctive inflection of Class III verbs was so radically modified by analogical change that the prior conjugational regularity of Proto-Germanic was greatly disturbed and frequently obliterated. As a consequence of the resultant confusion, a majority of Old English verbs which had originally belonged to Class III, were transferred" to Classes I and II; Class III was thus so depleted that there are only four verbs remaining in West Saxon which legitimately constitute a separate conjugation: *habban* 'to have', *libban* 'to live', *secgan* 'to say', and *hycgan* 'to think'.

10.1.1   The following paradigms of the four weak verbs of Class III display those variations caused by analogical re-patterning.

Present Indicative
Singular

1	iċ	hæbb-e	libb-e, lifġ-e	secg-e	hycg-e
2	þū	hæf-st, haf-ast	leof-ast	sæġ-st, sag-ast	hyġ-st, hog-ast
3	hē	hæf-þ, haf-aþ	leof-aþ	sæġ-þ, sag-aþ	hyġ-þ, hog-aþ

Present Indicative
Plural

1	wē	habb-aþ	libb-aþ	secg-aþ	hycg-aþ
2	ġē	habb-aþ	libb-aþ	secg-aþ	hycg-aþ
3	hīe	habb-aþ	libb-aþ	secg-aþ	hycg-aþ

Preterite Indicative
Singular

1	iċ	hæfd-e	lifd-e	sæġd-e	hogd-e
2	þū	hæfd-est	lifd-est	sæġd-est	hogd-est
3	hē	hæfd-e	lifd-e	sæġd-e	hogd-e

Plural

1	wē	hæfd-on	lifd-on	sæġd-on	hogd-on
2	ġē	hæfd-on	lifd-on	sæġd-on	hogd-on
3	hīe	hæfd-on	lifd-on	sæġd-on	hogd-on

10.1.2   The past participles of *habban, libban, secgan* and *hycgan* are *ġehæfd, ġelifd, ġesæġd* and *ġehogod*.

10.1.3   The present subjunctive roots are *hæbb-, libb-, secg-* and *hycg-;* the preterite subjunctive roots are *hæfd-, lifd-, sæġd-* and *hogd-*. For the imperative formations see 8.1.

10.1.4   Contracted negatives are formed with *habban* and the adverb *ne* 'not'; examples include *næbban* (*ne habban*), *nafað* (*ne hafað*), *nabbað* (*ne habbað*), and *næfdon* (*ne hæfdon*).

10.2   *The Gerund*   The gerund is a verbal that is used as a noun. In the sentence 'Running is good exercise' the word 'running' is not only the subject but also a derived form of the verb 'to run'. The mark of a gerund in Modern English is *-ing*, and hence there is no difference between the *shape* of gerunds and present participles; the difference between the two parts of speech lies in their respective *functions:* the gerund functions as a noun, and the present participle functions as an adjective (see 8.3). In Old English the gerund resembles, not the present participle, but the infinitive (see 3.8). Both gerund and infinitive are merely different cases of what was originally a neuter verbal substantive in Indo-European that ended in *-n-om,* e.g., **bhero-n-om* 'bearing'. The Germanic infinitive derives from the accusative singular of that noun (**bhero-n-om* becomes OE *beran* 'to bear'), and the gerund, a development of West Germanic only, derives from the dative singular, the termination for which ultimately came to be *-enne* or *-anne* in Old English; for some exceptions see 10.2.1. The Old English gerund is always preceded by the preposition *tō,* a construction that later supplied the source for Modern English infinitives. Because it is historically akin to the Old English infinitive, the gerund may be viewed as simply an inflected form of the infinitive possessing special uses, and may be translated either as an infinitive with nominal capacity, or as a verbal noun in its own right. There is no single, consistent translation for the gerund; a satisfactory interpretation depends largely upon the nature and meaning of the words that accompany the gerund in a given clause or sentence. With copulas, or linking verbs, the gerund may be a subject or a predicate nominative: *hū him tō drohtniġenne wǣre betwux ðām nīġhworfenum folce* 'how for him the leading of his life (subject) should be among the newly converted people'; *wundor is tō secganne hū. . . .* 'a wonderful thing is the telling (predicate nominative) how. . . .' A smoother translation of the latter example is, of course, achieved *inter alia* by regarding the gerund as infinitival: 'it is a wonderful thing to tell how. . . .' With transitive verbs the gerund may be a direct object: *ongann ðā Augustīnus mid his munecum tō ġeefenlǣċenne þǣra apostola līf* 'then Augustine with his monks commenced to imitate (the imitating) the life of the apostles'; being a verbal the gerund may have an object of its own as in the preceding example. Not solely a stylistic device, the Old English gerund possessed certain idiomatic uses, among them the expression of purpose: *God sylf wāt ġeare þæt wē winnað rihtlīċe wið þysne rēðan cyning tō āhreddenne ūre lēode* 'God himself knows that we are fighting righteously against this cruel king for (the purpose of) saving our people'; *ongunnon ðā dæġhwōmlīċe for wel meniġe efstan tō ġehȳrenne ðā hālgan bodunge* 'then began daily a great multitude to hasten for (the purpose of) hearing the holy preaching'. Other specialized constructions involving the gerund are no less obvious in context, and do not require enumeration here.

10.2.1   Some gerunds not ending in *-enne* or *-anne* are: *tō bēonne* 'being', *tō donne* 'doing', *tō fōnne* 'seizing', *tō gānne* 'going', *tō sēonne* 'seeing', and *tō tēonne* 'pulling, drawing'.

10.3   *The Possessive Pronoun*   Sometimes termed possessive adjectives, the Old English possessive pronouns are identical with the genitival forms of the personal pronouns (see 6.5 and 7.5). Possessive pronouns of the first and second persons are declined as strong adjectives (see 5.2.1); they include *mīn* 'mine'; *þīn* 'your' (singular); *uncer* 'of us two'; *incer* 'of you two'; *ūre, ūser* 'our'; and *ēower* 'your' (plural). Thus *mīn*, for instance, is either *mīnne* (masculine), *mīne* (feminine), or *mīn* (neuter) in the accusative singular depending upon the gender of the noun modified. Those possessive pronouns of the third person (*his* 'his', *hiere* 'her', *his* 'its', and *hiera* 'their') are not declined, and retain the same form no matter what the gender, number, or case of the noun modified. It is occasionally possible to confuse the personal pronoun in the genitive with the possessive pronoun, particularly when pronouns of the third person are involved; only an unsatisfactory meaning results from translating *his* as a possessive in the following two excerpts: *brūn on bāne bāt unswīðor þonne his ðīodcyning þearfe hæfde* 'the bright (sword) bit less strongly into the bone when the king had need of it'; *þā ġefēoll hire mōd on his lufe* 'then her heart fell in love with (literally: of) him'.

10.3.1   *The Possessive Pronoun sīn*   From an Indo-European locative (**sei-*) of the third person personal pronoun, Proto-Germanic developed a reflexive possessive (**sī-na-z*) for all genders and both numbers of the third person; *cf.* Gothic *seins* [si:ns], Old Norse *sinn*, and Old English *sīn* 'his', 'her', 'its', 'their'. During the historical period of Old English, *sīn* was restricted chiefly to poetry; elsewhere it was largely replaced by the genitival forms of *hē*. Like *mīn* and *þīn*, which share a similar Indo-European heritage, *sīn* was declined as a strong adjective. The following illustrations are drawn from *Beowulf:* . . . *syþðan æfen cwōm, ond him Hrōþgār ġewāt, tō hofe sīnum.* . . . '. . . after evening came and Hrothgar went to his (own) dwelling. . . .'; *bær þā sēo brimwylf, þā hēo tō botme cōm, hringa þenġel tō hofe sīnum.* . . . 'then the she-wolf, when she had reached the bottom, bore the ring-clad prince to her (own) dwelling. . . .'; . . . *wīsdōme hēold ēðel sīnne* '[he] ruled his native country with wisdom'.

10.4   *The u-declension*   Conspicuously absent from those nouns of close family relationship encompassed by the *r*-declension (see 8.5) is the word for 'son'. Even in Indo-European the designation for a male offspring was not included in that declension, and Old English *sunu* derives from **sūnu-* which initially meant 'birth, offspring' and only later 'son'. By its stem vowel *sunu* is a member of the *u*-declension, a declension that contains a limited number of nouns in all three genders. In Proto-Old English many masculine and all neuter nouns (except the indeclinable *fela* 'much') of the *u*-declension were absorbed by the *a*-declension; almost all feminine nouns were absorbed by the *a*- and *ō*-declensions. It is, consequently, not uncommon to encounter a *u*-stem noun in literary Old English that has endings belonging to its original declension and also endings belonging to one of the others; thus, the genitive singular of a masculine noun like *feld* 'field' may be either *feld-a* or *feld-es*.

10.4.1   The following paradigms of *sunu* 'son' (masculine) and *duru* 'door' (feminine) are representative of the *u*-declension.

	Singular	
N	sun-u, -o, -a	dur-u
G	sun-a	dur-a
D	sun-a	dur-a, -u
A	sun-u, -o, -a	dur-u
I	sun-a	dur-a, -u
	Plural	
N	sun-a	dur-a, -u
G	sun-a	dur-a
D	sun-um	dur-um
A	sun-a	dur-a, -u
I	sun-um	dur-um

10.4.2   With due allowance for frequent analogical disturbance, other masculine nouns of the *u*-declension include: *bregu* 'prince', *eard* 'native country', *feld* 'field', *lagu* 'sea', *medu* 'mead', *weald* 'forest', and *wudu* 'wood'; other feminines are *eweorn* 'mill', *flōr* 'floor', *hand* 'hand', and *nosu* 'nose'.

10.5   *Syntax (I): The Accusative Case*   The employment of a given case for several semantic purposes is a practice common to the Indo-European languages; in Classical Latin, for example, the ablative case developed some twenty and more distinct uses. Although the Germanic dialects lost the formal ablative, a similar situation, even if less exaggerated, prevails in Old English with regard to the genitive, dative-instrumental, and accusative cases. The nominative case, apart from being the medium for subjects and predicate nominatives, serves only for nouns in direct address. After the nominative, the next most diversified case is the accusative, which, in addition to its basic function as the indicator of direct objects, has two other well-defined capacities: adverbial and prepositional.

10.5.1   *The Adverbial Accusative*   The accusative is used to measure the extent of space: *nelle iċ beorges weard oferflēon trem fōtes*

'I do not intend to flee the space (*trem*) of a foot from the guardian of the barrow'; and to measure the duration of time: *swā wē þǣr inne andlangne dæ̅ȝ nīode nāman* 'thus we there within took pleasure the entire day'. See also 9.3.2.

10.5.2   *The Prepositional Accusative*   In yet another Old English reflex of Indo-European, the accusative is governed by certain prepositions for the expression of various concepts, prominent among which are movement, and 'place to which' or destination, both literal and metaphorical. The prepositions, some of which combine alike with the dative to specify 'place where' or location, include: *fore* 'before', *ȝeond* 'throughout, through, over', *in* 'into', *ofer* 'beyond, across', *on* 'into, against, up to', *onȝēan* 'towards', *oð* 'to, up to, as far as', *þurh* 'through', *wið* 'with, against, through', *ymbe* 'around'. The distinction between movement and location was not consistently distributed between the two cases; the dative could be used with *onȝēan*, for example, to express movement: . . . *þonne scyldfreca onȝēan gramum gangan sceolde* 'when the shield-warrior was destined to advance against foes'.

10.5.3   *Miscellaneous Uses of the Accusative*   a) Not only the direct object but also the subject of an infinitive is in the accusative: *hēt þā hyssa hwæne hors forlǣtan* '(he) then commanded each one of the young men to turn loose (his own) horse'. b) Instead of the dative, the accusative is found with some impersonal verbs: *hine nānes ðinges ne lyste* 'he desired no thing' (literally: 'it desired him not of no thing'). c) The accusative may have a double object: *þā hē biorges weard sōhte searonīðas* 'when he sought the guardian of the barrow, (and) battles'.

10.6   The Historia aduersum Paganos *of Paulus Orosius and an Alfredian Interpolation*   Among the disciples of the illustrious Church Father, Saint Augustine of Hippo (354–430), was an Hispanic monk, Paulus Orosius, born toward the close of the fourth century, perhaps in the Galician town of Braga (Portugal). As an adjunct to his *City of God*, a defense of Christianity against those non-Christians who claimed that the gods of Rome were punishing the Empire with barbarian invasions and natural calamities because Roman citizens were embracing the religion of Christ, Augustine requested Orosius to write a narrative based, as Orosius himself describes it, "on all the histories and annals available, of all the grievous wars, foul epidemics, baneful times of famine, ghastly earthquakes, unheard-of floods, fearful conflagrations, savage blasts of lightning, storms of hail, wretched murders and crimes,"[1] which had blighted the human condition even before the advent of Christianity, and for which Christianity could in nowise be, or have been, responsible.

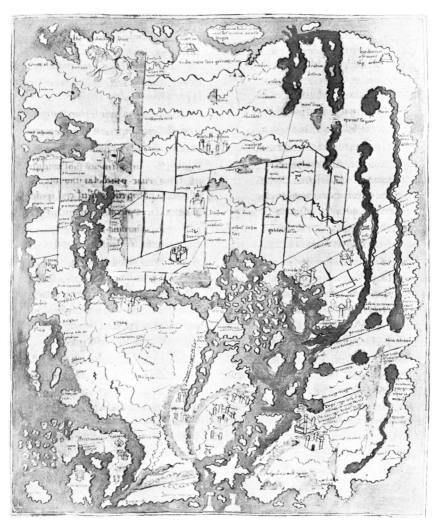

Figure 5. WORLD MAP. Ms. Tiber B. V. (1) 56ᵛ c. 11th century. Courtesy British Museum.

The new religion was not to be found guilty of having offended the Roman deities or of having corrupted Roman virtues; mankind was, in fact, to be recognized as less well off before the coming of Christ. Dedicated to Saint Augustine and didactic in the extreme, the *Historia*, or *Seven Books of History against the Pagans* (*Historiarum aduersum Paganos Libri* vii) was completed by 418, eight years after the devastating sack of Rome by the Visigoths; because Orosius extended his researches as far into the past as he was able, and then brought his story forward to the civilization of his own time, the work is sometimes called the *Compendious* (or *Universal*) *History of the World.*

The fact that the exoneration of Orosius was mediocre history at best did not prevent it from becoming a standard sourcebook in the early Middle Ages, especially for members of the Christian community who could not help being impressed by arguments which, to them, quite successfully refuted a part of the so-called pagan fallacy regarding the decline of Imperial Rome; testimony to its erstwhile popularity are the nearly two hundred manuscripts of the *Historia* that survive today. The necessity for its translation into English would have been obvious to King Alfred; in the *Historia* he had a work that not only told the story of the world, but strenuously vindicated the Christian religion as well. The problem of educating an unenlightened populace and of dealing simultaneously with obstreperous heathens was one that Alfred and Orosius had more or less in common. At a time presumably subsequent to his translation of Pope Gregory's *Pastoral Care*, Alfred took the history of Orosius in hand.

To the modern reader the Alfredian translation, as such, is of negligible value; the seven books of Orosius were reduced to six by Alfred, and errors of the original were not only "retained" by Alfred but, indeed, compounded. "Names are continually misspelled by him; persons and places are confused; words are entirely misunderstood, causing complete mistranslation."[2] By specific design, the West Saxon version is in every way a simplification intended to appeal to the widest audience. Of enduring significance, however, are those departures from the text before him which the king of Wessex deemed imperative for *his* readers. "On almost every page of the history Alfred launches out into comments, moralizings, and attempted explanations; and the generally fluent and natural language displays a marked advance on the clumsy faithfulness of the *Pastoral Care*."[3] Near the beginning of Alfred's rendition occurs the most famous of all his interpolations: a digression on the peoples and geography of ninth-century Germania and Scandinavia. Orosius had prefaced his argument proper with a survey of world geography which concluded with an allusion to the countries of Scandinavia. At that point Alfred interrupts the narrative with a more extensive discussion of Northern tribes and countries, and then proceeds with an account of the exploratory voyages made by Ohthere and Wulfstan, two seamen who had visited his court and had told him at first hand about their experiences in northerly latitudes.

Interestingly enough, Alfred's fundamental view of the world is not appreciably different from that outlined by the Greek geographer, Strabo, in his celebrated *Geographica* of the early first century. The three major landmasses of the world were Asia, Africa, and Europe, each one surrounded by the ocean. Far to the east and south of Britain lay India; less distant was the Mediterranean littoral. The existence of any territory beyond Iceland to the north and west was unknown to Alfred. With the information that he gleaned from Ohthere, however, the king was able to extend the northeastern limits of his world past the North Cape (of Norway) to the White Sea and the Kola Peninsula; from Wulfstan he learned about the southeastern shores of the Baltic Sea, in particular the area where the Vistula flows into that body of water. Such was the flat *middangeard* with which Alfred evinces a passing acquaintance. In no other section is his adaptation of Orosius augmented with detail of comparable interest and appeal.

10.7   *The Voyage of Wulfstan*   In addition to citing geographical landmarks, both Ohthere and Wulfstan supplied King Alfred with descriptions of human life in regions foreign to Anglo-Saxon England. The Scandinavian chieftain, Ohthere (Old Norse *Óttar*), whose home was Helgeland (Old Norse *Hálogaland*) along the far northern coast of Norway, had made one voyage north from there around the North Cape to the waters of the Kola Peninsula, and two voyages to the south; on the first of those he explored the Norwegian Coast from Helgeland to Oslofjord, and on the second he travelled from Oslofjord to the Schlei estuary in southern Jutland. He told Alfred about the excellent whale hunting in Helgeland; with five companions he had once killed sixty whales in two days. He explained that his considerable income was derived from two sources: reindeer, which were hunted and sold, and a tribute paid to him by the Lapps living (under Norwegian domination?) just north of Helgeland; the tribute, or tax, consisted of skins from wild animals (reindeer, bear, marten, otter), eiderdown (birds' feathers), walrus ivory, and ship cables made from hides of walrus and seal. He spoke about those "Beormas" who dwelled along the south shore of the White Sea, and how their language seemed almost identical to that spoken by the Lapps; from the "Beormas" he had heard many stories of their own and surrounding territory—stories, unfortunately, not repeated by Alfred. The following account by Wulfstan incorporates much the same sort of material reported by Ohthere. Probably an Anglo-Saxon, Wulfstan might have been a Scandinavian, perhaps a Dane or a Swede. The dialect is Late West Saxon.

> Wulfstān sǣde þæt hē ġefōre of Hǣðum, þæt hē wǣre on Trūsō on syfan dagum and nihtum, þæt þæt scip wæs ealne weġ yrnende under seġle. Weonoðland him wæs on stēorbord, and on bæcbord him wæs Langaland, and Lǣland, and Falster, and Scōneġ;
> 5   and þās land eall hȳrað tō Denemearcan. And þonne Burgenda

land wæs ūs on bæcbord, and þā habbað him sylfe cyning. þonne
æfter Burgenda lande wǣron ūs þās land, þā synd hātene ǣrest
Blēcinga ēġ, and Mēore, and Ēowland, and Gotland on bæcbord;
and þās land hȳrað tō Swēom. And Weonodland wæs ūs ealne
10   weġ on stēorbord oð Wīslemūðan. Sēo Wīsle is swȳðe myċel ēa,
and hīo tōlīð Wītland and Weonodland; and þæt Wītland belimpeð
tō Estum; and sēo Wīsle līð ūt of Weonodlande, and līð in Estmere;
and sē Estmere is hūru fīftēne mīla brād. þonne cymeð Ilfing
ēastan in Estmere of ðǣm mere, ðe Trūsō standeð in staðe; and
15   cumað ūt samod in Estmere, Ilfing ēastan of Estlande, and Wīsle
sūðan of Winodlande. And þonne benimð Wīsle Ilfing hire naman,
and liġeð of þǣm mere west and norð on sǣ; for ðȳ hit man hǣt
Wīslemūða.

þæt Estland is swȳðe myċel, and þǣr bið swȳðe maniġ burh,
20   and on ælċere byriġ bið cyningc. And þǣr bið swȳðe myċel huniġ,
and fiscað, and sē cyning and þā rīcostan men drincað mȳran
meolc, and þā unspēdigan and þā þēowan drincað medo. þǣr bið
swȳðe myċel ġewinn betwēonan him. And ne bið ðǣr nǣniġ ealo
ġebrowen mid Estum, ac þǣr bið medo ġenōh. And þǣr is mid
25   Estum ðēaw, þonne þǣr bið man dēad, þæt hē līð inne unforbærned
mid his māgum and frēondum mōnað, ġe hwīlum twēġen; and þā
kyningas, and þā ōðre hēahðungene men, swā miċle lencg swā hī
māran spēda habbað, hwīlum healf ġēar, þæt hī bēoð unforbærned
and licgað bufan eorðan on hyra hūsum. And ealle þā hwīle þe
30   þæt līċ bið inne, þǣr sceal bēon ġedrynċ and plega, oð ðone dæġ
þe hī hine forbærnað. þonne þȳ ylcan dæġe þe hī hine tō þǣm āde
beran wyllað, þonne tōdǣlað hī his feoh, þæt þǣr tō lāfe bið æfter
þǣm ġedrynċe and þǣm plegan, on fīf oððe syx, hwȳlum on mā,
swā swā þæs fēos andefn bið. Ālecgað hit ðonne forhwæga on ānre
35   mīle þone mǣstan dǣl fram þǣm tūne, þonne ōðerne, ðonne þæne
þriddan, oþ þe hyt eall ālēd bið on þǣre ānre mīle; and sceall bēon
sē lǣsta dǣl nȳhst þǣm tūne ðe sē dēada man on līð. Ðonne
sceolon bēon ġesamnode ealle ðā menn ðe swyftoste hors habbað
on þǣm lande, forhwǣga on fīf mīlum oððe on syx mīlum fram
40   þǣm fēo. þonne ærnað hȳ ealle tōweard þǣm fēo: ðonne cymeð
sē man sē þæt swiftoste hors hafað tō þǣm ǣrestan dǣle and tō
þǣm mǣstan, and swā ælċ æfter ōðrum, oþ hit bið eall ġenumen;
and sē nimð þone lǣstan dǣl sē nȳhst þǣm tūne þæt feoh ġeærneð.
And þonne rīdeð ælċ hys weġes mid ðan fēo, and hyt mōtan habban
45   eall; and for ðȳ þǣr bēoð þā swiftan hors unġefōge dȳre. And
þonne hys ġestrēon bēoð þus eall āspended, þonne byrð man hine
ūt, and forbærneð mid his wǣpnum and hræġle; and swīðost ealle
hys spēda hȳ forspendað mid þan langan leġere þæs dēadan mannes

inne, and þæs þe hȳ be þǣm wegum ālecgað, þe ðā fremdan tō
50   ærnað, and nimað. And þæt is mid Estum þēaw þæt þǣr sceal
ælċes ġeðēodes man bēon forbærned; and ġyf þār man ān bān
findeð unforbærned, hī hit sceolan miclum ġebētan. And þǣr is
mid Estum ān mǣġð þæt hī magon ċyle ġewyrċan; and þȳ þǣr
licgað þā dēadan men swā lange, and ne fūliað, þæt hȳ wyrċað þone
55   ċyle him on. And þeah man āsette twēġen fætels full ealað oððe
wæteres, hȳ ġedōð þæt ōþer bið oferfroren, sam hit sȳ sumor sam
winter.

10.8   Notes

1.   *Hæðum*, Hedeby or Haddeby, the ancient name of Slesvig (Schleswig), a town about thirty miles northwest of modern Kiel.

2.   *Trūsō*, an unidentified town, possibly Elbing, almost forty miles east of Gdansk (Danzig) in Poland.

3.   *Weonoðland* (*Weonodland, Winodland*) the land of various Slavic tribes called the Wends; probably the area inland and along the coast of the Baltic between the Elbe and the Vistula.

4.   *Langaland* (*Langeland*), *Lǣland* (*Laaland*) *Falster,* Danish islands; *Scōnēġ*, in southwest Sweden (modern Skåne).

5.   *Denemearcan*, much of southern Sweden was then occupied by Danes.

5–6.   *Burgenda land,* the island of Bornholm; before their migration south the home of the East Germanic Burgundians; *cf.* the French province *Bourgogne*.

6.   *ūs*, at this point Wulfstan is quoted directly.

6.   *sylfe* modifies *þā*.

8.   *Blēcinga ēġ* and *Mēore* the Swedish districts of Blekinge and Möre; *Eowland* (*Öland*) and *Gotland* are Swedish islands.

11.   *Wītland*, the region east of the Vistula.

12.   *Estum*, the *Este* were a Baltic tribe.

12.   *Estmere*, the *Frisches Haff* (*Fresh Bay*) into which an eastern branch of the Vistula, called the Nogat, flows.

13.   *Ilfing*, the river Elbing.

14.   *of ðǣm mere* 'from that lake' (the *Drausensee*).

14.   *ðe Trūsō standeð in staðe* 'on the shore of which stands Truso'.

16.   *and þonne benimð Wīsle Ilfing hire naman,* the Elbing merges with and loses itself in the Vistula.

17.   *of þǣm mere west and norð on sǣ,* through the *Frisches Haff* into the *Baltic Sea.*

33.   *on fīf oððe syx* 'into five or six (parts)'.

34–35.   *Alecgað hit ðonne forhwǣga on ānre mīle* . . . "the dead man's treasures, those which could be carried, were divided into five or six or even more shares, according to their number and value. The richest portion was laid on the ground about a mile from the dead man's home, and all the other portions at points between the first one and the home, the portion of least value being placed nearest the house.

After this had been carefully done, all the men who owned the swiftest horses rode from a point five or six miles distant in a race to pick up these treasures, and the prizes fell to those who reached them first."[4]

    44. *hys weġes* 'on his (own) way', an adverbial genitive.

    47. *swīðost* 'for the most part'.

    49. *and þæs þe* 'and with that which'.

    53. *hī magon ċyle ġewyrċan*, the corpse may have been laid on top of some sort of an ice pit; see the note by Dorothy Whitelock in her revision of Sweet's *Anglo-Saxon Primer* (Oxford, 1967), page 231.

    54. *þæt hȳ wyrċað þone ċyle* 'because they effect the refrigeration'.

    55. *fætels full*, for the more regular *fætelsas fulle*.

    56. *ōþer* 'both', or, perhaps, 'one of the two'.

References

1. Eleanor Shipley Duckett, *Alfred the Great* (Chicago, 1956), p. 160.
2. Duckett, p. 161.
3. R. H. Hodgkin, *A History of the Anglo-Saxons,* 3rd ed. (Oxford, 1952), II, p. 629.
4. Duckett, pp. 167–168.

Chapter 11

11.1   *The Strong Verb: Classes VI and VII*   Old English strong verbs of Classes I through V have root vowels in the present and in the preterite (exclusive of the second singular) which are based, for the most part, upon an Indo-European alternation of *e* and *o* respectively (see 5.1.4.1); the verbs of Classes VI and VII, however, clearly stem from ablaut of a divergent sort. From the Germanic evidence an earlier alternation of *a* (*o*, *ə*): *ā* must be assumed for Class VI; with the customary shift of Indo-European *ā* to Germanic *ō*, the principal parts of Class VI verbs are thus satisfactorily accounted for, e.g., *dragan, drōg, drōgon, dragen* 'to drag, draw'. In Class VI no distinction is made between the root vowel of the preterite singular and the preterite plural. Because they originally had a present-tense suffix containing *-j-*, some verbs of Class VI have an umlauted root vowel or diphthong and a geminated consonant at the appropriate places in their conjugational pattern (see 7.2.2), e.g., *steppan* 'to step' from Proto-Germanic **stapjanan*, but (*hē*) *stōp* '(he) stepped' from **stōpe*. For Class VII verbs the ablaut in Indo-European was fundamentally *ē:ō*. Although that variation is not always clear from the Old English data, upon which analogical deflection has had an influence, a contrast in Gothic such as *lētan: lailōt* [lelo:t] 'permit: permitted' does indicate the prehistoric situation. In Old English the infinitive may have *ā, a, ea, ēa, æ, ō* or *ē* as the root vowel or diphthong; like the verbs of Class VI, those of Class VII have the same root vowel (or diphthong) for both preterite singular and preterite plural. The preterite is marked by *ē* or *ēo;* both characteristic of Class VII only. Two representative verbs are *lǣtan, lēt, lēton, lǣten* 'permit' and *healdan, hēold, hēoldon, healden* 'hold'.

11.2   *Reduplicating Verbs in Germanic and in Old English*   A few West Saxon verbs of Class VII have alternative formations in the preterite singular which are vestiges of an ancient method for signifying completed action resulting in a present state, namely reduplication. In addition to the standard preterites *drēd, hēt, lēc, lēt,* and *rēd,* the verbs *drǣdan* 'to be afraid', *hātan* 'to be called', *lācan* 'to jump', *lǣtan* 'to permit', and *rǣdan* 'to advise' also have the attested variants *dreord, heht, leolc, leort* (from **leolt*), and *reord.* The latter group is derived from the reduplicated perfect of Indo-European, a verbal type that is common in Sanskrit and Greek, e.g., *dadāu* 'I have given', *leloipa* 'I have left'; there are token traces of reduplication in Latin, among them the perfects *cecīdī* 'I have fallen', *dedī* 'I have given', and *stetī* 'I have stood'. The characteristic feature of reduplicated perfects is an intensifying stem prefix that consists of the initial consonant, or consonant-cluster, of the root plus the neutral vowel *e* [e]; if successive consonant clusters result, one of them is likely to be simplified, as in Latin *stetī* from *stāre* 'to stand' or Gothic *saislēp* [sesle:p] 'slept' from *slēpan* 'to sleep'. Among the older Germanic dialects, Gothic is unique in regularly preserving the reduplicated perfect of Indo-European; having undergone a semantic shift from 'perfect' to 'preterite', the old reduplicated forms are standard indicators of past time for Class VII verbs. The Gothic parallels of West Saxon *heht, leolc, leort,* and *reord* are *haihait, lailaik, lailōt* and *rairōþ* respectively. It is obvious, then, that a preterite formation like *heht* can be explained only on the basis of reduplication, with concomitant syncope of the root vowel; the *eo*-diphthong of *leort* and *reord* represents the normal development of Proto-Old English short *e* before *r* or *l* plus a single consonant, a sound change sometimes called "breaking" (see 14.3.1). (Because *e* before *lc* did not become a diphthong unless preceded by *s, leolc,* a problematic form, may be analogical.) The etymologies of *heht* and *hēt,* and of the other pairs like them, are independent of one another; *heht* goes back to a reduplicating perfect and *hēt* to an aorist. In North and West Germanic the aorist reflexes are predominant.

11.2.1   The foregoing discussion of reduplication in Old English summarizes traditional views; they are not, however, immune from challenge. For example, the American scholar, W. P. Lehmann, has plausibly argued that reduplication is not attested in North and West Germanic, and that formations like *leort* derive from Indo-European roots containing a laryngeal consonant which, under certain circumstances, became a preterite marker in *-r-;* see W. P. Lehmann, "Old English and Old Norse Secondary Preterits in *-r-*," *Language,* 30. 202–210 (1954).

11.3   *Preterite-Present Verbs*   Apart from the four anomalous verbs (see 6.5), the irregular verbs of Old English are limited to a group of twelve others known as preterite-presents. Like reduplicated verbs, they are also Germanic adapations of an Indo-European perfect formation, but of a formation that lacked reduplication and had a different semantic thrust. Whereas the reduplicating perfects indicated completed action resulting in a present state, the other type placed a psychological emphasis "on the state attained and not on the action of which it was a result."[1] A good example of the non-reduplicating perfect is Greek *oîda;* with an *o*-grade diphthong marking the perfect stem, *ôida*, literally 'I have seen', was used as a present in the sense 'I know', for that which one has seen, is known. The Old English cognate of *ôida* is *wāt* 'I know' (from **woid-*); the present meaning is firmly established, but the form, like that of *ôida*, is clearly an old perfect. Through a process that is not entirely clear, the preterites of eleven other Old English verbs also acquired present meanings by the historical period; that the shift in meaning occurred during the time of Proto-Germanic unity is demonstrated by the presence of preterite-present verbs in both Gothic and Old Norse. Because those preterites which became presents were originally perfect formations only, and not the mixture of perfect and aorist typical in "regular" strong verbs, the root vowel is the same for all three persons in the singular, e.g., *iċ wāt, þū wāst, hē wāt;* ablaut of the former perfect stem accounts for the difference between the root vowel of the singular and that of the plural, e.g., *iċ wāt,* but *wē witon.* When the Germanic preterites developed present meanings, new weak preterites were created to take their place, e.g., *iċ āh* 'I own', but *iċ āhte* 'I owned'. Preterite-present verbs are drawn from each of the first six strong conjugations.

11.3.1   The principal parts of a preterite-present verb are the infinitive, the present third singular (formerly the strong preterite), the present plural (formerly the strong preterite), and the preterite third singular (the new weak formation). The infinitive always has the vowel of the present plural.

Original Class	Infinitive	Present Third Singular	Present Plural	Preterite Third Singular
I	āgan 'to possess'	āh	āgon	āhte
I	witan 'to know'	wāt	witon	wisse, wiste
II	dugan 'to avail'	dēag	dugon	dohte
III	cunnan 'to know, be able'	cann, conn	cunnon	cūþe
III	durran 'to dare'	dearr	durron	dorste
III	þurfan 'to need'	þearf	þurfon	þorfte

Original Class	Infinitive	Present Third Singular	Present Plural	Preterite Third Singular
III	unnan 'to grant'	ann, onn	unnon	ūþe
IV	munan 'to remember'	man, mon	munon	munde
IV	sculan 'to be obliged'	sceal	sculon	sceolde
V	(ġe) nugan 'to suffice'	neah	nugon	nohte
VI	magan 'to be able'	mæġ	magon	meahte, mihte
VI	mōtan 'to be permitted'	mōt	mōton	mōste

11.3.2   The only attested imperatives are *wite, witaþ* and *ġemun, ġemunaþ*. The present subjunctive is formed from the infinitival root, with the exception of *magan* for which the present subjunctive root is *mæġ-;* the preterite subjunctive of all twelve verbs is based on the root of the (new) preterite. If the root vowel of the preterite is *u*, it may be fronted to *y* by umlaut. The only past participles recorded are *āgen* (or *ǣġen*), *ġemunen, ġeunnen* and *witen;* a past participle for *cunnan* exists only from the compound *oncunnan* 'to accuse' (*oncunnen*).

11.3.3   The verb *witan* forms contracted negatives with the adverb *ne* 'not', of which the following are some examples: *nāt* (*ne wāt*), *nyton* (*ne witon*), *nyste* (*ne wiste*), and *nyte* (*ne wite*).

11.4   *The Preterite-Present Verbs in Modern English*   The development of preterite-present verbs subsequent to the Old English period is of some interest. During the century that immediately followed the Norman Conquest in 1066, English, as a language of any standing, was largely eclipsed by Norman French (Anglo-Norman). Through a lack of use by educated classes, the vocabulary of English was considerably diminished; the language was not taught in the schools, nor was any literature created by people who had largely ceased to read or write their former national tongue. In the course of time, almost all the learned words of Old English were simply lost.[2] Early in the Middle English period nearly one-third of the strong verbs disappeared, and today less than one-half the original total remains. Strong verbs were already recessive in Old English, and they were further affected by the normal process of lexical attrition that continued even after the fourteenth century when English was restored to its previous status. The preterite presents were, of course, not excepted. Only six of the twelve now survive: *can, dare, may, must, ought,* and *shall*. Except in the case of *dare* which has become a weak verb in Modern English, the third singular, present indicative is not inflected with -*s*, a lingering sign of the erstwhile preterite nature of the forms. The current present tense paradigms of *must* and *ought* are examples of linguistic history repeating itself. They are the modern equivalents of Old English forms, *mōste* and *āhte; must* and *ought* acquired a present meaning, and then replaced the Old English present forms *mōt-* and *āh-,* which were themselves at one time indicators of past action. In effect, *must* and *ought* do not have a formal imperfect in Modern English. The modern preterites *could* (*can*), *might* (*may*), and *should* (*shall*) derive from their earlier counterparts; the *l* of *could* is a sixteenth-century innovation on the analogy of *should* and *would; dare* has developed a new weak preterite, *dared*. A completely "new" verb has been fashioned from the past participle of *āgan;* used only as an attributive adjective in Old English, *āǵen* is the source for the weak verb *own, owned, owned.* Together with *would* (from *willan, wolde*), *may, might, ought, could,* and *should* often function as indicators of the subjunctive, or conditional, mood, in Modern English.

11.5   *The Demonstrative Pronoun* þēs   In all the Germanic languages a compound demonstrative of rather strong deictic force was constructed from the roots **te-/to-* and **se-/so-* which, singly, supplied the forms for the Old English definite article, itself a demonstrative in origin (see 3.7). In historical Old English, the dithematic pronoun appears as *þēs,* meaning 'this, these'. The Gothic adverb *sai* [sai] 'see! behold!' may be related to **se-/so-,* which is always the second element of the compound demonstrative and intensifies the first; *cf.* the Latin intensive pronoun *ip-se, ip-sa* 'himself, herself'. Some runic inscriptions in Old Norse contain examples of the strong demonstrative that indicate its compound nature more clearly than the Old English paradigms. Part of an inscription (c.985) on a stone from Hällestad in Skåne (southern Sweden) reads: *askil sati stin þansi ifti[R] tuka kurms sun* 'Askel set up this stone (*stin þansi*) in memory of (literally: after) Toki, Gorm's son'. The earlier condition of Old English is seen in the etyma of the nominative singular, masculine and feminine, and the nominative plural (all genders): **te-se, *tjā-se,* and **toi-se*.[3] On the analogy of the oblique cases, **t-* was regularized for the nominative singular, masculine and feminine, where *s-* (from **se-/so-*) would normally be expected as the initial consonant; *cf.* inscriptional Old Norse *sasi* (masculine), *susi* (feminine) 'this', and Old English *sē, sēo.*

11.5.1   *The Declension of* þēs *'this'*

	Singular		
	Masculine	*Feminine*	*Neuter*
N	þĕs	þīos, þēos	þis
G	þis(s)es	þisse, þisre	þis(s)es
D	þis(s)um	þisse, þisre	þis(s)um
A	þisne	þās	þis
I	þȳs	þisse, þisre	þȳs, þīs

Plural

All Genders

N	þās
G	þissa
D	þis(s)um
A	þās

11.5.2   The neuter singular *þis* develops into Modern English *this,* and the plural *þās* into *those.* Modern English *these* comes from Middle English *thise, these, theos,* a new plural of *this.*

11.6   *Syntax (II): The Dative-Instrumental*   Because the various functions of the instrumental case were in large part transferred to the dative, and because inflection of the dative and instrumental is practically identical, it is convenient to regard both cases as a single unit of Old English syntactic processes. Fundamentally, the dative is "the case of the noun in regard to which something is done," and the instrumental the case expressing "the means by which something is done."[4] The semantic resemblance between the two is sufficient to account for an eventual overlapping of functions, especially given the roughly similar character of their endings in Indo-European and Proto-Germanic. The more important specialized uses of the dative-instrumental are cited in the following paragraphs.

11.6.1   *The Dative as Object*   Although the dative case is most often associated with expression of the indirect object, it may also indicate the direct object after certain verbs: *þǣr him hel onfēng* 'there hell received him'. Some common verbs construed with the dative are: *andswarian* 'to answer', *bedrēosan* 'to deprive (of)', *bēodan* 'to offer', *bodian* 'to announce', *breġdan* 'to pull', *dēman* 'to judge', *ġefēon* 'to rejoice', *folgian* 'to follow', *helpan* 'to help', *hȳrsumian* 'to obey', *līcian* 'to please', *ġelȳfan* 'to believe', *miltsian* 'to pity', *onfōn* 'to receive', *wealdan* 'to rule', and *wiðstandan* 'to resist'.[5] The dative as direct object may be reflexive: *ðā him Hrōþgār gewāt* 'then Hrothgar departed'; or it may be connected with an impersonal verb: *ne ofþyncð hit ðē ġif iċ þus wer ġeċēose?* 'will it not displease you, if I should choose a husband thus?' The dative is also the object of prepositions, more frequently, in fact, than any other case in Old English. Some prepositions, like *ofer* and *under,* indicate 'place to which' with the accusative (see 10.5.2), but 'place where' with the dative: *mæst hlīfade ofer Hrōðgāres hordġestrēonum* 'the mast towered above the treasures of Hrothgar'.

11.6.2   *The Possessive Dative*   This idiomatic use of the dative occurs in a frequently encountered sentence pattern: *subject—verb—(ob-*

ject)—*preposition*—*noun;* although the word order need not always be the same, the *noun* is identified or defined by a noun or pronoun in the dative.[6] That construction is illustrated by *hire* in the following sentence: *hond sweng ne oftēah, þæt hire on hafelan hringmǣl āgōl grǣdiġ gūðlēoð* '(his) hand did not hold back the blow, so that the ring-sword sang a fierce war-song on her head'; and by *him* in: *dyde him of healse hring gyldenne þīoden þrīsthȳdiġ* 'the brave prince took a golden torque from his (own) neck'. A particularized use of the possessive dative involves the preposition *tō: wāt sē þe cunnað hū slīþen bið sorg tō ġefēran* 'that man, who experiences (it), knows how cruel sorrow is for his companion'.

11.6.3   *The Adjectival Dative*   Certain adjectives denoting proximity or an emotional attitude are regularly construed with the dative; among them is *anlīċ* 'like': *for þām is heofona rīċe anlīċ þam cyninge þe his þēowas ġerādegode* 'therefore, the kingdom of heaven is like the king who called his servants to account'. Other adjectives with the dative include: *fāh* 'hostile (to)', *hold* 'loyal (to)', *lēof* 'dear (to)', and *nēah* 'near (to)'.

11.6.4   *The Temporal Dative*   Like the accusative, the dative may also be an indicator of time: *þāra heord him wæs þǣre neahte beboden* 'the tending of which was entrusted to him at night'. A rather common adverbial dative is *hwīlum* 'sometimes, now and again, formerly' from *hwīl* (feminine) 'time, space of time': *hwīlum on beorh æthwearf* 'now and again he turned back into the barrow'.

11.6.5   *Idiomatic Uses of the Instrumental*   Insofar as it remains a distinct entity in Late West Saxon, the instrumental continues to express *agency* or *means,* either with or without a preposition: *þæt hē mid ðȳ wīfe wælfǣhða dǣl sæċċa ġesette* 'that he should settle a portion of the deadly feuds, of the battles, by means of a wife'; *ealdorlangne tīr ġeslōgon æt sæċċe sweorda ecgum* '(they) struck out everlasting glory at battle by means of edges of swords'. In some contexts, the basic function of the instrumental may easily approach that of an adverb: *stondeð nū on lāste . . . weal wundrum hēah* 'now a rampart, wondrously high, remains behind'; this adverbial usage is relatively common (see also 9.3.2). The instrumental is used idiomatically in causal constructions, in constructions involving the comparative degree, and after a few prepositions. A causal relationship may be stated by the instrumental of *hwā* 'who, what' and *sē: hwī synt ġē forhte* 'why (for what cause) are you afraid?'; *ðȳ hē þone fēond ofercwōm* 'therefore (by that) he overcame the fiend'. Prepositions are also used with the instrumental to express causation: *for hwȳ God is ġehaten sīo hēhste ēcnes* 'why God is called the Supreme Eternity'; *be þȳ þū meaht ongitan* 'by which you may perceive'; the prepositional phrase *for þon* (*for þȳ*) 'therefore, for this reason' is very frequent. The comparative degree of adjectives and adverbs is often accompanied by the instrumental: *þæt hī fōr nānum ermðum bīoð ne þȳ betran, ac þȳ wyrsan* 'that they for no miseries will be better, but rather (will get) worse'; *sē eorl wæs þē blīþra* 'the warrior was the happier'; *þæt þū meaht þȳ sweotolor onġitan* 'that you may the more clearly perceive'. The comparative of the adverb *lȳt* 'little' forms a conjunction with *þȳ* that customarily introduces the subjunctive: *ðȳ læs hī hwæm leohte ðynċen* 'lest (by that much less) they may seem to anyone light to assume'. The instrumental occurs in a non-specific sense after certain prepositions, among which are *æfter, be, for, mid,* and *on: raþe æfter þon on fagne flōr fēond treddode* 'quickly after that the fiend stepped on to the decorated floor'; *ðū þē lær be þon* 'teach yourself by that'; *ond hē swā wæs hine ġetrymmende mid þȳ heofonlecan weġneste* 'and thus he was preparing himself with the heavenly viaticum'. But note the highly idiomatic *mid þȳ* (*þe*) 'when'.

11.7   *The Anglo-Saxon Chronicle*   Associated with the increased literary activity of King Alfred's reign is an original work in the vernacular which has inestimable value for historians and philologists, the *Anglo-Saxon Chronicle*. Surviving in seven manuscript versions, the *Chronicle* is a continuous record of annual events from the first landing of Julius Caesar in Britain (55 BC) to the coronation of Henry II in 1154. Just when, or by whom the *Chronicle* was started is not clear. The oldest manuscript, the *Parker Chronicle,* so-called because it was donated by Mathew Parker, archbishop of Canterbury (1559–1575) to Corpus Christi College at Cambridge, is written down to the year 891 in the hand of a single scribe, a circumstance which suggests 891 as the *terminus a quo* for inception of that particular annal, and, consequently, all others. From the description in the *Parker Chronicle* of events after 891 it further appears that later scribes were writing at Winchester, the capital of Wessex, and it may well be that "the manuscript was from the first written at the Old Minster, Winchester."[7]

In spite of the proposed date of origin and the place of production, however, there is no direct evidence connecting the *Parker Chronicle,* or any other, with King Alfred personally; if a patron is necessary, a possible candidate might be some nobleman of the southwest since the "early annals give prominence to events in Dorset and Somerset, rather than to those which took place in Hampshire."[8] Nevertheless, the *Anglo-Saxon Chronicle* does represent the sort of project that would certainly have received enthusiastic encouragement from King Alfred, and that may explain the circulation of copies of the *Parker,* or "Alfredian," *Chronicle* to various educational centers in England during the king's lifetime, a distribution recalling that of Pope Gregory's *Pastoral Care.* The relationship to one another of the extant recensions of the *Chronicle* is extremely complicated, to say the least, but they did all spring "originally from the Alfredian chronicle, and were [then] reared independently in different parts of the country."[9]

The *Parker Chronicle* itself is unique as a document only, not as a concept; it, too, was derived from an earlier source, vestiges of which are apparent in the language of the manuscript. Commenting upon the value of entries for the fifth and sixth centuries, Sir Frank Stenton, observes that that chronicle would be less credible "if the occasional preservation of an archaic case-ending or a pre-Alfredian form of a proper name did not show that it incorporates ancient matter. The foundation of the work was a set of West Saxon annals, possibly written in Latin, which came down to the middle of the eighth century."[10] Now lost, the West Saxon annals which formed the basis of the *Parker Chronicle* would seem to have been a compilation of various chronological summaries, royal genealogies, a list of the bishops of Winchester to 754, and other like material.

The *idea* of annalistic writing derives from the custom of keeping Easter Tables for the purpose of determining the day upon which the resurrection of Christ was to be celebrated in any given year. Occasionally the calculator would make use of marginal space for the citation of some particularly important death or event; marginalia of that sort were in fact later transferred to the *Anglo-Saxon Chronicle* where, for example, entries relating to the Germanic settlement of England tend to be spaced out at intervals of four or eight years, simply because the margin of the Easter Tables was divided into separate spaces by the recurrent indications of successive leap years.[11] Until the third decade of the ninth century when the events recorded begin to fall within living memory of the chronicler, there is a frequent paucity of detail for the annual listings, which are often no more than a single, short sentence. The entry for 588 states only that "In this year King Ælle died, and Æthelric ruled after him for five years"; the notice for 741 is even more laconic: "In this year York burned down." There were, of course, exceptions to such brief reports and one of them occurs for the year 755 wherein the savage feud between King Cynewulf of Wessex and his retainer, Cyneheard, is related at some length and with considerable vigor. Very likely an interpolation resting upon oral tradition, that account qualifies as the first English short story.

Poetic insertions are likewise found; the first and best-known example occurs after the expanded entries of the ninth century. It is the *Battle of Brunanburh*, a seventy-three line poem commemorating a victory of King Æthelstan of Wessex over the combined forces of Norwegian Vikings and Scotsmen who had crossed over to England from Ireland in 937; the anonymous poet concludes his encomium of the English with the remark that "according to what books or venerable scholars tell us, there never was yet before this a greater slaughter of an army carried out with the edges of swords on this island, since Angles and Saxons came ashore here over the broad waters (the North Sea and the English Channel) from the east (the Continent); since the proud warriors, nobles eager for glory, sought Britain, overcame the Welsh, and acquired a homeland." Yet, the tenth century was to see a disastrous decline of Anglo-Saxon might, and there were few subsequent occasions for such happy self-congratulation. Throughout the times of future adversity the *Chronicle* was nevertheless maintained. The unfortunate reign of the West Saxon king, Æthelred (978–1016), under whom England was ultimately subjected to Scandinavian control for twenty-five years, is well documented, and events before and after the unpalatable Conquest of 1066 are also fully described. Save for the chronicle of Peterborough Cathedral, however, no version of the Old English annals is carried beyond 1079, and the *Peterborough Chronicle* itself is discontinued after 1154. What now remains is the first example of historical writing in any Germanic language, a superb attestation of English prose during a period of some two hundred years, and the most significant primary source for the history of early England.

11.8   *The Annal for 1009 in the* Peterborough Chronicle   As the *Battle of Brunanburh* shows, King Alfred's containment of the Danes did not permanently secure the country from foreign attack; during the tenth century internal strife and increased Viking activity were to lead to the collapse of the Old English monarchy. In 980 a series of Danish raids began that culminated with the occupation of the English throne in 1017 by the Danish king, Knut. To more readily meet the threat of a Danish invasion, the English forces were placed under the central control of the Mercian, Eadric, in 1007; the annal for 1009 tells of dissension in the English ranks, and an unsuccessful attempt to thwart the Danes who were once again challenging the English levy. "The history of England in the next generation was really determined between 1009 and 1012."[12] The dialect is Late West Saxon.

    1009   Hēr on þissum ġēare ġewurdon þā scipu ġearwe þe wē ǣr
    ymbe sprǣcon, and heora wæs swā feala swā nǣfre ǣr þes ðe ūs
    bēċ secgað on Angelcynne ne ġewurdon on nānes cynges dæġ. And
    hī man þā ealle tōgædere ferode tō Sandwīċ, and þǣr sceoldan
 5 licgan, and þisne eard healdan wið ǣlcne ūthere. Ac wē ġyt næfdon
    þā ġesēlða, ne þone wurðscipe þet sēo scipfyrd nytt wǣre ðisum
    eard þē mā þe hēo oftor ǣr wæs.

Ðā ġewearð hit on þisum ilcan tīman oððe litle ǣr þet
Brihtrīċ Ēadrīċes brōðor ealdormannes forwreġde Wulfnōð ċild
10   þone Sūðseaxscian tō þām cyning, and hē þa ūt ġewende and him
þā tō āspēon þet hē heafde .xx. scipa, and hē þā hergode ǣġhwēr
be ðām sūðriman; and ǣlċ yfel wrohton. þā cȳdde man in tō þǣre
scipfyrde þet hī mann ēaðe befaran mihte ġif man ymbe bēon
wolde. Ðā ġenām sē Brihtrīċ him tō hundeahtatiġ scipa, and þōhte
15   þet hē him myċeles wordes wirċean sceolde, and þet hē Wulfnōð
cuconne oððe dēadne beġytan sceolde. Ac þā hī þyderweard wǣron
þa cōm him swilċ wind onġēan swilċe nān mann ǣr ne ġemunde
and þā scipo ðā ealle tōbēot and tōþræsc and on land wearp; and
cōm sē Wulfnōð sōna and ðā scipo forbærnde. Ðā þis cūð wæs tō
20   ðām ōðrum scipon þǣr sē cyng wæs, hū ðā ōðre ġefērdon, wæs þā
swilċ hit eall rǣdlēas wǣre, and fērde sē cyng him hām and þā
ealdormenn and þā hēahwitan, and forlēton þā scipo þus lēohtlīċe.
And þet folc þā þe on ðām scipe wǣron fǣrcodon ðā scipo eft tō
Lundene, and lēton ealles ðēodscipes ġeswincg þus lēohtlīċe
25   forwurðan; and næs sē siġe betera þe eall Angelcynn tō hopode.

    þā ðēos scipfyrd ðus ġeendod wæs, þā cōm sōna æfter
Hlāmmessan sē unġemetlīca unfriðhere, þe wē hēton Ðurkilles
here, tō Sandwīċ and sōna wendon heora fōre tō Cantwarbyriġ,
and þā burh raðe ġeēodon ġif hī þē raðor tō him friðes tō ne
30   ġirndon. And ealle Ēast Centingas wið þone here frið ġenāmon,
and him ġesealdon .iii. þūsend punda. And sē here þā sōna æfter
þām ġewendon ābūton oð þet hī cōmon tō Wihtlande, and þǣr
ǣġhwēr on Sūðseaxum and on Hamtūnscīre, and ēac on Bearrucscīre hergodon and bærndon swā heora ġewuna wæs. þā hēt
35   sē cyng ābannan ūt ealne þēodscipe þet mann on ǣlċe healfe wið
hī ġehealdan sceolde; ac þēahhweðere hī fērdon lōc hū hī woldon.

    þā sum sīðe heafde sē cyng hī fōrebegān mid ealre fyrde þā
hī tō scipan woldon, and eall folc ġearu wæs heom on tō fōnne,
ac hit wæs ðā þurh Ēadrīċ ealdorman ġelet swā hit þā ǣfre wæs.
40   Ðā æfter Sanctus Martinus messan þā fērdon hī eft onġēan tō
Cent, and nāmon him winter settl on Temesan and lifedon of Ēast
Seaxum and of ðām scīrum þe þǣr nyxt wǣron on twām healfum
Temese, and oft hī on þā burh Lundene ġefuhton. Ac sī Gode lof
þet hēo ġyt ġesund stent, and hī þǣr ǣfre yfel ġefērdon. Ðā æfter
45   middanwintra hī nāmon þā ǣnne ūpgang ūt þurh Ċiltern, and swā
tō Oxneforda, and þā burh forbærndon, and nāmon hit þā on twā
healfe Temese tō scipan weard. þā ġewarnode man hī þet þǣr wæs
fyrd æt Lundene onġēan; hī ġewendon þā ofer æt Stāne. And þus
fērdon ealne þone winter, and ðone lencten wǣron him on Cent
50   and bēttan heora scipa.

11.9   *Notes*

1. *hēr* 'in this year', the customary introduction for each entry; the entry for 1009 "seems to begin the year either with March 25 or with Easter, for the first date under 1010 is 'ofer Eastron'."[13]

2–3. *þes ðe* for *þæs ðe; bēð* may be an allusion to earlier chronicles.

4. *Sandwīð,* Sandwich, on the coast north of Dover.

7. *þē mā þe* 'any more than'.

9. Brihtric and Eadric were Mercians.

9. *ðild,* a title, meaning 'of noble birth'; Wulfnoth was the grandfather of King Harold who was killed fighting against William, Duke of Normandy, at the Battle of Hastings in 1066.

10. *tō þām cyning,* Æthelred Unrǣd.

10. *hē* [Wulfnoth] *þā ūt ģewende.*

13. *þet hī* [Wulfnoth's force] *mann ēaðe befaran mihte.*

13. *ymbe bēon* 'to set about it'.

15. *myðeles wordes* 'a great reputation'.

27. *Hlāmmessan,* Lammas Day, 1 August.

27–28. *Ðurkilles here.* The Danish force of 1009 was augmented by other Viking companies, one of which came from Jómsborg, a Danish settlement of professional soldiers at the mouth of the Oder, and was led by Thorkell the Tall.

28. *Cantwarbyriģ,* Canterbury.

32. *Wihtlande,* the Isle of Wight.

33. *Hamtūnscīre,* Hampshire; *Bearrucscīre,* Berkshire.

40. *Sanctus Martinus messan,* the feast of Saint Martin of Tours, November 11.

45. *Ċiltern,* the Chilterns; a range of chalk hills extending northeast for forty-five miles from the Thames at Goring, through Oxford and beyond to the border of Suffolk.

48. *Stāne,* Staines; a settlement southwest of London, in Middlesex.

References

1. Eduard Prokosch, *A Comparative Germanic Grammar* (Philadelphia, 1939), p. 188.

2. Margaret Bryant, *Modern English and Its Heritage,* 2nd ed. (New York, 1962), p. 59.

3. Prokosch, p. 272.

4. Prokosch, p. 231.

5. This list is largely derived from Randolph Quirk and C. L. Wrenn, *An Old English Grammar,* 2nd ed. (London, 1958), p. 65.

6. Quirk and Wrenn, p. 66.

7. Dorothy Whitelock, with David C. Douglas and Susie I. Tucker, eds., *The*

Anglo-Saxon Chronicle, A Revised Translation (New Brunswick, New Jersey, 1961), p. xi.

8. G. N. Garmonsway, trans., *The Anglo-Saxon Chronicle,* Everyman's Library 624 (London, 1953), p. xxxi.

9. Garmonsway, p. xxxiii.

10. *Anglo-Saxon England,* 2nd ed. (Oxford, 1947), p. 15.

11. Sir Frank Stenton, *Anglo-Saxon England,* pp. 15–16.

12. Stenton, p. 379.

13. C. Plummer, ed., *Two of the Saxon Chronicles Parallel,* based on an earlier edition by J. Earle, II (Oxford, 1899, reprinted 1952), p. 187.

Chapter 12

12.1 *Contract Verbs* A comparison of the Old English infinitive *nēotan* 'to use, enjoy' with its cognates in Gothic and Old Saxon, *niutan* and *niotan*, shows the Old English form to have developed in a regular fashion from Proto-Germanic **neutanan*, but a comparison of Old English *tēon* 'to draw, pull' with Gothic *tiuhan* and Old Saxon *tiohan* indicates the presence of certain sound changes peculiar to the insular dialect. Both *tēon* and *nēotan* are strong verbs of Class II, but *tēon* also belongs to a small subcategory of strong verbs known as "contract verbs." Very late in the Proto-Old English period, intervocalic *h* [χ] was lost, and the two newly juxtaposed vowels (or diphthong and vowel) coalesced, or contracted, into a single long vowel or diphthong; thus Proto-Old English **wrīhan* became *wrēon* 'to cover', and **tēohan* (from Proto-Germanic **teuhanan*) became *tēon*. Because *Beowulf* was written down at least two hundred years after the probable date of composition, the uncontracted forms of the manuscript must sometimes be restored when the meter of the poem calls for a dissyllabic word rather than a monosyllabic one; line 1036 contains a case in point: (1035) *heht ðā eorla hlēo eahta mēaras/ fǣtedhlēore on flet tēo[ha]n* 'then the protector of warriors commanded eight horses with gold-plated bridle(s) to be brought into the hall'. When *h* was not intervocalic it was, of course, not lost; it is preserved in the second and third person singular, present indicative (*tīehst, tīehþ*) and in the second singular of the imperative (*tēoh*) of all contract verbs. In the present, *h* was kept after syncopation of the suffix vowel obliterated its former intervocalic status; in the imperative singular, *h* always was in word-final position, and, hence, never intervocalic. All contract verbs were subject to *i*-umlaut (see 6.3) in the second and third person singular

114

of the present indicative, and it is, therefore, clear that syncopation of the suffix vowel came after mutation and before the disappearance of *h*, which would otherwise not have remained. Verner's Law (see 6.1) was also operative in contract verbs, accounting for preterite plurals and past participles like *tugon* and *togen* for *tēon*. Contract verbs occur in all classes of the strong verb except Class IV.

12.1.1   The following conjugation of *tēon* in the present and preterite indicative typifies the contract verbs.

Present

	Singular	*Plural*
1	iċ tēo	wē tēoþ
2	þū tīehst	ġē tēoþ
3	hē tīehþ	hīe tēoþ

Preterite

	Singular	*Plural*
1	iċ tēah	wē tugon
2	þū tuge	ġē tugon
3	hē tēah	hīe tugon

12.1.2   The present participle is *tēonde*, the past participle *togen*, and the gerund *tō tēonne;* the present subjunctive, singular and plural are *tēo* and *tēon;* the preterite subjunctive, singular and plural are *tuge* and *tugen*. In contract verbs, the forms for the present subjunctive singular and plural are always identical with the first singular, present indicative, and the infinitive respectively. The imperative singular and plural are *tēoh* and *tēon*.

12.1.3   Other common contract verbs include *fēolan* (Class I) 'to reach', *fēon* (V) 'to rejoice', *flēon* (II) 'to flee', *fōn* (VII), 'to seize', *hōn* (VII) 'to hang', *sēon* (V) 'to see', *slēan* (VI) 'to strike', and *ðēon* (I) 'to thrive'.

12.2   *Numerals*   The counting system of Old English was well developed, and could be used for the expression not only of cardinals and ordinals, but also for collectives (*bēġen* 'both'), distributives (*ānlīepiġ* 'one each' *ġetwinne* 'two each'), multiplicatives (*fēowerfeald* 'fourfold'), and some fractions (*þridda dǣl* 'one-third').[1] The Germanic method of counting was based upon ten and reflects the decimal system achieved by Indo-European, apparently in its later stages and only after experimentation with competing numerical schemes. The fact that the first four cardinals, and no others, are fully declined in some Indo-European languages, plus the fact that the reconstruction for *eight* (*$oktōu$) is in the dual, points to the previous existence of a tetradic system that must have stemmed from the practice of touching the other four fingers consecutively with the thumb. Furthermore, the etymology of *nine* connects that word with the root for 'new', *$newo$-; nine is the 'new number' (*cf.* Gothic *niujis* 'new', *niun* 'nine' and Latin *nouus* 'new', *nouem* 'nine'). Application of the thumb to the joints of the other figures on one hand yields a base of twelve, and a duodecimal system is doubtless reflected in the earliest meaning of *hund*- which was 'a gross' or 'six score'; *cf.* Old Norse *hundrað* '120', Modern German *Grosshundert* '120', and English *long hundred* '120'. The etymologies of *eleven* and *twelve*, 'one left (over)' and 'two left (over)', also suggest the sometime use of a duodecimal system in Indo-European. In the historical period, however, the decimal system is universally employed, and the numbers for one through ten are exceedingly stable cognates among the Indo-European dialects.

12.2.1   *The Old English Cardinals*   A selected list of cardinal numbers includes the following:

1	ān	16	siextīene
2	twēġen, tū, twā	17	seofontīene
3	þrīe, þrīo, þrēo	18	eahtatīene
4	fīower, fēower	19	nigontīene
5	fīf	20	twēntiġ
6	siex, six	21	ān ond twēntiġ
7	siofon, seofon	30	þrītiġ
8	eahta	40	fēowertiġ
9	nigon	50	fīftiġ
10	tīen, tȳn	60	siextiġ
11	endlefan, -leofan, -lufan	70	(hund) seofontiġ
12	twelf	80	(hund) eahtatiġ
13	þrēotīene, -tēne, -tȳne	90	(hund) nigontiġ
14	fēowertīene	100	hundtēontiġ, hund, hundred
15	fīftīene	1000	þūsend

All cardinals could function grammatically as both nouns and adjectives, but only *ān, twēġen,* and *þrīe* were consistently inflected for each case and gender; when not immediately preceding the noun modified,[2] the numbers from 4 through 12 could be declined with a nominative-accusative singular in -*e* (in the neuter also -*u*, -*o*), a genitive in -*a*, and a dative in -*um;* those from 13 through 19 form the genitive in -*a*, and the dative in -*um;* numerals from 20 upward have a genitive in -*es*, -*a*, or -*ra*, and a dative in -*um*. When not invariable, *hund* and *þūsend* are declined as neuter nouns. The following excerpt from the *Voyage of Ohthere* (see 10.6) illustrates the usage of cardinals:

> *Sē hwǣl bið micle lǣssa þonne ōðre hwalas: ne bið hē lenġra ðonne syfan elna lang; ac on his āgnum lande is sē betsta hwǣlhuntað; þā bēoð eahta and fēowertiġes elna lange, and þā mǣstan fīftiġes elna lange; þāra hē sǣde þæt hē syxa sum ofslōge syxtiġ on twām dagum.*

'The whale (walrus) is much smaller than the other whales: it is not longer than seven (of) ells long: but the best whaling is in his own country; they (the whales) are (of) eight and forty (of) ells in length, and the biggest (of) fifty (of) ells in length; of those, he said that he, of six a certain one (i.e., he and five others), killed sixty in two days'. On the genitive plural for *eln* see 12.5.5; *sum* plus a numerical genitive is a common and idiomatic way of separating an individual from the total number in a group: *fīftȳna sum sundwudu sōhte* 'a certain one of fifteen sought the ship'.

12.2.1.1   *The Declension of* ān, twēġen, *and* þrīe.

		Masculine	Feminine	Neuter
Singular	N	ān	ān	ān
	G	ānes	ānre	ānes
	D	ānum	ānre	ānum
	A	ānne, ǣnne	āne	ān
	I	āne, ǣne	ānre	āne, ǣne
Plural	N	āne	āna, āne	ān, āne
	G	ānra	ānra	ānra
	D	ānum	ānum	ānum
	A	āne	āna, āne	ān, āne
	I	ānum	ānum	ānum

		Masculine	Feminine	Neuter
Plural	N	twēġen	twā	tū, twā
	G	twēga, twēġra	twēga, twēġra	twēga, twēġra
	D	twǣm, twām	twǣm, twām	twǣm, twām
	A	twēġen	twā	tū, twā
	I	twǣm, twām	twǣm, twām	twǣm, twām
Plural	N	þrīe, þrī	þrēo	þrēo
	G	þrēora	þrēora	þrēora
	D	þrim	þrim	þrim
	A	þrīe, þrī	þrēo	þrēo
	I	þrim	þrim	þrim

12.2.1.2   It should be noted that *ān* is declined like a strong adjective; grammatically it alternates between a numeral and an adjective, sometimes becoming an indefinite article in the latter capacity when declined according to the weak declension (see 4.3.1), *ān* means 'alone'. Plural forms of *ān* have the meaning 'only, unique', except for *ānra* in phrases like *ānra ġehwylċ* 'each of the individuals, each of those'.

12.2.2   *The Old English Ordinals*   A selected list of ordinal numbers includes the following:

1	forma, fyrmest, fyrst, ǣrest	16	siextēoþa
2	ōþer	17	seofontēoþa
3	þridda	18	eahtatēoþa
4	fēowerþa, fēorþa	19	nigontēoþa
5	fīfta	20	twēntigoþa, -tiġþa, -tiga
6	siexta	21	ān ond twēntigoþa
7	seofoþa, -eþa	30	þrītigoþa
8	eahtoþa, -eþa, -eoþa	40	fēowertigoþa
9	nigoþa, -eþa, -eoþa	50	fīftigoþa
10	tēoþa	60	siextigoþa
11	endlefta, ellefta	70	(hund) seofontigoþa
12	twelfta	80	(hund) eahtigoþa
13	þrēotēoþa	90	(hund) nigontigoþa
14	fēowertēoþa	100	hundtēontigoþa
15	fīftēoþa		

The synonymns for *first* are not connected with the cardinal *ān,* but derive instead from Indo-European **pro* 'before, in front'; *ǣrest* is an adjective in the superlative degree formed from the adverb *ǣr* 'early, formerly'; the word survives in Modern English *erstwhile*. *ōþer* comes from the Indo-European root **ono-* 'that one' plus the comparative suffix **-tero-;* except for *ōþer*, which is declined like a strong adjective (see 5.2.1), all the ordinals are declined according to the weak adjectival pattern (see 4.3.1). In Middle English *ōþer,* as an ordinal, was replaced by French *secounde;* Modern English phrases like 'every other day' preserve the earlier meaning of 'second'. The original *-n* of numbers like *seofon,* for example, which was lost before *þ* in Old English (*seofoþa*), was restored during the Middle English period by analogy with the cardinal formations, giving *sevenþe; ninþe, tenþe, fourtenþe,* and so forth.[3]

12.3   *The i-declension*   Before the historical period of Old English, many nouns of the *i*-stem declension were affected by umlaut and by analogical change. Because the stem vowel was capable of causing *i*-mutation, a shift of the root vowel took place, wherever possible, in all cases and both numbers; in contrast to the *r*-declension where some forms of a noun are umlauted and others are not (see 8.5), there is no paradigmatic variation of the root vowel for any umlauted noun of the *i*-declension. Except as a matter of historical interest, however, the process of mutation is irrelevant to a consideration of attested forms; some nouns, of course, did not have a radical vowel susceptible to umlaut. The *i*-declension contains nouns of all three genders, but the inflectional endings of masculine and neuter nouns show a strong tendency to conform to those of the *a*-declension.

12.3.1   The following paradigms of *ġiest* 'guest', *tīd* 'time', and *spere* 'spear' are representative of the *i*-declension.

Singular

	Masculine	*Feminine*	*Neuter*
N	ġiest	tīd	sper-e
G	ġiest-es	tīd-e	sper-es
D	ġiest-e	tīd-e	sper-e
A	ġiest	tīd	sper-e
I	ġiest-e	tīd-e	sper-e

Plural

	Masculine	*Feminine*	*Neuter*
N	ġiest-as	tīd-e, -a	sper-u, -o
G	ġiest-a	tīd-a	sper-a
D	ġiest-um	tīd-um	sper-um
A	ġiest-as	tīd-e, -a	sper-u, -o
I	ġiest-um	tīd-um	sper-um

12.3.2   Like certain neuter nouns of the *a*-declension, some masculine nouns of the *i*-declension retain a vocalic ending in the nominative and accusative singular because the root was originally short (see 3.5.3). The "ending" is really the old thematic vowel *-i-;* the Indo-European suffix **-i-s* became **-i-z* in Proto-Germanic, and was then reduced to *-i* which developed into *-e* in Old English, thus yielding a formation like *wine* 'friend' from Proto-Germanic **winiz*. Except for the nominative and accusative singular, *wine* has inflectional endings identical to those of *ġiest*. Other nouns of the same type include: *bite* 'bite', *byre* 'son', *ċiele* 'cold', *cwide* 'saying, speech', *dryre* 'fall', *dyne* 'din', *flyġe* 'flight', *gryre* 'terror', *hryre* 'fall', *hyġe* 'mind', *hyse* 'son, young man', *lyġe* 'lie, falsehood', *mete* 'food', *sele* 'hall', *stede* 'place', *stiġe* 'ascent', and *wlite* 'brightness, beauty'.

12.3.3   Except in the nominative-accusative singular and in the dative-instrumental singular, all the inflectional endings of masculine nouns like *ġiest* are taken over by analogy from the *a*-declension; in the singular the etymologically correct forms would have been: *ġiest, ġieste, ġieste, ġiest, ġieste;* and in the plural: *ġieste, ġiest(i)ga, ġiestim, ġieste, ġiestim.* The old nominative-accusative plural is, in fact, preserved in a few nouns which name tribal groups: *Dene* 'Danes', *Engle* 'the English', *Mierċe* 'the Mercians', *Norþhymbre* 'the Northumbrians', *Seaxe* 'the Saxons'; the original genitive plural is attested by *Deniġea* 'of the Danes'. Other masculine nouns which also retain the non-analogical nominative and accusative plural are: *ielde* 'men', *ielfe* 'elves', *lēode* 'peoples', *stede* 'places', and *wine* 'friends'. In neuter nouns of the *i*-declension the ending of the genitive singular and all plural endings are taken over from the neuter *a*-declension. All feminine nouns with short roots were absorbed by the *ō*-declension, and those feminine nouns with long roots which remained a part of the *i*-declension have endings much influenced by the *ō*-declension.

12.3.4   Declined like *ġiest* are the masculines: *æsc* 'ash tree', *dǣl* 'portion', *drenċ* 'drink', *ent* 'giant', *feng* 'grasp', *flyht* 'flight', *gylt* 'guilt', *hyht* 'hope', *līeġ* 'flame', *list* 'skill, cunning', *sweġ* 'sound, noise', *wyrm* 'worm'. All feminine *i*-stem nouns are declined like *tīd;* they include: *ǣht* 'property', *ansīen* 'face', *benċ* 'bench', *brȳd* 'bride', *cwēn* 'queen', *dǣd* 'deed', *dryht* 'troop', *hyrst* 'ornament', *meaht, miht* 'might, power', *scyld* 'guilt', *spēd* 'success', *wēn* 'hope, expectation', *wyrd* 'fate'. Other than *spere*, neuter *i*-stem nouns are few and inconsequential.

12.4   *The Interrogative Pronoun* hwā   The Indo-European root **kwo-/kwi-* appears in all the derivative languages as both an interrogative pronoun and a relative (indefinite) pronoun; the "true" function cannot be determined historically, but the fact that the indefinite meaning is so frequently indicated by some sort of suffix or prefix suggests that it may well be secondary.[4] In Old English, for example, *hwā* means 'who', but *āhwā* means 'any one'. By itself, however, *hwā* may also be an indefinite: *sibbe ne wolde wið manna hwone* '[he] did not wish peace with any one of men'. The interrogative pronoun has a common form for both masculine and feminine; there is no declension in the plural.

12.4.1   *The Declension of* hwā *'who'*

	Masculine-Feminine	**Neuter**
N	hwā	hwæt
G	hwæs	hwæs
D	hwǣm, hwām	hwǣm, hwām
A	hwone, hwane, hwæne	hwæt
I	hwon, hwī, hwȳ	hwon, hwī, hwȳ

12.4.2   Modern English *who* derives from Middle English *hwō*, the normal development of *hwā;* *whom* derives from Old English *hwām* which became *hwōm, whōm* in Middle English. Old English *hwæs*, for which the regular development in Middle English would have been *hwas*, became, instead, *hwōs, whōse* on the analogy of *who* and *whom*.

12.4.3   *Some Indefinite Pronouns*   Old English had a multiplicity of indefinite pronouns; those which derive from *hwā* include *æġhwā* 'each one, every one', *æġhwæþer* 'each of two, both', *æthwā* 'each', *āhwā* 'any one', *āhwæþer* 'one of two' *ġehwā* 'each one, every one', and *hwæthwugu* 'somewhat, something'. Other indefinite pronouns are: *æġhwilċ* 'each one', *ælċ* 'each, every', *æniġ* 'any', *āwiht* 'anything', *ġehwilċ* 'each, every one', *hwilċ* 'anyone, some one', *nāht (nāwiht)* 'nothing', *nānþing* 'nothing', *sum* 'a certain (one)', *swilċ* 'such', and *þyslīċ* 'such'. Note also the idioms with the correlative, *swā . . . swā: swā hwā swā* 'whosoever, whoever', *swā hwæt swā* 'whatsoever, whatever', *swā hwilċ swā* 'whichever'.

12.5   *Syntax (III): The Genitive Case*   As in the other dialects of Indo-European, the case system inherited by Old English was used to establish various relationships among the discrete units of a completed utterance, or sentence; that a given case might express more than one relationship has already been demonstrated (see 10.5 and 11.6). A consideration of the Old English genitive, however, reveals the very wide range of techniques by which elements of a sentence could be related to one another through the medium of a single case. Historically, "the *genitive* with verbs indicates a less direct and complete influence of the verb concept on the noun concept than the accusative. With nouns it implies various types and degrees of connection between the two nouns."[5] The following paragraphs cite the major uses of the Old English genitive, a complex case that signifies a number of things besides 'possession'; the several categories are not necessarily mutually exclusive.

12.5.1   *The Complementary Genitive*   The genitive may simply modify a noun or adjective without suggesting possession as such: *næs hearpan wyn* '[there] was not joy of the harp'; *ār wæs on ofoste, eftsīðes ġeorn* 'the messenger was in haste, eager of return'. The basic function of the complementary genitive is somewhat allusive of description or definition.

12.5.2   *The Possessive Genitive*   In its best-understood use the genitive indicates possession or ownership: *Grendles hond* 'Grendel's hand'; *wine mīn Bēowulf* 'my friend Beowulf'; *Godes andsaca* 'God's adversary'; *tō his hūse* 'to his house'; *þīn abal and cræft* 'your strength and power'; *cwēn Hrōðgāres* 'Hrothgar's queen'.

12.5.3   *The Genitive of Origin*   The genitive may denote a person's lineage or family: *bearn Ecgþēowes* 'son of Ecgtheow'; *sunu Bēanstānes* 'son of Beanstan'; *Ecglāfes bearn* 'son of Ecglaf'; *Gaddes mǣġ* 'the kinsman of Gadd'; *ides Helminga* 'the woman of the Helmings'; *ides Scyldinga* 'the woman of the Scyldings'. The genitive of origin is often employed as a formulaic device in poetry.

12.5.4   *The Instrumental Genitive*   Occasionally the genitive expresses agency: *nīða ġenǣġed* 'attacked by force(s)'; *hē hine eft ongon wæteres weorpan* 'he began again to sprinkle him with water'; *ac mǣst ǣlċ swicode and ōþrum derede wordes and dǣde* 'but almost everyone was deceitful, and did injury to others by word and deed'; *wendon him sūðweard ōðres weġes* 'they turned (them) southward by another way'.

12.5.5   *The Partitive Genitive*   This common use of the genitive indicates the whole from which a part is taken; the partitive genitive is often accompanied by *fela* 'much, many', *mā* 'more', a superlative, *sum* 'a certain (one)', some other indefinite pronoun, or a number. Examples are: *fela gōdra monna* 'many of good men'; *hyra mā* 'more of them'; *bēama beorhtost* 'brightest of crosses (trees)'; *mynte sē mānscaða manna cynnes sumne besyrwan* 'the evil-doer intended to ensnare a certain one of mankind'; *ǣniġe þinga* 'by any (of) means'; *twēntiġ hrȳðera, and twēntiġ scēapa, and twēntiġ swȳna* 'twenty cattle, and twenty sheep, and twenty hogs'.

12.5.6   *The Genitive of Measure*   The genitive may delimit the extent of time or space: *ānes mōnðes fyrst* 'the time of one month'; *twelf wintra tīd* 'the time of twelve winters'; *syxtiġ mīla brād* 'sixty miles broad'. For further examples of the genitive as an indicator of time see 9.3.2.

12.5.7   *The Adverbial Genitive*   Like the dative-instrumental and the accusative the genitive may function as an adverb: *þæt hīe ǣr tō fela micles in þǣm wīnsele wældēað fornam* 'that a murderous death had previously carried them off, far (*micles*) too many in the wine-hall'; *hwǣr mīn lēodfruma londes wǣre* 'where in the country my lord might be'. For additional examples of the genitive used adverbially see 9.3.2.

12.5.8   *The Prepositional Genitive*   Although none does so exclusively, a few prepositions govern the genitive case; among them are *tō, toweard, þurh,* and *wið* meaning 'towards': *and ēode wið þæs Hǣlendes* 'and [he] went towards the Saviour'.

12.5.9   *The Genitive with Verbs*   Certain verbs require the genitive instead of the dative or accusative; they include a number of verbs denoting an emotional state and verbs of using or partaking. Examples are: *āmyrran* 'to hinder (from)'; *bedǣlan* 'to deprive (of)'; *beniman* 'to deprive (of)'; *bīdan* 'to wait (for)'; *blissian* 'to rejoice (at)'; *brūcan* 'to enjoy'; *cunnian* 'to try, have experience (of)'; *ēhtan* 'to pursue'; *fæġnian* 'to rejoice'; *ġefēon* 'to rejoice'; *ġyrnan* 'to desire', *ġelȳfan* 'to believe, trust'; *nēosian* 'to seek'; *nēotan* 'to make (of)'; *ofhrēowan* 'to feel pity (for)'; *onfōn* 'to receive, accept'; *reċċan* 'to care for'; *þurfan* 'to be in need (of)'; *wealdan* 'to rule (over), have control (of)'; *wēnan* 'to hope'; *wilnian* 'to desire'; *wundrian* 'to wonder (at)'; *ġewyrċan* 'to strive (for)'. If a verb has two objects, one of them may be in the genitive: *God ēaþe mæġ þone dolsceaðan dǣda ġetwǣfan!* 'God may easily deprive the wild ravager of his deeds'.

12.6   *Wulfstan*   One important witness to the discouraging events of 1009 (see 11.8) was a highly placed English cleric, Wulfstan, the archbishop of York (1002–1023). Very little is known about his life, but the details of his professional career reveal that he exercised an influence upon his contemporaries in both spiritual and temporal affairs. Wulfstan was appointed bishop of London in 996 and held that position until 1002 when he became not only bishop of Worcester but also archbishop of York. In 1016 he relinquished the see of Worcester to Abbot Leofsige of Thorney, but it is probable that Leofsige was only Wulfstan's suffragan. Wulfstan died at York on May 23, 1023, and was buried at Ely (north of Cambridge); his death was duly recorded in the chronicle kept at Peterborough. Because he was never a member of the monastery at Ely, the place of burial so far removed from York is difficult to account for. It may, however, suggest some connection with the east of England during his early years.[6]

From his writings, Wulfstan would seem to have been a Benedictine. While bishop of London he had already attracted attention as a writer, or preacher, in the vernacular, probably through his eschatological homilies, which were prompted by the approach of the millenium and the gravity of the Danish incursions;[7] during his tenure in London the surrounding areas suffered so severely from Danish harassment that by the end of 1001 the forces of Hampshire, Devon, and Somerset were completely defeated. London itself continued to manage a successful resistance, but, like other citizens, Wulfstan must have recognized the Scandinavian threat to English independence for what it was. When he assumed his duties in the north, it was only to be confronted anew with the consequences of Danish ferocity. The northern Church had not escaped the disruptive force of Danish raids and, as archbishop of York, Wulfstan was obliged to institute some stabilizing reforms; it is also likely that he encouraged the collection of manuscripts for the purpose of restoring the library at York.[8]

No later than 1008 Wulfstan became involved in the affairs of secular government as well. In that year he drafted the first of several law codes for Æthelred, king of Wessex. Wulfstan was a strong supporter of the English monarchy although Æthelred himself was far less than a paragon of its embodiment. Æthelred, whose name means 'noble counsel', was, in fact, nicknamed *unræd,* or 'no-counsel' by his contemporaries. (In the course of time *unræd* became 'unready' by the process of folk etymology; the second epithet is equally appropriate.) In 1013 Æthelred was unable to check the advance of Svein ("Forkbeard"), king of Denmark, who had determined to secure the English throne for himself, and when at last even London submitted to the foreigner, Æthelred was forced to flee across the Channel to Normandy whither his Norman wife, Emma, had preceded him. Expulsion of the incompetent king was nevertheless regarded by Wulfstan the loyalist as a "very great treachery" (*mæst hlāfordswice*). Although Æthelred was brought back to England early in 1014, he was not able to lead his people to a victory over the Danes. Upon Æthelred's death two years later, his son, Edmund ("Ironside"), was obliged to cede all of England, except Wessex, to Knut, the younger son of Svein (who had died in 1015). When Edmund himself died on November 30, 1016, the West Saxons also accepted Knut as their king. Danish hegemony was to last from 1017 until 1042.

Because Knut intended to rule as a king chosen by the people, he convened a national assembly at Oxford in 1018, the purpose of which was an agreement for peaceful relations between the Danes and the English, an agreement duly produced and approved by representatives of both peoples. The text of the entente survives in a manuscript of Corpus Christi College, Cambridge, and "the style, sources and method of work"[9] show the author to have been archbishop Wulfstan. Having served as an adviser to Æthelred, Wulfstan was not loath to function in the same capacity under Knut, for whom he also drafted a code of laws. The confidence which the Danish ruler presumably placed in Wulfstan may well have been partly inspired by the *Institutes of Polity,* the latter's "greatest accomplishment in the fields of law and politics."[10]; although it is not possible to give an exact date of composition to the *Institutes,* the work was probably written during the reign of Æthelred. There are two extant versions, one being an expansion of the other.

The treatise "defines the duties of all classes of men, though it does not include the specific lay obligations of thegns, *ceorlas,* and slaves except as they impinge upon their religious duties. Beginning with the responsibilities of the king, Wulfstan moves to the doctrine (taken from Ælfric's *Letter to Ligeweard*) of the three supports of the throne: preachers, workers, and warriors—then to the duties of those in authority, starting with the highest ecclesiasts, and moving to secular government in the persons of such as earls, reeves, judges, and lawyers. By defining the limits of power, Wulfstan tries to clarify the interrelationship of the Church and the secular state."[11]

Among Wulfstan's several other legal writings is yet another code, the *Laws of Edward and Guthrum,* a set of regulations concerning the observance of ecclesiastical laws, especially in the Danelaw for which it seems to have been primarily intended.[12] Whatever the greatness of his contributions to the administration of Church and state, Wulfstan also claims recognition as a literary stylist of considerable stature, and his skillful manipulation of English is nowhere seen to better advantage than in his homilies, the outstanding example of which is his impassioned "Address to the English" of 1014.

12.7   *Wulfstan's* Address to the English, *or the* Sermo Lupi ad Anglos *(I)*   Like his esteemed contemporary, Ælfric (c. 955–c. 1025). Abbot of Eynsham, with whom he corresponded and from whom he occasionally did some literary borrowing, Wulfstan was adept at phrasing homilies in an idiom that combined the elements of both prose and poetry. Editors and critics have often pointed out Wulfstan's use of repetition, lists, and intensifiers; his tendency to pair words, sometimes by means of rhyme and alliteration; his fondness for underscoring a completed sequence of ideas with a rhetorical question; his care in fashioning balanced sentences; and his characteristic sense of rhythm, manifested in a continuing series of two-stress phrases.[13] Wulfstan avoids poetical imagery as such, but instead draws to a large extent upon the structural resources of the language at his disposal. A fine exemplification of his style, the "Address to the English," was composed in 1014 after the expulsion of Æthelred late in the previous year; that it was a period of great troubles for the English is made abundantly clear by the Latin rubric which (with some variation of the second clause) heads the text in the surviving manuscripts: *Sermo Lupi ad Anglos quando Dani maxime persecuti sunt eos, quod fuit anno millesimo XIIII ab incarnatione Domini Nostri Iesu Cristi.* Wulfstan's appropriation of the Latin word *lupus* 'wolf' as a *nom de plume* dates from his years as bishop of London. A document of high exhortation which was directed to the whole nation, the sermon also reveals much through implication about the conditions of daily life in Anglo-Saxon England at the time of intensified persecutions by the Danes. The dialect is Late West Saxon.

Lēofan men, ġecnāwað þæt sōð is: ðēos worold is on ofste, and
hit nēalǣċð þām ende, and þȳ hit is on worolde ā, swā leng, swā
wyrse, and swā hit sceal nȳde for folces synnan ǣr Antecrīstes tōcyme
yfelian swȳþe, and hūru hit wyrð þænne eġeslīċ and grimlīċ wīde on
5   worolde. Understandað ēac ġeorne þæt dēofol þās þēode nū fela
ġēara dwelode tō swȳþe, and þæt lȳtle ġetrēowþa wǣran mid
mannum, þēah hȳ wel spǣcan, and unrihta tō fela rīcsode on lande;
and næs ā fela manna þe smēade ymbe þā bōte swā ġeorne swā man
scolde, ac dæġhwāmlīċe man īhte yfel æfter ōðrum and unriht rǣrde
10   and unlaga maneġe ealles tō wīde ġynd ealle þās þēode. And wē
ēac for þām habbað fela byrsta and bysmara ġebiden, and, ġif wē
ǣniġe bōte ġebīdan scylan, þonne mōte wē þæs tō Gode ernian bet
þonne wē ǣr þysan dydan. For þām mid miclan earnungan wē
ġeearnedan þā yrmða þe ūs on sittað, and mid swȳþe miċelan
15   earnungan wē þā bōte mōtan æt Gode ġerǣċan, ġif hit sceal
heonanforð gōdiende weorðan. Lā hwæt, wē witan ful ġeorne þæt tō
miclan bryċe sceal miċel bōt nȳde, and tō miclan bryne wǣter
unlȳtel, ġif man þæt fȳr sceal tō āhte ācwenċan; and miċel is
nȳdþearf manna ġehwilcum þæt hē Godes lage ġȳme heonanforð
20   ġeorne and Godes ġerihta mid rihte ġelǣste. On hǣþenum þēodum
ne dear man forhealdan lȳtel ne miċel þæs þe ġelagod is tō
ġedwolgoda weorðunge; and wē forhealdað ǣġhwǣr Godes ġerihta
ealles tō ġelōme. And ne dear man ġewanian on hǣþenum þēodum
inne ne ūte ǣniġ þǣra þinga þe ġedwolgodan brōht bið and tō
25   lācum betǣht bið; and wē habbað Godes hūs inne and ūte clǣne
berȳpte. And Godes þēowas syndan mǣþe and munde ġewelhwǣr
bedǣlde; and ġedwolgoda þēnan ne dear man misbēodan on
ǣniġe wīsan mid hǣþenum lēodum, swā swā man Godes þēowum
nū dēð tō wīde, þǣr crīstene scoldan Godes lage healdan and Godes
30   þēowas griðian.
   Ac sōð is þæt iċ secge, þearf is þǣre bōte, for þām Godes
ġerihta wanedan tō lange innan þysse þēode on ǣġhwylcan ænde
and folclaga wyrsedan ealles tō swȳþe, and hāliġnessa syndan tō
griðlēase wīde, and Godes hūs syndan tō clǣne berȳpte ealdra
35   ġerihta and innan bestrȳpte ǣlcra ġerisena; and wydewan syndan
fornȳdde on unriht tō ċeorle, and tō mæneġe foryrmde and
ġehȳnede swȳþe; and earme men syndan sāre beswicene and
hrēowlīċe besyrwde and ūt of þysan earde wīde ġesealde swȳþe
unforworhte fremdum tō ġewealde; and cradolċild ġeþēowede þurh
40   wælhrēowe unlaga for lȳtelre þȳfþe wīde ġynd þās þēode; and
frēoriht fornumene and þrǣlriht ġenyrwde and ælmæsriht
ġewanode; and hrædest is tō cweþenne, Godes laga lāðe and lāra
forsawene; and þæs wē habbað ealle þurh Godes yrre bysmor

ġelōme, ġecnāwe sē þe cunne; and sē byrst wyrð ġemǣne, þēh man
45   swā ne wēne, eallre þysse þēode, būtan God beorge.

For þām hit is on ūs eallum swutol and ġesēne þæt wē ǣr
þysan oftor brǣcan þonne wē bēttan, and þȳ is þysse þēode fela
onsǣġe. Ne dohte hit nū lange inne ne ūte, ac wæs here and hunger,
bryne and blōdġyte on ġewelhwylcan ende oft and ġelōme; and ūs
50   stalu and cwalu, strīċ and steorfa, orfcwealm and uncoþu, hōl and
hete and rȳpera rēaflāc derede swȳþe þearle, and unġylda swȳðe
ġedrehtan, and ūs unwedera foroft wēoldan unwæstma; for þām on
þysan earde wæs, swā hit þinċan mæġ, nū fela ġēara unrihta fela
and tealte ġetrȳwða ǣġhwǣr mid mannum. Ne bearh nū foroft
55   ġesib ġesibban þē mā þe fremdan, ne fæder his bearne, ne hwīlum
bearn his āgenum fæder, ne brōþor ōþrum; ne ūre ǣniġ his līf
fadode swā swā hē sceolde, ne ġehādode regollīċe, ne lǣwede lahlīċe.
Ac worhtan lust ūs tō lage ealles tō ġelōme, and nāþor ne hēoldan
ne lāre ne lage Godes ne manna swā swā wē scoldan. Ne ǣniġ wið
60   ōþerne ġetrȳwlīċe þōhte swā rihte swā hē scolde, ac mǣst ǣlċ
swicode and ōþrum derede wordes and dǣde; and hūru unrihtlīċe
mǣst ǣlċ ōþerne æftan hēaweþ mid sceandlīcan onscytan, dō māre,
ġif hē mæġe. For þām hēr syn on lande unġetrȳwþa micle for Gode
and for worolde, and ēac hēr syn on earde on mistlīċe wīsan
65   hlāfordswican maneġe. And ealra mǣst hlāfordswice sē bið on
worolde þæt man his hlāfordes sāule beswice; and ful miċel
hlāfordswice ēac bið on worolde þæt man his hlāford of līfe forrǣde,
oððon of lande lifiendne drīfe; an ǣġþer is ġeworden on þysan
earde: Ēadweard man forrǣdde ond syððan ācwealde and æfter
70   þām forbærnde and Æþelred man drǣfde ūt of his earde. And
godsibbas and godbearn tō fela man forspilde wīde ġynd þās þēode;
and ealles tō mæneġe hāliġe stōwa wīde forwurdan þurh þæt þe
man sume men ǣr þām ġelōgode, swā man nā ne scolde, ġif man
on Godes griðe mæþe witan wolde; and crīstenes folces tō fela man
75   ġesealde ūt of þysan earde nū ealle hwīle; and eal þæt is Gode lāð,
ġelȳfe sē þe wille. And scandlīċ is tō specenne þæt ġeworden is tō
wīde, and eġeslīċ is tō witanne þæt oft dōð tō maneġe, þe drēogað þā
yrmþe, þæt scēotað tōgædere and āne cwenan ġemǣnum ċēape
bicgað ġemǣne, and wið þā āne f ȳlþe ādrēogað, ān æfter ānum.
80   and ælċ æfter ōðrum, hundum ġelīccast, þe for f ȳlþe ne scrīfað,
and syððan wið weorðe syllað of lande fēondum tō ġewealde Godes
ġesceafte and his āgenne ċēap, þe hē dēore ġebohte. Ēac wē witan
ġeorne hwǣr sēo yrmð ġewearð þæt fæder ġesealde bearn wið
weorþe, and bearn his mōdor, and brōþor sealde ōþerne fremdum
85   tō ġewealde; and eal þæt syndan micle and eġeslīċe dǣda, understande sē þe wille. And ġȳt hit is māre and ēac mæniġfealdre þæt

dereð þysse þēode: mæniġe synd forsworene and swȳþe forlogene, and wed synd tōbrocene oft and ġelōme; and þæt is ġesȳne on þysse þēode þæt ūs Godes yrre heteliċe on sit, ġecnāwe sē þe cunne.

12.8   *Notes*

2–3.   *swā lenġ, swā wyrse* 'as longer, so worse'; as the end of the world approaches, the worse things get.

5.   *dēofol,* Wulfstan characteristically uses the word without an article.

7.   *tō fela rīcsode,* Wulfstan uses *fela* with a singular verb.

15–16.   *ġif . . . gōdiende weorðan,* if things are going to start improving.

18.   *tō āhte,* at all.

36.   *fornȳdde . . . tō ċeorle* 'forced to [take] a husband'.

42.   *hrædest is tō cwepenne,* to sum up briefly.

48.   *inne ne ūte,* at home or abroad.

51.   *unġylda,* the Danegeld, money paid to the Danes; also taxation to support the English levies.

54–55.   *ne bearh nū foroft ġesib gesibban . . . ne brōþor ōþrum,* an allusion to Matthew 10:21, though taken here by Wulfstan from a homily which he had written earlier.[14]

58.   *ac [wē] worhtan lust ūs tō lage.*

63–64.   *for Gode and for worolde,* for Church and state.

69.   *Eadweard,* Edward the Martyr, who at the age of twelve succeeded his father, Edgar, to the throne of England in 975; he was assassinated at Corfe on March 18, 978, and the crown then passed to his older half-brother, Æthelred. Although Æthelred was too young to have been an accomplice, Sir Frank Stenton suggests that the murder was planned and carried out by the men of Æthelred's household who wished to see their master king.[15] There is no outside evidence to support Wulfstan's possibly demagogic assertion that Edgar's body was burned.

77–78.   *þe drēogað þā yrmþe* 'who commit the crime'.

78.   *sċēotað tōgædere* 'get together'.

81.   *wið weorðe syllað* 'sell'.

References

1.   A. Campbell, *Old English Grammar* (Oxford, 1959), p. 287.

2.   Campbell, p. 284.

3.   E. E. Wardale, *An Introduction to Middle English* (London, 1937), p. 85.

4.   Eduard Prokosch, *A Comparative Germanic Grammar* (Philadelphia, 1939), p. 278.

5.   Prokosch, p. 230.

6.   Dorothy Whitelock, ed., *Sermo Lupi ad Anglos,* 3rd ed. (New York, 1966), p. 7.

7.   Stanley B. Greenfield, *A Critical History of Old English Literature* (New York, 1965), p. 53.

8. Greenfield, p. 53.
9. Whitelock, *Sermo Lupi ad Anglos*, p. 25.
10. Greenfield, p. 53.
11. Greenfield, pp. 53–54.
12. Whitelock, *Sermo Lupi ad Anglos*, p. 24.
13. Greenfield, pp. 56–57; Whitelock, *Sermo Lupi ad Anglos*, pp. 18–19.
14. Henry Sweet, *Anglo-Saxon Reader in Prose and Verse*, 15th ed., revised by Dorothy Whitelock (Oxford, 1967), p. 256.
15. Sir Frank Stenton, *Anglo-Saxon England*, 2nd ed. (Oxford, 1947), p. 368.

Chapter 13

13.1 *Minor Nominal Declensions* Although the inflectional endings of nouns were not to be completely eliminated until the Middle English period, the actual number of different nominal declensions inherited from Proto-Germanic underwent a preliminary reduction of sorts in Old English. Evidence of that reduction has already been presented, as, for example, in the case of feminine *i*-declension nouns with short roots, all of which were shifted by analogy to the *ō*-declension (see 12.3.3). Although it produced a simplification of the Proto-Germanic declensional system, the analogical force exerted by the *a*-declension and the *ō*-declension also introduced an ambivalency into the declensional status of many Old English nouns. The ambivalence in turn was often resolved when those nouns were regularly declined according to the pattern of a declension to which they had not originally belonged. That practice, however, resulted in a considerable depletion of certain declensions, in particular those consequently termed the minor nominal declensions of Old English.

13.1.1 *The Indo-European* s-*stem Declension in Old English* Neuter nouns with stems ending in -*s* were an important class in Indo-European, and were also fairly numerous in the prehistoric period of Germanic.[1] Sometimes called *es*- and *os*-stems, or (in terms of Germanic grammar) *iz*- and *az*-stems, the nouns of this declension correspond to Latin neuters like *genus,* in the genitive singular *generis* (from older **genes-os*) 'race'. Only a handful of these neuter nouns remains in Old English; the characteristic -*s* of their declension is present only in the plural where by Verner's Law (see 6.1) it has become -*r*. The paradigm of *lamb* 'lamb' is representative.

	Singular	Plural
N	lamb	lamb-ru
G	lamb-es	lamb-ra
D	lamb-e	lamb-rum
A	lamb	lamb-ru
I	lamb-e	lamb-rum

Declined like *lamb* are *ǣġ* 'egg', *ċealf* 'calf', and sometimes *ċild*. Original *s*-stem nouns transferred to the *a*-declension are *gāst, gǣst* (with umlaut) 'spirit', and *sigor* 'victory'; the neuter *a*-declension includes *dōgor* 'day', *ēar* 'ear of corn', *ġewealc* 'rolling', *hālor* 'salvation, health', and *salor* 'hall'.

13.1.2   *Three Declensions of Feminine Abstract Nouns*   Proto-Germanic developed three new declensions of feminine nouns, most of which were abstractions; in Old English they were largely absorbed by the *ō*-declension. One of the two groups based upon adjectives was formed with a suffix in *-iþō;* after causing umlaut the *i* was syncopated, and the ending became -*þu* in Old English. An example is *strenġþu* 'strength', from the adjective *strang* 'strong'.

	Singular	Plural
N	strenġþu, -o	strenġþa, -e, -u, -o
G	strenġþe, -u, -o	strenġþa
D	strenġþe, -u, -o	strenġþum
A	strenġþe, -u, -o	strenġþa, -e, -u, -o
I	strenġþe, -u, -o	strenġþum

Other nouns like *strenġþu* are *cȳþþu* 'native country', *fǣhþu* 'fend', *ġesǣlþu* 'prosperity', *hīehþu* 'height', *iermþu (yrmþu)* 'misery', *lenġþu* 'length', *mǣġþu* 'family,' *mǣrþu* 'fame, glory', and *trēowþ (trīewþ)* 'truth, fidelity'; the ending -*u* often does not appear in the nominative singular. Another class of feminine abstracts, also from adjectives, was formed with the suffix *-īn-;* in Old English these nouns were completely remodeled on the pattern of the *ō*-declension and no trace of the distinguishing suffix is preserved. Before being removed, however, the high front vowel of the suffix caused umlaut of the radical vowel; thus, from *brād* 'broad' is derived *brǣdu* 'breadth', originally an -*īn*-stem, for which the Proto-Old English nominative singular was *brādi*. Other *ō*-declension nouns from the same source are *bieldu (byldu)* 'boldness', *engu* 'narrowness', *fyllu* 'fullness', *hǣlu* 'health', *hyldu* 'favor', *ieldu (yldu)* 'age', *lenġu* 'length', *meniġu* 'multitude', *snytru* 'wisdom', *þīestru (þēostru, þȳstru)* 'darkness', and *wlencu* 'pride'; the ending -*u* is frequently replaced by -*o*. A third group of feminine abstracts was fashioned with the suffixes *-ingō, *-ungō, and *-angō;*

these nouns were chiefly derived from weak verbs of Class II. In Old English the suffix *-unga* (from *-ungō*) is predominant; the final *-a* was dropped in the nominative singular, and elsewhere often replaced with *-e* on the analogy of *ō*-declension nouns. The noun *leornung* 'learning' is an example; *cf.* the Class II weak verb *leornian* 'to learn'.

	Singular	**Plural**
N	leornung	leornunga, -e
G	leornunga, -e	leornunga
D	leornunga, -e	leornungum
A	leornunga, -e	leornunga, -e
I	leornunga, -e	leornungum

Other nouns with *-ung* are *ǣfnung* 'evening', *costung* 'temptation', *ġemiltsung* 'pity', *ġeþafung* 'consent', *lēasung* 'lying, falsehood', *rihtung* 'direction', *þeġnung* 'service, ministration', and *wēnung* 'hope, expectation'; the smaller number of formations with *-ing* includes *ærning* 'riding, racing', *grēting* 'greeting'; *ielding* 'delay', *rǣding* 'reading', and *wending* 'turning'. As noted above (see 8.3), the *-ing* termination was later used to mark the present participle.

13.1.3   *Root Consonant Stems*   A relatively large number of Indo-European nouns did not have a thematic vowel or a suffix of any kind interposed between the root and the case endings; the endings were attached directly to the final consonant of the root, e.g., *pōd-s* 'foot' (nominative), *pōd-m̥* (accusative). In Germanic the inherited nouns of this class were for the most part shifted to the *a-*, *i-*, and *u-* declensions,[2] and, although the consonant stems originally included all three genders, Old English preserves no neuters, only two masculines (*fōt* 'foot' and *tōþ* 'tooth'), and a few feminines. The Germanic reflexes of certain Indo-European endings for the genitive and dative-instrumental singular, and the nominative plural sometimes caused umlaut in those cases; umlaut in the accusative plural is by analogy with the nominative. Examples of the consonant stems distinguishable in Old English are *fōt* (masculine) and *gōs* 'goose' (feminine).

	Singular		**Plural**	
N	fōt	gōs	fēt	gēs
G	fōt-es	gēs	fōt-a	gōs-a
D	fēt	gēs	fōt-um	gōs-um
A	fōt	gōs	fēt	gēs
I	fēt	gēs	fōt-um	gōs-um

The genitive singular of *fōt* (and *tōþ*) is patterned after the *a*-declension, and therefore does not have umlaut. Declined like *fōt* and often regarded as a root consonant stem, the noun *mann* 'man' belongs etymologically to the *n*-stems (see 4.4); *cf.* the alternative nominative and accusative forms, *manna, mannan.* Other feminines like *gōs* are *āc* 'oak', *burg* 'city', *cū* 'cow', *gāt* 'goat', *lūs* 'louse', *mūs* 'mouse', and *niht* (*neaht*) 'night'.

13.1.4   *Stems in* -þ   Old English preserves four nouns belonging to the *t*-stems of Indo-European, a declension very similar to that of the root consonant stems; in Latin it is represented by nouns of the type *nepōt-* 'nephew'. The declension occurs in Old English with the customary Germanic shift of Indo-European [t] to [θ]; at an early date the dental consonant was lost in the nominative singular, but was later restored, except in the neuter *ealu* 'beer', by influence of the oblique cases. In addition to *ealu* the other *þ*-stem nouns in Old English are the masculines *hæleþ* 'hero', *mōnaþ* 'month', and the feminine *mæġ(e)þ* 'maiden'. The *þ*-stems are declined as follows.

Singular

N	hæle, hæleþ	mōnaþ	mæġ(e)þ	ealu
G	hæleþ-es	mōn(e)þ-es	mæġ(e)þ	ealoþ
D	hæleþ-e	mōn(e)þ-e	mæġ(e)þ	ealoþ
A	hæle, hæleþ	mōnaþ	mæġ(e)þ	ealu
I	hæleþ-e	mōn(e)þ-e	mæġ(e)þ	ealoþ

Plural

N	hæleþ	mōnaþ	mæġ(e)þ	
G	hæleþ-a	mōn(e)þ-a	mæġ(e)þ-a	ealeþ-a
D	hæleþ-um	mōn(e)þ-um	mæġ(e)þ-um	
A	hæleþ	mōnaþ	mæġ(e)þ	
I	hæleþ-um	mōn(e)þ-um	mæġ(e)þ-um	

The only plural formation recorded for *ealu* is *ealeþa.*

13.2   *The Runic Alphabet*   Among the many different writing systems adopted by·speakers of Indo-European languages is the runic alphabet, an exclusive property of the Germanic community. Although runic writing was employed more extensively in Scandinavia than elsewhere, it was also used in England by the Anglo-Saxons who recorded some very early examples of their speech with runic characters. The origin of the runic alphabet has been disputed, and various scholars have favored the Greek alphabet or the Roman alphabet as a prototype; in view of certain graphic parallels, however, a more probable source than either would appear to be some North Italic alphabet related to, but not derived from, the Roman characters. Just as the speech of Rome was only one subcategory of the Italic branch of Indo-European, the Roman alphabet was only one of several local alphabets in use on the Italian peninsula during the period of Roman military and political ascendency. Almost all Italic dialects attested, including Latin, were written in alphabets that were a modified form of a script brought to Italy by the (non-Indo-European) Etruscans in their assumed migration from the east where they somehow acquired a version of the western Greek alphabets; thus, there was a limited similarity between the writing system of Rome and the writing systems of other Italic settlements, some of which were located in the alpine regions of northern Italy.

Resemblances among the Italic alphabets notwithstanding, an examination of runic symbols clearly shows them to possess a far closer affinity to the North Italic alphabets as a group than to the graphic system developed in Latium. The northwestern Alps are, furthermore, known to have been penetrated by some Germanic tribes who could easily have become acquainted there with North Italic writing, perhaps as early as the fourth century BC.[3] The hypothesis that runic letters were based upon a North Italic alphabet, or alphabets, is given very strong support by the most ancient example of Germanic yet recovered, a votive inscription on the brim of a bronze helmet from Negau in southeastern Austria. Written in North Italic characters that are practically identical to their Etruscan counterparts, the inscription reads (in transliteration): *harigastiteiwai;* although interpretations vary, a probable translation is 'To Tīw (Proto-Germanic **Tīwaz*), guest of the army'. The name of a Germanic god of war, Tīw survives in Old and Modern English *tīwesdæġ* 'Tuesday'; *cf.* the Latin semantic parallel *dies Martis* 'day of Mars', and Italian *martedi,* French *mardi* 'Tuesday'. The other two nominal roots of the inscription are also unmistakably Germanic; *har-* means 'army' (*cf.* Gothic *harjis,* Old Icelandic *herr,* Old English *here*), and *gast-* 'guest' (*cf.* Gothic *gasts,* Old Icelandic *gestr,* Old English *ġiest*).

The Negau helmet was found (1812) stacked with twenty-five others, suggesting that the helmets might have been part of a trader's depot; its provenance is unknown, but the inscription is not likely to have originated outside the North Italic region.[4] As the helmet itself is dated from the third to second century BC, an initial Italo-Germanic contact cannot have taken place any later, but, given the graphic nature of the Negau inscription, it would seem a fair assumption that a specifically Germanic writing system was at that time yet to be devised; nevertheless, the three words scratched in bronze point directly to the subsequent configuration of that system. The earliest runic inscriptions now extant were recovered in Scandinavia and date from the third century AD, but, on the authority of the Roman historian, Tacitus, the use of runes was already widely known by 100 AD. In Chapter X of the *Germania,* his survey of Germanic tribes and customs written in 98 AD, Tacitus refers to the practice of divination by means of runes: "For auspices and the casting of lots they have the highest possible regard. Their procedure in casting lots is uniform. They break off a branch of a fruit-tree and slice it into strips; they distinguish these by certain runes and throw them, as random chance will have it, on to a white cloth. Then the priest of the State if the consultation is a public one, the father of the family if it is private, after a prayer to the gods and an intent gaze heavenward, picks up three, one at a time, and reads their meaning from the runes scored on them. If the lots forbid an enterprise there can be no further consultation that day; if they allow it, further confirmation by auspices is required."[5] Even if the ritual described by Tacitus involved nothing more sophisticated than "reading" the runes in the manner of tea leaves, the Scandinavian inscriptions prove that a tradition of genuine literacy, however tenuous, was never lost altogether.

Since time must be allowed for a knowledge of writing to have spread within the Germanic community by 100 AD, the creation of a runic alphabet probably occurred in the century between 250 BC and 150 BC. There is no reason to doubt that the runes were indeed created by an enterprising individual who was inspired to fashion a series of characters which would symbolize the sounds of his Germanic speech; because he initiated a system that embodied the acrophonic principle of a separate letter for each vowel and consonant, his script was also truly alphabetic. The runic alphabet is often called the *fuþark* from the fact that the first six letters of its customary sequence represent the six sounds [f], [u], [θ], [a], [r], and [k]. Initially, there was a common Germanic *fuþark* which consisted of twenty-four letters and which was uniformly employed throughout the Germanic world, dialectal boundaries being no impediment to its diffusion; early in the fifth century the common alphabet as such was incised on a stone from Kylver on the island of Gotland, Sweden, and incomplete sequences also occur on various objects of later date from two places in Sweden proper, from Charnay in Burgundy, France, and from Breza near Sarajevo in Yugoslavia.

In addition to standing for a given speech sound, each runic letter bore an identifying name, a feature that only enhanced its value for ritualistic purposes. The eighteenth rune (ᛒ), for example, was 'birth', from Proto-Germanic *berkana- literally 'birch twig', and "is undoubtedly to be connected with fertility cults, symbolizing the awakening of nature in spring and the birth of new life generally. In many parts of Europe the birch has long played a role in popular beliefs and customs going back beyond Christianity. To promote fruitfulness among men and beasts birch saplings were placed in houses and stables, and young men and women as well as cattle were struck with birch twigs;"[6] other rune-names were 'year' (ᛄ), 'giant' (ᚦ), the god 'Ing' (ᛜ), 'Tīw' (ᛏ), 'hail' (ᚺ), 'yew'

(S), 'water' ($\mathit{\uparrow}$), 'cattle' (F), 'day' (◪), 'joy' (P), and 'gift' (✗). The word *rune* itself means 'mystery, secret' (*cf.* Gothic *rūna*, the Old Icelandic plural *rūnar*, and Old English *rūn*, all with the primary denotation), an indication of the non-utilitarian purposes which the letters so frequently served. From the beginning runic characters were allied with the recondite pursuits of magic and religion, wherein the primary motive for their creation and design almost certainly resides. North of Rome the Italic alphabets were not a medium for historical records or literature, but were instead largely restricted to dedications, memorial notices, supplications, ceremonial procedure, and to the names of individuals who wished to identify objects of their manufacture or ownership.

Containing some pre-runic symbols that doubtless had a connection with magic, the common *fuþark* became a device of even greater cultic significance in the hands of those who knew the secret of its manipulation. In addition to their reputed efficacy for sortilege, runes were separately credited with numerous specialized powers which could influence not only fertility, as previously mentioned, but also birth, health, speech, victory, thought, love, and the weather; "the scratching of runes on to staffs or objects of various kinds for immediate practical purposes, such as curing a disease, frequently no doubt went hand in hand with the re-citing of charms or spells in order to enhance their potency."[7] Runic inscriptions on stones placed inside a grave were viewed as a defense against evil spirits and a means of confining the corpse to its appointed location. In Norse mythology, the runes were held to have been a gift to men from Óðinn, the chief member of the Nordic pantheon and the god of wisdom, poetry, war, and death; thus, their magical properties were readily accounted for.

The belief in runes as a source of supernatural aid was so strong that even the sanctions of the Christian church were slow to take effect, and runic lore and practice survived the Conversion for varying periods of time both in England and the Scandinavian countries; in Iceland, where Christianity was not declared the national religion until 1000, people were burned to death as late as the seventeenth century for the mere possession of runes.[8] Eventually, however, the Roman alphabet, so intimately con-nected with the Church, entirely superseded the angular Germanic letters, which had been intentionally designed for being cut into or scratched upon materials like metal, bone, wood, and stone; when ink and parch-ment, along with cursive writing, became a staple of northern European civilization, the Roman alphabet offered the advantages of a far more flexible script. A cursive form never developed, and when the ritualistic use of runes began to decline, their existence as a practical writing system was not long perpetuated either.

In a purely secular manner, the names of proud artisans and owners, the names of weapons, memorial inscriptions, messages, and even poetry had all been expressed with runes, which now and then also contributed something to the decoration of a particular ring, sword, coin, medallion, fibula, drinking horn, or similar object. Literature and the law, however, continued to be sustained by oral tradition. In the fourteenth century a runic manuscript containing the law code of Skåne was produced in Denmark, but the so-called *Codex Runicus* is largely a monument to the "archaic dignity and antiquarian interest" which "would attach to runic writing in a medieval scriptorium,"[9] and no lasting manuscript tradition was established by it. Carried by Vikings to such distant places as Greenland and Greece (Piraeus), the angular runic letters are now one of the few tangible remains of early Germanic society.

13.3   *Linguistic Change*   An understanding of those features which characterize the structure of any language at a given point in time often rests solely upon a knowledge of what the language was like in a considerably earlier stage of its development. The reason for so self-evident a statement has, of course, to do with the slow rate at which linguistic change proceeds; even the life span of a human being is never long enough to afford a person any substantial information about the future of his vernacular. Nevertheless, changes are continually accumlating, and subtle modifications in pronunciation, meaning, word forms, and syntactical patterns are always being instituted here and there. Tracing the derivation of Old English inflectional categories, for example the personal pronoun, from Proto-Germanic and Indo-European, involved mainly the alteration of morphological entities (words), and although Verner's Law, *i*-umlaut, and gemination have all concerned phonological alternation further attention will be given to that subject in this and succeeding chapters. The changes manifested by vowels and consonants as such, are frequently important for ascertaining the pronunciation of Old English words and do much to clarify unexpected variations within declensions and conjugations. The regularity of phonetic change should be kept in mind; if a sound shifts its quality or quantity under certain conditions, it will always do so whenever those conditions are present unless a determinable, inhibiting factor causes a suspension of the shift. At the same time, however, a given sound may undergo (consistent) changes of a widely varying kind depending upon its position (initial, medial, final) in a word and whether it does or does not bear the primary stress accent; also, a sound may shift its value in "isolation" or in combination with others which comprise its phonetic context. Because so many possibilities thus exist for the development of speech sounds, especially vowels, only the most significant modifications can be considered in the discussions which follow.

13.4   *Sound Changes (I): Proto-Germanic and West Germanic*
For practical purposes, the history of Old English speech sounds begins
not with Indo-European but with the common source for all Germanic
dialects: Proto-Germanic. The phonological system of Proto-Germanic
was the immediate basis for a West Germanic system from which the
vowels and consonants of Old English were in turn derived; the con-
tinuum of change ends with those innovations of a specifically West-
Saxon nature.

13.4.1   *Vowels and Diphthongs*   Proto-Germanic had the
following vocalic system:

Short vowels: i, e, a, o, u

Long vowels: ī, ē, ǣ, ā, ō, ū

With the exception of *ǣ*, which became *ā*, all the vowels remained unchanged in West Germanic. At an early stage of Proto-Germanic the
diphthongs were *ai, au,* and *eu;* in the form of West Germanic from which
Old English is derived, the Proto-Germanic diphthong *eu* was preserved
without change. In a later period of Proto-Germanic itself, *eu* was shifted
to *iu* when followed by *ī, i,* or *j;* the *iu* was also retained in West Germanic.
The other two diphthongs did not change; and hence, a West Germanic
diphthongal series consisting of *ai, au, eu,* and *iu* may be posited for Old
English.

13.4.2   *Consonants*   Proto-Germanic had the following consonantal system:

		Labial	Dental	Alveolar	Palatal	Velar
I.	Stops					
	a) voiceless	p	t			k
	b) voiced	b	d			g
II.	Fricatives					
	a) voiceless	f	þ	s		χ
	b) voiced	ƀ	ð	z		ǥ
III.	Resonants					
	a) nasals	m	n			ŋ
	b) liquids		l	r		
	c) semi-vowels	w			j	

The consonants remained the same in West Germanic, except for *z* and *ð*
which became *r* and *d* respectively; *cf.* Proto-Germanic *wǣzún, Old Eng-

lish *wǣron* 'were', and Proto-Germanic **faðér*, Old English *fǣder* 'father'. The *z* and *ð* were sounds that resulted from the operation of Verner's Law (see 6.1). In word-initial position before a vowel, the voiceless velar fricative [χ] was "weakened" to simple aspiration [h] in all Germanic dialects, a sound identical to that represented by *h* in Old and Modern English *horn*.

13.5   *Syntax IV: Word Order (Noun and Verb Modifiers)* The fact that there is a fair degree of similarity between the word order of Old English and Modern English has been amply borne out by the reading selections; many word patterns are common to the language in both the earliest and most recent stages of its development. Adjectival modifiers, for example, have traditionally stood close to the noun which they qualify and have, in general, preceded that noun. Because of the grammatical meaning carried by inflectional endings, however, a somewhat greater variety of sentence structure is permitted in Old English than in Modern English where the meaning of a word may often depend solely upon its position in an utterance. The variety was nevertheless limited, for all languages, even the most highly inflected, are governed by rules on all levels; simple, declarative statements, for example, continued to reflect the actor-action syntax of Indo-European with the characteristic word order: subject-verb-object (or complement). The remarks on word order contained in this and succeeding chapters will necessarily be confined to those arrangements of greatest frequency.

13.5.1   *Adjectives* In prose the attributive adjective customarily stands before the noun, but in poetry the positions are often reversed: *hæle hildedēor* '(a) warrior brave-in-battle', *mundgripe māran* '(a) handgrip greater'. When two adjectives modify a noun, they may be linked by *and* to form a unit that follows the noun: *þǣr æt hȳðe stōd hringedstefna īsiġ ond ūtfūs* 'there at the harbor stood the ring-prowed ship, icy and ready'; but two, or more, adjectives may also precede a noun: *þæt hīe gesāwon swylċe twēġen micle mearcstapan* 'that they saw two such great moorstalkers', *oþ ðæt semninga tō sele cōmon frome fyrdhwate fēowertȳne Ġeata gongan* 'until presently to the hall came walking, brave (and) war-like, fourteen of the Gauts'. Less frequently, two adjectives may occur separately, one before the noun and one after: *ne seah iċ elþēodiġe þus maniġe men modiġlícran* 'I never saw foreigners, so many men braver', *and þǣr sint swīðe micle meras fersce ġeond þā mōras* 'and there, there are very large fresh-water lakes throughout the mountains'. The adjectives *eall* and *ġenōh* are often placed after the noun: *Denum eallum* 'to all the Danes', *duguð eal ārās* 'the retainers all arose', *ac þǣr bið medo ġenōh* 'but there is enough mead'.

13.5.2   *The Definite Article, Demonstrative Pronoun, and Possessive Pronoun*   As in Modern English, the forms of *sē*, *þēs*, and *mīn* normally precede a noun and any adjective which may also modify the noun, but a metathesis of positions also occurs: *Wulfmǣr sē ġeonga* 'Wulfmær the younger', *on sele þām hēan* 'in the lofty hall', *þe wile ġeealgian ēþel þysne* 'who will defend this homeland', *wine mīn Unferð* 'my friend Unferth', *dryhten sīnne* 'his lord', *Nerġend ūser* 'our Saviour'. In the case of phrases like *Wulfmǣr sē ġeongra*, the adjective may also be construed as a noun in apposition ('Wulfmær, the younger one') and the word order viewed as unexceptional since epithets are placed after the names which they modify, e.g., *Ælfrēd cyning; Mathēus, mīn sē lēofa, beheald on mē* 'Matthew, my beloved, look upon me'. If the adjective *eal* is used with *sē* or *þēs*, then it customarily comes first: *fram eallum þām gōdum* 'from all those good things', *eall ðios unstille ġesceaft* 'all this moving creation'; if an adjective ending in -*weard* occurs with *sē* or *þēs*, it may come first: *on sūðeweardum þǣm lande* 'in the southward (part of the) land', but *on ðisse andweardan bēċ* 'in this present book'.

13.5.3   *Genitival Constructions*   Both the complementary genitive (see 12.5.1) and the possessive genitive (see 12.5.2) are essentially nominal modifiers, and they are most frequently placed directly before the noun in question: *dēaðes nyd* 'the distress of death', *his sylfes hām* 'his own dwelling'.

13.5.4   *Adverbs*   Although adverbs enjoy a somewhat freer distribution than adjectives, they generally precede the item to which they relate: *hwider hyra ġehwylċ faran scolde tō lǣranne* 'whither each of them should go to teach', *wel þū hit onġitst* 'well you perceive it', *swā dōð ðā sēlestan men* 'thus do the best men', *oft ēac becymð sē anwald þisse worulde tō swiðe goodum monnum* 'often, too, the power of this world (i.e., temporal authority) comes to very good men'. On many occasions, however, the adverb will follow the item qualified; that is especially true of compound adverbs and adverbial phrases: *saga ūs þæt hrædlīċe* 'tell us that quickly', *and hē āstāg on heofonas* 'and he ascended to heaven'.

13.6   *King Knut and the Danish Domination of England*   Archbishop Wulfstan's concern about the Danish attacks and conditions in his country was fully justified. From 1017 to 1042 the Danes, who had previously controlled a large portion of England (the Danelaw) granted to them by King Alfred until the land was gradually reconquered by the Anglo-Saxons, were masters of the entire state. For almost all of that

Figure 6.　PANEL FROM THE FRANKS CASKET.　Courtesy British Museum.

quarter century, the Danish leader, Knut, held the English throne, and he was not unsuccessful in restoring a measure of political and social stability to the English scene; because Knut was required by his Scandinavian interests to be absent from England on four occasions, he was obliged to delegate his authority over domestic affairs, and the consequence was the "resultant growth of powerful subjects. Towards the end of his reign interest begins to shift, for the first time in the narrative of English history, from the king himself towards the more ambitious of his noblemen."[10]

An opportunity for Scandinavian culture to influence that of the Anglo-Saxons never really arose, and native customs were not profoundly affected by the Danish presence. For his part, Knut desired to reign in the tradition of an English king, and, furthermore, "for all their skill in warfare, the intricacy of their decorative art, and the elaboration of their encomiastic verse, the northern peoples of Knut's age belonged in spirit to a remote, barbaric world;"[11] the Danes were a people, in other words, who might better learn than teach. In a move to emphasize his position as king of England and to minimize the danger of Norman interference, Knut disassociated himself from his first consort, Ælgifu of Northampton, and in the summer of 1017 took Æthelred's widow, Emma of Normandy, as his queen; Emma agreed that any children whom she might bear to Knut would have rights to the throne which superceded those of her sons by Æthelred. At the Oxford meeting of 1018 in which Wulfstan figured, the legal system adopted was that promulgated by Edgar, king of England (959–975); although the "Laws of Edgar" had been favorable to the Danes by granting them administrative autonomy in return for loyalty to the English throne, and were thus readily acceptable to Knut and his followers, the laws were, nevertheless, of English and not Danish origin. If Knut was disposed to honor English law, he was also willing to respect the native church; "accepting from its leaders the traditional English conception of the king as an agent appointed by God for the promotion of religion and the protection of its ministers, he identified himself with them in their task of restoring ecclesiastical authority among a people demoralized by thirty years of war. Through them he was brought into contact with the court of Rome, and thereby into intimacy with the members of a political circle which no one of his race had ever entered. He was the first viking leader to be admitted into the civilized fraternity of Christian kings."[12]

In 1027 Knut even journeyed to Rome to be present at the coronation of Conrad II as Holy Roman Emperor. At that time Knut had also been king of Denmark for nine years, having succeeded to the throne upon the death of his older brother, Harald, who left no other heir. Upon his return from Rome, Knut sailed for Norway, and managed to have himself proclaimed king of that country at Nidaros in 1028, an event which marked the apogee of his power. Knut sent Ælfgifu of Northampton and their son, Svein, to govern in his place, but the pair was expelled by the Norwegians in 1035 after an extremely oppressive reign, and when Knut died on November 12 of that same year Norway was under the control of Magnus, the son of Olaf II (Saint Olaf). In England Knut's death was followed by an interregnum which lasted until 1037 when Harald (Harefoot), the son of Knut and Ælgifu was recognized as king; Harald's rival for the English throne was his half brother, Harthaknut, born to Knut and Emma.

When his father died, Harthaknut was the ruler of Denmark, and because he was expecting an invasion of that country by Magnus of Norway he was prevented from leaving in order to assert his claim of being Knut's legitimate successor. By the end of 1039, however, Harthaknut was on his way to England with a fleet of sixty-two warships. Harald's death from illness on March 17, 1040, removed the necessity of armed conflict, and Harthaknut reigned as king until June 8, 1042, when, according to the *Chronicle,* he was seized by convulsions, while he *æt his drince stōd,* and died. The previous year Harthaknut had invited his half brother, Edward, who was living in Normandy, to reside in England; although Edward's father had been the late king, Æthelred, he and Harthaknut had the same mother in Emma, and Harthaknut rather charitably "adopted him as a member of his household, and, almost certainly, put him forward as his heir."[13] Even before Harthaknut's interment, Edward (the Confessor) was proclaimed king in London, and the native dynasty was thus restored—but only temporarily, for twenty-four years later Edward was to be succeeded by his vigorous cousin, William, the duke of Normandy.

13.7   *Wulfstan's Address to the English (II)*

And lā, hū mæġ māre scamu þurh Godes yrre mannum
ġelimpan þonne ūs dēð ġelōme for āgenum ġewyrhtum? Ðēh þræla
hwylċ hlāforde æthlēape and of crīstendōme tō wīċinge weorþe, and
hit æfter þām eft ġeweorþe wæpnġewrixl weorðe ġemǣne þeġene
5 and þræle, ġif þræl þæne þeġen fullīċe āfylle, licge æġylde ealre
his mæġðe; and, ġif sē þeġen þæne þræl þe hē ǣr āhte fullīċe āfylle,
ġylde þeġenġylde. Ful earhlīċe laga and scandlīċe nȳdġyld þurh
Godes yrre ūs syn ġemǣne, understande sē þe cunne; and fela
unġelimpa ġelimpð þysse þēode oft and ġelōme. Ne dohte hit nū
10 lange inne ne ūte, ac wæs here and hete on ġewelhwilcan ende oft
and ġelōme, and Engle nū lange eal siġelēase and tō swȳþe ġeyriġde
þurh Godes yrre; and flotmen swā strange þurh Godes þafunge

þæt oft on ġefeohte ān fēseð tȳne, and hwīlum lǣs, hwīlum mā,
eal for ūrum synnum. And oft tȳne oððe twelfe, ǣlċ æfter ōþrum,
15 scendað tō bysmore þæs þeġenes cwenan, and hwīlum his dōhtor
oððe nȳdmāgan, þǣr hē on lōcað, þe lǣt hine sylfne rancne and
rīcne and ġenōh gōdne ǣr þæt ġewurde. And oft þrǣl þæne þeġen þe
ǣr wæs his hlāford cnyt swȳþe fæste and wyrcð him tō þrǣle þurh
Godes yrre. Wālā þǣre yrmðe and wālā þǣre woroldscame þe nū
20 habbað Engle, eal þurh Godes yrre! Oft tweġen sǣmen, oððe þrȳ
hwīlum, drīfað þā drāfe crīstenra manna fram sǣ tō sǣ, ūt þurh
þās þēode, ġewelede tōgædere, ūs eallum tō woroldscame, ġif wē
on eornost ǣniġe cūþon āriht understandan; ac ealne þæne bysmor
þe wē oft þoliað wē ġyldað mid weorðscipe þām þe ūs scendað: wē
25 him ġyldað singāllīċe, and hȳ ūs hȳnað dæġhwāmlīċe; hȳ herġiað
and hȳ bærnað, rȳpað and rēafiað and tō scipe lǣdað; and lā, hwæt
is ǣniġ ōðer on eallum þām ġelimpum būtan Godes yrre ofer þās
þēode swutol and ġesǣne?

Nis ēac nān wundor þēah ūs mislimpe, for þām wē witan ful
30 ġeorne þæt nū fela ġēara mænn nā ne rōhtan foroft hwæt hȳ
worhtan wordes oððe dǣde: ac wearð þēs þēodscipe, swā hit þinċan
mæġ, swȳþe forsyngod þurh mæniġfealde synna and þurh fela
misdǣda: þurh morðdǣda and þurh māndǣda, þurh ġītsunga and
þurh ġīfernessa, þurh stala and þurh strūdunga, þurh mannsylena
35 and þurh hǣþene unsida, þurh swicdōmas and þurh searacræftas,
þurh lahbrycas and þurh ǣswicas, þurh mǣġrǣsas and þurh
manslyhtas, þurh hādbrycas and þurh ǣwbrycas, þurh sibleġeru
and þurh mistlīċe forliġru. And ēac syndan wīde, swā wē ǣr
cwǣdan, þurh āðbricas and þurh wedbrycas and þurh mistlīċe
40 lēasunga forloren and forlogen mā þonne scolde; and frēolbricas
and fæstenbrycas wīde ġeworhte oft and ġelōme. And ēac hēr syn
on earde apostatan ābroþene and ċyriċhatan hetole and lēodhatan
grimme ealles tō maneġe, and oferhogan wīde godcundra rihtlaga
and crīstenra þēawa, and hōcorwyrde dysiġe ǣġhwǣr on þēode
45 oftost on þā þing þe Godes bodan bēodaþ, and swȳþost on þā þing
þe ǣfre tō Godes lage ġebyriað mid rihte. And þȳ is nū ġeworden
wīde and sīde tō ful yfelan ġewunan þæt menn swȳðor scamað
nū for gōddǣdan þonne for misdǣdan, for þām tō oft man mid
hōcere gōddǣda hyrweð and godfyrhte lehtreð ealles tō swȳðe, and
50 swȳðost man tǣleð and mid olle ġegrēteð ealles tō ġelōme þā þe
riht lufiað and Godes eġe habbað be ǣnigum dǣle. And þurh þæt
þe man swā dēð þæt man eal hyrweð þæt man scolde hereġian and
tō forð lāðet þæt man scolde lufian, þurh þæt man ġebringeð ealles
tō maneġe on yfelan ġeþance and on undǣde, swā þæt hȳ ne
55 scamð nā , þēh hȳ syngian swȳðe and wið God sylfne forwyrċan
hȳ mid ealle, ac for īdelan onscytan hȳ scamað þæt hȳ bētan heora

misdǣda swā swā bēċ tǣċan, ġelīċe þām dwǣsan þe for heora
prȳtan lēwe nellað beorgan ǣr hȳ nā ne magan, þēh hȳ eal willan.
Hēr syndan þurh synlēawa, swā hit þinċan mæġ, sāre ġelēwede
60 tō maneġe on earde. Hēr syndan mannslagan and mǣġslagan and
mæsserbanan and mynsterhatan, and hēr syndan mānsworan and
morþorwyrhtan, and hēr syndan myltestran and bearnmyrðran and
fūle forleġene hōringas maneġe, and hēr syndan wiċċan and
wælcyrian, and hēr syndan rȳperas and rēaferas and worolstrūderas,
65 and hrædest is tō cweþenne, māna and misdǣda unġerim ealra.
And þæs ūs ne scamað nā, ac ūs scamað swȳðe þæt wē bōte
āginnan swā swā bēċ tǣċan, and þæt is ġesȳne on þysse earman
forsyngodan þēode. Ēalā, miċel magan maneġe ġȳt hērtōēcan ēaþe
beþenċan þæs þe ān man ne mehte on hrædinge āsmēagan, hū
70 earmlīċe hit ġefaren is nū ealle hwīle wīde ġynd þās þēode. And
smēage hūru ġeorne ġehwā hine sylfne and þæs nā ne latiġe ealles
tō lange. Ac lā, on Godes naman, utan dōn swā ūs nēod is, beorgan
ūs sylfum swā wē ġeornost magan, þē læs wē ætgædere ealle
forweorðan.
75 Ān þēodwita wæs on Brytta tīdum, Gildas hātte, sē āwrāt be
heora misdǣdum, hū hȳ mid heora synnum swā oferlīċe swȳðe
God ġegræmedan þæt hē lēt æt nyhstan Engla here heora eard
ġewinnan and Brytta dugeþe fordōn mid ealle. And þæt wæs
ġeworden, þæs þe hē sǣde, þurh rīcra rēaflāc and þurh ġītsunge
80 wōhġestrēona, þurh lēode unlaga and þurh wōhdōmas, þurh biscopa
āsolcennesse and unsnotornesse, and þurh lȳðre yrhðe Godes
bydela, þe sōþes ġeswugedan ealles tō ġelōme and clumedan mid
ċeaflum þǣr hȳ scoldan clypian. þurh fūlne ēac folces gǣlsan and
þurh oferfylla and mæniġfealde synna heora eard hȳ forworhtan
85 and selfe hȳ forwurdan. Ac wutan dōn swā ūs þearf is, warnian ūs
be swilcan; and sōþ is þæt ic secge, wyrsan dǣda wē witan mid
Englum þonne wē mid Bryttan āhwǣr ġehȳrdan; and þȳ ūs is
þearf miċel þæt wē ūs beþenċan and wið God sylfne þingian ġeorne.
And utan dōn swā ūs þearf is, ġebūgan tō rihte, and be suman
90 dǣle unriht forlǣtan and ascunian, and bētan swyðe ġeorne þæt
wē ǣr brǣcan; and utan God lufian and Godes lagum fylġean, and
ġelǣstan swȳðe ġeorne þæt þæt wē behētan þā wē fulluht underfēngan, oððon þā þe æt fulluhte ūre forespecan wǣran; and utan
word and weorc rihtlīċe fadian, and ūre inġeþanc clǣnsian ġeorne,
95 and āð and wed wǣrlīċe healdan, and sume ġetrȳwða habban ūs
betwēonan būtan uncræftan; and utan ġelōme understandan þone
miclan dōm þe wē ealle tō sculon, and beorgan ūs ġeorne wið þone
weallendan byrne helle wites, and ġeearnian ūs þā mǣrþa and
þā myrhða þe God hæfð ġeġearwod þām þe his willan on worolde
100 ġewyrċað. God ūre helpe. *Amen.*

13.8   *Notes*

2–6.   *ðēh . . . ealre his mǣ͡gðe* At the time of Wulfstan's writing, the word *þe͡gen* had come to mean a man of the upper classes;[14] if such a man were slain by a thrall, or slave, who had deserted the English, no monetary compensation (*wergild*) could be collected by the dead person's kinsmen. The Danes, who had the right to demand the *wergild* from the English for a fallen Danish freeman, were, however, also insisting upon payment for the death of a former English slave who had gone over to their side.

38.   *and ēac syndan,* the subject of *syndan* is *mā þonne scolde* 'more (people) than should be'.

53.   *lāðet,* third singular, present indicative of *lāðettan* 'to hate, loathe'.

57.   *bēc,* books of penances used in the Anglo-Saxon Church.[15]

57–58.   *þe for heora prȳtan lēwe nellað beorgan* 'who are not willing to seek a cure for (their) imperfection(s) because of their pride'.

64.   *wælcyrian,* the word *wælcyrie,* which literally means 'chooser of the slain' (cf. *cyre* 'choice', *wæl* 'slaughter, dead body'), seems here to indicate a witch or sorceress of some kind.

75.   *Gildas,* a Welshman and a Christian, who in the early or middle sixth century, had addressed his countrymen in terms similar to those used by Wulfstan; known as 'the wise' (*sapiens*), Gildas was the author of a homiletic work often called the *De Excidio Britanniae* (*On the Destruction of Britain*) in which he lamented the sorry conditions in Britain, produced, as he saw them, by corruption in the Church and the Germanic invasions alike.

100.   *God ūre helpe,* here *helpan* takes the genitive.

References

1.   Eduard Prokosch, *A Comparative Germanic Grammar* (Philadelphia, 1939), p. 256.
2.   Prokosch, p. 256.
3.   Ralph W. V. Elliott, *Runes, an Introduction* (Manchester, England, 1959), p. 9.
4.   Elliott, p. 9.
5.   *Tacitus on Britain and Germany,* a new translation of the 'Agricola' and the 'Germania' by H. Mattingly (Baltimore, Maryland, 1948), p. 108.
6.   Elliott, p. 47.
7.   Elliott, p. 68.
8.   Elliott, p. 30.
9.   Elliott, p. 62.
10.   Peter Hunter Blair, *An Introduction to Anglo-Saxon England* (Cambridge, England, 1956), pp. 99–100.
11.   Sir Frank Stenton, *Anglo-Saxon England,* 2nd ed. (Oxford, 1947), p. 405.
12.   Stenton, pp. 390–391.
13.   Stenton, p. 417.
14.   Dorothy Whitelock, ed., *Sermo Lupi ad Anglos,* 3rd ed. (New York, 1966), p. 58.
15.   Whitelock, p. 63.

Chapter 14

14.1   *Word Formation in Old English* (I)   One aspect of Old English, heretofore touched upon only incidentally, is the way in which words are put together. Polysyllabic words, for instance, often contain component elements, one or more of which may recur elsewhere in the language and have a meaning that is either grammatical or semantic. The suffixation of *-e* to adjectives in order to form adverbs involves an element (or morpheme) that carries grammatical meaning, while the prefixation of *ūt* 'out' to the verb *gān*, for example, involves an element with semantic meaning: *ūtgān* 'to go out'. The process of building words by means of affixation is common among the Indo-European languages, and, from one point of view, the thematic vowels and the inflectional endings of nouns and verbs may be regarded as just so many limiting suffixes attached to various roots. In the matter of word formation as such, however, attention focuses upon the creation of words rather than upon their classification or inflection; the morphological devices which a language has for enlarging its vocabulary are the primary concern. The formation of words is also an aspect of linguistic change. The lexical inventory of a living language is never completely stable, and words are continually being dropped from or added to a given vernacular, the new terms always being fashioned according to recognized principles such as affixation. The following paragraphs indicate how the vocabulary of Proto-Old English and of Old English proper was developed through the use of prefixes; suffixes are listed and explained in the next chapter (see 15.1), and another major technique for forming words, namely compounding, is examined in Chapter 16 (see 16.1). An additional method of word formation productive in Old English was the derivation of verbs from nouns, adjectives, and other verbs (see 7.2).

14.1.1 *Common Old English Prefixes* Some prefixes serve more than one function, and some may be attached to several different parts of speech; some prefixes (like *ofer*) are also independent units that may stand by themselves, whereas some (like *ġe-*) never occur except in conjunction with other linguistic forms. On occasion, a prefix may have no discernible function.[1]

ā-   A modifier of many verbs, and, thereby, of nouns and adjectives derived from those verbs. When it has a recognizable semantic effect, the prefix is an intensifier of action: e.g., *bītan* 'to bite', *ābītan* 'to bite in pieces, devour'; *swāpan* 'to sweep', *āswāpan* 'to sweep away, devour'. Sometimes, however, the two forms of a given verb, one with *ā-* and one without, do not contrast in meaning; that happens when the prefix has no clear semantic force (e.g., *bōdian* and *ābōdian* both mean 'to announce, proclaim'), or when the form without *ā-* has also acquired an intensified denotation (*wringan* and *āwringan* both mean 'to wring, to squeeze out').

æġ-   Imparts an indefinite meaning to pronouns and adverbs: *hwā* 'who' but *ǣġhwā* 'whoever, everyone'; *hwǣr* 'where' but *ǣġhwǣr* 'everywhere, in every direction'.

an-   See *and-*.

and-   Combines with nouns, verbs which are usually denominative, and also
(ond-)   appears in some adjectives and adverbs. Although it occasionally appears to have little semantic function, the prefix usually signifies 'against', 'opposite' or 'toward': *cf.* the nouns *andfang* 'acceptance', *andġyt* 'understanding, intellect', *andsaca* 'adversary', *andswaru* 'answer', *andwiġ* 'resistance'; the verbs *andhweorfan* 'to move against', *andspurnan* 'to stumble against', *andswarian* 'to answer'; the adjectives *andġytful* 'intelligent', *andlang* 'entire, continuous', *andweord* 'present', *andwīs* 'expert, skilful'; and the adverbs *andġytfullīċe* 'intelligently', *andlangnes* 'along', *andweardlīċe* 'actually'. Before some nouns the prefix also appears in an unstressed, reduced form, *an-/on-*: *onlīcnes* 'resemblance', *onrǣs* 'onrush, assault', *onsagu* 'affirmation, accusation', *onspeca* 'accuser'.

be-, bī- Chiefly a modifier of verbs *be-* may lend the dimension 'round, over' (*licgan* 'to lie', *belicgan* 'to lie round'; *gān* 'to go', *begān* 'to go over, traverse'), may convert an intransitive verb to a transitive verb (*sittan* 'to sit', *besittan* 'to besiege'; *wēpan* 'to weep', *bewēpan* 'to bewail'), or exert a privative force (*niman* 'to take', *beniman* 'to deprive'). Along with its stressed counterpart bī/biġ-, the prefix *be-* also combines to form nouns, but the meaning which it carries is far less distinct: e.g., *behǣs* 'vow', *behāt* 'promise', *belimp* 'event', *beswic* 'treachery, deceit'; *bismer* 'insult', *bīword* 'proverb'. In like manner, *be-* is also the first element of some common adverbs and prepositions: *beforan* (both adverb and preposition) 'before', *behindan* (both adverb and preposition) 'behind', *benorðan* 'northwards (of)', *betwēonum* (both adverb and preposition) 'between'.

ed- A prefix meaning 'again, repetition, back' (*cf.* Latin *et* 'and'), *ed-* modifies several different parts of speech: *edcennan* 'to regenerate', *edgift* 'restitution', *edhwyrfan* 'to return', *edlæstan* 'to repeat', *edlēan* 'reward', *ednīwe* 'renewed' (as an adverb 'anew, again'), *edstaðelian* 'to re-establish'.

el- A prefix signifying 'foreign, strange' (*cf.* Latin *alius* and the Old English comparative adjective *elra* 'other'): *elcor* (adverb) 'elsewhere', *elreordig* 'of foreign speech', *elþēodian* 'to live abroad', *elþēodisc* 'foreign, strange'.

for- Used primarily to intensify the action of verbs, often with pejorative effect: *forbrecan* 'to break into pieces', *forcweðan* 'to speak ill of', *fordōn* 'to undo, destroy,' *forhogian* 'to neglect, despise', *forlǣdan* 'to mislead', *forsendan* 'to send away, banish', *forweorðan* 'to perish'. The prefix also occurs in some nouns based upon verbs: *forfang* 'capture', *forleornung* 'deception', *forsewen* 'contempt'; *for-* is a straightforward intensifier meaning 'very' when used with adjectives and adverbs: *fordyslīc* 'very foolish', *forgeare* 'very certainly', *forgeorne* 'very earnestly', *forheard* 'very hard', *foroft* 'very often'.

fore- The prefix combines with verbs, nouns, adjectives, and adverbs to imply 'precedence' or 'pre-eminence': *foregān* 'to go before, precede', *foreċeorfend* 'front tooth', *foresǣd* 'aforesaid', *forðanclīce* 'thoughtfully, prudently'.

for- As a prefix *forð-* carries with it the sense of 'forward motion': *forðdōn* 'to put forth', *forðgang* 'going forth, progress', *forðheald* 'bent forward, stooping', *forðlīce* 'forwardly'; but may also be a simple intensifier: *forðmǣre* 'very glorious', *forðriht* 'direct, plain'.

ful(l)- Combines with different parts of speech to intensify the meaning or to denote 'completeness': *fullblīðe* 'very glad', *fullfremman* 'to fulfil, complete', *fullgrōwan* 'to grow to perfection', *fullhāl* 'thoroughly well', *fullraðe* 'very quickly', *fullrīpod* 'mature', *fulnēah* 'very near', *fultum* 'help, protection'.

ġe- The perfective particle, frequently joined to the past participle of verbs to indicate action completed: *ġecoren* 'chosen', *ġefunden* 'found'; used throughout the conjugation of a given verb it may impart a specialized meaning (*hātan* 'to call, name', *gehātan* 'to promise'), or it may be of no apparent significance (*sprecan* 'to speak', *ġesprecan* 'to speak'). With other parts of speech, *ġe-* may also impart a sense of 'completeness', it may signify 'collectiveness, association', or it may be semantically inert: *ġenīp* 'darkness' (from *genīpan* 'to grow dark'), *ġebrōðor* 'brothers', *ġelīċ* 'alike', *ġereord* 'speech'. It should be noted that scholarly opinion has not been uniform regarding the function and meaning of *ġe-;* for a useful summary of the situation see J. W. Richard Lindemann, "Old English Preverbal *ge-:* A Re-Examination of Some Current Doctrines," *Journal of English and Germanic Philology* 64.65–83 (1965).

in- Occasionally spelled *inn-*, this prefix can modify different parts of speech as an indicator of direction and place where, or as an intensifier: *insendan* 'to send in, put in', *ingenġa* 'visitor, intruder'; *incempa* 'soldier of the same company', *inwræc* 'internal pain'; *indryhten* 'distinguished, noble', *infrōd* 'very aged, wise'.

mis-   A modifier of various parts of speech signifying 'wrong(ly), amiss': *misfaran* 'to go wrong, transgress', *misġelimp* 'misfortune', *mislīcian* 'to displease', *mistēd* 'evil time', *miswerde* 'erring, ill-behaving'.

ō-   See *ā-*.

of-   Chiefly, but not exclusively, a modifier of verbs, *of-* sometimes adds a perfective aspect, and sometimes intensification: *ofbēatan* 'to beat to death', *ofdrincan* 'to intoxicate', *ofġeorn* 'elated', *ofrǣċan* 'to reach, obtain', *ofrīdan* 'to overtake (by riding)', *ofsceotan* 'to shoot down, kill', *oftēon* 'to withhold, take away'.

ofer-   A widely used prefix, *ofer-* occurs most often with verbs where it customarily retains the adverbial meaning 'over'; with nouns, adjectives, adverbs, and some verbs, however, the prefix also implies 'excessiveness' or 'superiority': *oferbreġdan* 'to draw over, cover', *oferfaran* 'to go over', *oferġeotan* 'to pour upon', *oferstīgan* 'to climb over', *oferǣt* 'gluttony', *oferhyġd* 'pride, conceit', *oferspreca* 'one who talks too much', *ofereald* 'very old', *oferhāt* 'over-hot', *ofermōdlīċe* 'proudly, arrogantly', *oferðēon* 'to excel, surpass'.

on-   Often prefixed to verbs, *on-* signifies that the action is incipient: *onǣlan* 'to set fire to, ignite, inflame', *onbryrdan* 'to excite, inspire', *onstellan* 'to institute, create, originate'. See also *and-*.

or-   Converts nouns into adjectives, lending a privative force to them, and intensifies original adjectives: *orhlȳte* 'destitute', *orsorg* 'unconcerned, without care', *orwēne* 'hopeless', *oreold* 'very old', *ormǣte* 'boundless, huge', *orðanc* 'ingenious, skillful'.

oð-   A verbal modifier, usually meaning 'away (from)': *oðfeallan* 'to fall off, decline', *oðflēon* 'to flee away, escape', *oðswerian* 'to abjure', *oðtēon* 'to take away'.

tō-   A very common prefix used with various parts of speech; *tō-* implies 'motion towards' or acts as an intensifier: *tōgædre* (adverb) 'together', *tōgān* 'to go to', *tōsprǣċ* 'conversation, speaking to (another)', *tōwæard* (adjective) 'facing, approaching'; *tōbrecan* 'to break into pieces', *tōsendan* 'to send out, disperse'.

þurh-   A modifier of verbs, nouns, adjectives and adverbs *þurh-*, which often indicates 'through', is also an intensifier and a marker of 'completeness': *ðurhflēon* 'to fly through', *ðurhsċēotan* 'to pierce'; *ðurhbeorht* 'very bright', *ðurhspēdiġ* 'very rich', *ðurhendian* 'to accomplish, perfect'.

un-   Commonly used with adjectives and adverbs *un-* negates or reverses the meaning of the root to which it is attached: *unġesund* 'unsound, unhealthy', *unlǣne* 'permanent', *unrihtlīċe* 'unrighteously'; it is also used in the same capacity with some nouns: *unmōd* 'depression', *unspēd* 'want, poverty'. As a qualifier of verbs, *un-* appears in the unstressed form *on-*: *onsǣlan* 'to untie, loosen', *onwrīðan* 'to unbind, unwrap'.

under-   With the literal or figurative sense of 'under, underlying' the prefix modifies several different parts of speech, especially verbs: *underberan* 'to support, endure', *underdōn* 'to put under', *underflōwan* 'to flow under', *underscyte* 'passage underneath, transit', *underdrifennes* 'subjection', *underbæc* (adverb) 'backwards'.

up-   Used with various parts of speech in its adverbial meaning of 'up, upwards': *upcuman* 'to arise', *upeard* 'land above, heaven', *uphēah* 'uplifted, tall', *uprihte* (adverb) 'straight up'.

ūt-   Combines with different parts of speech to add the sense of 'out, away': *ūtādrīfan* 'to drive out, dispel', *ūtlǣdan* 'to lead out', *ūtfaru* 'going out', *utgenga* 'exit', *utanweord* 'external', *ūtfūs* 'ready to start out', *ūtanbordes* (adverb) 'from abroad'.

wan-/   Combining primarily with nouns and adjectives, *wan-* is a prefix with a
won-   negative, sometimes privative, force: *wanǣht* 'want, poverty' *wanhāl* 'unsound, weak', *wonhȳd* 'carelessness', *wansǣliġ* 'unhappy'.

wiÐ-   Qualifies various parts of speech by adding the sense of 'away, against': *wiÐcweÐan* 'to speak against', *wiÐfeohtan* 'to fight against' *wiÐlǣdnes* 'abduction', *wiÐmetennes* 'comparison', *wiÐrǣde* 'contrary', *wiÐneoþan* (adverb) 'beneath', *wiÐġeondan* (preposition) 'beyond'.

wiÐer- Modifies most parts of speech with the sense of 'opposing, counter': *wiÐersacian* 'to renounce, become apostate', *wiÐerstandan* 'to resist', *wiÐerlēan* 'requital, compensation', *wiÐersaca* 'adversary', *wiÐerrǣde* 'contrary', *wiÐermōd* 'unwilling, contrary' *wiÐerrǣdlīċ* 'contrary, adverse', *wiÐerræhtes* (adverb) 'opposite'.

ymb(e)- Combines with various parts of speech to add the sense of 'around': *ymbfōn* 'to surround, encompass', *ymbwerdan* 'to turn around', *ymbfæstnes* 'enclosure', *ymbeÐanc* 'thought, reflection', *ymbhȳdiġ* 'anxious, solicitous', *ymbsett* 'neighboring', *ymbūtan* (adverb and preposition) 'around, about, outside'.

14.2   *The Use of Runes in Anglo-Saxon England*   Evolved at a time when Britain was Keltic-speaking, the runic alphabet, as a parcel of Germanic culture, was eventually transported across the Channel by Angles and Saxons who had become acquainted with that form of writing on the Continent. Writing systems are, of course, as vulnerable to change as speech itself, and the runic letters employed in England were not completely identical in shape, phonetic value, or number with those of the common Germanic *fuþark*. Traditionally written ⟨, the sixth rune (Old English *cēn*, probably 'torch') consistently assumes the derived shape ʰ in Anglo-Saxon inscriptions, the upper stroke having simply been extended downward to a length equal to that of the lower stroke; although the rune is transliterated *c* in Old English, the phonetic value [k] remained the same. Because Proto-Germanic [a] underwent a triple development in Old English, the original symbol (ᚠ) for that sound acquired the value [æ] in Anglo-Saxon orthography, and a new letter (ᚪ) was devised for [a]; a second new letter (ᚩ) was introduced to represent the Old English shift of [a] before nasals to [o]. With (ᚩ) replacing (ᚠ) in fourth position, the runes (ᚠ) and (ᚪ) were relegated to the end of the series; hence, the Old English runic alphabet is known as the *fuþorc*, a name that conveniently distinguishes it from the earlier *fuþark*. As a consequence of additional, similar modifications, the standard Germanic alphabet of twenty-four characters was initially expanded to a *fuþorc* of twenty-eight; that development probably took place in Frisian territory, for "Old Frisian shared certain linguistic changes with Old English, and some of the new runes actually occur in Frisian inscriptions of the fifth to seventh century."[2] A later augmentation of the *fuþorc* brought the total number of characters to a maximum of thirty-three in ninth-century Northumbria. (In Scandinavia, by contrast, the *fuþark* was reduced to sixteen letters.) Although the twenty-eight-letter *fuþorc* as such seems not to have been recorded until the late eighth century or early ninth, the history of runic writing in England almost certainly begins with the advent of the Anglo-Saxons.

If a gold coin now in the British Museum is indeed English, and not Frisian, the earliest native inscription yet recovered can probably be assigned to the sixth century. A somewhat questionable item (its provenance is not known), the coin is a barbarous copy of a *solidus* of Flavius Honorius, Roman emperor in the west from 395 until his death in 423, but it cannot have been reproduced before the middle of the sixth century when the Anglo-Saxons apparently began to use coined money.[3] In any event, the nine runic letters appearing on the coin read *scanomodu*, very likely the name of a person; the presence of final *-u* after a long root, *mōd-* is good evidence of the inscription's considerable antiquity (*cf.* the Old English neuter noun *mōd* 'heart, mind, spirit'). Another early inscription, and one that is indisputably English, occurs on a pagan sepulchral stone found about 1830 near the town of Sandwich in Kent; now housed in the Royal Museum, Canterbury, the stone measures one foot four inches in height, is six square inches at the base and four square inches at the top. There are seven runes on the stone, and they read *ræhæbul*, either the name of the deceased or of the rune-master; "the rough nature of the stone, the absence of any Christian marks or ornamentation, as well as the archaic nature of the name, preserving intervocalic *h*, speak for an early date, certainly before the middle of the seventh century."[4] Sometime in the latter decades of the same century, or in the first half of the eighth, the magnificent Ruthwell Cross of Dumfriesshire was created; about eighteen feet tall, the stone monument is decorated with sculptured panels, a number of which depict scenes from the life of Christ, with vinescroll ornamentation, and with runic characters that spell out passages parallel to sections of *The Dream of the Rood*, a poem of religious ecstasy (see 15.7). The purpose of the Ruthwell Cross, and others like it, most notably the similarly ornamented Bewcastle Cross in Cumberland, may have been to mark a site of worship where no church had yet been erected.[5]

The early eighth century also yields another beautifully crafted object bearing runic letters, the Franks casket, so-called from the name of its former owner, Sir Augustus Wollanston Franks, who presented the lid and three sides of the walrus-bone box to the British Museum in 1867. (In 1890 the missing fourth side was discovered in the Museo Nazionale, Florence, and a cast of that side has since been joined to the others in the British Museum.) The casket is nine inches long, seven and one-half inches wide, and, in its present condition, just over five inches high; on each of the four sides a runic inscription forms a border surrounding an intricately carved center panel (for example, one shows the fall of Jerusalem in 70 AD to Titus, son of the then Roman Emperor, Vespasian). The Christian theme is not absent; the Adoration of the Magi constitutes the partial subject matter of another panel. The dialect of the inscriptions is Northumbrian, and it follows that Northumbria must have been the casket's place of origin. An exquisite relic, the Franks casket is justifiably termed "a unique and priceless specimen"[6] of the English runic heritage.

The use of runic letters in England was, of course, not confined to epigraphy alone; in a continuation of Continental practices, the Anglo-Saxons also relied upon the Germanic characters for their magical powers, and, from time to time, even made some use of them in poetry. Six riddles from the *Exeter Book* contain interpolated runes which serve as clues to the solution; the *Husband's Message,* a lyric addressed to his wife by a man absent in a distant land, has a concluding passage with five runes that presumably represent a secret five-word communication intended for the woman alone. Three lines (520, 913, 1702) in the *Beowulf* manuscript, which dates from the end of the tenth century, contain the *ēþel-* or 'homland'-rune, used as a kind of shorthand; line 520, for example, reads *ðonon hē ġesōhte swǣsne*   'thence he sought his own homeland'. The first English author to sign his work was the early ninth-century poet, Cynewulf (or Cynwulf), who 'wove' the spelling of his name into various passages by means of runes; *cf. Christ* 1. 797 ff., *Elene* 1. 1256 ff., *Fates of the Apostles* 1. 96 ff., and *Juliana* 1. 704 ff. The most direct utilization of the *fuþorc,* however, is found in the *Rune Poem* (c.775–800), where the name of each rune introduces a short verse on the object in question. There are twenty-nine stanzas, of which the following three (1, 11, 19) are representative:

> (ᚠ) *Feoh* byþ frotur   fira ġehwylcum;
>   sceal ðēah manna ġehwylċ   miclun hyt dǣlan
>   ġif hē wile for Drihtne   dōmes hlēotan.
>   (*Wealth* is a comfort to each of men; but each man
>   must share it generously if he wishes to obtain
>   glory in the sight of God.)

(|) *Īs* byþ oferċeald,   unġemetum slidor,
       glisna glæshlūttur   ġimmum ġelīcust,
       flōr forste ġeworuht,   fæġer ansȳne.
       (*Ice* is intensely cold, excessively slippery,
       it glistens glass-clear, most like gems,
       it is a floor created by frost, a beautiful sight.)

(M) *Eh* byþ for eorlum   æþelinga wyn,
       hors hōfum wlanc,   ðǣr him hæleþe ymb
       weleġe on wicgum   wrixlaþ sprǣce,
       and biþ unstyllum   ǣfre frotur.
       (*Horse* in the presence of warriors is a joy to noblemen,
       a steed proud of its hooves where mounted heroes
       and wealthy men exchange speech about him,
       and is ever a joy to the restless.)

An example of oral poetry later copied down, the *Rune Poem* has several parallels in early Norwegian and Icelandic literature. Although runes did become the object of an antiquarian interest, particularly in monastic *scriptoria,* their employment as any part of a living tradition probably ceased no later than the tenth century, by which time the Roman alphabet had long been the only writing system in daily use throughout England.

   14.3   *Sound Changes (II): The Old English Development of West Germanic Stressed Vowels and Diphthongs*   Because the development of Old English from West Germanic involved an extremely large number of changes on the phonological level, the following survey of vowels and diphthongs is restricted solely to those modifications which occurred in accented (root) syllables. A further limitation excludes minor changes that do not show Old English in clearest relation to other Germanic dialects, and changes that do not shed much light on the growth of Old English itself; an exhaustive list of sound shifts is not the aim here. The designation *Old English* is always synonymous with *West Saxon*.

   14.3.1   *West Germanic Short Stressed Vowels in Old English*

West Germanic	Old English Development
i	a) Short *i* generally remained without change: OS *biddian*, OHG *bitten*, OE *biddan* 'to pray, request, entreat'.
	b) Short *i* was lengthened to ī in Old English when it preceded a nasal consonant which was lost before a following voiceless fricative: OHG *fimf*, OE *fīf* 'five'.
	c) When *i* occurred before *r* plus a consonant (except *j* [y]), before *l* plus *h* [χ], or before single *h* it was

broken to the diphthong *io* in eOE: O Fris. *lirmia,* eOE *liormian* 'to learn'; otherwise there was no change. Even in eOE, however, the *io-* diphthong was regularly shifted to *eo* (*leornian*). When affected by *i*-umlaut, *io* became *ie* which then developed into lOE *i/y:* OHG *hirti,* OE *hierde, hirde, hyrde* 'shepherd'.

e

a) Short *e* often remained in Old English: OS *helpan,* OHG *helfan,* OE *helpan* 'to help'.

b) When followed by [m], *e* became *i* in Old English: OHG *neman,* OE *niman* 'to take'.

c) Like short *i*, *e* was broken to a diphthong (*eo*) before r plus a consonant (except *j* [y]), before *l* plus *h* [χ], or before single *h:* OS *fehu,* OHG *feho,* OE *feoh* 'cattle'; otherwise there was no change.

d) After the palatal consonants *ċ* [c], *ġ* [y], and *sc* [š], *e* was diphthongized to *ie* in Old English: OS *ge an,* OHG *geban,* OE *ġiefan* 'to give'. In lOE the diphthong *ie* became *i/y: ġifan,* ME *yive.*

a

a) When uninfluenced by surrounding sounds, *a* normally became *æ* in Old English: OS *dag,* OHG *tag,* OE *dæg;* if subject to *i*-umlaut, *æ* was in turn raised to *e:* Gothic *badi,* OE *bedd* 'bed'.

b) The change of *a* to *æ* was inhibited when *a* preceded [w], a nasal, or a single consonant followed by one of the back vowels [a], [o], [u]: hence the plural forms *dagas, daga, dagum.* Before a nasal, *a* frequently became *o:* OS *hand,* OHG *hant,* OE *hond* 'hand'; in lOE, however, forms with *a* once again prevailed (*hand*). If subject to *i*-umlaut, *o* became *e:* Gothic *sandjan,* OE *sendan* 'to send'.

c) Like *i* and *e*, *æ* (from *a*) was broken to a diphthong (*ea*) when followed by r plus a consonant (except *j* [y]), *l* plus any consonant, and before *h* [χ]: OS *haldan,* OHG *haltan,* OE *healdan* 'to hold'. The diphthong *ea* in turn became *ie* (later *i/y*) through *i*-umlaut: Gothic *hlahjan,* OE *hliehhan* 'to laugh'.

d) After the palatal consonants *ċ* [c], *ġ* [y], and *sc* [š], *æ* (from *a*) was diphthongized to *ea:* OS *forgat,* OE *forġeat* 'he forgot'. By *i*-umlaut *ea* in turn became *ie* (later *i/y*): Gothic *skapjan,* OE *scieppan* 'to create'.

e) When *a* preceded a nasal (*n/m*) that was subsequently lost before one of the voiceless fricatives *s*, *f*, or *þ* then *a* became *ō* in Old English: OHG *gans,* OE *gōs* 'goose', OHG *samfto,* OE *sōfte* 'softly'.

o a) In general *o* remained unchanged in Old English: OS *dohtar*, OHG *tohter*, OE *dohtor* 'daughter'. (The vowel in question here does not derive from IE *o*, which became *a* in PGmc, but from PGmc *u*.) When subject to *i*-umlaut, *o* became the unrounded vowel *e* through the intermediate stage of the rounded vowel *oe* (akin to *ö* in Modern German *Mönch* 'monk'): PGmc **dohtri* (dative singular), eOE *doehter*, lOE *dehter*.

    b) Before nasals *o* became *u* in Old English: OHG *gomo*, OE *guma* 'man'; when subject to *i*-umlaut the *u* was fronted to *y* [ü], as in *mynster* borrowed from Latin *monasterium* 'monastery'.

    c) In the neighborhood of labial consonants, *o* sometimes became Old English *u:* OHG *fogal*, OE *fugol* 'bird', OHG *wolf*, OE *wulf* 'wolf '.

u Short *u* generally remained without change: OS *hund*, OHG *hunt*, OE *hund* 'dog'; when subject to *i*-umlaut, *u* was fronted to *y* [ü]: OS and OHG *kuning*, OE *cyning* 'king'.

14.3.2   *West Germanic Long Stressed Vowels in Old English*

West Germanic **Old English Development**

ī a) Long *ī* generally remained without change in Old English: OS, OHG, OE *sīn* 'his'.

    b) Before *h* [χ], *ī* was diphthongized to *īo* which in turn became *ēo* at an early period: POE **līht*, eOE *līoht*, OE *lēoht* 'light' (adjective). When subject to *i*-umlaut, *īo* (*ēo*) became *īe:* POE **līohtjan*, OE *līehtan* 'to lighten, make easier'.

ē The long *ē* of PGmc and WGmc remained the same in Old English: Gothic, OS, OI, OE *hēr* 'here'. (The vowel in question does not derive from IE *ē*, which became *ǣ* in PGmc and OE, but primarily from the IE long diphthong *ēi*.)

ā a) The primary source for this WGmc vowel was PGmc *ǣ* from IE *ē*. In OS and OHG the *ā* was retained from PGmc, but in Gothic it became *ē:* OS *dād*, OHG *tāt*, Gothic *gadēþs* 'deed'. In Old English, *ā* was preserved before [w], [p], [k], or [g] plus a back vowel: OHG *knāen*, OE *cnāwan* 'to know', OHG *slāfan*, OE *slāpan* 'to sleep', OE plurals like *māgas* 'kinsmen' (*cf. mǣġ* 'kinsman'). Before nasals, *ā* became *ō* in Old English: Gothic *mēna,* OS and OHG *māno,* OE *mōna* 'moon'. When subject to *i*-umlaut, *ō* became *ē* (through intermediate *ōē*): POE **wōnjan,* OE *wēnan* 'to believe, expect'. Elsewhere, *ā* (PGmc *ǣ*) reverted to *ǣ:* OE *dǣd* 'deed'.

b) In West Saxon *ǣ* was diphthongized to *ēa* before *h* [χ]: *nēah* 'near' from older **nǣh, cf.* OS and OHG *nāh* 'near'. When subject to *i*-umlaut, *ēa* became *īe* (later *ī/ȳ*): POE **nēahista,* OE *nīehsta* 'nearest'.

c) Under the influence of the initial palatals *ċ* [č], *ġ* [y], *sc* [š], *ǣ* also became the diphthong *ēa:* POE **ġǣr,* OE *ġēar* 'year', *cf.* OS and OHG *jār.*

d) A secondary source for WGmc *ā* was the nasalized and lengthened *ā* of PGmc which resulted from the loss of *n* [ŋ] in the sound cluster *-anh-* [-aŋχ-]; in Gothic, OS, and OHG the long *ā* was retained but in OE it became *ō:* PGmc **þanhtǣ,* Gothic *þāhta,* OS *thāhta,* OHG *dāhte,* OE *þōhte* 'he thought'.

ō   The long *ō* of PGmc and WGmc was generally retained without change in Old English: Gothic *brōþar,* OI *brōðer,* OS *brōðer,* OHG *bruoder,* OE *brōþor* 'brother'. When subject to *i*-umlaut, *ō* was fronted to *ē:* OS *fōti,* OE *fēt* 'feet'.

ū   The long *ū* of PGmc and WGmc generally remained without change in Old English: OI, OS, OHG, OE *hūs* 'house'. Through *i*-umlaut, *ū* was fronted to *ȳ* [ü:]: PGmc **brūdiz,* OE *brȳd* 'bride'.

14.3.3   *West Germanic Diphthongs in Old English*

West Germanic   **Old English Development**
   ai   The PGmc and WGmc diphthong *ai* became *ā* in Old English: Gothic *stains,* OI *steinn,* OS *stēn,* OHG *stein,* OE *stān* 'stone'. Through *i*-umlaut, the OE *ā* was raised to *ǣ:* Gothic *hailjan,* OS *hēlian,* OE *hǣlan* 'to heal'.

   au   The PGmc and WGmc diphthong *au* became *ēa* in Old English: Gothic *augō,* OI *auga,* OS *ōga,* OHG *ouga,* OE *ēage* 'eye'. When subject to *i*-umlaut, *ēa* became *īe* in the earliest period of West Saxon, but the *īe* was soon monothongized to *ī/ȳ:* Gothic *hausjan,* OS *hōrian,* eWS *hīeran,* WS *hȳran* 'to hear'.

eu	That the PGmc and WGmc diphthong *eu* survived into Old English is shown by a form such as *steupfædaer* 'stepfather' from the Epinal Glosses (before 700). At a very early period, however, *eu* became *ēo* (sometimes *īo*) in West Saxon and Mercian: Northumbrian *lēaf*, Kentish *līof*, but West Saxon and Mercian *lēof* 'dear' (Gothic *liufs*, OS *liof*, OHG *liob*). In late West Saxon the most common spelling is *eo*.
iu	From PGmc *eu* before *ī, i,* or *j, iu* normally became *īo* in Old English: OS *lindi*, OHG *liuti*, OE *līode* 'people'. When affected by *i*-umlaut, *īo* became West Saxon *īe* (later *ī/ȳ*): POE **biudiþ*, West Saxon *bīett* 'he commands'. In non-umlauted words, early West Saxon *īo* was often shifted to *ēo*, the diphthong that eventually prevailed (*lēode*).

14.3.4   *The Accented Vowels and Diphthongs of Germanic and Their Development in Old English: A Tabular Summary*

PGmc	WGmc	OE	umlauted
i	i	i	
		ī	
		io	ie, i, y
		eo	
e	e	e	
		i	
		eo	
		ie, i, y	
a	a	æ	
		a	
		o	e
		ea	ie, i, y
		ō	
o	o	o	e
		u	y
u	u	u	y
ī	ī	ī	
		īo	īe
		ēo	īe
ē	ē	ē	
æ	ā	ā	
		ō	ē
		æ	
		ēa	īe, ī, ȳ
ā	ā	ō	
ō	ō	ō	ē

PGmc	WGmc	OE	umlauted
ū	ū	ū	ȳ
ai	ai	ā	ǣ
au	au	ēa	īe, ī, ȳ
eu	eu	eu	
		ēo	
		īo	
iu	iu	īo	īe, ī, ȳ
		ēo	

14.4 *Syntax V: Word Order* (*Prepositions, Questions, Imperatives*)   The following sections consider the salient features of word arrangement connected with a part of speech and with completed utterances of two different types. Once again, similarities between the practices of Old and Modern English will be evident.

14.4.1 *Prepositions*   By virtue of their etymology, prepositions ought to precede the word or words which they organize into a discrete grammatical unit, the prepositional phrase; and, more often than not, they do: *hē tō healle ġēong* 'he went to the hall', *on his suna būre* 'in his son's dwelling'; but the syntax of Old English permits several other arrangements as well. Sometimes a preposition will follow the item(s) to which it must be linked. A postpositive placement is not infrequent with pronouns: *forðon iċ mē on hafu bord and byrnan* 'therefore, I shall have shield and corslet on me', *þæt hīe him tō mihton ġeġnum gangan* 'that they might go directly to it', and postpositional constructions that effect a juxtaposition of preposition and verb are common in both prose and poetry:[7] *þe þū hēr tō lōcast* 'at which you are here looking', *þe wē ġefyrn ymbe sprǣcon* 'about which we spoke earlier'. Finally, the two elements of a compound preposition such as *betwēonum* or *tōweard* may be separated in order to enclose the object: *sē wæs Hrōþgār hæleþa lēofost . . . be sǣm twēonum* 'he was to Hrothgar the dearest of warriors . . . between the seas (i.e., on earth)'.

14.4.2 *Questions, Imperatives*   In declarative utterances the subject customarily precedes the verb, but the order of the two units is reversed for questions and imperatives: *wāst þū þone forlidenan monn* 'do you know the shipwrecked man?' *æt þisses ofetes* 'eat of this fruit!'. It should be noted, however, that there are numerous exceptions to the general formulation (for example, *þū on sǣlum wes* 'be happy!'). When a question contains an interrogative word or phrase, or the negative particle *ne*, then the verb, although still followed by the subject, once again becomes the second element: *hwæt drincst þū* 'what do you drink?', *hwæt* *māre ytst þū* 'what more do you eat?', *hwylċe þinc ġelǣdst þū ūs* 'what thing do you bring to us?', *ne drincst þū wīn* 'do you not drink wine?'. Imperatives with *ne* are similarly constructed: *ne frīn þū æfter sǣlum* 'do not ask about happiness!'. In both questions and imperatives, a noun in direct address may be positioned in various ways.

14.5   *William, Duke of Normandy, and the Conquest of 1066*
In 911, thirty-three years after Alfred the Great had allotted English territory to the Danish Vikings under Guthrum, the king of France, Charles III ("the Simple"), was forced to cede control of upper Normandy to another Scandinavian marauder, the Viking Hrolf, and his followers. Probably a Norwegian in command of Danes, Hrolf (OI *Hrólfr*) (or Rollo, as he was known among the Franks) thus became the first duke of Normandy, in return for which he did homage to the French king, and accepted baptism in 912 from the archbishop of Rouen. The holdings and power of Hrolf and his successors continued to increase until Normandy was eventually organized into an efficient feudalistic state; at the same time, use of the *dönsk tunga* declined, as the Northmen, or Normans, moved ever further away from their native institutions and modes of thought.[8] When Edward, the surviving son of King Æthelred and Emma of Normandy, returned to England from his Norman refuge in 1041, he was a man who had been exposed to twenty-five years of a culture that was no longer Norse but French in its orientation; although not documented until after the Conquest, the influence of Norman French upon English almost certainly dates not from 1066 but from the acclamation of Edward as king of England in 1042. Surrounding himself with Norman friends and officials, the pious Edward maintained a court that was characterized by "a strong French atmosphere."[9]
Across the Channel, Normandy was then ruled, at least nominally, by Edward's cousin, William, the illegitimate son of Robert I, sixth duke of Normandy, and Herleve of Falaise. Born in 1027 or 1028, William managed to survive a precarious minority and to consolidate his position as *dux* by 1060 after fourteen years of continuous warfare.[10] Some nine years earlier William, accompanied by a large retinue, appears to have paid a visit upon his friend and cousin, King Edward; according to the *Worcester Chronicle* for 1052 (in reality, 1051), "Ðā sōne cōm Willelm eorl fram ġeondan sǣ mid mycclum werode Frencis[c]ra manna, and sē cynning hine underfēng. And swā feola ġefēran swā him tō onhagode. And lēt hine eft onġēan." Nothing is known about the conversations which the two men had, but "it was so unusual for a reigning prince to leave his own dominions that the visit is unlikely to have been a mere act of courtesy. It is in every way probable that the duke came in order to receive a recognition of his standing as successor-designate to the

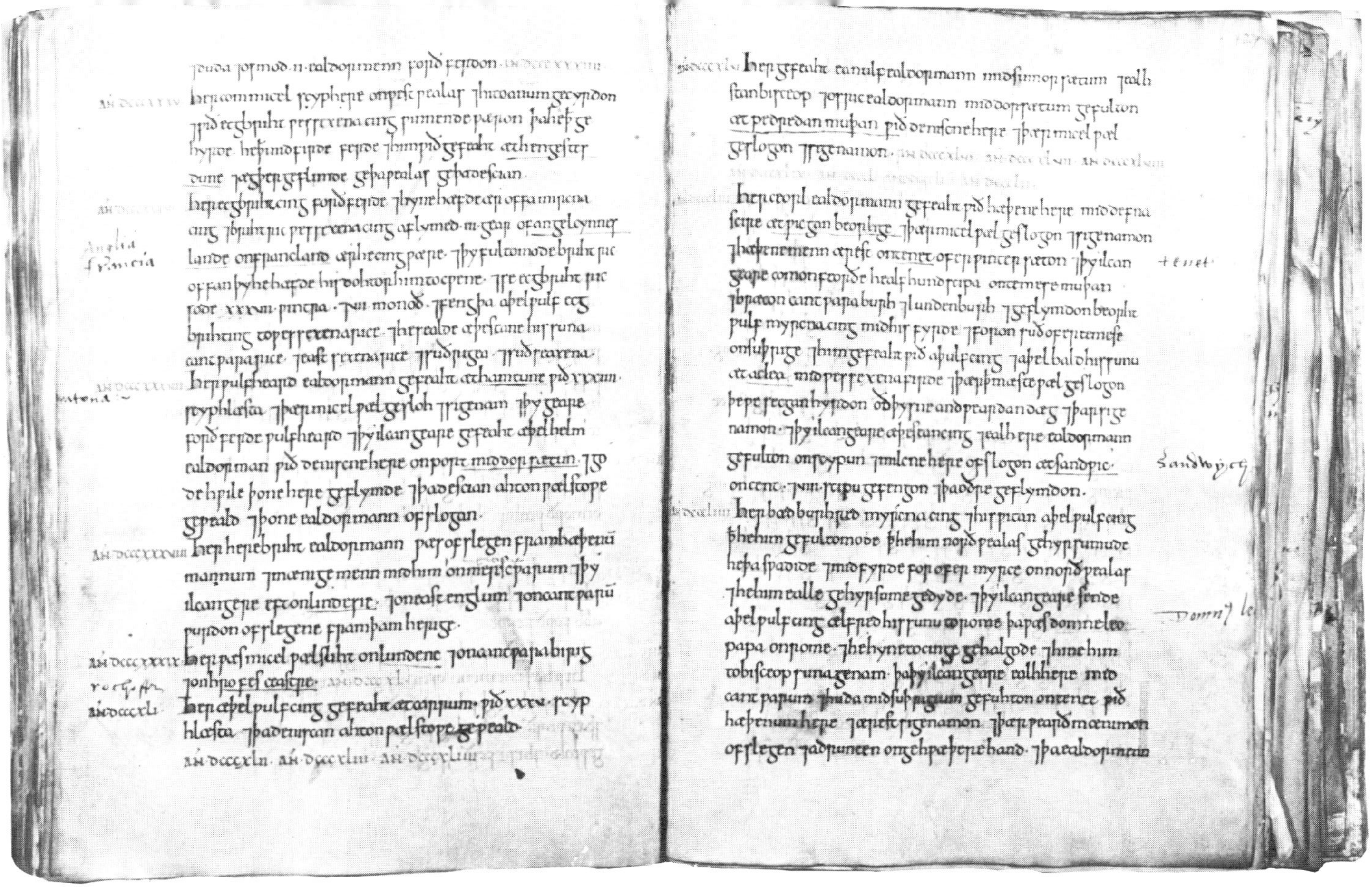

Figure 7. A PAGE FROM THE ANGLO-SAXON CHRONICLE. Courtesy Department of Mss., British Museum.

crown."[11] At that time Edward, who was about fifty and had been married for six years, lacked an heir (he was never to have one). William's subsequent claim to the English throne was further strengthened by an oath of allegiance sworn to him (presumably in 1064) by Edward's chief counsellor, Harold, earl of Wessex, who had emerged as a clear contender for the crown; Harold's future actions, however, would seem to indicate that his journey to Normandy was only undertaken at the behest of King Edward who wished to see William's rival personally confirm the agreement existing between the English sovereign and the Norman duke.

In failing health since the autumn of 1065, Edward died on January 5, 1066, at Westminster where he had gone to attend the consecration of his new abbey of Saint Peter on December 28; he was buried on January 6 (Epiphany), and on that same day Harold was crowned as king. "The indecent haste of these proceedings indicates that the earl's seizure of the throne was premeditated, and that he feared opposition."[12] It is possible that on his deathbed Edward himself had, willingly or not, nominated Harold to be his successor; the leading members of the Confessor's council seem to have been in favor of Harold's selection. But Harold had no claims to royal lineage and owed his elevation primarily to the successful defense of his countrymen that he was expected to make against foreign attack. The king of Norway, Harald Hardrada ("Hard-Counsel"), was known to be projecting an invasion of England, while in nearby Flanders the new king's brother, Tostig (Tosti), deposed earl of Northumbria, was not thought to be immune from a similar ambition.

Harold's coronation elicited an immediate protest from Normandy, but William knew that "his whole political future now depended upon his ability to vindicate his claims by force."[13] The appearance of Halley's comet on April 24 was regarded as a momentous portent by contemporary observers who knew that a crisis impended. Just five months later, on Monday, September 25, Harold defeated the Norwegian king at the Battle of Stamfordbridge (Yorkshire); both Harald Hardrada and Tostig, his ally in the conflict, were killed. Three days later, William who had been waiting in preparation for more than a month, landed at Pevensey on the coast of Sussex. After a hurried march south, Harold engaged William in battle some nine miles north of the (then coastal) town of Hastings on Saturday, October 14. Although probably outnumbered, William's army knew how to fight on horseback and with concerted action; the English lacked a cavalry and archers, which the Normans had as well. Throughout the daylight hours the English held their position, but when Harold was felled by a random arrow their line was broken and by dusk the battle was beyond recovery.[14] The significance of William's victory over Harold would be clear in time; the Anglo-Saxon state had come to a permanent end.

14.6   *A Biographical Sketch of William the Conqueror from the*
Peterborough Chronicle Although William was crowned as King
(William I) of England on Christmas Day in 1066, several years were to
pass before his *de facto* realm extended beyond the southeastern part of
the country; throughout most of his reign, which lasted until his death on
September 9, 1087, he was obliged to rule as a conqueror rather than as a
duly constituted tenant of the kingship. Like Knut before him, William
wished to be regarded as a protector of English law and custom, but he
was well aware that the exigencies of governing a state acquired by force
carried with them the necessity of instituting political and social change.
In general he succeeded in superimposing the feudal structure of his
Norman duchy upon a country which had not known the mounted knight
or castle. Some particulars of his administration, and his character, are
contained in the following excerpt from the *Peterborough Chronicle* for
1086 (in reality, 1087), written by an anonymous Englishman who had at
one time been attached to the king's household. The dialect is Late West
Saxon.

      Ēalā, hū lēas and hū unwrēst is þysses middaneardes wela.
Sē þe wæs ǣrur rīċe cyng, and maniġes landes hlāford, hē næfde
þā ealles landes būton seofon fōtmǣl. And sē þe wæs hwīlon
ġescrīd mid golde, and mid ġimmum; hē læġ þā oferwrogen mid
5   moldan.

      Hē lǣfde æfter him þrēo sunan. Rōdbeard hēt sē yldesta; sē
wæs eorl on Normandīġe æfter him. Sē ōðer hēt Willelm, þe bǣr
æfter him on Engleland þone kinehelm. Sē þridda hēt Heanrīċ,
þām sē fæder becwæð ġersuman unāteallendlīċe.

10   Ġif hwā ġewilniġeð tō ġewitane hū ġedōn mann hē wæs, oððe
hwilċe wurðscipe hē hæfde, oððe hū fela lande hē wǣre hlāford,
ðonne wille wē be him āwrītan swā swā wē hine āġēaton ðe him on
lōcodan and ōðre hwīle on his hīrēde wunedon. Sē cyng Willelm þe
wē embe specað wæs swīðe wīs man and swīðe rīċe, and wurðfulre
15 and strenġere þonne ǣniġ his foregenġa wǣre. Hē wæs milde þām
gōdum mannum þe God lufedon, and ofer eall ġemett stearc þām
mannum þe wiðcwǣdon his willan. On ðām ilcan steode þe God
him ġeūðe þet hē mōste Engleland ġegān, hē ārērde mǣre mynster,
and munecas þǣr ġesætte and hit wæll ġegōdade. On his dagan wæs
20 þet mǣre mynster on Cantwarbyriġ ġetymbrad and ēac swīðe maniġ
ōðer ofer eall Englaland. Ēac þis land wæs swīðe āfylled mid
munecan, and þā leofodan heora līf æfter Sanctus Benedictus
regule; and sē crīstendōm wæs swilċ on his dæġe þet ælċ man
hwæt his hāde tō belumpe, folgade sē þe wolde.

25   Ēac hē wæs swīðe wurðful: þriwa hē bǣr his cynehelm ælċe

ġēare, swā oft swā hē wæs on Englelande. On Ēastron hē hine bær
on Winċeastre, on Pentecosten on Westmynster, on midewintre on
Glēawċeastre; and þænne wǣron mid him ealle þā rīċe men ofer
eall Englaland: arcebiscopas and lēodbiscopas, abbodas and eorlas,
30   þeġnas and cnihtas. Swilċe hē wæs ēac swȳðe stearc man and rǣðe,
swā þet man ne dorste nān þing onġēan his willan dōn. Hē hæfde
eorlas on his bendum þe dydan onġēan his willan. Biscopas hē
sætte of heora biscoprīċe and abbodas of heora abbodrīċe and
þeġnas on cweartern, and æt nēxtan hē ne sparode his āgenne
35   brōðor, Ōdo hēt; hē wæs swīðe rīċe biscop on Normandīġe, on
Baius wæs his biscopstōl, and wæs manna fyrmest tō ēacan þām
cynge, and hē hæfde eorldōm on Englelande, and þonne sē cyng
wæs on Normandīġe, þonne wæs hē mæġester on þissum lande,
and hine hē sætte on cweartern.
40   Betwyx ōðrum þingum nis nā tō forġytane þet gōde frið þe
hē macode on þisan lande, swā þet ān man þe him sylf āht wǣre
mihte faran ofer his rīċe mid his bōsum full goldes unġederad, and
nān man ne dorste slēan ōðerne man, næfde hē nǣfre swā myċel
yfel ġedōn wið þone ōðerne. And ġif hwilċ carlman hǣmde wið
45   wīmman hire unðances, sōna hē forlēas þā limu þe hē mid pleagode.
Hē rīxade ofer Englæland and hit mid his ġēapscipe swā
þurhsmēade þet næs ān hīd landes innan Englalande þet hē nyste
hwā hēo hæfde, oððe hwæs hēo wurð wæs, and syððan on his ġewrit
ġesætt. Brytland him wæs on ġewealde and hē þǣr inne castelas
50   ġewrohte, and þet manncynn mid ealle ġewealde, swilċe ēac Scotland, hē him underþǣdde for his myċele strengþe. Normandīġe þet
land wæs his ġecynde, and ofer þone eorldōm þe Mans is ġehāten
hē rīxade, and ġif hē mōste þā ġȳt twā ġēar libban, hē hæfde Yrlande
mid his werscipe ġewunnon, and wiðūtan ælcon wǣpnon. Witodlīċe
55   on his tīman hæfdon men myċel ġeswinċ and swīðe maniġe tēonan:

castelas he lēt wyrċean,
and earme men swīðe swenċean.
Sē cyng wæs swā swīðe stearc,
and benām of his underþēoddan man maniġ marc
60   goldes and mā hundred punda sēolfres.
Ðet hē nam be wihte and mid myċelan unrihte
of his landlēode for littelre nēode;
hē wæs on ġitsunge befeallan,
and grǣdinæsse hē lufode mid ealle.
65   Hē sætte myċel dēorfrið and hē læġde laga þǣrwið,
þet swā hwā swā slōge heort oððe hinde,

þet hine man sceolde blendian.
Hē forbēad þā heortas, swylċe ēac þā bāras.
Swā swīðe hē lufode þā hēadēor,
70   swilċe hē wǣre heora fæder.
Ēac hē sætte be þām haran þet hī mōsten frēo faran.
His rīċe men hit mǣndon and þā earme men hit beceorodan.
Ac hē wæs swā stīð þet hē ne rōhte heora eallra nīð,
ac hī mōston mid ealle þ·es cynges wille folgian
75   ġif hī woldon libban oððe land habban,
land oððe ēahta, oððe wel his sehta.
Wālāwā þet ǣniġ man sceolde mōdigan swā
hine sylf ūpp āhebban, and ofer ealle men tellan.
Sē ælmihtiga God cȳþæ his sāule mid mildheortnisse
80   ond dō him his synna forġifenesse.

Ðas þing wē habbað be him ġewritene, ǣġðer ġe gōde ġe yfele,
þet þā gōdan men niman æfter þeora gōdnesse and forflēon mid
ealle yfelnesse, and gān on ðone weġ þe ūs lētt tō heofonanrīċe.

14.7   *Notes*

6. *hē lǣfde . . . þrēo sunan.* William and his consort, Matilda (d. 1083),
the daughter of Baldwin V, count of Flanders, had four sons: Robert (Rodbeard),
later Robert II, duke of Normandy, born c.1051–1054, died February 10, 1134;
Richard, born before 1056, accidentally killed in the New Forest c.1075; William
(Willelm), later William II of England, born c.1056–1060, died August 2, 1100;
and Henry (Heanric), later Henry I of England, born 1068, died December 1, 1135.
William's fruitful marriage was further blessed with four, possibly six, daughters.

18. *Hē ārērde mǣre mynster,* Battle Abbey, founded on the site of the
Battle of Hastings by William to commemorate his victory over the English.

20. *mǣre mynster on Cantwarbyriġ,* a rebuilding of Christ Church,
Canterbury, under Lanfranc, archbishop of Canterbury (1070–1089) and a close
adviser to William.

25. *þriwa hē bær his cynehelm* "It was sort of a minor coronation. The
crown was placed on the king's head by one or both of the archbishops, and the
ceremony sometimes occasioned an outbreak of the never-ending jealousy between
Canterbury and York."[15]

27. *midwintre,* Christmas.

35. *Ōdo hēt* The legitimate son of William's mother, Herlene, and
Herluin, *vicomte* of Conteville, Odo was bishop of Bayeux from 1049 to 1090. It is
not clear why William arrested and imprisoned his half brother.

43. *slēan* 'to strike', possibly 'to kill'.

46–47. *hit . . . swā þurhsmēade* a reference to Domesday Book, compiled in
1086 for the purpose of taxation; a survey of all England, "it covered the lands of

every shire, and the property of every magnate in fields, manors, and men—whether slaves or free men, cottagers or farmers—in plough-teams, horses, and other stock, in services and rents."[16]

49. *Brytland,* Wales.

50. *manncynn,* the Welsh.

52. *Mans,* the county of Maine, south of Normandy to which it was annexed by William in 1063.

56. *castelas* "The employment of the castle, not only as a fortified centre of administration but also as a means for conducting a campaign, had already before 1066 become a normal feature of Norman military life. In England, on the contrary, except in Normanized Herefordshire, its use had hardly been adopted, and it was regarded as a continental innovation of doubtful value."[17]

59. *underþēodan man,* the second word is probably a scribal error for *men.*

References

1. The compilation of prefixes, and of suffixes (15.1), is derived from Randolph Quirk and C. L. Wrenn, *An Old English Grammar,* 2nd ed. (London, 1958), pp. 109–119.

2. Ralph W. V. Elliott, *Runes, an Introduction* (Manchester, England, 1959), p. 33.

3. Peter Hunter Blair, *An Introduction to Anglo-Saxon England* (Cambridge, England, 1956), p. 285.

4. Elliott, p. 81.

5. Sir Frank Stenton, *Anglo-Saxon England,* 2nd ed. (Oxford, 1947), p. 151.

6. Elliott, p. 108.

7. Quirk and Wrenn, p. 90.

8. Gwyn Jones, *A History of the Vikings* (London and New York, 1968), p. 232.

9. Albert C. Baugh, *A History of the English Language,* 2nd ed. (New York, 1957), p. 129.

10. David C. Douglas, *William the Conqueror* (Berkeley and Los Angeles, 1964), p. 83.

11. Stenton, pp. 557–558.

12. Douglas, p. 182.

13. Douglas, p. 184.

14. Stenton, p. 587.

15. C. Plummer, ed., *Two of the Saxon Chronicles Parallel,* based on an earlier edition by J. Earle, II (Oxford, 1899, reprinted 1952), p. 274.

16. Stenton, p. 609.

17. Douglas, p. 216.

Chapter 15

15.1 *Word Formation (II): Common Old English Suffixes*
From a functional viewpoint, a prefix generally shifts the semantic force of a given noun, verb, adjective, or adverb; a suffix, however, customarily transforms one part of speech into another, and is therefore a marker of grammatical rather than semantic meaning. Unlike prefixes, which may often be attached to more than one part of speech, suffixes are consistently identified with a specific form only; in themselves, suffixes *define* nouns, verbs, adjectives, and adverbs. The following list includes those suffixes which occur most frequently in Old English:

-að See -*oð*

-bora Also an independent word meaning 'ruler', the suffix *-bora* forms masculine agent nouns from other nouns: *rǣd* 'advice, counsel', *rǣdbora* 'counsellor'. Nouns with *-bora* are declined according to the weak declension (see 4.4.1); other examples are: *æscbora* 'spear-bearer', *mundbora* 'protector', *wǣpenbora* 'warrior'.

-cund An adjectival suffix that imparts the sense 'of the nature of' to the meaning of the root: *æðelcund* 'noble', *dēofolcund* 'devilish', *godcund* 'sacred, divine', *weoroldcund* 'worldly, secular'.

-dōm Also an independent word meaning 'judgment', the suffix *-dōm* forms abstract nouns from other nouns and from adjectives: *þēow* 'slave', *þēowdōm* 'slavery'. Nouns in *-dōm* are always masculine and are declined according to the *a*-declension (see 3.5.1); other examples are: *crīstendōm* 'Christianity', *cynedōm* 'kingdom', *frēodōm* 'freedom', *hlāforddōm* 'lordship', *swicdōm* 'treachery', *wīsdōm* 'wisdom'.

-ed A suffix for the derivation of adjectives, customarily from nouns: *hringed* 'made of rings'.

-en	Used for the derivation of adjectives from nouns: *ǣttren* 'poisonous', *fȳren* 'fiery', *gylden* 'golden', *hwǣten* 'wheaten', *stǣnen* 'stony'.
-end	Used to form masculine agent nouns from verbs: *rǣdan* 'to advise, counsel', *rǣdend* 'ruler'; see 8.4.
-ettan	Used to form weak verbs that are intensive or frequentative in nature: *lāðettan* 'to hate', *ōnettan* 'to hasten'.
-ere	Originally used to form agent nouns from other nouns, *-ere* was ultimately applied to verbal roots as well. Nouns in *-ere* are declined like the *ja-* stem *here* 'army' (see 3.5.4); examples include: *bæcere* 'baker', *bōcere* 'scholar', *cwellere* 'killer', *drincere* 'drinker', *hearpere* 'harper', *leornere* 'learner', *sangere* 'singer', *scipere* 'sailor'. The suffix was occasionally attached to Latin loan words: Latin *grammaticus,* Old English *grammaticere* 'grammarian'.
-fæst	Also an independent word meaning 'firm, fixed', *-fæst* is an adjectival suffix combining with nouns and existing adjectives: *blǣdfæst* 'glorious', *leġerfæst* 'sick', *scamfæst* 'modest', *siġefæst* 'victorious', *sōðfæst* 'righteous', *wīsfæst* 'wise'. Old English *scamfæst,* incidentally, became *shamefaced* in Modern English by the process of folk etymology.
-feald	An adjectival suffix, often combined with numerals to form multiplicatives: *ānfeald* 'single', *hundfeald* 'hundredfold', *maniġfeald* 'manifold, various', *þrīfeald* 'threefold'.
-ful(l)	An adjectival suffix added to existing adjectives and to nouns (especially abstractions): *andġytfull* 'sensible', *eġesfull* 'terrible', *ġeornfull* 'eager', *nīþfull* 'envious', *synnfull* 'sinful'.
-hād	Also an independent word with the meanings 'condition, state, nature', *-hād* forms masculine abstract nouns from concrete nouns; the abstractions with *-hād* are declined according to the *a*-declension (see 3.5.1). Examples are: *camphād* 'warfare', *ċildhād* 'childhood', *cynehād* 'kinghood', *crithād* 'boyhood', *mæġðhād* 'virginity', *þēowhād* 'servitude', *woruldhād* 'secular state'.
-iġ	Used to form adjectives, primarily from nouns: *blōdiġ* 'bloody', *ġeþyldiġ* 'patient', *grǣdiġ* 'greedy', *spēdiġ* 'wealthy', *wlitiġ* 'beautiful'.
-ing	A nominal suffix that forms concrete nouns from adjectives and from other nouns; *-ing* often imparts a sense of 'derived from' or 'associated with' to the meaning of the root, and, hence, is sometimes the mark of a patronymic, e.g., *Hrēþling* 'son of Hrethel', *Wǣlsing* 'son of Wæls'. Nouns in *-ing* are masculine and are declined according to the *a*-declension (see 3.5.1); examples include: *æðeling* 'prince, son of a noble', *cyning* 'king', *earming* 'poor wretch', *wīċing* 'viking'. From nouns like *æðeling* and *lȳtling* 'child', a suffix *-ling* was detached and often used to form nouns designating a person: *dēorling* 'favorite, darling', *ġeongling* 'a youth', *sibbling* 'relative', *yrðling* 'farmer'.
-isc	Converts nouns, often having a national or ethnic denotation, into adjectives, some of which may themselves function as substantives: *ċildisc* 'childish', *denisc* 'Danish', *englisc* 'English, the English language', *entisc* 'of giants', *mennisc* 'human, mankind', *samaritanisc* 'Samaritan', *tigrisc* (from Latin *tigris* 'tiger') 'of tigers'.

-lāc   Forms neuter abstract nouns declined according to the *a*-declension (see
3.5.2); examples include: *feohtlāc* 'fighting', *rēaflāc* 'robbery', *wedlāc* 'wed-
lock', *wītelāc* 'punishment'.

-læċan   Forms weak verbs from adjectives and nouns: *ānlǣċan* 'to unite', *nēalǣċan*
'to approach'.

-lēas   An independent adjective meaning 'without, free from, bereft of', *-lēas*
combines with nouns to form adjectives in which the sense 'bereft of' is
applied to the root: *ārlēas* 'impious', *bānlēas* 'boneless', *cwidelēas* 'speech-
less', *drēamlēas* 'joyless', *mæġenlēas* 'powerless', *tōþlēas* 'toothless', *winelēas* 'friendless'.

-līċ   Used with high frequency to form adjectives from nouns and existing adjectives: *ǣnlīċ* 'unique', *cynelīċ* 'royal', *ġeomorlīċ* 'sad', *heofonlīċ* 'heavenly',
mǣrlīċ 'famous', *sellīċ* 'rare', *torhtlīċ* 'glorious'; see also 9.3.

-ling   See *-ing*.

-oð(-að) A nominal suffix, *-oð* forms masculine nouns many of which are abstractions; nouns in *-oð* are declined according to the *a*-declension (see 3.5.1).
Examples include: *drohtoð* 'way of life', *faroð* 'sea', *hlēonað* 'shelter', *langað*
'longing', *waroð* 'share'.

-nes(s) A nominal suffix, also spelled *-nis, -nys,* used to form feminine abstract
nouns, often from adjectives; nouns in *-nes* are declined according like
the *jō*-stem noun *ecg* 'edge' (see 4.1.4). Examples include: *æþelnes* 'nobility',
beorhtnes 'brightness', *ēadiġnes* 'prosperity', *mildheortnes* 'mercy', *strangnes*
'strength', *þrīnes* 'trinity'.

-scipe   Used to form masculine abstract nouns from adjectives and other nouns;
nouns in *-scipe* are declined according to the *i*-declension (see 12.3.1). Examples include: *bēorscipe* 'feast', *eorlscipe* 'courage', *frēondscipe* 'friendship', *gōdscipe* 'goodness', *hǣþenscipe* 'paganism', *þeġenscipe* 'service',
wǣrscipe 'prudence'.

-sian   Forms weak verbs from adjectives and nouns: *mǣrsian* 'to proclaim',
yrsian 'to be angry'.

-ung   Often spelled *-ing,* used in the formation of feminine abstract nouns like
leornung 'learning'; see 13.1.2.

-weard   An adjectival suffix that imparts the meaning 'in the direction of' to the
root: *ēastenweard* 'eastward', *hāmweard* 'homeward', *niþerweard* 'downward'.

15.2   *The Old English Alphabet*   As noted above, the only
writing system which served Anglo-Saxon scribes in their daily labors
was a form of the Roman alphabet; it was not, however, a script that had
been directly acquired from the Italian peninsula. When the Roman
legions withdrew from Britain in the first half of the fifth century they
took their alphabet with them, and it did not reappear on the island until
the coming of Saint Augustine in 597. The sixth-century Italian hand
introduced by the Roman missionaries was then used in England into
the eighth century, during which it was gradually but completely superseded by an Irish modification of the Roman alphabet, a national hand

known as "Insular." As the power and influence of Imperial Rome declined, five national scripts began to assume distinctive characteristics; among those of Italy, Spain, Gaul, and Germania was the handwriting of Ireland, which in one variety consisted of long and narrow minuscules often marked by initial strokes tapered downward into points. That so-called "pointed" hand (still used for the writing of Irish today) was to become the predominant script of the Anglo-Saxons until the Norman Conquest.

Begun in the fourth century, the conversion of the Irish to Christianity was completed in the fifth by the legendary Saint Patrick (?385–?461), who, depending upon the reliability of tradition, may also have been responsible for the introduction of the "Irish" hand from Gaul where he had trained for the priesthood. In any event, Irish missionaries of the seventh century brought the Insular script to Northern England, where it spread to the south and ultimately eclipsed the style of writing employed by the first missionaries from Rome;[1] the Italian hand, incidentally, had been largely restricted to the transcription of Latin and was never more than an experimental medium for Old English. The oldest documents in that language show the adoption of Keltic lettering.

The Insular hand underwent some inevitable alterations in England before being stabilized in a form that was specifically Anglo-Saxon; individual characters were to a certain extent transformed, and the alphabet, originally designed for Latin, was slightly adjusted for the necessary expression of several Old English speech sounds. In the later stages of Classical Greek, the letter *thēta* (θ) stood for the voiceless dental fricative [θ], a speech sound alien to Latin; the Romans, therefore, used the digraph *th* to represent that consonant in words which they transliterated from Greek, e.g., *theatrum* 'theater' from *theatron* (θέατρον). Following Roman practice Anglo-Saxon scribes at first wrote [θ], as in *þū*, with the same digraph, but *th* "in such Greek words having it as entered (through Latin) into the vernaculars of Western Europe, was pronounced [t] by the relatively unlearned, to whom therefore *th* suggested rather [th] or even merely [t] (hardly distinguishable from [th]), and it was accordingly always in danger of seeming to be merely a complex and pretentious way of writing *t*."[2] An attempt to resolve the ambiguity of *th* occurred about 900 when the runic symbol þ (*thorn*), which had the sound value [θ], was appropriated for the Old English alphabet. But then the runic character acquired the further value of [ð], as in *ōþer*, the voiced counterpart of [θ]; that voiced fricative had initially been written with a crossed Insular *d*, now called *eth* (ð). Somewhat illogically, both þ and ð were standardized for both [θ] and [ð], with no consequent advance in the clarity of Old English spelling. During the Middle English period ð disappeared before þ, which continued in use until about 1400 when the digraph *th* was reintroduced for the consonantal values still carried by it in Modern English. The Anglo-Saxon alphabet also contained one other runic symbol, namely Ᵽ (*wynn* 'joy') which stood for the semi-vowel [w]. Although the earliest manuscripts show *u* and *uu* for that sound, the fact that *u* had come to signify [v] instead of [w] in Latin long before the seventh century interferred with the status of *u* as a designation for [w] in Old English. Maintained into Middle English, Ᵽ was eventually replaced by *w,* a ligatured form of *uu* (double-*u*) that was brought to England by Norman scribes from the Continent where the original English spelling had in the meantime gained currency.[3] (Some modern editions of Old English texts are printed with Ᵽ rather than with *w.*) Also lost from the Old English version of the Insular hand was the Anglo-Latin digraph *æ* (*ash*), distinctive forms of *f, g, i, r, s, t, y,* and, among other abbreviations, the very common one for the conjunction 'and' (ꝛ); conversely, the previously rare letters, *k, q,* and *z,* were employed with increasing frequency after the close of the Old English period. After 1000, the Carolingian hand of France, developed at the end of the eighth century (probably under the influence of the Anglo-Irish script), begins to appear in Old English manuscripts, "at first only in French and Latin words and passages, but later in English ones as well."[4] By the middle of the twelfth century French handwriting had become the established norm in England.

15.3   *Sound Changes (III): The Old English Development of West Germanic Consonants*   The immediate source of the Old English consonantal system had the following configuration in West Germanic:

voiceless stops:	p	t	k	
voiced stops:	b	d	g	
voiceless fricatives:	f	þ	s	χ h
voiced fricatives:	ƀ	ǥ		
nasals:	m	n	ŋ	
liquids:	l	r		
semi-vowels:	w	j		

On an individual basis, the consonants of West Germanic underwent fewer modifications than the vowels as they assumed forms characteristic of Old English; some consonantal sounds did not change at all, and others were affected only in rather limited phonetic contexts. Often the word position (initial, medial, final) of a particular consonant is an important factor in its development.

West Germanic	**Old English Development**
p	The voiceless bilabial stop [p] remained unmodified in all positions: Gothic *páida,* OE *pād* 'cloak'; OI *openn,* OS *opan,* OE *open* 'open'; Gothic *diups,* OS *diop,* OE *dēop* 'deep'.

t   The voiceless dental stop [t] remained unmodified in all positions: Gothic *tunþus,* OS *tand,* OE *tōþ* 'tooth'; Gothic *itan,* OI *eta,* OS and OE *etan* 'to eat'; Gothic *nahts,* OS and OHG *naht,* OE *neaht* 'night'.

k   a) The voiceless velar stop [k], written *c* in Old English, remained unmodified in initial position when followed by a consonant, a back vowel, or a front vowel produced by *i*-mutation of an orginal back vowel: Gothic *kniu,* OE *cnēo* 'knee'; Gothic *kunþs* OE *cūþ* 'known'; OE *cemban* 'to comb' from earlier **kambjan.* In medial position, [k] also remained when contiguous to a consonant, or to original back vowels: Gothic *akrs,* OE *æcer* 'field' from earlier **akraz;* OE *macian* 'to make' from earlier **makōjan.* In final position, [k] remained when preceded by a consonant, or an original back vowel: OS and OHG *werk,* OE *weorc* 'work'; OE *blæc* from earlier **blakaz.*

b) When [k] was contiguous to a front vowel (*ĭ, ē̆, æ̆*) or the umlaut of a front vowel, either singly or as the first element of a diphthong, the point of articulation was fronted and the manner of articulation eventually shifted to the voiceless, alveopalatal, affricated stop [č]; the spelling of the new sound remained *c* (*ċ*). The change of [k] to [č] was effected in initial, medial, and final position; in medial position it also occurred before a following *i, ī,* or *j.* Under the conditions stated, a geminated [kk] became [čč], and the consonant cluster [ŋk] became [ŋč]. Some examples of the sound shift are: *ċēosan* 'to choose' (*cf.* Gothic *kiusan*), *ċinn* 'chin' (*cf.* Gothic *kinn* 'cheek'); *sēċan* 'to seek' from earlier **sōkjan, læ̆ċe* 'physician' (*cf.* Gothic *lēkeis*); *benċ* 'bench' from earlier **bankiz, bēċ* 'books' from earlier **bōkiz, iċ* 'I' (*cf.* Gothic *ik*).

b   The voiced bilabial stop [b], remained unmodified in all positions: OS, OHG, OE *beran* 'to bear'; OHG and OE *climban* 'to climb'; Gothic *dumbs,* OI *dumbr,* OHG *tumb,* OE *dumb* 'dumb'.

d   The voiced dental stop [d] remained the same in all positions: Gothic *dags,* OI *dagr,* OS *dag,* OHG *tag,* OE *dæġ;* OI *faðer,* OS *fadar,* OHG *fater,* OE *fæder* 'father'; Gothic *blōþ,* OI *blōð,* OS *blōd,* OHG *bluot,* OE *blōd* 'blood'.

g   In West Germanic, the voiced velar stop [g] occurred only in the two clusters [gg] and [ŋg]; the doubled consonant had a dual source in Proto-Germanic: *ɡn* and *ɡj.* When derived from *ɡn,* West Germanic [ɡɡ] remained the same in Old English (*dogga* 'dog', *frogga* 'frog'), but when derived from *ɡj,* the West Germanic cluster became the voiced, alveopalatal, affricated stop [ǰ] in Old English, generally represented by the digraph -*cg*-*:* Gothic *bugjan,* OE *bycgan* 'to buy', Gothic *lagjan,* OE *lecgan* 'to lay'. In the West Germanic combination [ŋɡ], the velar stop remained unmodified in Old English when followed by a back vowel: *cyning* 'king' from earlier **kuniŋgaz, lang* 'long' from earlier **laŋgaz.* When followed by a front vowel or *j,* the [g] became [ǰ]: *senġān* [senǰan] 'to singe' from earlier **saŋgjan, streŋ* [strenǰ] 'string' from earlier **straŋgiz.*

f   The voiceless labial fricative [f] was at first retained in all positions, but became the corresponding voiced fricative [v] by about 700 when it occurred medially between two voiced sounds: Gothic and OHG *fimf,* OS and OE *fīf* 'five', OI, OS, OHG, OE *hof* 'court, dwelling', Gothic *gaskafts,* OE *ġesceaft* 'creation'; but *heofon* 'heaven', *seolfor* 'silver', *wulfas* 'wolves', etc. where *f* represents [v] as in *even.*

þ   The voiceless dental fricative [θ] was at first retained in all positions, but became the corresponding voiced fricative [ð] by about 700 when it occurred medially between two voiced sounds: Gothic *þūsundi,* OHG *dūsunt,* OE *þūsend* 'thousand', Gothic *áiþ* (accusative), OHG *eid,* OE *āþ* 'oath'; but *brōþor* 'brother', *eorþe* 'earth', *feþer* 'feather', etc. where *þ* represents [ð], the initial sound of *then.* When doubled, *þ* was always voiceless.

s   The voiceless alveolar fricative [s] was at first retained in all positions, but became the corresponding voiced fricative [z] by about 700 when it occurred medially between two voiced sounds: Gothic *sáiws,* OS and OHG *sēo,* OE *sǣ* 'sea', Gothic, OI, OS, OHG, OE *hūs* 'house', OS *gēst,* OHG *geist,* OE *gāst* 'spirit'; but *ċēosan* 'to choose', *hǣsl* 'hazel bush', *nosu* 'nose', *wesan* 'to be', etc. where *s* represents [z], the initial sound of *zone.* The consonant cluster *sk* [sk] became the voiceless alveopalatal fricative [š] (spelled *sc*) in most positions during the Old English period: Gothic *fisks,* OI *fiskr,* OE *fisc* 'fish' (see 2.4.7).

χ

Spelled *h* in Old English, the voiceless, velar fricative [χ] occurred in word-initial position before other consonants: OS *hwē,* OHG *hwer,* OE *hwā* 'who'. Medially, [χ] was retained before voiceless consonants and when doubled: Gothic, OS, OHG *brāhta,* OE *brōhte* 'he brought'; *teohhian* 'to intend, propose'. The combination [χs] (spelled *hs*) became [ks] (spelled *x*): *weahsan* 'to grow', later *weaxan.* About 700, medial [χ] was lost between two vowels or between a diphthong and a vowel: *tā* 'toe' from earlier **tāhe, flēon* 'to flee' from earlier **flēohan;* see also 12.1. Medial [χ] also disappeared before *s* plus a consonant (*fȳst* 'fist' from earlier **fūχstiz*); between a vowel or diphthong and a following liquid or nasal (*hēla* 'heel' from earlier **hōhila*); and between a liquid and a following vowel (*mēares* 'of a horse' from earlier **mearhes*). In final position, [χ] was retained: OS and OHG *hōh,* OE *hēah* 'high', OS *thurh,* OHG *durh,* OE *þurh* 'through'.

h

Reflecting the situation in West Germanic, where the voiceless glottal fricative [h] arose from [χ] in word-initial position before vowels, the distribution of [h] in Old English is restricted to that same environment: Gothic *haban,* OI *hafa,* OHG *habēn,* OE *habban* 'to have'.

ƀ

The voiced bilabial fricative [ƀ] occurred only in medial and final position in West Germanic. Medial [ƀ] became [v] (spelled *f*): Gothic *giban,* OHG *geban,* OE *ġiefan* 'to give'; OHG *wībe* (dative), OE *wīfe* (dative) 'woman'. Final [ƀ] became [f] (also spelled *f*): OHG *wīb,* OE *wīf* 'woman'.

ɡ

The voiced velar fricative [ɡ] occurred in all positions in West Germanic; it underwent a varied development in Old English. In initial position before a back vowel, a consonant, or a front vowel produced by *i*-umlaut of an original back vowel [ɡ] became the voiced velar stop [g]: Gothic *gōþs,* OI *gōðr,* OS *gōd,* OHG *guot,* OE *gōd* 'good'; Gothic, OS, OHG *gras,* OE *græs* 'grass'; OE *gēs* 'geese' from earlier **gōsi.* Before a front vowel (or the umlaut of a front vowel), either singly or as the first element of a diphthong, [ɡ] was at first fronted, and then shifted to the palatal glide [y]; the spelling remained *g* (*ġ*). Examples of the shift include: Gothic, OI, OS, *gaf* 'he gave', but OE *ġeaf;* Gothic *giutan,* OS *giotan* 'to pour out' but OE *ġeotan;* Gothic *gasts,* OI *gestr,* OS and OHG *gast* 'guest', but OE *ġiest.* In medial position, [ɡ] remained when contiguous to original back vowels: Gothic *áugō,* OI *auga,* OS *ōga,* OHG *ouga,* OE *ēage* 'eye'. When originally followed by a front vowel or by *i, ī,* or *j,* [ɡ] became [y]: *bīeġan* 'to bend' from earlier **baugjan; wǣġ* 'wave' from earlier **wǣɡiz; byrġ* (dative singular) 'city' from earlier **burġi.* At the end of a syllable within a word, [ɡ] also became [y] when preceded by a front vowel: *breġdan* 'to move quickly', *sæġde* 'he said'. Between two front vowels, [ɡ] likewise became [y]: *fæġer* 'fair', *mæġen* 'strength', *weġes* (genitive singular) 'way'. The West Germanic geminate [ɡɡ] became [ǰ] (spelled with the digraph *-cg-*) when followed by *i, ī,* or *j:* WGmc **hruɡɡjaz,* OE *hrycg* 'ridge'. In word-final position [ɡ] was palatalized to [y] when preceded by a front vowel: *dæġ* 'day', *weġ* 'way', *æniġ* 'any', *hāliġ* 'holy'. Otherwise, final [ɡ] was unchanged in early Old English, but later tended to become the corresponding voiceless fricative [χ] (spelled *h*); the de-voicing of [ɡ] is attested by pairs such as *bēag, bēah* 'ring', *burg, burh* 'fortress', *dāg, dāh* 'dough', *ġenōg, ġenōh* 'enough', *stāg, stāh* 'he ascended'.

m

The bilabial nasal [m] was customarily retained in all positions: Gothic *mēna,* OS and OHG *māno,* OE *mōna* 'moon'; Gothic *guma,* OS *gumo,* OHG *gomo,* OE *guma* 'man'; OS, OHG, OE *rūm* 'room'. When preceded by a vowel and followed by *f, þ,* or *s,* however, [m] disappeared with compensatory lengthening of the vowel: OHG *fimf,* OE *fīf* 'five'.

n

The dental nasal [n] was customarily retained in all positions: Gothic *namō,* OS and OHG *namo,* OE *nama* 'name'; Gothic *sunus,* OS, OHG, OE *sunu* 'son'; Gothic *stains,* OS *stēn,* OHG *stein,* OE *stān* 'stone'. Like [m], [n] disappeared when preceded by a vowel and followed by *f, þ,* or *s:* Gothic *uns,* OE *ūs* 'us' with compensatory lengthening of the vowel.

ŋ

The velar nasal [ŋ] occurred only in medial position before [g] and [k]; and its Old English development was dependent upon the two stop consonants. If [g] and [k] were not palatalized, then [ŋ] likewise did not change: Gothic *briggan* [*briŋgan*], OHG *bringan,* OE *bringan* 'to bring' with *n* for [ŋ]; Gothic *drigkan* [*driŋkan*], OS *drinkan,* OHG *trinkan,* OE *drincan* 'to drink' with *n* for [ŋ]. If [g] and [k] were palatalized, then [ŋ] became [n]: *strenġ* [*strenĵ*] 'string' from earlier **straŋgiz; benċ* [*benc*] 'bench' from earlier **baŋkiz.*

l

The dental liquid [l] remained in all positions: OI *ljōðr,* OS *liud,* OHG *liut,* OE *lēod* 'people, nation'; Gothic *hilpan,* OI *hjalpa,* OS *helpan,* OHG *helfan,* OE *helpan* 'to help'; Gothic *fugls,* OI *fugl,* OS *fugal,* OHG *fogal,* OE *fugol* 'bird'.

r

The alveolar liquid [r] remained in all positions: Gothic *ráups,* OI *rauðr,* OS *rōd,* OHG *rōt,* OE *rēad* 'red'; Gothic *waúrd,* OS *word,* OHG *wort,* OE *word* 'word'; OI *mōðir,* OS *mōdar,* OHG *muoter,* OE *mōdor* 'mother'.

w

The labial semi-vowel, or glide, [w] generally remained in initial and medial position: OS *wīd,* OHG *wīt,* OE *wīd* 'wide'; Gothic *speiwan,* OS, OHG, OE *spīwan* 'to spit, spew'. In final position [w] became the vowel [u], later [ɔ]: *bearu* (*bearo*) 'grove', *bearwes* 'of a grove'. When preceded by a short vowel, [u] combined with that vowel to form a long diphthong: *cnēo* 'knee' from earlier **knew, trēo* 'tree' from earlier **trew.* When preceded by a long vowel, a long diphthong, or a long root, the [u] disappeared: Gothic *áiw,* OE *ā* 'always', Gothic *hráiw,* OE *hrā* 'corpse'. In time, however, the [w], which had become [u] before being lost, was frequently restored on the analogy of inflected forms like *bearwes* where it had been retained.

j

The palatal semi-vowel, or glide, [y] was retained in initial position where it is represented by various spellings: *g* (*ġ*), *ge* (*ġe*), *gi* (*ġi*), and *i;* thus a word like *ġeong* 'young' (OS and OHG *jung*) was also written *ġiong* and *iung.* In medial position between vowels, where the sound was also kept, [y] is spelled *g* (*ġ*) or *ge* (*ġe*): *ċīeġan, ċīeġean* 'to call, name' from earlier **kaujan.* Medial [y] was likewise retained after a short syllable ending in [r], and again written in different ways: *g* (*ġ*), *ge* (*ġe*), *i, ig* (*iġ*), *ige* (*iġe*); thus *herġan, herġean, herian, heriġan,* or *heriġean* 'to praise'. After a long syllable ending in a consonant, medial [y] became at first vocalic ([i]) and then disappeared about 700: PGmc *satjan, WGmc *sattjan, POE *sættjan, later *settian, OE settan 'to set' (cf. OS settian). In final position, [y], spelled g (ġ), was retained after long vowels and diphthongs: ēġ, īeġ 'island' (cf. OI ey).

15.3.1   *The Consonants of Germanic and Their Development in Old English: A Tabular Summary*

PGmc	WGmc	Old English					
		Initial		Medial		Final	
		Sound	Spelling	Sound	Spelling	Sound	Spelling
p	p	[p]	p	[p]	p	[p]	p
t	t	[t]	t	[t]	t	[t]	t
k	k	[k]	c	[k]	c	[k]	c
		[č]	ċ	[č]	ċ	[č]	ċ
b	b	[b]	b	[b]	b	[b]	b
d, ð	d	[d]	d	[d]	d	[d]	d
ɣn	gg			[g]	gg		
ɣj	gg			[ǰ]	cg	[ǰ]	cg
ŋg	ŋg			[ŋg]	ng	[ŋg]	ng
				[ŋǰ]	nġ	[ŋǰ]	nġ
				[nj]	nġ	[nj]	nġ
f	f	[f]	f	[f]	f	[f]	f
				[v]	f		
þ	þ	[θ]	þ, ð	[θ]	þ, þþ, ð, ðð	[θ]	þ, þþ, ð, ðð
				[ð]	þ, ð		
s	s	[s]	s	[s]	s	[s]	s
				[z]	s		
sk	sk	[š]	sc	[š]	sc	[š]	sc
χ	{ χ	[χ]	h	[χ]	h	[χ]	h
	h	[h]	h				
ƀ	ƀ			[v]	f	[f]	f
ǥ	ǥ	[g]	g	[ǥ]	g	[ǥ]	g
		[y]	ġ	[y]	ġ	[y]	ġ
m	m	[m]	m	[m]	m	[m]	m
n	n	[n]	n	[n]	n	[n]	n
ŋ	ŋ			[ŋ]	n		
				[n]	n		
l	l	[l]	l	[l]	l	[l]	l
r, z	r	[r]	r	[r]	r	[r]	r
w	w	[w]	w	[w]	w	[u]	u
j	j	[y]	ġ, ġe, ġi, i	[y]	ġ, ġe, i, iġ, iġe	[y]	ġ

15.4   *Loanwords in Old English* It is a fact without need of demonstration that the vocabulary of Modern English is a compound blended from native and foreign elements; although to a far lesser degree, the lexical inventory of Old English was also a mixture of the indigenous and the borrowed. A language with a historical span of six and one-half centuries, and one which was spoken by a people who were the recipients of attention from such diverse outside groups as the Roman Church and the Danish Vikings, and who at one time achieved the highest standards of learning and scholarship in western Europe, is a language not likely to have remained forever in a state of lexical purity. The confederation of low Germanic dialects that made its appearance in fifth-century Britain was, in fact, already marked by the importation of Latin words; Germanic tribes in contact with Roman civilization along the northern frontiers of the Empire appear to have adapted some 175 Latin terms to their own speech in the first centuries of the Christian era. At that time, the loanwords were drawn largely from the spheres of agriculture, trade, military affairs, and from the emollients of Roman daily life; Old English survivals include *ancor* 'anchor' from Latin *ancora, camp* 'battle' from *campus* 'field, field of battle', *cȳse* 'cheese' from *cāseus, mīl* 'mile' from *mīlia [passuum]* 'a thousand [of paces]', *miltestre* 'prostitute' from *meretrīx, mynet* 'coin, money' from *monēta, mydd* 'bushel' from *modius, strǣt* 'paved road' from *[uia] strāta* '[way] paved', *tæpped (teped)* 'tapestry, carpet' from *tapēte,* and *wīn* 'wine' from *uīnum.* The influence of foreign idioms upon Old English proper begins, of course, not on the Continent but in the new island home of the Anglo-Saxons where renewed borrowing from Latin was subsequently to occur in addition to borrowing from the Scandinavian dialects. (The history of French loanwords in English does not begin until after the Norman Conquest, and is therefore not a part of Old English studies.)

15.4.1   *The Latin Influence* It is convenient to distinguish two periods during which Latin loanwords were received into Old English. In the first period, extending to about 650, words from the Italic language were affected (when possible) by those sound changes that were operative in Old English until toward the end of the seventh century; thus, an early borrowing like Latin *cesta* (Classical Latin *cista*) 'chest, box' became *čiest, čyst* in Old English, the initial [k] of *cesta* being palatalized to [č] before a following front vowel (see 15.3). Having small opportunity for any direct contact with native speakers of Latin, the Anglo-Saxons clearly obtained some of their earliest borrowings from Keltic Britons who had accommodated over 600 Latin words in *their* speech;[5] in 650 the fullest impact of Christianity upon Anglo-Saxon culture was yet to come, and most Latin terms acquired before that time were of a practical and popular (non-scholarly) nature. Included among them are: *candel* 'candle' from *candēla, ċēac* 'jug' from *caucus, ċealc* 'plaster' from *calcem* (accusative singular of *calx* 'lime, chalk'), *copor* 'copper' from *cuprum, disċ* 'dish' from *discus, ġimm* 'gem' from *gemma, Lǣden* 'Latin' from *Latīna, leahtrīċ* 'lettuce' from *lactūca, mæġester* 'chief, teacher' from *magister, peru* 'pear' from *pirum, port* 'harbor' from *portus, senop* 'mustard' from *sināpi,* and *tīġle* 'tile' from *tēgula.* Probably through Keltic, a widespread early borrowing is the Latin neuter plural *castra* 'camp, encampment' for which the standard Old English *ċeaster* (from earlier **ċæster*) developed the meaning 'castle, fort, town'; by itself or as the second element of a compound, and with dialectal differences, the word was frequently used for place-names, some of which, like *Colchester,* do in fact commemorate the site of an ancient Roman settlement: *Caister, Casterton, Castor, Chester, Chesterfield, Chesterton, Colchester, Doncaster, Dorchester, Exeter* (earlier *Execestre*), *Gloucester, Lancaster, Manchester, Winchester,* and *Worcester.*

According to one authority,[6] 111 Latin words found their way into Old English between 450 and approximately 650; between 650 and the Norman Conquest the estimated number of borrowings increased more than twofold. As might be expected, the second period of borrowing is characterized by the importation of many scholarly and religious words; furthermore, the Old English sound changes having terminated by the close of the seventh century, the new expressions were not affected by phenomena like palatalization. The later group of loanwords included: *alter* 'altar' from *altar, apostol* 'apostle' from *apostolus, cālend* 'the beginning of a month' from *calendae* 'the first day of a month', *cell* 'cell' from *cella, crēda* 'creed' from *crēdō* 'I believe', *cristalla* 'crystal' from *crystallum, dēmon* 'demon' from *daemōn, īdol* 'idol' from *īdolum, mæsse* 'mass' from *missa, nepte* 'catnip' from *nepeta, paper* 'paper' from *papȳrus, scōl* 'school' from *schola, templ* 'temple' from *templum, tītol* 'title' from *tītulus;* and, in their Modern English spelling: *alb, antiphoner, balsam, basilica, cantor, circle, cloister, coriander, cucumber, dirge, font, history, laurel, martyr, plaster* (medicinal), *prophet, scorpion, scrofula, tiger, verse.* Although Latin was invariably the immediate source, some words, for example *basilica, martyr, school,* were ultimately of Greek origin. Not infrequently, only the meaning of a word was borrowed and then applied to an existing Old English term; thus, Latin *baptizāre* 'to baptize' was rendered by *fullian* 'to consecrate', *patriarcha* by *hēahfæder* 'high father', and *trinitas* 'trinity' by *þrines* 'threeness'. (Such words are called 'loan translations', or *calques* from the French noun meaning 'a tracing, copy'.) Proper names were occasionally declined with their Latin endings (*for ðiosum ðingum manade Paulus Tīmotheum his cniht* 'for these things Paul admonished his disciple,

Timothy'), but common nouns were inflected on the pattern of Old English paradigms; given the infinitival ending *-ian*, Latin verbs became weak: Latin *saltāre*, Old English *sealtian* 'to dance'. If Continental borrowings are included in the total, the attested number of Latin words to have entered Old English before 1066 exceeds 500.

15.4.2   *The Scandinavian Influence*   The influence of North Germanic speech upon Old English occurred at a time when the national languages, and the national states, of modern Scandinavia were in the initial stages of formation; the earliest Scandinavian loanwords in English, therefore, were extractions from a relatively undifferentiated idiom which may satisfactorily be described with general terms like "Norse" or "Scandinavian," even though it is convenient to cite cognates and the underlying forms for loanwords from Old Icelandic specifically. The respective homelands of those Scandinavians who came to England may enable historians to separate "Danes" from "Norwegians," but linguists are seldom in a position to view the origin of a borrowed word as specifically Danish or Norwegian. Although the Norse element in Old English documents is in reality small (about forty words), the fact that Anglo-Saxon speech was affected by the Viking presence is confirmed by the Scandinavian loanwords which later appear in Middle English texts; of approximately 2,650 words in *Sir Gawain and the Green Knight,* for example, some 250 are North Germanic by etymology.[7] In general, the borrowed words dealt with "ideas, persons, or things which were either peculiarly Scandinavian, or of which the OE conception had been modified by contact with the Scandinavian civilization. Naturally, they are found chiefly in late texts, especially in the *Chronicle* after 1000."[8]

The Scandinavian influence upon Old English was manifested in various ways. The North Germanic dialects were, of course, linguistically much closer to Old English than Latin, and both Vikings and Anglo-Saxons used words which were virtually identical in sound and meaning. If Old English were not attested until after the Scandinavian incursions, it would be impossible to recognize West Germanic as the true source for common nouns like *father, folk, house, man, summer, wife,* for verbs like *bring, can, come, see, stand, think,* and for modifiers like *best, better, full, under, well,* and *wise.*[9] The complete or partial assimilation to the phonological patterns of Old English was, therefore, greatly facilitated in the case of a lexical item with a Scandinavian pedigree; for example, Old Icelandic *brúðlaup, félagi, lög,* and *þjónusta* became Old English *brýdhlōp* 'wedding', *fēolaga* 'partner' ('fellow'), *lagu* 'law', and *þēnest* 'service' respectively. A few words required no Anglicization: OI, OE *grið* 'truce'; OI, OE *lið* 'fleet'; OI *rán*, OE *rān* 'robbery, rapine'. On the other hand, because all Scandinavian borrowings postdated the completion of Old English sound changes, many Norse loanwords are conspicuous for their "divergent" consonantal or vocalic structure. The Proto-Germanic consonant cluster [sk] which became [š] (*sc*) in Old English (see 15.3), remained the same in North Germanic, as reflected in the following Scandinavian importations: *scant, skill, skin, skirt* (*cf.* the native *shirt*), *skull, sky,* and *to bask, scare, scoff, scowl, scream, scrub, skip.* Also, initial [k] and [g] before front vowels were not palatalized to [č] and [y] in Norse (see 15.3), accounting for the pronunciation of loanwords like *kick, kindle, get, gift* (*cf.* Chaucerian *yift*), *give* (*cf.* Chaucerian *yive*), and *guild* (spelled *gilde* in Middle English). In addition, the Proto-Germanic diphthong *ai* became *ā* in Old English (later [ow] in Modern English), but *ei* or *ē* in Norse (OE *stān*, OI *steinn* 'stone'; OE *stāh*, OI *stē* 'he climbed'), from which were taken *aye, hale* (*cf.* the native *whole*), *nay* (*cf.* the native *no*), *reindeer,* and *swain.*

Sometimes the Scandinavian influence was exclusively semantic. An Old English word might keep its original form, but acquire the meaning of its Norse cognate; in the presence of Old Icelandic *draumr* 'dream, vision', Old English *drēam* 'joy' took on the meaning of the alien word, and Old English *brēad* 'a fragment' came to signify 'bread' after Old Icelandic *brauðr* 'bread'. But the opposite could also occur: a difference in form, and not in meaning, was involved when Old Icelandic *systir* replaced Old English *sweostor* 'sister' (Middle English *suster*), and when Old Icelandic *egg* replaced the native *ǣġ* 'egg'. Loan translations (*calques*) are represented by Old English *bōtlēas* 'unpardonable', *hāmsōcn* 'offense of attacking a man in his own house', *landċēap* 'the tax paid upon the purchase of land', *saclēas* 'innocent', and *wǣpenġetæc* 'subdivision of a riding, wapentake' which are paralleled in Old Icelandic by *bótlauss, heimsókn, landkaup, saklauss* and *vápnatak.* In the matter of place-names the Scandinavian influence was very great indeed; over 1400 localities in England bear names which contain a Nordic element, the most common being the Danish word *by* meaning 'farm' or 'town' (*Derby, Grimsby, Kirkby, Rugby, Selby, Whitby*). Other reminders of the Scandinavian occupation are *-thorp* 'village' (*Althorp, Linthorpe, Mablethorpe*), *-thwaite* 'an isolated piece of land' (*Applethwaite, Cowperthwaite, Satterthwaite*), and *-toft* 'a piece or ground' (*Brimtoft, Eastoft, Langtoft, Nortoft*). With an influence considerably less pervasive than that of Latin upon Old English the Norse dialects, nevertheless, rank immediately after the language of Rome in their contributions to Anglo-Saxon speech. Providing an oblique commentary on the initial contacts between two cultures, the following Scandinavian loanwords are a further part of the Old English lexicon: *barda* 'beaked ship' (Old Icelandic *barði*), *cnearr* 'small warship' (*knorr*), *genġe* 'troop' (*gengi*), *hāsæta* 'oarsman' (*háseti*), *hofding* 'chief, leader' (*höfðingi*), *hūsting* 'court, tribunal' (*hūsðing*), *liðsmen* 'sailors' (*liðsmenn*), *nīðing* 'evil man' (*niðingr*), *orrest* 'battle' (*orrusta*), *sceg* 'ship' (*skeið*), *tīdung* 'news' (*tiðindi*), *þrǣl* 'thrall' (*þrǽll*), and *ūtlaga* 'outlaw' (*útlagi*).

15.4.3   *The Keltic Influence*   That so few Keltic words found their way into Old English is probably explained by the subjugated position of Britons in Anglo-Saxon England; the tendency to borrow copiously, or at all, from the language of a conquered people is easily inhibited on social and political grounds. And yet, the confrontation of Anglo-Saxon and Kelt lasted so long that some British terms were inevitably made a part of the Old English wordstock; among them are: *ancora* 'hermit', *binn* 'basket, crib', *bratt* 'cloak', *brocc* 'badger', *cumb* 'valley, combe', *drȳ* 'magician' (*cf. druid*), and *torr* 'peak, crag'. Of the dozen or so Keltic words in Old English, however, only a few achieved permanent status. Keltic roots do survive in a number of English place-names (*Brockhall, Bryn Mawr* 'great hill', *Devon, Duncombe, Kent, Pendle, York*), and in the names of some rivers (*Avon, Thames, Wye*), but they do not constitute substantiating evidence for any significant influence of Keltic speech upon the vocabulary of English in its earliest phase.

15.5   *Syntax VI: The Order of Clauses*   A subunit of the sentence, a clause is a group of words which, as a minimum, contains a subject and a verb. If the meaning of a clause is felt to be complete, then the clause is called independent, or principal; if the meaning is not complete, the clause is called dependent, or subordinate. Thus, in the maxim of La Rochfoucauld, "When our integrity declines, our taste does also,"[10] the words preceding the comma constitute a dependent clause, and those following, an independent clause. Dependent clauses function in a nominal, an adjectival, or an adverbial capacity; independent clauses state the major predication. If at least one dependent clause is included in a sentence, then the sentence is said to be "complex." "Although the criteria distinguishing dependent from nondependent clauses in OE have not yet been completely worked out,"[11] it is generally not impossible to separate one type of clause from the other. The structure of complex sentences in Old English prose and poetry favors a clausal order wherein dependent clauses follow the other clauses, both principal and subordinate, to which they are related:[12] *hē forġifð trūwan ūre forhtunge, sē þe þurh his witegan clypað,* "*Nylle iċ þæs synfullan dēað, ac iċ wille þæt hē ġeċyrre and lybbe* 'He gives confidence to us in (our) fear, he who calls out through his prophet, "I do not wish the death of the sinner, but rather I wish that he should convert and live" ', *þū ġelīċ ne bist/ ǣnegum his engla, þe iċ ǣr ġeseah,/ ne þū mē oðīewdest ǣniġ tācen,/ þe hē mē þurh trēowe tō onsende,/ mīn Hearra, þurh hyldo* 'you are not like any one of his angels, whom I saw before, nor have you shown me any sign which he may be sending to me through faith, my Lord, through grace'; *tō hēanlīċ mē þinceð/ þæt* *ġē mid ūrum sceattum tō scype gangon/ unbefohtene, nū ġē þus feor hider/ on ūrne eard in becōmon* 'it seems too ignominious to me that you should go unopposed aboard ship with our tribute, now (that) you have come thus far hither into our country'. Almost any kind of dependent clause can occur medially, but correlation is commonly the prerequisite for the appearance of a dependent clause in initial position: *þā hī þider ūt cōmon, þā stefnede man heom man tō ġemōte* 'when they had come out thither, then they were summoned to a meeting'. If correlation is lacking, a subordinate clause that introduces a principal clause is likely to be a conditional clause or an indefinite relative clause: *ġif þū hit witan wilt, ðū scealt habban ǣr þīnes mōdes ēagan clǣne ond hlūtor* 'if you want to know it, you must first have your mind's eye pure and clear'; *and swā hwǣr swā hē wæs, hē wurðode ǣfre God ūpāwendum handbredum wið þæs heofones Weard* 'and wherever he was, he always worshipped God with the palms of his hands upturned toward the Guardian of Heaven'.

15.6   *Old English Versification*   Although no example of East Germanic poetry has survived, the poems which have come down in North and West Germanic indicate that the pre-literate Germanic community evolved a verse technique based upon stress and alliteration; early Germanic verse was, of course, exclusively oral, and consequently formulaic in nature. End-rhyme was entirely absent. Old English poetry represents a continuation of the ancient tradition, and is not, in that respect, innovative in style. The principles of Germanic versification were first codified by the German scholar, Eduard Sievers, in his *Altgermanische Metrik* (Halle, 1893), and if later scholars have made refinements in his work they have not discarded the fundamental tenets of his theory. Viewed according to Sievers' hypothesis, each line of Old English poetry is divided by a caesura into two half-lines (a and b) which are in turn linked together by alliterative elements. Each half-line contains two syllables, called lifts, which bear the primary stress ($\stackrel{\prime}{}$), and it is there that the alliteration occurs; the number of unaccented syllables, or dips (x), per half-line is not constant and may range from two to eight, the average being four. The first half-line is more frequently expanded with unaccented syllables than the second. Allowance is also made for syllables with a secondary stress-accent ($\stackrel{\prime}{}$). Every half-line has an independent scansion, and Sievers distinguished five main types:[13]

A	$\acute{-}$ x | $\acute{-}$ x	*stīðum wordum*
B	x $\acute{-}$ | x $\acute{-}$	*þīn āgen bearn*
C	x $\acute{-}$ | $\acute{-}$ x	*on flōt feran*
D¹	$\acute{-}$ | $\acute{-}$ $\grave{-}$ x	*hring gyldenne*
D²	$\acute{-}$ | $\acute{-}$ x $\grave{-}$	*hār hilderinc*
E	$\acute{-}$ $\grave{-}$ x | $\acute{-}$	*andlangne dæġ*

In the foregoing examples the lifts ($\_'$) are all coincidental with long syllables (one containing a long vowel or diphthong, or a short vowel or diphthong followed by two or more consonants), but the primary stress may also be resolved: that occurs when the stress is placed upon "two syllables, of which the first (with one of the word-accents) is short in quantity and the second is light enough in accent to combine with the first to produce with it the metric equivalent of a long syllable":[14] thus, *eaforan þīnne* x͡x x | ͟ʹ x, exemplifying Type A. Among the numerous other variations in scansion is anacrusis, or presence of an additional syllable (rarely two) which stands at the beginning of a half-line and is not a part of the metrical pattern proper: thus, *ġeslogon æt sæċċe* x | ͟ʹ x x | ͟ʹ x, exemplifying Type A (with an expanded first measure). The alliterative elements may be vocalic as well as consonantal, e.g., *eald inwitta* ͟ʹ | ͟ʹ ͟ʹ x (D¹), and sometimes there may be no alliteration at all, e.g.' *wīs ealdorman* ͟ʹ | ͟ʹ x ͟ʹ (D²). In a full line the first lift in the second half alliterates with one or both lifts in the first half: *cōm þā tō reċede rinc sīþian* ͟ʹ x x | x͡x x (A) ‖ ͟ʹ | ͟ʹ x ͟ʹ (D¹); *mynte sē māscaþa manna cynnes* x͡x x | ͟ʹ x x (A) ‖ ͟ʹ x | ͟ʹ x (A); the second lift of the second half-line almost never shares in the alliteration. As indirect testimony to the antiquity of the verse form, the Old English consonants [k] and [č] were considered a legitimate alliterative pair, along with [g] and [y]: *onġietan sceal glēaw hæle* x | x͡x x x | ͟ʹ ͟ʹ x (D¹ with anacrusis). Some Old English poems (*The Dream of the Rood, Genesis B, The Phoenix, The Wanderer*) contain hypermetric lines, or lines in which an additional measure precedes each half-line: *mōdiġ meahtum spēdiġ   sē þā moldan ġesette* ͟ʹ x | ͟ʹ x | ͟ʹ x ‖ ͟ʹ x | ͟ʹ x x | ͟ʹ x; hypermetric lines are generally grouped and may have been used to somehow heighten or shift the emotional response of the poet's audience. In contrast, it is unlikely that a poet ever arranged normal half-lines according to any design; the many variations possible for even a single type suggest that half-lines were ordered unconsciously and at random.

If one chooses to regard Old English verse as isochronous, however, then the poet or singer must be credited with the facility for maintaining an equal number of beats per measure. In his book, *The Rhythm of Beowulf* (New Haven, Conn., 1942), John C. Pope argues for a reading of Old English poetry which differs from that proposed by Sievers; briefly, Pope asserts that each measure was recited in 4/8 time (eight eighth notes to a half-line), and that the poet made use of a harp in order to supply whatever beats were not present in the verse itself. There is little doubt that a harp was actually used in the recitation of Old English poetry (*cf.*6.8; *Beowulf* lines 896–90a, 2107–2110, and 2262b–2263a), and Pope's hypothesis is attractive for the clarification and insights which it gives with regard to the harp as an instrument of accompaniment. There are, then, two schools of thought on the reading of Old English poetry: the older, or nonisochronous, and the more recent, or isochronous; each has its merits and each is worthy of serious consideration.

15.7   *The Dream of the Rood* A poem of great religious intensity, *The Dream of the Rood* is generally felt by modern critics to be an outstanding example of the passionate lyricism which, here and there, infuses the extant corpus of Old English verse. It is quite legibly preserved in folios 104b–106a of the *Vercelli Book*, a manuscript of Old English prose and poetry (discovered in 1823) that for many centuries has belonged to the Cathedral Library at Vercelli in northern Italy near Milan. Incidentally, the presence of such a manuscript at Vercelli has never been satisfactorily explained, although it may have something to do with Cardinal Guala, papal legate in England from 1216 to 1218, and founder of the Church of Saint Andrew at Vercelli; for an examination of the problem and an entirely different hypothesis for its solution see Kenneth Sisam, *Studies in the History of Old English Literature* (Oxford, 1953), pages 116–118. The manuscript dates from the latter half of the tenth century (or, perhaps, from the first half of the eleventh), and among its selections records the Old English poems *Andreas, Elene,* and *The Fates of the Apostles,* as well as twenty-three homiletic pieces.

As its modern title suggests, *The Dream of the Rood* concerns an experience not derived from wakeful consciousness. In the poem a human being who is overcome with a sense of sin, and who has fallen asleep, is addressed by a personified True Cross, now adorned with gold and radiant jewels and now drenched with blood; the dreamer learns that the Cross, ultimately to be identified with the crucified Christ, has itself become a genuine instrument of salvation. Veneration of the Cross developed into an element of Christian worship in the sixth century, but the present poem was probably not composed until the second half of the eighth century. The runic inscriptions on the Ruthwell Cross (see 14.2) which parallel portions of the speech of the Cross in *The Dream of the Rood* show the early popularity of a poem or poems on the subject of the Cross, and *The Dream of the Rood* may represent a later expansion of the Ruthwell Cross fragments, or it may be a West Saxon version of an original work (possibly Anglian), now lost, from which the Ruthwell Cross selections were excerpted. Closer in tone to the school of Cynewulf than to that of Cædmon, *The Dream of the Rood* is of anonymous authorship; the dialect is Late West Saxon with a small admixture of Anglian forms.

> Hwæt, iċ swefna cyst   secgan wylle,
> hwæt mē ġemǣtte   tō midre nihte,

Figure 8. RUTHWELL CROSS. Ruthwell Church, Dumfriesshire, Scotland. Courtesy, The British Tourist Authority.

syðþan reordberend   reste wunedon.
þūhte mē þæt iċ ġesāwe   syllicre trēow

5   on lyft lǣdan   lēohte bewunden,
beama beorhtost.   Eall þæt bēacen wæs
begoten mid golde;   ġimmas stōdon
fæġere æt foldan scēatum,   swylċe þǣr fīfe wǣron
uppe on þām eaxlġespanne.   Behēoldon þǣr engeldryhta feala

10   fæġere þurh forðġesceaft;   ne wæs ðǣr hūru fracodes ġealga,
ac hine þǣr behēoldon   haliġe gāstas,
men ofer moldan,   and eall þēos mǣre ġesceaft.
Sylliċ wæs sē siġebēam,   and iċ synnum fāh,
forwundod wid wommum.   Ġeseah iċ wuldres trēow

15   wǣdum ġeweorðod   wynnum scīnan,
ġeġyred mid golde;   ġimmas hæfdon
bewriġen weorðlīċe   Wealdendes trēow.
Hwæðre iċ þurh þæt gold   onġytan meahte
earma ǣrġewin,   þæt hit ǣrest ongan

20   swǣtan on þā swīðran healfe.   Eall iċ wæs mid sorgum
    ġedrēfed,
forht iċ wæs for þǣre fæġran gesyhðe;   ġeseah iċ þæt fūse
    bēacen
wendan wǣdum and blēom: hwīlum hit wæs mid wǣtan
    bestēmed,
beswyled mid swātes gange,   hwīlum mid since ġeġyrwed.
Hwæðre iċ þǣr licgende   lange hwīle

25   behēold hrēowċeariġ   Hǣlendes trēow,
oð ðæt iċ ġehȳrde   þæt hit hlēoðrode;
ongan þā word sprecan   wudu sēlesta:
"þæt wæs ġeara iū   (iċ þæt ġyta ġeman)
þæt iċ wæs āhēawen   holtes on ende,

30   āstȳred of stefne mīnum.   Genāman mē ðǣr strange fēondas,
ġeworhton him þǣr tō wæfersȳne,   hēton mē heora wergas
    hebban;
bǣron mē þǣr beornas on eaxlum,   oð ðæt hīe mē on beorg
    āsetton;
ġefæstnodon mē þǣr fēondas ġenōge.   Ġeseah iċ þā Frēan
    mancynnes
efstan elne micle,   þæt hē mē wolde on ġestīgan.

35   þǣr iċ þā ne dorste   ofer Dryhtnes word
būgan oððe berstan,   þā iċ bifian ġeseah
eorðan scēatas.   Ealle iċ mihte
fēondas gefyllan   hwæðre iċ fæste stōd.

Onġyrede hine þā ġeong hæleð,   þæt wæs God ælmihtiġ,
40   strang and stīðmōd;   ġestāh hē on ġealgan hēanne,
mōdiġ on maniġra ġesyhðe,   þā hē wolde mancyn lȳsan.
Bifode iċ þā mē sē beorn ymbclyppte;   ne dorste iċ hwæðre
    būgan tō eorðan,
feallan tō foldan scēatum,   ac iċ sceolde fæste standan.
Rōd wæs iċ ārǣred,   āhōf iċ rīcne cyning,
45   heofona hlāford,   hyldan mē ne dorste.
þurhdrifan hī mē mid deorcan næġlum;   on mē syndon þā
    dolg ġesīene,
opene inwidhlemmas;   ne dorste iċ hira ǣnigum sceððan.
Bysmeredon hīe unc būtū ætgædere;   eall iċ wæs mid blōde
    bestēmed,
begoten of þæs guman sīdan,   siððan hē hæfde his gāst
    onsended.
50   Feala iċ on þām beorge   ġebiden hæbbe
wrāðra wyrda: ġeseah iċ weruda God
þearle þenian;   þȳstro hæfdon
bewriġen mid wolcnum   Wealdendes hrǣw,
scīrne scīman.   Sceadu forðēode,
55   wann under wolcnum.   Wēop eal ġesceaft,
cwīðdon cyninges fyll: Crīst wæs on rōde.
Hwæðre þǣr fūse   feorran cwōman
tō þām æðelinge;   iċ þæt eall behēold.
Sāre iċ wæs mid sorgum gedrēfed,   hnāg iċ hwæðre þām
    secgum tō handa
60   ēaðmōd elne mycle.   Ġenāmon hīe þǣr ælmihtiġne God,
āhōfon hine of ðām hefian wīte;   forlēton mē þā hilderincas
standan stēame bedrifenne;   eall iċ wæs mid strǣlum for-
    wundod.
Ālēdon hīe hine limwēriġne,   ġestōdon him æt his līċes
    hēafdum;
behēoldon hīe ðǣr heofenes Dryhten,   and hē hine ðǣr hwīle
    reste
65   mēðe æfter ðām miclan ġewinne.   Ongunnon him þā moldern
    wyrċan
beornas on banan ġesyhðe,   curfon hīe ðæt of beorhtan stāne;
ġesetton hīe ðǣron sigora Wealdend.   Ongunnon him þā
    sorhlēoð galan
earme on þā ǣfentīde,   þā hīe woldon eft sīðian
mēðe fram þām mǣran þēodne;   reste hē ðǣr mǣte weorode.
70   Hwæðre wē ðǣr grēotende   gōde hwīle
stōdon on staðole;   stefn ūp gewāt

hilderinca;   hrǣw cōlode,
fǣġer feorgbold.   þā ūs man fyllan ongan
ealle tō eorðan;   þæt wæs eġeslīċ wyrd!
75   Bedealf ūs man on dēopan sēaþe;   hwæðre mē þǣr Dryhtnes þeġnas,
frēondas ġefrūnon   [. . . . .],
ġyredon mē   golde and seolfre.
Nū ðū miht ġehȳran,   hæleð mīn sē lēofa,
þæt iċ bealuwara weorc   ġebiden hæbbe,
80   sārra sorga.   Is nū sǣl cumen
þæt mē weorðiað   wīde and sīde
menn ofer moldan   and eall þēos mǣre ġesceaft,
ġebiddaþ him tō þyssum bēacne.   On mē bearn Godes
þrōwode hwīle;   for þan iċ þrymfæst nū
85   hlīfiġe under heofenum,   and iċ hǣlan mæġ
ǣġhwylcne ānra   þāra þe him bið eġesa tō mē.
Iū iċ wæs ġeworden   wīta heardost,
lēodum lāðost,   ǣr þan iċ him līfes weġ
rihtne ġerȳmde,   reordberendum.
90   Hwæt, mē þā ġeweorþode   wuldres Ealdor
ofer holtwudu,   heofonrīċes Weard,
swylċe swā hē his mōdor ēac,   Marian sylfe,
ælmihtiġ God   for ealle menn
ġeweorðode   ofer eall wīfa cynn.
95   Nū iċ þē hāte,   hæleð mīn sē lēofa,
þæt ðū þās ġesyhðe   secge mannum;
onwrēoh wordum   þæt hit is wuldres bēam,
sē ðe ælmihtiġ God   on þrōwode
for mancynnes   manegum synnum
100   and Ādōmes   ealdġewyrhtum.
Dēað hē þǣr byriġde;   hwæðre eft Dryhten ārās
mid his miclan mihte   mannum tō helpe.
Hē ðā on heofenas āstāg.   Hider eft fundaþ
on þysne middanġeard   mancynn sēċan
105   on dōmdæġe   Dryhten sylfa,
ælmihtiġ God,   and his englas mid,
þæt hē þonne wile dēman,   sē āh dōmes ġeweald,
ānra ġehwylcum,   swā hē him ǣrur hēr
on þyssum lǣnum   līfe ġeearnaþ.
110   Ne mæġ þǣr ǣniġ   unforht wesan
for þām worde   þe sē Wealdend cwyð:
frīneð hē for þǣre mǣniġe   hwǣr sē man sīe,
sē ðe for Dryhtnes naman   dēaðes wolde

biteres onbyriġan,   swā hē ǣr on ðām bēame dyde.
115 Ac hīe þonne forhtiað,   and fēa þenċaþ
hwæt hīe tō Crīste   cweðan onginnen.
Ne þearf ðǣr þonne ǣniġ   anforht wesan
þe him ǣr in brēostum bereð   bēacna sēlest;
ac ðurh ðā rōde sceal   rīċe ġesēċan
120 of eorðweġe   ǣġhwylċ sāwl,
sēo þe mid Wealdende   wunian þenċeð."
Ġebæd iċ mē þā tō þān bēame   blīðe mōde,
elne mycle,   þǣr iċ āna wæs
mǣte werede.   Wæs mōdsefa
125 āfȳsed on forðweġe,   feala ealra ġebād
langunghwīla.   Is mē nū līfes hyht
þæt iċ þone siġebēam   sēċan mōte
āna oftor   þonne ealle men,
well weorþian.   Mē is willa tō ðām
130 myċel on mōde,   and mīn mundbyrd is
ġeriht tō þǣre rōde.   Nāh iċ rīcra feala
frēonda on foldan,   ac hīe forð heonon
ġewiton of worulde drēamum,   sōhton him wuldres Cyning;
lifiaþ nū on heofenum   mid Hēahfædere,
135 wuniaþ on wuldre;   and iċ wēne mē
daga ġehwylċe   hwænne mē Dryhtnes rōd,
þe iċ hēr on eorðan   ǣr scēawode,
on þysson lǣnan   līfe ġefetiġe,
and mē þonne ġebringe   þǣr is blis myċel,
140 drēam on heofonum,   þǣr is Dryhtnes folc
ġeseted tō symle,   þǣr is singāl blis;
and mē þonne āsette   þǣr iċ syððan mōt
wunian on wuldre,   well mid þām hālgum
drēames brūcan.   Sī mē Dryhten frēond,
145 sē ðe hēr on eorðan   ǣr þrōwode
on þām ġealgtrēowe   for gumena synnum;
hē ūs onlȳsde,   and ūs līf forġeaf,
heofonlīcne hām.   Hiht wæs ġenīwad
mid blēdum and mid blisse,   þām þe þǣr bryne þolodan.
150 Sē Sunu wæs sigorfæst   on þām sīðfate,
mihtiġ and spēdiġ,   þā hē mid maniġeo cōm,
gāsta weorode,   on Godes rīċe,
Anwealda ælmihtiġ,   englum tō blisse
and eallum ðām hālgum   þām þe in heofonum ǣr
155 wunedon on wuldre   þā heora Wealdend cwōm,
ælmihtiġ God,   þǣr his ēðel wæs.

15.8   *Notes*

4. *syllicre,* an absolute comparative.

8. *æt foldan scēatum* 'at the corners of the earth'.

10. *forðġesceaft,* an ambiguous word; *forð* may mean either 'preceding' or 'succeeding', and *ġesceaft* either 'creation' or 'decree'. Suggested translations include 'fair through the future', 'created fair',[15] 'beautiful in virtue of an ancient decree'.[16]

15. *wǣdum,* the standard meaning would be 'garments'; here, perhaps 'banners', 'pennants' or 'streamers'.

21. *fūse* 'shining'.

31. *mē* is to be understood after *þǣr.*

37f. *mihte . . . ġefyllan* 'could have felled'.

43. *tō foldan scēatum* 'to the surface(s) of the earth'.

46. *deorcan* with the color of blood(?).

52. *þenian* 'to be stretched out'.

57. *fūse* 'the hastening ones', in particular Joseph of Arimathea and Nicodemus.

63. *heafdum,* with singular meaning.

66. *banan,* the Cross.

69. *mǣte weorode,* the real meaning is 'alone'; *cf.* line 124.

70. *wē,* there were, of course, three crosses on Calvary.

76. At least one half-line is missing.

77. *nū ðū miht ġehȳran,* the Cross is now famous, and its story may be heard everywhere.

86. *æġhwylcne ānra þāra þe him bið eġesa tō mē* 'everyone who fears me'; *þe him* 'to whom'.[17]

109. *ġeearnaþ,* to be construed as a future perfect.

126. *langunghwīla* 'times of weariness (of spirit)';[18] perhaps the sin of slothfulness is implied.

148–156. Christ's descent into hell after the crucifixion and his triumphant return to heaven with those (*gāsta weorode*) whom he had redeemed.

References

1. Berthold Louis Ullman, *Ancient Writing and Its Influence* (New York, 1932; reprinted with an introduction by Julian Brown, Cambridge, Massachusetts, 1969), p. 83.
2. John Williams Clark, *Early English* (London, 1957), p. 78.
3. Thomas Pyles, *The Origins and Development of the English Language* (New York, 1964), p. 30.
4. Clark, p. 79.
5. Albert C. Baugh, *A History of the English Language,* 2nd ed. (New York, 1957), p. 93.

6. Pyles, p. 327, from Mary S. Serjeantson, *A History of Foreign Words in English* (London, 1935), Appendix A, pp. 277–288.

7. J. R. R. Tolkien and E. V. Gordon, eds., *Sir Gawain and the Green Knight,* 2nd ed., revised by Norman Davis (Oxford, 1967), p. 138.

8. A. Campbell, *Old English Grammar* (Oxford, 1959), pp. 220–221.

9. Otto Jespersen, *Growth and Structure of the English Language,* First Free Press Paperback Edition (New York, 1968), p. 60.

10. Louis Kronenberger, trans., *The Maxims of La Rochefoucauld,* The Modern Library (New York, 1959), p. 103.

11. Randolph Quirk and C. L. Wrenn, *An Old English Grammar,* 2nd ed. (London, 1958), p. 95.

12. Quirk and Wrenn, p. 95.

13. Almost all the examples in 15.6 are drawn from James W. Bright, *Anglo-Saxon Reader,* revised and enlarged by James R. Hulbert (New York, 1963), pp. 231–240.

14. Bright, p. 229.

15. Henry Sweet, *Anglo-Saxon Reader in Prose and Verse,* 15th ed., revised by Dorothy Whitelock (Oxford, 1967), p. 273.

16. Bruce Dickins and Alan S. C. Ross, eds., *The Dream of the Rood* (New York, 1966), p. 22.

17. Sweet, p. 274.

18. Dickins and Ross, p. 33.

Chapter 16

16.1 *Word Formation (III): Compounds* Any linguistic form which is not *simple* may be regarded as a compound of sorts, and consequently those Old English words created by means of affixation (14.1 and 15.1) are indeed compounds in the most general sense of the term. Traditional usage, however, often restricts the label to certain nouns and adjectives composed of two elements which invariably exist as independent words elsewhere in the language. The fact that some affixes are also independent words (or, free morphemes) does not impede recognition of "compounds" from the narrower viewpoint; in general, a given affix will combine with different words with a higher frequency than will either part of a nominal or adjectival compound customarily defined. Like other Germanic dialects, past and present, Old English relied upon compounding as a major technique for increasing its vocabulary.

16.1.1 *Nominal Compounds* The second element of any nominal compound is always a noun, and the gender of that noun determines the gender of the compound as a whole. The first element, however, may be a) another noun: *brōþor-sunu* 'nephew', *lār-hūs* 'school', *tungol-cræft* 'astronomy'; b) an adjective: *ān-haga* 'solitary man', *dim-hūs* 'prison', *middel-niht* 'midnight'; or c) an adverb: *eft-cyme* 'return', *eft-lēan* 'recompense'. Occasionally the first member of a nominal compound will appear in some inflected form: *dæges-ēage* 'daisy', *Engla-land* 'England', *helle-bryne* 'hell-fire', *sunnan-niht* 'Saturday evening'.

16.1.2 *Adjectival Compounds* Compounds functioning in an adjectival capacity customarily conclude with an adjective, preceded by

a) a noun: *blōd-rēad* 'blood-red', *dǣd-cēne* 'bold in deed(s)', *sigor-ēadiǵ* 'victorious'; b) another adjective: *eall-gōd* 'all-good', *efen-eald* 'contemporary', *scīr-mǣled* 'brightly-adorned'; or, c) an adverb: *ǣr-wacol* 'early awake', *fela-synniǵ* 'very guilty'. Being adjectives, both present and past participles may contribute the second element of an adjectival compound: *cyne-boren* 'of royal birth', *eall-wealende* 'omnipotent', *gold-hroden* 'adorned with gold', *lēoht-berende* 'luminous'. A special group of adjectival compounds, for which there are parallel formations in Sanskrit, Greek, and Latin, attesting the Indo-European origin of the class, contained a noun instead of an adjective as the second element: *brūn-ecg* 'bright-edged', *drēoriǵ-mōd* 'sad', *glæd-mōd* 'glad-hearted', *mild-heort* 'gentle', *strang-mōd* 'resolute', *yrre-mōd* 'angry'. Such compounds are sometimes identified by the generic term *bahuvrīhi* (literally 'much rice'), the description reserved for them in Sanskrit grammar.

16.2   *Anglo-Saxon Personal Names*   In the matter of personal names the Anglo-Saxons rather consistently followed common Germanic practices which themselves stemmed from the period of Indo-European unity. As family names did not come into use until the late Middle Ages, each person customarily bore a single name that was either one word or a (dithematic) compound of two. Compound names are widely attested among the dialects of Indo-European, Italic being the only major branch to have discarded them in favor of a different system of nomenclature (*Gaius Julius Caesar*); *cf.* in Sanskrit *Dēva-datta* 'God-given', in Greek *Eteo-klēs* 'true fame', in Keltic (Gaulish) *Catu-rīx* 'battle ruler', and in Russian *Bole-slav* 'more fame'. Either part of a double name may be either a noun or an adjective. In Germanic, names for men often had reference to warfare, power, fame, religion, and personal qualities; women's names were distinguished by means of certain second components such as *-burg, -gard, -hild,* and *-rūn*.[1] Within a family, names which repeated some particular element were frequently favored; *cf.* in *Beowulf* the two sons, *Heorogar* and *Hrothgar,* of the Danish king, *Healfdene,* and, in the Old High German *Hildebrandslied, Heribrand, Hildebrand,* and *Hadubrand,* father, son, and grandson respectively. Unlike the Scandinavian dialects, for example, which formed patronymics with *-son,* Old English did not have a ready technique for designating the father-son relationship, although the element *-ing* 'son of' does occur with limited application; *cf.* in *Bēowulf* ('Bee-wolf', hence 'bear'), *Hrēþling* 'son of Hrethel' *Hūnlāfing* 'son of Hunlaf', *Wælsing* 'son of Wæls', and *Wonrēding* 'son of Wonred'. Among the most popular words used by the Anglo-Saxons for dithematic names were *æþel, bēorht, ēad, ōs, stān, wine* and *wulf;* the following names, which appear in the *Anglo-Saxon Chronicle,* are representative: *Æsc-wine, Æþel-gar, Æþel-wulf, Bēorht-wulf, Ēad-mund, Hēah-stān, Hyġe-briht, Lēof-wine, Ōs-wine,* and *Wulf-heard.* Noble ladies named in the *Chronicle* include *Ēad-burg,* the daughter of King Offa of Mercia; *Seax-burg,* a queen of the West Saxons; and *Wǣr-burg,* a queen of the Mercians. As the name *Offa* indicates, the Anglo-Saxons, like other Indo-European groups, also used single words for personal appellations; among them, the *Chronicle* records: *Ælle, Acca, Cissa, Cnebba, Dudda, Goda, Gyrð, Penda,* and *Worr.* The dithematic compounds, however, were more numerous.

16.3   *Kentish, Mercian, and Northumbrian*   With the exception of West Saxon the dialectal situation of Old English must be retrieved from an extreme paucity of surviving texts, with occasional help being provided by alien forms occurring in West Saxon manuscripts, by the evidence of Middle and Modern English dialects, and by proper names of every period, in particular, place names.[2] The Old English dialects no doubt reflect speech differentiations which originated on the Continent in the former homelands of the Angles, Saxons, and Jutes, but those differentiations, on the Continent and later in Britain, were never so great that communication among the three groups of invaders was in any way rendered difficult or unsatisfactory. In addition to West Saxon, the existence of three other dialects is commonly recognized: *Kentish,* spoken by the Jutes, *Mercian* and *Northumbrian* both spoken by the Angles; see also 1.4, 1.5, and 1.6. (Mercian, however, is a cover term for what appear to have been several dialects, exclusive of Northumbrian, spoken by the Angles.) All three dialects had much in common with West Saxon, with which they all preserved a West Germanic wordstock and the major inflectional categories (e.g., various nominal declensions, the strong and weak adjective, strong and weak verbs, and so forth) of Proto-Germanic. The differences among them, as might be expected, do not reside in their respective structures but rather in particular inflectional endings (*cf.* Northumbrian *-es, -as,* a sometime ending for the third person singular, present indicative of Class I weak verbs, as opposed to *-eþ* in standard West Saxon) and in the phonological shape of shared cognates. A detailed survey of dialectal idiosyncracies is not practicable here, but the following phonological disparities will indicate something about the nature of Kentish, Mercian and Northumbrian.

16.3.1   Proto-Germanic *ǣ,* which under certain circumstances yielded *ǣ* in West Saxon (see 14.3.2), became *ē* in Kentish and Anglian (Mercian and Northumbrian): *cf. bēron* 'they bore', *dēd* 'deed', *slēpan;* West Saxon *bǣron, dǣd, slǣpan.* The foregoing distinction probably arose on the Continent.

16.3.2   In the matter of *i*-umlaut West Saxon shifts the diphthongs *ĕa* and *ĭo* to *ĭe* whereas the non-West Saxon dialects shift *ĕa* to *ĕ*

and retain *ĭo* unchanged: *ċerr* 'turn', *hēran* 'to hear', *nēd* 'need' but West
Saxon *ċierr, hīeran, nīed; hiorde* 'shepherd', *onsīon* 'face', but West Saxon
hierde, onsīen.

16.3.3   A phonetic phenomenon known as *u*-umlaut, or back
mutation, took place in all the dialects but was more restricted in West
Saxon than elsewhere. Toward the end of the prehistoric period of Old
English the short front vowels *i, e, æ* were diphthongized to *io, eo, ea*
when they occurred in open syllables and when the following syllable contained a back vowel. In West Saxon the shift was inhibited unless the
consonant intervening between the front vowel and the back vowel was
a labial (*f, p, w*) or a liquid (*m, l, r*); in Anglian, back mutation took place
before all consonants except velar [k] and [g], and in Kentish before any
consonant. (Back mutation was usually inoperative in all dialects if two
consonants, either the same or different, intervened.) Representative of
u-umlaut are Anglian and Kentish *nioman*, West Saxon *niman* 'to take';
Mercian and Kentish *eotan*, West Saxon *etan* 'to eat'; Mercian *fearan*,
West Saxon *faran* 'to go'. (West Saxon did not have short *æ* in open syllables preceding a back vowel; see 14.3.1.) Forms with back mutation in
West Saxon are *heorot* 'hart' from earlier **herot*, and *siofun* 'seven' from
earlier **sifun*; because of the double consonant there was no umlaut in
words like *drincan* 'to drink' and *swimman* 'to swim'.

16.3.4   The diphthongization of front vowels (*e, æ, ǣ*) after
the word-initial palatal consonants *ċ* [c], *ġ* [y], and *sc* [š] is a phenomenon
(see 14.3.1) that separates West Saxon from Kentish and Mercian where
no such modification ever developed: *sceld* 'shield', *ċæster* 'town, fortress',
gēr 'year' in contrast to West Saxon *scield, ċeaster, ġēar*. Diphthongization
by palatals also occurred in Northumbrian, but less consistently than in
West Saxon. Unknown in Kentish and Mercian, the subsequent shift of
ĕa to *ĭe* by *i*-umlaut is possibly confined to West Saxon; since both *æ* and
ea mutate to *e* in Northumbrian a determination of the "true" process
cannot be made for that dialect.

16.3.5   The Anglian dialects are marked by a phonetic change
known as "smoothing," the reduction, or monothongization, of a diphthong to a single vowel. When *ĕa, ĕo,* and *ĭo* stood immediately before the
velar consonants [k], [g], or [χ] the diphthongs were simplified to *ǣ, ē,* and
ī respectively; the monothongization also took place before an intervening
r or *l*. Hence, the Anglian forms *mæht* 'might', *feh* 'money', *werc* 'work',
ġesihð 'sight', *hēh* 'high', and *betwīh* 'between' correspond to West Saxon
meaht, feoh, weorc, ġesiehð, hēah, and *betwīoh.*

16.3.6   In Anglian the *i*-umlaut of $\breve{o}$ remained a front rounded vowel $\bar{oe}$, which in West Saxon was unrounded to $\bar{e}$: Anglian *oele* 'oil', *grōēne* 'green', but West Saxon *ele, grēne*.

16.3.7   Anglian keeps the etymologically correct *-u* (or *-o*) as an ending for the first person singular, present indicative, but West Saxon has the termination *-e*, taken from the subjunctive: Anglian *bindu* 'I bind', *dōēmu* 'I judge', but West Saxon *binde, dēme*.

16.3.8   A further distinguishing feature of Anglian is the retraction, or lowering, of *æ* (from Germanic *a*) before *l* plus a consonant to *a;* in Kentish and West Saxon *æ* was dipthongized to *ea* (see 14.3.1): Anglian *cald* 'cold', *fallan* 'to fall', *haldan* 'to hold'; West Saxon *ċeald, feallan, healdan*. The diphthongization of *i, e,* and *æ* (to *io, eo, ea*) before *r* plus a single consonant and before single *h* is far more regular in Kentish and West Saxon than in Anglian, as well as the diphthongization of *e* and *i* before *l* plus a single consonant. In Northumbrian exclusively, *æ* before *r* plus a consonant is retracted to *a* (*barn* 'child', *hard* 'hard'; West Saxon *bearn, heard*), and *e* between *w* and *r,* in that order, is retracted to *o* (*sword* 'sword', *worpa* 'to throw'; West Saxon *sweord, weorpan*).

16.3.9   Syncopation of the thematic vowel in the second and third person singular, present indicative, of strong verbs resulting in consonantal assimilation (see 6.3) was the norm in West Saxon but not in Anglian where *brecest* 'you break', *breceþ* 'he breaks', *cumest* 'you come', *cumeþ* 'he comes' parallel West Saxon *bricst, bricþ, cymst, cymþ* (all of which also have *i*-umlaut).

16.3.10   A peculiarity of Kentish is the lowering and unrounding of $\breve{\bar{y}}$ (the *i*-umlaut of $\breve{\bar{u}}$) to $\breve{\bar{e}}$: Kentish *efel* 'evil', *senn* 'sin', *mēs* 'mice', *ontēnan* 'to open', but West Saxon *yfel, sinn, mȳs, ontȳnan*.

16.3.11   In late Kentish, *æ*, the *i*-umlaut of *ā* (from Proto-Germanic *ai*), was raised to $\bar{e}$: Kentish *clēne* 'clean', *hēlan* 'to heal', *mēst* 'most', but West Saxon *clǣne, hǣlan,* and *mǣst*.

16.3.12   In general the consonants are less revealing of dialectal differences than the vowels and diphthongs simply because phenomena like palatalization and metathesis, for example, were common to the Old English speech community. A few minor distinctions do nevertheless present themselves. Characteristic of West Saxon is the loss of *ġ* [y] before the dentals *þ, d,* and *n* with compensatory lengthening of the preceding vowel, thus forms like *frīnan* 'to ask', *mǣden* 'maiden, girl', *rēn* 'rain', and *ðēnung* 'service' from earlier *friᵹnan, mæᵹden, reᵹn,* and *ðeᵹnung.* In Northumbrian final *-n* began to disappear at an early date, and by the end of the Old English period most parts of speech were affected; *cf. eorðu* (accusative singular feminine) 'earth', *herᵹa* 'to praise', *cwōmu* 'they came', *biᵹeonda* 'beyond' and *seofo* 'seven' with West Saxon *eorðan, herian, c(w)ōmon, beoᵹeondan,* and *seofon.* Speakers of West Saxon tended to convert fricatives to stops when the former stood before liquids and nasals, and so, for example, *þl* and *þm* became *tl* and *tm* after short vowels: *setl* 'seat', *bytme* 'keel', but Anglian *seþel* (from earlier **sepla-*) and *bythne;* after long vowels West Saxon *þl* became *dl: ādl* 'disease', *wǣdla* 'poor man', but Northumbrian *āðl, wīðlia.* (In late Old English [ð] before liquids and nasals became [d], and *dl* consonant clusters were then frequent everywhere except in some Mercian areas.)

16.3.13   *An Example of Kentish* The following passage, dated 833–839, begins a document (the will of a man named Abba) originally housed in the archives of Christ Church Cathedral at Canterbury but now preserved in the British Museum. The words for this selection, and for those in 16.3.14 and 16.3.15, are listed in the Glossary.[3]

Ic Abba gerōēfa cȳðe ond wrītan hāte hū mīn willa is þæt mon ymb mīn ærfe gedōē æfter mīnum dæge. Ærest ymb mīn lond þe ic hæbbe, ond mē God lāh, ond ic æt mīnum hlāfordum begæt, is mīn willa, gif mē God bearnes unnan wille, ðæt hit fōē tō londe æfter
5   mē, ond his brūce mid mīnum gemeccan, ond sioððan swǣ forð mīn cynn ðā hwīle þe God wille ðæt ðeara ænig sīe þe londes weorðe sīe ond land gehaldan cunne. Gif mē ðonne gifeðe sīe ðæt ic bearn begeotan ne mege, þonne is mīn willa þæt hit hæbbe mīn wiif ðā hwīle ðe hīa hit mid clēnnisse gehaldan wile; ond mīn brōðar
10   Alchhere hire fultume ond þæt lond hire nytt gedōē; ond him man selle ān half swulung an Ciollandene tō habbanne ond tō brūcanne, wið ðan ðe hē ðȳ geornliocar hire ðearfa begā ond bewiotige; ond mon selle him tō ðēm londe IIII oxan, ond II cȳ, ond L scēpa, ond ænne horn. Gif mīn wiif ðonne hīa nylle mid clēnnisse swǣ
15   gehaldan, ond hire līofre sīe ōðer hēmed tō nīomanne, ðonne fōēn mīne mēgas tō ðēm londe, ond hire āgefen hire āgen.

16.3.14   *An Example of Mercian* The *Vespasian Psalter* is a collection of psalms and hymns, or canticles, in Latin which were set down in the eighth century; late in the ninth century the *Psalter* received an interlinear gloss in Mercian. The following excerpt is the first part of King Hezekiah's prayer from the Old Testament book of Isaiah (chapter thirty-eight, verses ten through seventeen) as glossed in the vernacular.[4]

Ic cweð in midum daega mīnra: Ic fearu tō gete helle. Ic sōhte lāfe gēra mīnra; ic cweð: Ic ne gesīo Dryhten God in eorðan lifgendra. Ne gelōciu ic mon māē ond eardiend. Gestilde cnēoris mīn;
20 wiðlāēded is ond befalden is from mē swē swē geteld heorda. Forcorfen is swē swē from ðǣm weofendan līf mīn; mit te nū gēt gehefeldad ācearf mec. Of marne oð ēfen geendas meç; from ēfenne oð margen swē swē lēa swē fordrǣste all bān mīn; of marne ot ēfen geendas mec. Swē swē brid swalwan swē ic cleopiu; ic smēgu
25 swē swē culfre. Geðynnade sind ēgan mīn gelōcendu in hēanis. Dryhten, nēd ic ðrōwiu; ondsweora fore mē, hwet ic cweðe, oððe hwet ondsweorað mē ðæt ic seo[l]fa dōa. Ic ðencu all gēr mīn in bitternisse sāwle mīnre. Dryhten, gif swē bið lifd, oððe in weolerum līf gāstes mīnes, geðrēas mec, ond gelīffestes mec. Sehðe, in sibbe
30 bitternis mīn sīe bittreste; ðū sōðlīce generedes sāwle mīne, ðet ic ne forwurde.

16.3.15 *Two Examples of Northumbrian* Among the four extant Northumbrian versions of Cædmon's *Hymn* (see 6.9) is the following; it is contained in the Leningrad (Public Library) Manuscript of Bede's *History*, a copy of the Latin original made toward the middle of the eighth century (probably in 746).

Nū scilun herga   hefenrīcæs Uard,
Metudæs mehti   and his mōdgithanc,
uerc Uuldurfadur,   suē hē uundra gihuæs,
35 ēci Dryctin,   ōr āstelidæ.
Hē ǣrist scōp   aeldu barnum
hefen tō hrōfæ,   hālig Sceppend.
Thā middingard   moncynnæs Uard,
ēci Dryctin   æfter tīadæ
40 f īrum foldu,   Frēa allmehtig.

A tenth-century gloss of the Rushworth Gospels (c.800) provides a late Northumbrian version of the Gospel of Matthew from which verses one through six of chapter seven are here excerpted.[5] The symbol 7 stands for the word 'and'.

1. ne dōēmeþ gē þȳles gē sīen dōēmed 2. in ðǣm wiotudlīce dōme þe gē dōēmeþ gē bēoþ dōēmde 7 in ðǣm gemete þe gē metaþ bið ēow meten 3. for hwon þonne gesihstū strēu in ēge brōþer þīne 7

bēam in ēge þīnum ne gesees *vel* sis 4. oþþa hū cweþestū brōþer
45 þīnum brōþer ābīd þæt ic ofdō þæt strēu of ēge þīnum 7 sihþe bēam
in ēge þīnum is 5. þū līcettere geþō ǣrǣst þone bēam of ēge þīnum
7 þonne gesihst þū āwearpe þæt strēu of þīnes brōþer ēge 6. ne
sellað gē hālig hundum ne gewearpaþ ercnanstānas ēowre beforan
swīnum þyles hīæ tredan ðā heora fōtum 7. gehwerfæþ tōslīte
50 ēowic.

16.4   *Syntax VII: Parataxis and Hypotaxis*   When a language
or a stage thereof ceases to be spoken, certain aspects of its pronunciation,
vocabulary and structure remain moot and problematic for those subsequently interested in the surviving documents; the precise meaning of
æstel in King Alfred's *Preface* to the *Pastoral Care* (see 9.10 note 16), or
the etymology of *garsecg* 'sea' (*Beowulf* lines 49, 515, 537) are cases in
point for investigators of Old English lexical affairs. Similar difficulties
arise in the area of Old English syntactical studies when it becomes necessary to consider the stylistic devices of parataxis and hypotaxis. The
former term refers to the absence of grammatical subordination and the
latter to the opposite situation. Thus defined, the words are simple enough
in application to Old English texts, but if the meaning of parataxis is
extended to imply hypotaxis idiomatically expressed (without benefit of
conjunctions) then questions of interpretation enter upon the scene,
questions which only a native speaker could be in a position to answer.
In the narrower sense, however, parataxis in Old English is customarily
unmistakable; the following sequence, no matter how punctuated by a
modern editor, can hardly be said to contain an example of subordination:
Sē hāliga Andrēas þā ġebǣd on his heortan and raðe hīo wǣron dēade. Sē
hālga Andrēas þā ēode tō þæs carcernes duru and hē worhte Crīstes rōde
tācen and raþe þā dura wǣron ontȳnede and hē in ēode on þæt carcern mid
his discipulum and hē ġeseah þone ēadigan Mathēus ǣnne sittan singende
'Holy Andrew then prayed in his heart and quickly they were dead. Holy
Andrew then went to the door of the prison and he made the sign of the
Cross and quickly the doors were opened and he went in to the prison
with his disciples and he saw blessed Matthew sitting alone singing'. And,
similarly, hypotaxis is clear in *nū cwæð sē hālga Bēda þe ðās bōc ġedihte*
þæt hit nān wundor nys þæt sē hālga cynincg untrumnysse ġehǣle nū hē on
heofonum leofað for ðan þe hē wolde ġehelpan þā þā hē hēr on līfe wæs
þearfum and wannhālum and him biġwiste syllan 'now holy Bede, who
wrote this book [the *Historia Ecclesiastica*], said that it is no wonder that
the holy king may cure illness now that he is living in heaven, because he
wanted to help, when he was alive here, the needy and sick and to give
them sustenance'. The use of correlative elements may involve either
coordination or subordination: *þæt hē ealle þā tīd meahte ġe sprecan ġe*

gongan 'that all the time he could both speak and walk'; *þā hē ðā þær in ġelimplīċe tīde his leomu on reste ġesette ond onslēpte, þā stōd him sum mon æt þurh swefn* 'when he then there at a suitable time had set his limbs at rest and was sleeping, then a certain man stood before him through a dream'.

On the surface, paratactic sentences seem to predominate in Old English and that has led to a frequently stated view that a lack of sub-ordination is the chief characteristic of Old English syntax (a condition perhaps not to be unexpected for a language without a relatively long literary tradition); in any event, the matter is of no great consequence. Generalized statements about parataxis and hypotaxis have little meaning when they do not refer to some specific text or writer; that the *Homilies* of Ælfric contain many more periodic sentences than do earlier sections of the *Chronicle* is demonstrable in a way that remarks about the corpus of Old English as a whole are not. What remains of interest, however, is the possibility of hypotaxis expressed by certain "paratactic" constructions; as noted above, that involves judgments which cannot be entirely objective.

In 1940 S. 0. Andrew suggested that parataxis in Old English was the sometime equivalent of various constructions associated with periodic sentences.[6] He pointed out that a paratactic sentence, usually introduced by *wolde, wēnde,* or *cwæð,* could in fact function as an adverbial clause of reason or purpose; thus, *hēo ēode of ðām stæpum tō ðām hālgan cyðere, wolde hī gebiddan* 'she went from the steps to the holy martyr, she wanted to pray' is properly 'she went from the steps to the holy martyr in order to pray'; and, likewise, *hī ġelȳfdon on manega ōðre ġesceafta: cwædon þæt hī for heora fæġernysse godas wæron* is 'they believed in many other creatures, saying that they were gods because of their beauty'. A para-tactic sentence may also be a defining clause, commonly after *swā dōn* or a similar phrase: *ond hīe þā swā dydon: worhton ðā tū ġeweorc on twā healfe* 'and they did so, building two forts, one on either bank'; a com-parative clause: *hī sind ōðre ōðre hī wæron* 'they are other than they were'; or an adjectival phrase or clause, usually with *hātan: ðā wæs sum consul. Boetius wæs hātan* 'there was at the time a consul called Boetius'. Since formal hypotaxis was undeniably a feature of Old English syntax, An-drew's proposed interpretations are in all likelihood correct; but with no evidence to the contrary, it must be conceded that a native speaker might never have taken the foregoing examples in anything except their "literal" sense; the absence of subordinating elements might not have been felt as awkward, and perhaps the need to "smooth out" sentences mentally did not exist. Fortunately, a modern translator is not required to choose one approach over the other, but he ought to realize that the syntactical pat-terns of Old English will occasionally permit both.

16.5 *Some Stylistic Devices of Old English Poetry*   Although
the total surviving corpus of Anglo-Saxon poetry (about 30,000 lines)
is less extensive than one might wish, it is sufficiently large for an apprecia-
tion of the prevailing stylistic devices used by the earliest poets to have
composed in English. The structure of Old English verse (see 15.6) is the
feature which most immediately sets it apart from prose, but obviously
the structure of any poem reveals only a single aspect of creative endeavor. If poetry is at least a specialized use of words, then diction and
idiom require attention in themselves for a clearer understanding of their
contribution to the themes and motifs they were chosen to express. Just
as the most productive period of Middle High German literature (1190–
1250) was to see the evolution of a common poetic language, or *Dich-
tersprache,* in which the regionalisms of *Minnesänger* like Walter von der
Vogelweide and Wolfram von Eschenbach were suppressed, so do the
initial centuries of versification in English indicate the existence of a
literary koine. The four manuscripts which contain almost all the poetry
of Anglo-Saxon England now extant (see 1.2) date from about 1000 and
are written in a dialect that is mainly, but not exclusively, late West Saxon;
Mercian and Northumbrian forms are also present, probably as vestiges
of a poetic dialect employed on a national basis from the seventh to the
early ninth century. Such a dialect would have been practical. "A poem,
wherever composed, might win its way into the common stock. The native
metre, based primarily on the alliteration of stressed syllables, carried well
because in this essential the usage of seventh-century Northumbria and
tenth-century Wessex was the same; but any local dialect forms that
affected the verse-structure were a handicap to circulation. A poet might
prefer to take his models from the common stock rather than from the
less-known work of his own district. In this way poems could be produced
that do not belong to any local dialect, but to a general Old English poetic
dialect, artificial, archaic, and perhaps mixed in its vocabulary, conservative in inflections that affect the verse-structure, and indifferent to
non-structural irregularities, which were perhaps tolerated as part of the
colouring of the language of verse."[7]

Granting the universal tendency of poets to search out the unusual
or unexpected word, the assumption that the vocabulary of an artificial
dialect would *ipso facto* not fully coincide with that of everyday speech is
given support by the fair proportion of words in the Old English lexicon
which occur only or chiefly in poetry. Sometimes a poetical word merely
reflects its immediate context and could have had small chance to gain
further currency, e.g., *byrnġield* 'burnt-offering' from the story of Abra-
ham and Isaac in *Genesis A*. In the case of *ālimpan* 'to happen, occur',
beadu 'war, battle', *brytta* 'giver, lord', *dēmend* 'judge', *freca* 'warrior',

ġēaðˀ 'foolishness, mockery', gūð 'battle', mēċe 'sword', swearte 'miserably', and others like them, however, it is less easy (for a modern reader at any rate) to see why such "serviceable" terms should have been confined to verse unless they were the recognized property of poets and no one else. Certain poetic compounds like gūðfreca 'battle-warrior' were constructed from the restricted wordstock, whereas others like brandhāt 'burning hot' were composed of elements that enjoyed a distribution in prose as well.

Highly characteristic of Old English poetic diction is the type of compound known as a kenning (Old Norse kenningar 'symbols'). The term has been applied to various figurative expressions and its meaning thereby somewhat widened, but the true kenning (so-called) refers to two nouns, in a compound or as a phrase, which imply a third although neither names the suggested object directly. In Beowulf, hronrād 'whale-road', seġlrād 'sail-road', and swanrād 'swan-road' are true kennings for 'sea'; in a poetic passage from the Laud Chronicle (975 AD) the metaphor is ganotes bæð 'gannet's bath'. Additional true kennings in Beowulf include bānhūs 'body' ('bone-house'), beadolēoma 'sword' ('battle-light'), bronda lāfe 'ashes' ('leavings of fires'), heofones ġim 'sun' ('jewel of heaven'), homera lāfe 'swords' ('leavings of hammers'), rodores candel 'sun' ('candle of the sky'), and ȳðlāf 'sand (on the shore)' ('leaving of waves'). Also frequent in Beowulf and elsewhere is the half kenning, a compound or phrase in which one of the two elements does cite a particular attribute of the referend, e.g., hæðstapa 'heath-stepper' for 'stag', helmberend 'helmet-bearer' for 'warrior', and goldwine gumena 'gold-friend (generous friend) of men' for 'lord, chief'. The kenning, incidentally, is a device which Old English and Old Icelandic poetry have in common; the skaldic, or court, poets who began to flourish in the latter half of the ninth century were extremely partial to such metaphors and constructed them with considerable inventiveness, e.g., Isakar ís 'ice of battle', hence 'gleaming sword'. It is, of course, now impossible to know the effect which kennings may have had upon an Anglo-Saxon audience, but it may be that, as stereotypes of a sort, their impact was less intense than it is for a modern addressee who is necessarily obliged to dissect them literally. At the same time, there can be something of the riddle about a kenning, e.g., freoðuwebbe 'peace-weaver' meaning 'woman', and that must occasionally have commanded more than passive notice; in that connection, it has been pointed out that the Old English riddles themselves "are frequently nothing more than elaborate, successive kennings."[8] Later poems like the Battle of Brunanburh (937) and the Battle of Maldon (991) contain few kennings, the vogue for which had apparently begun to wane in the tenth century. Figurative speech was also realized with single words that embodied synecdoche, the part for the whole (e.g., ċeol 'keel' meaning 'ship'), or metonymy, the use of a word to suggest something associated with it, e.g., *æsc* 'ash (wood)' for 'spear', *lind* 'linden' for 'shield'; *Beowulf* provides examples of anaphora (l. 864 ff., l. 2107 ff.), antithesis (l. 183 ff.), hysteron proteron (l. 1114 ff.), and polysyndeton (l. 1392 ff., l. 1763 ff.), all of which may, however, reflect a Latin influence.[9]

Beowulf likewise records several instances of the *apo koinou* construction; the Greek phrase means 'from the common' and applies to two parts of a sentence related to one another through the medium of a third to which they are both directly linked; thus, in *þǣr wæs mādma fela/of feorwegum   frætwa ġelǣded* 'there was much of treasures, of ornaments brought from distant lands', both *mādma* and *frætwa* are related to the phrase between them, *of feorwegum* (see also lines 1316, 754, 935, and 3067). The simile is occasionally encountered: *fugle ġelīcost* 'most like a bird', *stȳle ġelīcost* 'most like steel', but for comparisons the kenning takes a consistent precedence. Far more typical of Old English verse than any other classical figure is the trope of litotes, the expression of a concept by the negation of its reverse, e.g., "This is not untrue"; litotes often represents the Anglo-Saxon fondness for understatement and irony. Speaking of death the *Beowulf* poet says *nō þæt ȳðe byð/tō befleonne   —fremme sē þe wille—* 'that is not easy to escape—try who will—'; and after Beowulf has killed Grendel the poet remarks *nō his līfġedāl/sārlīċ þūhte secga ǣnegum* 'his parting from life did not seem sad to any of men'. Defeated at Brunanburh by the Anglo-Saxons, Constantine, leader of the Scots, *hrēman ne ðorfte/mēċa ġemānan* 'had no need (cause) to boast of the joining of swords'; cast into hell, and mindful of certain restraints placed upon his former power, Satan reproaches God, saying *næfð hē þeah riht ġedōn* 'nevertheless He has not done right' (*Genesis B*). The illustrations are numerous.

Another notable convention of the Old English poetic style is *variation,* "a double or multiple statement of the same idea, each restatement suggesting through its choice of words either a general or more specific quality, or a different attribute of that concept; and such statements may, as in the first example, or may not, as in the second, be grammatically parallel."[10] Once again *Beowulf* supplies good examples: *Wīġlāf wæs hāten Wēoxstānes sunu/lēoflīċ lindwiga,   lēod Scylfinga,/mæġ Ælfheres* 'he was called Wiglaf, the son of Weohstan, an admirable shield-warrior, a man of the Scylfings (Swedes), the kinsman of Ælfhere'; *ġeseah ðā on weorðmynd; þæt [wæs] wæpna cyst—* 'he saw then among the armour a victory-blessed sword, an ancient sword made by giants, strong in its edges, the glory of warriors; that was the best of weapons—'; *men ne cunnon/secgan tō sōðe,   selerǣdende,/hæleð under heofenum,   hwā þǣm hlæste onfēng* 'men do not know, to tell the truth, counsellors in the hall, heroes under heaven, who received that cargo'. Cædmon's *Hymn* is remarkable for its variation; the nine-line poem has no less than seven different epithets for 'God', most of which (e.g., *ēċe Drihten, monncynnes Weard*) are formulaic in nature, thus exemplifying another major feature of the earliest English verse.

Like all poets who ever worked within an oral tradition, the Anglo-Saxon *scop* relied not only upon variation but also upon stock phrases, or formulas, in his compositions. (Formulas, kennings, and variations were by no means mutually exclusive.) "The poet could find among his formulaic resources almost any semantic values he needed for the immediate sense or ornamentation of the poem he was creating. Conveniently, he could substitute individual words within the grammatical and rhythmic patterns either for contextual or alliterative purposes."[11] Simple formulas like *mīne ġefrǣġe* 'I have heard say', *iċ ġefræġn* 'I have learned', and *iċ hyrde* 'I heard' are repeated five, seven, and nine times respectively in *Beowulf,* where the customary verb, (there are twenty-six instances) for the introduction of direct discourse is *maþelian* 'to say, make a speech': *Wulfgār maþelode   —þæt wæs Wendla lēod* 'Wulfgar spoke, he was a man of the Vandals'; *Hrōðgār maþelode,   helm Scyldinga* 'Hrothgar spoke, protector of the Scyldings'; *Bēowulf maðelode   —on him byrne scān* 'Beowulf spoke, his coat of mail shone'; *Bēowulf maþelode,   bearn Ecþēowes* 'Beowulf spoke, the son of Ecgtheow'; *Unferð maþelode, Ecglāfes bearn* 'Unferth spoke, the son of Ecglaf'; and so forth. The brief description which follows a person's name is also a formulaic device; *cf. Byrhtnōð maþelode   bord hafenode* 'Byrhtnoth spoke, he raised his shield', *Ælfwine þā cwæð,   hē on ellen spræc* 'Ælfwine then spoke, he spoke bravely', *Offa ġemǣlde,   æscholt āscēoc* 'Offa spoke, he brandished his ash (wood)-spear', *Byrhtwold maþelode   bord hafenode* 'Byrhtwold spoke, he raised his shield' in the *Battle of Maldon.* Because of its length, *Beowulf* is a text wherein the variations on a given formulaic theme are well exemplified; there are several involving the verb *cuman* 'to come'. One of these consists of a phrase beginning with an adverb which is followed by a noun or pronoun and then terminates in the third singular of *cuman;* without exception the formula comprises the second half of a line: *syþðan morgen cōm* (1077b), *syððan mergen cōm* (2103b), *þonan Bīowulf cōm* (2359b), *syþðan æfen cwōm* (1235b), *ond nū ōþer cwōm* (1338b), *syððan mergen cwōm* (2124b), *oð ðæt æfen cwōm* (2303b), *syððan Hiġelāc cwōm* (2914b), *þonne wiġ cume* (23b), *ær þon dæġ cwōme* (731b); to which may be added the expansions: *ðā iċ of searwum cwōm* (419b), and *nū iċ þus feorran cōm* (430b). Only *cume* (23b) is not a past-tense form. Furthermore, the formula *cōm (þā) tō* is used seven times, and *cōm þā,* or *þā cōm,* occurs six times. A final, prominent *Beowulf* formula is *mǣre þēoden* 'famous, illustrious prince', inserted fifteen times.

The list of formulaic elements in Old English poetry can be extended to a very great length; the examples above are merely intended to give some indication of their character. Whether Anglo-Saxon poems, early and late, were created according to the principles of a still living oral tradition has been disputed. (Certainly those of Cynewulf were written or dictated by a lettered man, containing as they do his signature in runes, but even his poems are not devoid of formulaic earmarks.) The debate, however, cannot be entered into here where the purpose has been to review the conspicuous devices of Anglo-Saxon poetic style without determining the extent to which those devices were legitimately operative, as opposed to being merely imitative of practices unquestionably stemming from a pre-literate (Proto-Germanic) society.

16.6   *The Wanderer* Among those poems in the *Exeter Book* which exemplify the elegiac strain in Old English poetry is *The Wanderer;* along with *Deor,* the *Husband's Message, Resignation,* the *Riming Poem,* the *Ruin, The Seafarer,* the *Wife's Lament,* and *Wulf and Eadwacer, The Wanderer* focuses chiefly upon loss and the possibility of subsequent consolation. Although the nine poems "are to differing degrees secular or Christian in their content and attitudes, they have in common two overlapping concerns: (1) a contrast between past and present conditions, and (2) some awareness of the transitory nature of earthly splendor, joy, and security."[12] The elegiac mood is also present in *Beowulf,* for example in the lament for happier days past recited by the last survivor of a 'noble race' (*æðlan cynnes*) who buries the ancient treasures of his people in the earth when there is no longer anyone alive to use or tend them (lines 2232b–2270a), treasures later discovered by Beowulf's final adversary, the dragon. Whereas the speaker in *Beowulf* endured his fate without consolation until, at last, 'the surge of death touched his heart' (*oð ðæt dēaðes wylm hrān æt heortan*), the lonely exile of *The Wanderer,* likewise bereft of kinsmen and comrades, concludes that true security for all lies with God in Heaven.

If the poem dates from the first half of the tenth century, as it may, then the Christian ending to what is otherwise an undeniably non-religious monologue, need not be considered unduly alien or falsely intrusive. *The Wanderer* may be regarded as a poem which relates the development of an aristocratic warrior in wisdom gained from experience, and, in the tenth century, ultimate wisdom would have had to have involved Christian doctrine. In his meditations the wanderer at first reflects upon his personal sorrows and then upon the impermanence of earthly things in general, his thoughts finding expression in the *ubi sunt* motif. Because of the shift in emphasis (at line 58), the poem has sometimes been regarded as a dialogue rather than a monologue; in that case the *eardstapa* of line 6 is not identified with the man who is *snottor on mōde* of line 111.

In lines 6–7, 88–91, and 111 the poet himself is clearly the commentator, but whether he introduces one or two speakers is contestable; lines 112–115 can, in fact, also be assigned to the poet if he is thought to continue the discourse after line 111. That, however, may be felt to disturb the unity of the poem by depriving the wanderer of having achieved consolation for himself, and is a reading not suggested in the text below. Lines 1–5 may constitute an impersonal introduction, or may be attributed to either the poet or the wanderer. Attempts to view the poem as an allegory of man's journey through life have received only limited support. The dialect is Late West Saxon, with retention of earlier *ie* (when it represents the diphthongization of *e* after *ġ* [y]) for the expected *i* or *y*.

<pre>
     Oft him ānhaga   āre ġebīdeð,
     Metudes miltse,   þēah þe hē mōdċeariġ
     ġeond lagulāde   longe sceolde
     hrēran mid hondum   hrīmċealde sæ,
5   wadan wræclāstas: wyrd bið ful āræd.
     Swā cwæð eardstapa   earfeþa ġemyndiġ,
     wrāþra wælsleahta,   winemæga hryre:
        'Oft iċ sceolde āna   ūhtna gehwylċe
     mīne ċeare cwīþan.   Nis nū cwicra nān,
10   þe iċ him mōdsefan   mīnne durre
     sweotule āsecgan.   Iċ tō sōþe wāt
     þæt biþ in eorle   indryhten þēaw,
     þæt hē his ferðlocan   fæste binde,
     healde his hordcofan,   hycge swā hē wille.
15   Ne mæġ wēriġmōd   wyrde wiðstondan,
     ne sē hrēo hyġe   helpe ġefremman.
     For ðon dōmġeorne   drēoriġne oft
     in hyra brēostcofan   bindað fæste;
     swā iċ mōdsefan   mīnne sceolde,
20   oft earmċeariġ   ēðle bidæled,
     frēomægum feor,   feterum sælan,
     siþþan ġeāra iū   goldwine mīnne
     hrūsan heolster biwrāh   and iċ hēan þonan
     wōd winterċeariġ   ofer waþema ġebind,
25   sōhte sele drēoriġ   sinces bryttan,
     hwær iċ feor oþþe nēah   findan meahte
     þone þe in meoduhealle   [mīn] mine wisse,
     oþþe mec frēondlēasne   frēfran wolde,
     wēman mid wynnum.   Wāt sē þe cunnað
30   hū slīþen bið   sorg tō ġefēran
</pre>

þām þe him lȳt hafað   lēofra ġeholena:
warað hine wræclāst,   nales wunden gold,
ferðloca frēoriġ,   nalæs foldan blǣd;
ġemon hē selesecgas   and sincþeġe,
35   hū hine on ġeoguðe   his goldwine
wenede tō wiste.   Wyn eal ġedrēas.
For þon wāt sē þe sceal   his winedryhtnes
lēofes lārcwidum   longe forþolian;
ðonne sorg and slǣp   somod ætgædre
40   earmne ānhagan   oft ġebindað,
þinċeð him on mōde   þæt hē his mondryhten
clyppe and cysse,   and on cnēo lecge
honda and hēafod,   swā hē hwīlum ǣr
in ġeārdagum   ġiefstōles brēac;
45   ðonne onwæcneð eft   winelēas guma,
ġesihð him biforan   fealwe wēgas,
baþian brimfuglas,   brǣdan feþra,
hrēosan hrīm and snāw   hæġle ġemenġed.
þonne bēoð þȳ hefiġran   heortan benne,
50   sāre æfter swǣsne;   sorg bið ġenīwad,
þonne māga ġemynd   mōd ġeondhweorfeð;
grēteð glīwstafum,   ġeorne ġeondscēawað.
Secga ġeseldan   swimmað eft on weġ,
flēotendra ferð   nō þǣr fela bringeð
55   cūðra cwideġiedda;   cearo bið ġenīwad
þām þe sendan sceal   swīþe ġeneahhe
ofer waþema ġebind   wēriġne sefan.
For þon iċ ġeþenċan ne mæġ   ġeond þās woruld
for hwan mōdsefa   mīn ne ġesweorce,
60   þonne iċ eorla līf   eal ġeondþenċe,
hū hī fǣrlīċe   flet ofġēafon,
mōdġe maguþeġnas.   Swā þēs middanġeard
ealra dōgra ġehwām   drēoseð and falleþ.
'For þon ne mæġ weorþan wīs   wer, ǣr hē āge
65   wintra dǣl in woruldrīċe.   Wita sceal ġeþyldiġ,
ne sceal nō tō hātheort   ne tō hrǣdwyrde,
ne tō wāc wiga   ne tō wanhȳdiġ,
ne tō forht ne tō fæġen,   ne tō feohġīfre,
ne nǣfre ġielpes tō ġeorn,   ǣr hē ġeare cunne.
70   Beorn sceal ġebīdan,   þonne hē bēot spriċeð,
oþ þæt collenferð   cunne ġearwe
hwider hreþra ġehyġd   hweorfan wille.
Onġietan sceal glēaw hæle   hū gǣstlīċ bið,
þonne eall þisse worulde wela   wēste stondeð,

75 swā nū missenlīċe   ġeond þisne middanġeard
    winde biwāune   weallas stondaþ,
    hrīme bihrorene,   hryðġe þā ederas.
    Wōriað þā wīnsalo,   waldend licgað
    drēame bidrorene;   duguð eal ġecrong
80 wlonc bī wealle: sume wīġ fornōm,
    ferede in forðweġe;   sumne fugel oþbær
    ofer hēanne holm;   summe sē hāra wulf
    dēaðe ġedælde;   sumne drēoriġhlēor
    in eorðscræfe   eorl ġehȳdde.
85 Ȳþde swā þisne eardġeard   ælda Scyppend,
    oþ þæt burgwara   breahtma lēase,
    eald enta ġeweorc   īdlu stōdon.
    Sē þonne þisne wealsteal   wīse ġeþōhte,
    and þis deorce līf   dēope ġeondþenċeð,
90 frōd in ferðe,   feor oft ġemon
    wælsleahta worn,   and þās word ācwið:
    'Hwǣr cwōm mearg, hwǣr cwōm mago?   Hwǣr cwōm
        māþþumġyfa?
    Hwǣr cwōm symbla ġesetu?   Hwǣr sindon seledrēamas?
    Ēalā beorht būne,   ēalā byrnwiga,
95 ēalā þēodnes þrym!   Hū sēo þrāg ġewāt,
    ġenāp under nihthelm,   swā hēo nō wǣre!
    Stondeð nū on lāste   lēofre duguþe
    weal wundrum hēah,   wyrmlīcum fāh;
    eorlas fornōmon   æsca þrȳþe,
100 wǣpen wælġīfru,   wyrd sēo mǣre;
    and þās stānhleoþu   stormas cnyssað,
    hrīð hrēosende   hrūsan bindeð,
    wintres wōma,   þonne won cymeð,
    nīpeð nihtscūa,   norþan onsendeð
105 hrēo hæġlfare   hæleþum on andan.
    Eall is earfoðlīċ   eorþan rīċe;
    onwendeð wyrda ġesceaft   weoruld under heofonum.
    Hēr bið feoh lǣne,   hēr bið frēond lǣne,
    hēr bið mon lǣne,   hēr bið mǣġ lǣne:
110 eal þis eorþan ġesteal   īdel weorþeð.'
        Swā cwæð snottor on mōde,   ġesæt him sundor æt rūne.
    'Til biþ sē þe his trēowe ġehealdeþ,   ne sceal nǣfre his torn tō
        rycene
    beorn of his brēostum ācȳþan,   nemþe hē ǣr þā bōte cunne,
    eorl mid elne ġefremman.   Wel bið þām þe him āre sēċeð,
115 frōfre tō Fæder on heofonum,   þǣr ūs eal sēo fæstnung
        stondeð.'

16.7   *Notes*

4.   *hrēran mid hondum* 'to stir, agitate with (his) hands', i.e., 'to row'.

7.   *winemǣga hryre,* the second word, 'fall, death', is something of a crux; a masculine, *i*-declension noun, *hryre* may be any case in the singular except genitive, which it ought to be if it is to strictly parallel *wrāþra wælsleahta* in being dependent upon *ġemyndiġ* 'mindful, remembering'. If *hryre* is accusative, then it can be construed as the direct object of *cwæð* (l. 4). If it is dative, then it could, in a fashion, parallel *wrāþa wælsleahta* by being a dative of reference: 'thus spoke a wanderer, mindful of hardships, of hostile bloody battles, (mindful) with respect to the death of kinsmen'.

10.   *þe . . . him* '(him) to whom'.

17.   *drēoriġne,* with 'mind' to be supplied. Line 17 begins a complex hypotactic sentence that does not conclude until *wēman mid wynnum* (l. 29a).

24.   *waþema ġebind* 'binding of the waves', i.e., 'frozen waves'.

25.   *drēoriġ* agrees with *iċ* in line 26.

27b.   The manuscript reading is *mine wisse,* a metrically defective half-line. The emendation to *mīn mine wisse* was suggested by F. Klaeber in his article, "Textual Notes on the Beowulf," in the *Journal of English and Germanic Philology* 8.254 (1909).

32.   *warað hine* 'is his portion'.

42.   *clyppe . . . hēafod,* as a sign of fealty.

44.   *ġiefstoles brēac,* i.e., enjoyed the gifts which were dispensed from the throne.

53–57.   A much discussed passage. One interpretation views the problematic *secga ġeseldan* 'companions of men' and *flēotendra ferð* 'the minds of the floating ones' as synonyms for 'sea-birds' (*brimfuglas,* l. 47); thus, freely, the lines may read: " 'The sea-birds swim away again, their minds do not bring any familiar speech to him who must very often send forth his weary heart across the frozen waves.' In his dream the wanderer has greeted his kinsmen, and has no doubt cried aloud in his sleep: he awakens to see only the sea-birds which, alarmed at his cries, swim away again; the *singende mǣw,* lacking human reason, cannot make the expected reply to the wanderer's greeting."[13]

54.   *fela* is an example of litotes.

65b–73.   A set of maxims.

80b–84.   The beasts of battle, despoilers of the bodies of slain warriors, are a formulaic theme in Old English poetry; cf. *Beowulf* lines 3024b–3027, *Brunanburh* 60–65a, *Judith* 296–297b, *Maldon* 106–107a. If *fugel* (l. 81) means a 'bird' literally, then only parts of the corpse could have been carried off; possibly it is a figurative expression for 'ship': cf. the ship burial of Scyld Scefing in *Beowulf,* lines 26–52. In 1939 an Anglo-Saxon ship cenotaph was discovered at Sutton Hoo (cf. Old English *hōh* 'headland') near Ipswich in Suffolk; see R. L. S. Bruce-Mitford, "The Sutton Hoo Ship-Burial," in R. H. Hogdkin, *A History of the Anglo-Saxons,* 3rd edition, London, 1952, Vol. Two, pp. 696–734, and Charles Green, *Sutton Hoo,* London and New York, 1963. Dating from about 670, the Sutton Hoo funeral ship parallels similar interments from ninth- and tenth-century Scandinavia.

87. *eald enta ġeweorc*, a phrase used to describe ancient ruins, including those from the period of Romano-British culture; *cf. Andreas*, line 1495, *Beowulf* line 2774.

93. *cwōm*, a singular verb followed by a plural subject (*ġesetu*) was not regarded as a solecism.

114b–115a.   The sentiment is reminiscent of *Beowulf* lines 186b–188: *wēl biŏ þæm þe mōt/æfter dēaŏdæġe Drihten sēċean/ond tō Fæder fæþmum freoŏo wilnian* 'Well is it for the one who may be allowed to seek God after (his) death-day, and to ask for peace in the Father's bosom'.

References

1. R. Priebsch and W. E. Collinson, *The German Language*, sixth edition (London, 1966), p. 285.
2. John Williams Clark, *Early English* (London, 1957), p. 96.
3. The example of Kentish is taken from Henry Sweet, *Anglo-Saxon Reader in Prose and Verse*, 15th edition, revised by Dorothy Whitelock (Oxford, 1967), p. 199.
4. Sweet, pp. 185–186.
5. Sweet, p. 217.
6. S. O. Andrew, *Syntax and Style in Old English* (Cambridge, 1940; reissued New York, 1966), p. 87 ff.
7. Kenneth Sisam, *Studies in the History of Old English Literature* (Oxford, 1953), p. 138.
8. George K. Anderson, *The Literature of the Anglo-Saxons* (Princeton, 1949), p. 173.
9. F. Klaeber, ed., *Beowulf and The Fight at Finnsburg*, 3rd ed. (New York, 1950), p. lxviii.
10. Stanley B. Greenfield, *A Critical History of Old English Literature* (New York, 1965), p. 77.
11. Greenfield, p. 74.
12. Greenfield, p. 214.
13. T. P. Dunning and A. J. Bliss, eds., *The Wanderer* (New York, 1969), p. 115.

Abbreviations

a., acc. *accusative*
adj. *adjective*
adv. *adverb*
anv. *anomalous verb*
cf. *compare*
cog. *cognate*
comp. *comparative*
conj. *conjunction*
cons. *consonant*
d., dat. *dative*
def. art. *definite article*
deg. *degree*
dem. *demonstrative*
dir. obj. *direct object*
e.g. *for example*
Eng. *English*
eOE *early Old English*
eWS *early West Saxon*
f., fem. *feminine*
g., gen. *genitive*
Ger. *German*
Gmc. *Germanic*
i., instr. *instrumental*
i.e. *that is*
IE *Indo-European*
imp. *imperative*
ind. *indicative*
indecl. *indeclinable*
indef. *indefinite*
inf. *infinitive*
interj. *interjection*
Lat. *Latin*
lit. *literally*
lOE *late Old English*
lWS *late West Saxon*
m., masc. *masculine*
ME *Middle English*
MnE *Modern English*
n. *neuter* or *nominative*

neg. *negative*
neut. *neuter*
nom. *nominative*
num. *numeral*
OE *Old English*
OFris *Old Frisian*
OHG *Old High German*
OI *Old Icelandic*
ON *Old Norse*
OS *Old Saxon*
p., pl. *plural*
pass. *passive*
PGmc *Proto-Germanic*
POE *Proto-Old English*
poss. *possessive*
pp. *past participle*
PP *preterite-present*
prep. *preposition*
pres. *present*
pret. *preterite*
pron. *pronominal* or *pronoun*
prp. *present participle*
rel. *relative*
s., sg. *singular*
subj. *subjunctive*
subst. *substantive*
supl. *superlative*
vb. *verb*
WGmc *West Germanic*
WS *West Saxon*

Glossary

1. All references are to page and line numbers.
2. Words beginning with *æ*- are listed after *a*-; when internal, -*æ*- follows -*ad*-. Word-initial *ð*- is regularized to *þ*- which follows *t*-.
3. Strong verbs are indicated by Arabic numerals that mark the class; weak verbs are similarly indicated by Roman numerals. The abbreviations 1s, 2s, and 3s stand for first singular, second singular, and third singular respectively.
4. The first letter of an abbreviation, like *nsn*, indicates the case, the second the number, and the third, when included, the gender; thus *nsn.* stands for nominative singular neuter.
5. For some adjectivals, the gender is not indicated if it is irrelevant or indeterminate, e.g. the plural of a past participle referring to a group of men and women.
6. No specific textual citation is provided for some extremely common forms (e.g. *sceal*) or for words which are not inflected (e.g. adverbs).
7. When a specialized definition precedes two or more citations it applies to all of them; when it follows a citation it applies to that citation alone.
8. The first Germanic consonant shift (Grimm's Law) produced the following equivalent sounds in Old English and Latin.

Old English	Latin
f	p
θ (spelled þ, ð)	t
h-, χ (spelled h)	k (spelled c)
p	b
t	d
k (spelled c)	g
b	f-, -b-
d	f-, -b-, -d-
g	h, g (before or after a cons.), f (before u)

These consonantal correspondences are, of course, found only in those Old English and Latin words that are genuine cognates (i.e. independently derived from Indo-European); the operation of Verner's Law in West Germanic further altered the general scheme (see 6.1). For the Old English palatalization of [k] to [č] as it affected Latin loanwords see 15.4.1.

A

ā adv. *ever, always, continuously*

ābannan (7) *to summon* ābannan inf. 111, 35

abbod m. *abbot* abbodas np. 164, 29, ap. 164, 33

abbodrīċe n. *office of an abbot* abbodrīċe ds. 164, 33

ābīdan (1) *to await* ābīd imp. sg. 200, 45

ābrēoþan (2) *to degenerate, fall away* ābroþene pp. npm. 144, 42

ābūton adv. *about, around*

ac conj. *but,* often with the force of *but rather*

ācennan (I) *to bring forth* ācenned pp. 36, 10

āceorfan (3) *to cut off* ācearf 3s pret. ind. 199, 22

ācwellan (I) *to kill* ācwealde 3s pret. ind. 127, 69

ācwenċan (I) *to quench, extinguish* ācwenċan inf. 126, 18

ācweðan (5) *to speak, utter* ācwið 3s pres. ind. 209, 91

ācwið see ācweðan

ācȳþan (I) *to make known* ācȳþan inf. 209, 113

ād m. *funeral pyre* āde ds. 98, 31

Ādam m. *Adam* Ādomes gs. 189, 100

ādl fn. *disease, infirmity* ādl ns. 29, 18

ādrēogan (2) *to practice* ādrēogað pl. pres. ind. 127, 79

aelde mp. *men* aeldu gp. 199, 36

āfeallan (7) *to fall, decay* āfeallen pp. nsf. 87, 25

āfyllan (I) *to fill* āfylled pp. nsn. 163, 21

āfyllan (I) *to slay, kill* āfylle sg. pres. subj. 143, 5; 143, 6

āfȳsan (I) *to impel* āfȳsed pp. nsm. 190, 125 [Cf. OE fūs *eager*]

āgan (PP) *own, have* nāh 1s pres. ind. neg. 190, 131. āh 3s pres. ind. 189, 107. āhte 3s pret. ind. 143, 6. age sg. pres. subj. 208, 64

āġeaton see āġietan

āgefen see āġiefan

āgen adj. *own* āgenum ds. 127, 56. āgenne asm. 127, 82; 164, 34. āgen asn. 76, 33; 86, 4; 86, 11; 87, 13. āgenum dpn. 143, 2

āgen n. *property* āgen as. 198, 16

āġiefan (5) *to give, return* āgefen pl. pres. subj. 198, 16

āġietan (5) *to know, perceive* āġēaton pl. pret. ind. 163, 12

āġinnan (3) *to begin, undertake* āġinnan pl. pres. subj. 145, 67

āh see āgan

āhēawan (7) *to cut down* āhēawen pp. ns. 187, 29

āhebban (6) *to lift up, raise* āhebban inf. 165, 78. āhebbað pl. pres. ind. 36, 3. āhōf 1s pret. ind. 188, 44. āhōfon pl. pret. ind. 188, 61

āhōf- see āhebban

āht n. *anything, ought* þe him sylf āht wǣre ns. *who amounted to anything, who was well to do* 164, 41

āhwār adv. *anywhere*

āht n. *anything, aught* tō āhte ds. *at all* 126, 18

āhte see āgan

Albion *England* Albion ns. 44, 1. [From Lat. Albion *England;* usually derived from Lat. albus *white;* the coastal cliffs of southeastern England are white.]

aldormann m. *magistrate, councilor, chief* aldormen np. 66, 27

ālecgan (I) *to lay down* ālecgað pl. pres. ind. 98, 34; 99, 49. ālēdon pl. pret. ind. 188, 63. ālēd pp. nsn. 98, 36

ālēd- see ālecgan

all see eall

allmehtig see ælmihtiġ

an same as **on**

ān adj., pron., and num. *one, a* ān nsm. 66, 19; 66, 21; 87, 36; 127, 79; 144, 13; 145, 69; 145, 75; 164, 41 nsf. 99, 53; 164, 47. āna nsm. *alone* 29, 13; 190, 123; 190, 128; 207, 8. ānes gs, 45, 21. ānum dsm. 127, 79. ānre dsf. 98, 34; 98, 36. ānne asm. 76, 18. āne asf. 87, 35; 12, 78; 12, 79. ænne 111, 45; 198, 14; 76 26 *alone.* ān asn. 75, 16; 99, 51; 198, 11. ānra gpm. 189, 86; 189, 108 *of those*

and **(ond)** conj. *and*

anda m. *enmity, malice, spite* andan ds. 209, 105

andefn f. *proportion* andefn ns. 98, 34

andettan (I) *to confess, acknowledge* andette 1s pres. ind. 65, 3

andġiet n. *sense, concept* andġiete ds. 87, 30. andġit as. 87, 30

andġitfullīcost adv. *most intelligibly* (supl. deg. of andġitfullīċe)

andswaru f. *answer* andsware as. 55, 17

andweard adj. *present* andwearde nsn. 65, 15

andwyrdan (I) *to answer* andwyrde 1s pret. ind. 86, 5

anforht adj. *afraid, terrified* anforht nsm. 190, 117

Angelcynn n. *England, the English people* Angelcynn ns. 111, 25. Angelcynne ds. 75, 14; 87, 19; 110, 3. Angelcynn as. 75, 3; 75, 5; 76, 30; 86, 2; 87, 25

ānhaga m. *solitary man, one who dwells alone* ānhaga ns. 207, 1. ānhagan as. 208, 40

ānlēp adj. *single, individual* ānlēpne asm. as subst. 76, 18

Antecrīst m. *Antichrist* Antecristes gs. 126, 3

anweald mfn. *authority, power* anwealdes gs. 29, 6. onwald as. 75, 5

anwealda m. *ruler, Lord* anwealda ns. 190, 153

apostata m. *apostate* apostatan np. 144, 42

ār f. *grace, favor, mercy* āre as. 207, 1; 209, 114

ār n. *copper* āres gs. 45, 18

ārās see **ārīsan**

ārǣd adj. *inexorable* ārǣd nsf. 207, 5

ārǣdan (I) *to read* ārǣdan inf. 87, 23; 87, 26

ārǣred see **ārēan**

arcebiscop m. *archbishop* ærcebiscepe ds. 87, 31. arcebiscopas np. 164, 29

areċċan (I) *to translate, interpret* areċċan inf. 75, 17; areċċean 87, 34

ārēran (I) *to set up* ārērde 3s pret. ind. 163, 18. ārǣred pp. nsf. 188, 44

āriht adv. *aright, properly*

ārīsan (1) *to arise, get up* ārās 3s pret. ind. 55, 5; 56, 29; 189, 101

āscunian (II) *to avoid, shun* āscunian inf. 145, 90

āsecgan (III) *to tell, say* āsecgan inf. 207, 11

āsettan (I) *to put, place* āsetton pl. pret. ind. 187, 32. āsette sg. pres. subj. 99, 55; 190, 142

āsmēagan (II) *to investigate* āsmēagan inf. 145, 69

āsolcennes f. *sloth, laziness* āsolcennesse as. 145, 81

āspanan (6, 7) *to allure, entice* āspēon 3s pret. ind. 111, 11

āspendan (I) *to spend, expend* āspended pp. npn. 98, 46

āstāg see **āstīgan**

āstelidæ see **onstellan**

āstīgan (1) *to ascend* āstāg 3s pret. ind. 189, 103

āstyrian (I) *to remove* āstyred pp. ns. 187, 30

að m. *oath* að as. 145, 95
āðbriċe m. *the breaking of oaths, perjury* āðbricas ap. 144, 39
āwendan (I) *to turn, translate* āwende 1s pret. ind. 87, 35
āweorpan (3) *to cast away* āwearpe imp. sg. *remove* 200, 47
āwrītan (1) *to write* āwrītan inf. 163, 12. āwrāt 3s pret. ind. 145, 75. āwritene pp. npf. 76, 33

Æ

ǣ f. *law* ǣ ns. 86, 9. [Related to Lat. īre *to go.*]
ǣfæstnes f. *religion, piety* ǣfæstnes ns. 65, 4. [Cf. OE ǣw *law, religion.*]
ǣfentīd f. *evening* ǣfentīde ds. 188, 68
ǣfre adv. *ever*
æftan adv. *from behind, in the back*
æfter adv. *afterwards, after*
æfter prep. *after* (with dat.) him . . . æfter as postposition 76, 36. æfter þām *thereafter* 143, 4
æfterfyliġan (III) *to follow after* æfterfyliġe sg. pres. subj. 66, 24
ǣ́ghwǣr adv. *everywhere*
ǣ́ghwēr same as **ǣ́ghwǣr**
ǣ́ghwylċ adj. *each, every* ǣ́ghwylċ nsf. 190, 120. ǣ́ghwylcan dsm. 126, 32. ǣ́ghwylcne asm. 189, 86
ǣ́ġðer pron. *each* (also a conj.) ǣ́ġþer *each one* 127, 68. ǣ́ġðer ġe . . . ġe *both . . . and* 75, 3; 75, 7; 75, 9; 75, 10; 76, 37; 165, 81. [MnE either]
ǣġylde adj. *without receiving compensation* ('wergild') ǣġylde nsm. 143, 5
ǣht f. *goods, possessions, wealth* (usually a plural) ǣhte ap. 29, 9. [Related to OE āgan *to own, have.*]
ǣlċ adj. and pron. subst. *each, any* ǣlċ nsm. 29, 12; 98, 42; 98, 44; 127, 80; 144, 14; 163, 23; mǣst

ǣlċ *almost everyone* 127, 60; 127, 62. ǣlċes gsn. 45, 13; 99, 51. ǣlcum dsm. 87, 35. ǣlċere dsf. 45, 17; 98, 20. ǣlcre as subst. 87, 36. ǣlċe dsn. 163, 25. ǣlċ asn. 111, 12. ǣlcra gpn. 126, 35. ǣlcon dpn. 164, 54. ǣlċe apf. 111, 35
ælde mp. *men* ælda gp. 209, 85
ælmæsriht n. *obligations to charity* ælmæsriht ns. 126, 41
ælmihtiġ adj. *almighty;* as subst. *The Almighty* ælmihtiġ nsm. 56, 28; 188, 39; 189, 93; 189, 98; 189, 106; 190, 153; 190, 156; ælmihtiga 165, 79; allmehtig 199, 40. ælmihtegum ds. 76, 19. ælmihtiġne as. 29, 18; 188, 60
ænde see **ende**
æniġ pron. and adj. *any* ǣniġ ns. 127, 56; 127, 59; 163, 15; 165, 77; 189, 110; 190, 117; ǣniġ (ōðer) *anything else* 144, 27; ǣnig 198, 6. ǣnigum dsm. 144, 51. ǣniġne asm. 76, 20. ǣniġe asf. 126, 12; 126, 28. ǣniġ as. 126, 24. ǣnigum dp. 188, 47. ǣniġe apf. 65, 9. ap. 144, 23 *any* (*things*)
ǣnne see **ān**
ǣr adv. *earlier, before, formerly*
ǣr prep. *before* (with dat.) ǣr ðǣm ðe *before the time when* 76, 28. ǣr þysan *until now* 127, 46. ǣr þām *formerly* 127, 73
ǣræst same as **ǣrest**
ærcebiscepe see **arcebiscop**
ǣrendġewrit n. *letter, epistle* ǣrendġewrit as. 75, 16
ǣrendwreca m. *minister, messenger* ǣrendwrecum dp. 75, 6
ǣrest adj. *first* (supl. deg. of ǣr *early*) ǣrestan dsm. 98, 41
ǣrest adv. *first* (supl. deg. of ǣr)
ærfe n. *property* ærfe as. 198, 2
ǣrġewinn n. *former agony, ancient strife* ǣrġewinn as. 187, 19
ǣrist same as **ǣrest** (adv.)

ærnan (I) *to gallop* ærnað pl. pres. ind. 98, 40; 99, 50

ǣrþan conj. *before*

ǣrur adv. *formerly* (comp. deg. of ǣr)

æsc m. *spear (of ashwood)* æsca gp. 209, 99

æstel m. *bookmark* æstel ns. 87, 36. æstel as. 87, 37. [Cf. Lat. hastula *a small spear.*]

ǣswic m. *deception, fraud* ǣswicas ap. 144, 36

æt prep. *in, at, from* (with dat.)

ætgædere adv. *together* ætgædre 208, 39

æthlēapan (7) *to run away (from), escape* æthlēape sg. pres, subj. 143, 3

ætȳwan (I) *to appear* ætȳweð 3s pres. ind. 66, 23

æþele adj. *noble* [Cf. Ger. edel *noble.*]

æþelest adj. *most noble* (supl. deg. of æþele) æþelestum dpf. 45, 21

æþeling m. *noble, prince, Lord* æþelinge ds. 188, 58

ǣwbryċe m. *adultery* ǣwbrycas ap. 144, 37

B

bǣcbord n. *port, left side of a ship* bǣcbord as. 97, 4; 98, 6; 98, 8

bær see **bēran**

bærnan (I) *to burn* bærnað pl. pres. ind. 144, 26. bærndon pl. pret. ind. 111, 34

bæð n. *bath* baðo ap. 45, 17

Baius *Bayeux* Baius ds. 164, 36

bām see **bēġen**

bān n. *bone* bān as. 99, 51. bān ap. 199, 23

bana m. *slayer, murderer* banan gs. 188, 66. [MnE bane.]

bār m. *boar* bāras ap. 165, 68

barnum see **bearn**

baðian (II) *to bathe* baþian inf. 208, 47

baðo see **bæð**

be prep. *by, near, with* (with dat.) be fullan *fully, perfectly* 86, 3

bēacen n. *beacon, vision, sign* eall þæt bēacen ns. *the whole vision* 187, 6. bēacne ds. 189, 83. bēacna gp. 190, 118

bēag m. *ring, bracelet* bēagum dp. 29, 17. [Cf. OE būgan *to turn, bend.*]

bealuware m. *wicked man* bealuwara gp. 189, 79

bēam m. *cross, beam, tree; beam in the eye* bēam ns. 189, 97; 200, 45. bēame ds. 190, 114; 190, 122. bēam as. 200, 44; 200, 46. bēama gp. 187, 6. [Cf. Ger. der Baum *tree.*]

bearh see **beorgan**

bearm m. *bosom, lap* bearm ns. 36, 23

bearn n. *child, son* bearn ns. 127, 56; 127, 84; 189, 83. bearnes gs. 198, 4. bearne ds. 127, 55. bearn as. 127, 83; 198, 7. bearnum dp. 56, 24; barnum 199, 36. [Allied to OE bearm *bosom, lap.*]

bearnmyrðra m. *slayer of a child* bearnmyrðran np. 145, 62

Bearrucscīr *Berkshire* Bearrucscīre ds. 111, 33

bebēodan (2) *to commit, entrust* bebīode 1s pres. ind. 76, 21; 87, 37. beboden pp. nsf. 55, 8

bebīode see **bebēodan**

bēċ see **bōc**

beceorian (II) *to complain, lament* beceorodan pl. pret. ind. 165, 72

becuman (4) *to come, befall* becōmon pl. pret. ind. 76, 24

becweðan (5) *to bequeath* becwæð 3s pret. ind. 163, 9

bedǣlan (I) *to deprive of* bedǣlde pp. npm. 126, 27

bedelfan (3) *to bury* bedealf 3s pret. ind. 189, 75

bedrīfan (1) *to besprinkle* bedrifenne pp. asm. 188, 62

beēodon see begān

befæstan (I) *to apply, utilize* befæstan inf. 76, 23. befæste sg. pres. subj. 76, 23

befaldan (7) *to fold, roll up* befalden pp. nsf. 199, 20

befaran (6) *to overtake, surround* befaran inf. 111, 13

befeallan (7) *to fall* befeallan pp. nsm. 164, 63

befēolan (3) *to apply oneself* (with dat.) befēolan inf. 87, 20

beforan prep. *before* (with dat.)

begæt see beġietan

begān (anv.) *to practice, serve* beēodon pl. pret. ind. 65, 5. begā sg. pres. subj. *may attend to* 198, 13

bēġen adj. *both* (declined like twēgen; see 12.2.1.1) bām dp. 29, 10

begeotan see beġietan

beġēotan (2) *to cover, suffuse* begoten pp. nsn. 187, 7; 188, 49

beġietan (5) *to get, acquire, obtain* beġietan inf. 75, 13, beġytan 111, 16, begeotan 198, 8 *beget.* begæt 1s pret. ind. 198, 3. beġēaton pl. pret. ind. 76, 35

beġiondan prep. *beyond* (with dat.)

begoten see beġeotan

beġytan see beġietan

behātan (7) *to promise, vow* behētan pl. pret. ind. 145, 92

behēaldan (7) *to behold, gaze upon, guard* behēold 1s pret. ind. 187, 25; 188, 58. behēoldon pl. pret. ind. 187, 9; 187, 11; 188, 64

behēold- see behēaldan

behētan see behātan

behionan prep. *on this side of* (with dat.)

belimpan (3) *to belong to, concern* belimpeð 3s pres. ind. 98, 11. belumpe sg. pret. subj. 163, 24

belumpe see belimpan

benām see beniman

bend mfn. *bond, chain, fetter* bendum dp. 164, 32

beniman (4) *to deprive* benimð 3s pres. ind. 98, 16. benām 3s pret. ind. 164, 59. The subject is cyng; see note under man, indef. pron.

benn f. *wound* benne np. 208, 49. [Cf. OE bana *murderer*.]

bēodan (2) *to command, bid* bēodaþ pl. pres. ind. 144, 45

bēom see bēon

bēon (anv.) bēon inf. 98, 30; 98, 38; 99, 51; ymbe bēon 111, 13 *to set about (a thing).* bēom 1s pres. ind. 36, 8. biþ 3s pres. ind.. bēoþ pl. pres. ind.

beorg m. *hill* beorge ds. 188, 50. beorg as. 187, 32. [MnE barrow.]

beorgan (3) *to save, protect* (with dat.) beorgan inf. 145, 97; *to seek a cure for,* 145, 58 *to cure* 145, 72. beorgað pl. pres. ind. 29, 5. bearh 3s pret. ind. 127, 54 *spare.* beorge sg. pres. subj. 127, 45. [Cf. OE burg *fort.*]

beorht adj. *bright, shining* beorht nsf. 209, 94. beorhtan dsm. 188, 66

beorhtost adj. *brightest* (supl. deg. of beorht) beorhtost asn. 187, 6

beorn m. *man, hero, warrior* beorn ns. 188, 42; 208, 70; 209, 113. beornas np. 187, 32; 188, 66

bēot n. *vow, boast* (before battle) bēot as. 208, 70

bēoþ see bēon

beran (4) *to bear, carry, bring* beran inf. 98, 32. byreð 3s pres. ind. 36, 6, byrð 98, 46, bereð 3s 190, 118. bær 3s pret. ind. *wore* 163, 7; 163, 25; 164, 26. bǣron pl. pret. ind. 187, 32. berende prp. nsf. 44, 9, nsn. 45, 18

berende see beran

berstan (3) *to burst, break* berstan inf. 187, 36

berȳpan (I) *to despoil* berȳpte pp.
nsm. 126, 26, npn. 126, 34

bestēman (I) *to make wet* bestēmed
pp. nsn. 187, 22, ns. 188, 48

bestrȳpan (I) *to strip, plunder* bestrȳpte pp. npn. 126, 35

beswīcan (1) *to betray, deceive* beswice
sg. pres. subj. 127, 66. beswicene
pp. npm. 126, 37

beswyllan (I) *to drench* beswyled pp.
nsn. 187, 23

besyrwan (I) *to defraud, ensnare* besyrwde pp. npm. 126, 38

bet adv. *better* (comp. deg. of gōde)

betǣċan (I) *to deliver, entrust* betǣht
pp. nsn. 126, 25

bētan (I) *to repair, restore, atone for*
bētan inf. 145, 90. bēttan pl. pret.
ind. 111, 50; 127, 47. bētan pl.
pres. subj. 144, 56

betera adj. *better* (comp. deg. of gōd)
betera nsm. 111, 25. betre nsn. 87,
15. beteran apn. 65, 11

betst adj. *best* (supl. deg. of gōd)
betstan npm. 44, 12

betwēonan prep. *between, among* (with
dat.)

betwyh prep. *between, among* (with
dat. and acc.)

betwyx same as **betwyh**

beþenċan (I) *to remember, call to mind*
beþenċan inf. 145, 69. beþenċan
pl. pres. subj. 145, 88

bewindan (3) *to envelop* bewunden
pp. asn. 187, 5

bewiotian (II) *to watch over* bewiotige sg. pres. subj. 198, 12

bewiotige see **bewiotian**

bewrēon (1) *to cover* biwrāh 3s pret.
ind. 207, 23. bewriġen pp. npm.
187, 17, npn. 188, 53

bewriġen see **bewrēon**

bewunden see **bewindan**

bī stressed form of **be**

bicgan (I) *to buy* bicgað pl. pres.
ind. 127, 79

bidǣlan (I) *to separate (from), deprive*

(of) (with dat. or inst.) bidǣled
pp. nsm. 207, 20

bidroren adj. *deprived of, bereft of*
(with dat.) (pp. of bidrēosan *to
overcome*) bidrorene npm. 209,
79

bifian (II) *to shake, tremble* bifian
inf. 187, 36. bifode 1s pret. ind.
188, 42

biforan prep. *before* (with dat.)

bīgang m. *worship* bīgange ds. 65, 6

bihroren adj. *covered with* (with instr.)
(pp. of bihrēosan *to fall, cover*)
bihrorene npm. 209, 77

bindan (3) *to bind* binde 3s pres. ind.
209, 102. bindað pl. pres. ind.
207, 18. binde sg. pres. subj. 207,
13

biscep m. *bishop* biscep ns. 87, 41,
biscop 164, 35. biscepe ds. 87, 31.
biscep as. 75, 1. biscepas np. 87,
39. biscopa gp. 145, 80. biscopas
ap. 164, 32. [From Lat. episcopus
bishop.]

biscepstōl m. *see, bishopric* biscopstōl ns. 164, 36. biscepstōle ds. 87,
35

biscop see **biscep**

biscoprīċe n. *bishopric* biscoprīċe
ds. 164, 33

bisigu f. *business, care, concern* bisgum dp. 87, 27

biter adj. *bitter, painful* bittreste nsf.
199, 30 *most bitter.* biteres gsm.
190, 114

bitternis f. *bitterness* bitternis ns.
199, 30. bitternisse ds. 199, 28

biþ see **bēon**

biwāwan (7) *to blow against, upon*
biwāune pp. npm. 209, 76

biwrāh see **bewrēon**

blǣd m. *joy, glory* blǣd ns. 208, 33

blæc adj. *black* blæc nsm. 45, 19

blǣċan (I) *to bleach* blǣċan inf. 45,
15

Blēcinga ēġ the Swedish district of
Blekinge ns. 98, 8

blēd m. *blessing* blēdum dp. 190, 149

blendian (I) *to blind* blendian inf. 165, 67

blēo n. *color* blēom ip. 187, 22

bliss f. *joy, merriment, happiness* blis ns. 190, 149; 190, 141. blisse gs. 55, 3. blisse ds. 190, 149; 190, 153

blīðe adj. *glad, joyful* blīðe dsn. 190, 122

blōd n. *blood* blōde is. 188, 48

blōdġyte m. *bloodshed* blōdġyte ns. 127, 49

bōc fn. *book* bēċ ds. 87, 38. bōc as. 87, 28; 87, 38. bēċ np. 29, 19; 110, 3; 145, 57; 145, 67. bōca gp. 76, 30; 76, 31. bēċ ap. 86, 2; 86, 11; 87, 15. [bōc also, and originally, means *beech-tree;* runic letters were incised upon staves from the beech.]

boda m. *messenger* bodan np. 144, 45

bodian (II) *to announce, proclaim, preach* bodad pp. nsf. 65, 2, npn. 65, 12. [Cf. OE boda *messenger.*]

boga m. *bow (weapon)* boga ns. 29, 10

bōsum m. *bosom* bōsum ds. 164, 42

bōt f. *remedy, atonement* bōt ns. 126, 17. bōte gs. 126, 31. bōte as. 126, 8; 126, 12; 126, 15; 145, 66; 209, 113

brād adj. *broad, wide* brād nsm. 98, 13, nsn. 44, 4

brǣdan (I) *to spread* brǣdan inf. 208, 47

brēac see **brūcan**

breahtm m. *noise, clamor* breahtma gp. 209, 86

brecan (4) *to break, transgress* brǣcan pl. pret. ind. 127, 47; 145, 91

brengán (I) *to bring* brenġe sg. pres. subj. 66, 25. [Cf. OE bringan *to bring.*]

brēost n. *breast* him ... in brēostum dp. *in his heart* 190, 118. brēostum dp. *breast* 209, 113

breostcofa m. *heart* breostcofan ds. 207, 18

Breoton f. *Britain* Breoton ns. 44, 1

brid m. *young bird, chick* brid ns. 199, 24

brimfugol m. *sea-bird* brimfuglas ap. 208, 47

bringan (I) *to bring* bringeð 3s pres. ind. 208, 54. broht pp. nsn. 126, 24

broht see **bringan**

brōðor m. *brother* brōðor ns. 111, 9; 127, 56; 127, 84; brōðar 198, 9; brōþer 200, 45. brōþer gs. 199, 43; 200, 47. brōþer ds. 200, 44. brōðor as. 164, 35. [Cognate with Lat. frāter *brother.*]

brūcan (2) *to enjoy, partake of, use* (with gen.) brūcan inf. 190, 144. brēac 3s pret. ind. 208, 44. brūce sg. pres. subj. 198, 5. brūcanne gerund 198, 11

bryċe m. *breach, offense, violation* bryċe as. 126, 17

brȳd f. *bride, wife* brȳde ds. 29, 19

bryhtm m. *glance, twinkling* bryhtm ns. 66, 22. [Cf. OE beorht, briht *bright.*]

bryne m. *burning, fire, conflagration* bryne ns. 127, 49. bryne ds. 126, 17. bryne as. 145, 98; 190, 149

Brytland *Wales* Brytland ns. 164, 49

brytta m. *giver, dispenser* bryttan as. 207, 25

Bryttas mp. the *Britons* Brytta gp. 145, 75; 145, 78. Bryttan dp. 145, 87

būan (anv.) *to dwell in, live in* būge 1s pres. ind. 36, 2. [Cf. Ger. bauen *to build.*]

bufan prep. *above* (with dat.)

būgan (2) *to bend, stoop* būgan inf. 187, 36. *to bend* (in obeisance) 188, 42

būge see **būan**

bune f. *cup, beaker* bune ns. 209, 94. bunum dp. 29, 17

Burgenda gpm. *of the Burgundians* Burgenda land the island *Bornholm* 97, 5, (lande) 98, 7

burgware mp. *townspeople, citizens* burgwara gp. 209, 86

burh f. *fortress, town, king's dwelling* burh ns. 98, 19. byriġ ds. 98, 20. burh as. 111, 29; 111, 43; 111, 46. [Cf. OE beorgan *to protect*.]

būtan conj. *unless, except that*

būtan prep. *besides, in addition to* (with dat.) būtan *without* 145, 96

būton same as **būtan** (conj. and prep.)

būtū adj. *both* unc būtū a. *both of us* 188, 48

bydel m. *officer* bydela gp. 145, 82

byht n. *dwelling* byht as. *dwelling(s)* 36, 3. [Cf. būan.]

byr(e)ð see **beran**

byriġ see **burh**

byriġan (I) *to taste* byriġde 3s pret. ind. 189, 101

byrnwiga m. *warrior in a coat of mail* byrnwiga ns. 209, 94

byrst m. *loss, injury* byrst ns. 127, 44. byrsta gp. 126, 11

bysmerian (II) *to mock, revile* bysmeredon pl. pret. ind. 188, 48

bysmor m. *insult, disgrace* bysmore ds. 144, 15. bysmor as. 126, 43; 144, 23. bysmara gp. 126, 11

C

Cantwarburh *Canterbury* Cantwarbyriġ ds. 111, 28; 163, 20

carlman m. *male, man* carlman ns. 164, 44

castel m. *castle, town* castelas ap. 164, 49; 164, 56. [Lat. castellum *castle, fortress*.]

ċeafl m. *jaw* ċeaflum dp. 145, 83

ċēap m. *goods, payment, purchase* ċēape ds. 29, 17; 127, 78. ċēap as. 127, 82. [MnE cheap.]

cearu f. *care, sorrow, anxiety* cearo ns. 208, 55. ċeare as. 207, 9

ċeaster f. *city, town* ċeastra gp. 45, 24. ċeastrum dp. 45, 21. [From Lat. castra (neut. pl.) *military camp*.]

cempa m. *warrior* cempan ds. 29, 19. [Cf. OE camp *fight, battle* from Lat. campus *field, field of battle*.]

cēn adj. *bold, brave, fierce* cēnum dsm. as subst. 30, 20. [Related to OE cunnan *to know*.]

Cent *Kent* Cent ds. 111, 41; 111, 49

ceorfan (3) *to carve, hew out* curfon pl. pret. ind. 188, 66

ċeorl m. *man, husband* ċeorle ds. 126, 36. [MnE churl.]

ċild n. *child, a young man of noble birth* ċild as. as a title 111, 9

Ċiltern the *Chilterns* Ciltern as. 111, 45

Ciollandene *Chillenden, Kent* Ciollandene ds. 198, 11

ċiriċe f. *church* ċiriċean np. 76, 29

clǣne adv. *fully, completely, entirely*

clǣnsian (II) *to cleanse, purify* clǣnsian inf. 145, 94

clēnnis f. *chastity, purity* clēnnisse ds. 198, 9; 198, 14

cleopiu see **clypian**

clumian (II) *to mumble* clumedan pl. pret. ind. 145, 82

clypian (II) *to cry out, call out* clypian inf. 145, 83. cleopiu 1s pres. ind. 199, 24

clyppan (I) *to embrace* clyppe sg. pres. subj. 208, 42. [MnE clip.]

cnēo n. *knee* cnēo ds. 208, 42

cnēoris f. *race, tribe* cnēoris ns. 199, 19

cniht m. *knight* cnihtas np. 164, 30

cnyssan (I) *to beat against* cnyssað pl. pres. ind. 209, 101

cnyttan (I) *to bind* cnyt 3s pres. ind. 144, 18. [MnE knit.]

cōlian (II) *to cool* cōlode 3s pret. ind. 189, 72

collenferð adj. *brave, ready for action* collenferð nsm. 208, 71

cōm see **cuman**

con see **cunnan**

cradolċild n. *infant, child in the cradle* cradolċild ns. 126, 39

Crēacas m. pl. the *Greeks* Crēacas np. 86, 10

Crīst m. *Christ* Crīst ns. 188, 56. Crīste ds. 190, 116

crīsten adj. *Christian* crīstenes gsn. 127, 74. crīstne np. as subst. 76, 26; 126, 29; crīstena 87, 14. crīstenra gp. 144, 21, gpm. 144, 44

crīstendōm m. *Christianity* crīstendōm ns. 163, 23. crīstendōme ds. 143, 3

cū f. *cow* cȳ ap. 198, 13. [Cf. Ger. die Kuh *cow*.]

cucu see **cwicu**

culfre f. *dove* culfre ns. 199, 25

cuman (4) *to come* cymeð 3s pres. ind. 66, 23; 98, 13; 98, 40; 209, 103. cumað pl. pres. ind. 98, 15. cōm 3s pret. ind. 75, 2; 111, 17; 111, 19; 111, 26; 190, 151. cwōm 190, 155; 209, 92 etc. cōmon pl. pret. ind. 111, 32; cwōman 188, 57. cume sg. pres. subj. 66, 19 (twice). cumen pp. ns. 189, 80

cunnan (PP) *can, be able, know* con 1s pres. ind. 55, 12. cunnun pl. pres. ind. 66, 24; cunnon 76, 36. cūðe 1s pret. ind. 55, 14. cūðon pl. pret. ind. 86, 8; 87, 26; 144, 23. cunne sg. pres. subj. 127, 44; 128, 89; 143, 8; 208, 69; 208, 71; 209, 113; 198, 7. cunnen pl. pres. subj. 87, 22. cūðen pl. pret. subj. 75, 15

cunnian (II) *to find out* (from experience) cunnað 3s pres. ind. 207, 29

curfon see **ceorfan**

cūð adj. *known, well known* cūð nsn. 111, 19. cūðra gpn. 208, 55

cūð- (vb.) see **cunnan**

cūðlīċe adv. *clearly, certainly*

cūðlīcre adv. *more clearly, more certainly* (comp. deg. of cūðlīċe)

cwǣd- see **cweðan**

cwǣð see **cweðan**

cwalu f. *murder, killing* cwalu ns. 127, 50

cweartern n. *prison* cweartern as. 164, 34; 164, 39

cwēn f. *wife, woman, queen* cwēne ds. 29, 17

cwene f. *woman, wife* cwenan as. 127, 78; 144, 15

cweðan (5) *to say, speak* cweðan inf. 190, 116. cweþes (tū) 2s pres. ind. 200, 44. cwyð 3s pres. ind. 189, 111. cwǣð 3s pret. ind. 55, 12; 55, 15; 55, 16; 86, 5; 207, 6; 209, 111; cweð 199, 17; 199, 18. cwǣdan pl. pret. ind. 144, 39. cweðe 1s pres. subj. 199, 26. cwǣden pl. pret. subj. 76, 34. hrædest is tō cweþenne gerund *to sum up most quickly* 126, 42

cweþestū (cweþes tū) see **cweðan**

cwicu adj. *alive, 'quick'* cuconne asm. 111, 16. cwicra gp. *among the living* 207, 9

cwideġiedd n. *spoken statement, utterance* cwideġiedda gp. 208, 55

cwīðan (I) *to lament, bewail* cwīþan inf. 207, 9. cwīðdon pl. pret. ind. 188, 56

cwōm- see **cuman**

cwyð see **cweðan**

cȳ see **cū**

cȳdde see **cȳðan**

ċyle m. *cold* ċyle as. 99, 53; 99, 55. [MnE chill.]

cymeð see **cuman**

cynehelm m. *royal crown* kinehelm as. 163, 8; cynehelm 163, 25.

cyng m. *king* (shortened form of cyning) cyng ns. 111, 20; 111, 21; 111, 35; 111, 37; 163, 2; 163, 13; 164, 37; 164, 58. cynges gs.

110, 3; 165, 74. cynge ds. 164, 37

cyning m. *king* cyning ns. 29, 6; 29, 17; 65, 15; 98, 21; kyning 75, 1; cyningc 98, 20. cyninges gs. 65, 13; 66, 27. cyning ds. 111, 10. cyning as. 98, 6; 188, 44; Cyning 190, 133; kyningas np. 75, 5; 98, 27. [Related to OE cynn *race, kind, family;* also to Greek genos, Lat. genus *kind, race.*]

cynn n. *kind, race, people* cynn ns. *family* 198, 6. wīfa cynn as. 189, 94 *womankind.* cynna gp. 44, 7; 44, 11. [See cyning.]

ċyriċhata m. *a persecutor of the Church* ċyriċhatan np. 144, 42

cyssan (I) *to kiss* cysse sg. pres. subj. 208, 42

cyst mf. *best, choice* cyst as. 185, 1. [Cf. OE ċēosan *to choose.*]

cȳðan (I) *to make known, show* cȳðan inf. 75, 2. cȳðe 3s pres. ind. 198, 1. cȳdde 3s pret. ind. 111, 12. cȳðæ his sāule mid mildheortnisse sg. pres. subj. *may* [almighty God] *show mercy to his soul* 165, 79. [Cf. OE cūð *known.*]

D

dǣd f. *deed, action* dǣde gs. *by deed* 127, 61; 144, 31. dǣda np. 127, 85. dǣda ap. 145, 86

dæġ m. *day* dæġ as. 98, 30; 110, 3. dæġe ds. 163, 23; dæge 198, 2. dæġe is. 98, 31. daga gp. 190, 136; daega 199, 17. dagum dp. 97, 2; dagan 163, 19

dæġhwāmlīċe adv. *daily*

dǣl m. *portion, part* dǣl ns. 98, 37. dǣle ds. 98, 41; be ænigum dǣle *to any extent* 144, 51; be suman dǣle *to some extent* 145, 89. dǣl as. 86, 3; 87, 14; 98, 35; 98, 43; 208, 65. dǣlum dp. 44, 3

dag- see **dæġ**

dēad adj. *dead* dēad nsm. 98, 25; dēada 98, 37. dēadan gs. 98, 48.

dēadne asm. 111, 16. dēadan npm. 99, 54

dear see **durran**

dēað m. *death* dēaðes gs. 189, 113; dēaðe ds. 209, 83. dēað as. 189, 101

dēman (I) *to deem, judge, determine* dēman inf. 189, 107. dōēmeþ pl. pres. ind. 199, 42. ġedēmed pp. nsm. 55, 3; dōēmed np. 199, 41. dōēmde np. 199, 42. dōēmeþ imp. pl. 199, 41

Denemearc f. *Denmark* Denemearcan ds. 97, 5

dēofol m. *devil* dēofol ns. 126, 5. [From Lat. diabolus *slanderer.*]

dēop adj. *deep* dēopan asm. 189, 75

dēope adv. *deeply*

dēor n. *animal, beast* dēor as. 29, 16. [Cf. Ger. das Tier *animal.*]

deorc adj. *dark* deorce asn. 209, 89. deorcan ipm. 188, 46

dēore adv. *at great expense*

dēorfrið n. *protection for game, or deer* dēorfrið as. 164, 65

derian (I) *to damage, injure* (with dat.) dereð 3s pres. ind. 128, 87. derede 3s pret. ind. 127, 51; 127, 61

dēð see **dōn**

dōēm- see **dēman**

dōgor m. *day* dogra gp. 208, 63

dohte see **dugan**

dōhtor f. *daughter* dōhtor as. 144, 15

dōm m. *judgment, doom* dōmes gs. 189, 107. dōme ds. 199, 41. miclan dōm as. the *Last Judgment* 145, 197

dōmdæġ m. *Judgment Day* dōmdæġe ds. 189, 105

dōmġeorn adj. *eager for praise, glory* dōmġeorne npm. as subst. 207, 17

dolg n. *wound* dolg np. 188, 46

dōn (anv.) *to do, make, put* dōn inf. 75, 11; 87, 24 *to bring;* 145, 72; 145, 85; 145, 89; 164, 31. dēð 3s pres. ind. 45, 20; 126, 29; 143, 2;

144, 52. dōð pl. pres. ind. 127, 77.
dyde 3s pret. ind. 55, 7; 190, 114.
dydan pl. pret. ind. 126, 13; 164,
32. dō sg. pres. subj. 76, 21; 87, 38
take; 127, 62; 165, 80; *grant;* dōa
199, 27. ġedōn pp. nsm. 164, 44

dorste see **durran**

drǣfan (I) *to drive* drǣfde 3s pret.
ind. 127, 70

drāf f. *band, group* drāfe as. 144, 21

drēam m. *joy, delight* drēam ns. 190,
140. drēames gs. 190, 144. drēame
ds. 209, 79. drēamum dp. 190,
133

dreċċan (I) *to trouble, vex, afflict*
dreċeþ 3s pres. ind. 29, 18

drēfan (I) *to stir up* drēfe 1s sg. pres.
ind. 36, 2. ġedrēfed pp. nsm. 187,
20 *troubled;* ns. 188, 59

drēogan (2) *to experience, suffer* drēogað pl. pres. ind. *commit* 127, 77

drēoriġ adj. *sad, dejected* drēoriġ
nsm. 207, 25. drēoriġne [hyġe]
asm. 207, 17

drēoriġhlēor adj. *sad-faced* drēoriġhlēor nsm. 209, 83

drēosan (2) *to fail, come to an end*
drēoseð 3s pres. ind. 208, 63

drīfan (1) *to expel, drive* drīfað pl.
pres. ind. 144, 21. drīfe sg. pres.
subj. 127, 68

drihten see **dryhten**

drincan (3) *to drink* drincað pl. pres.
ind. 98, 21; 98, 22

Dryctin see **dryhten**

dryht f. *people* dryhtum dp. 36, 11

dryhten m. *lord, chief, ruler* Drihten
ns. 56, 23; 56, 27; Dryhten 189,
101; 189, 105; 190, 144; 199, 26;
199, 28. Dryctin 199, 35; 199, 39.
Dryhtnes gs. 187, 35; 189, 75; 189,
113, 190, 136; 190, 140. Dryhten
as. 188, 64; 199, 18

dugan (PP) *avail, prosper* ne dohte
hit 3s pret. ind. *there has been no
prosperity* 127, 48; 143, 9

duguþ f. *power, host, band of retainers*

duguð ns. 209, 79. duguþe ds. 209,
97. duguþe as. 145, 78. [Cf. OE
dugan *to avail.*]

dumb adj. *mute, silent* dumbum dpn.
as subst. 36, 11

durran (PP) *dare* dear 3s pres. ind.
126, 21; 126, 23; 126, 27. dorste
1s pret. ind. 187, 35; 188, 42; 188,
45; 188, 47; 3s pret. ind. 164, 31;
164, 43. durre sg. pres. subj. 207,
10

duru f. *door* duru as. 66, 20. [Cf.
Ger. die Tür *door.*]

dwǣs adj. *foolish* dwǣsan dp. as
subst. 145, 57

dwelian (II) *to deceive, lead astray*
dwelode 3s pret. ind. 126, 6. [Cf.
OE dwola *error, heresy.*]

dyd- see **dōn**

dȳre adj. *dear, expensive* dȳre npn.
98, 45. [Cf. Ger. teuer *dear, expensive.*]

dysiġ adj. *foolish* dysiġ np. as subst.
144, 44

E

ēa f. *river* ēa ns. 98, 10. [Allied to
Lat. aqua *water.*]

ēac adv. *also* [Cf. ME a nekename
(= an ekename) *a nickname, an
'also' name.*]

ēaca m. *addition* tō ēacan ds. *next
to, after* 164, 36

ēadig adj. *wealthy, prosperous, blessed,
happy* ēadiġ nsm. 29, 14. ēadi-
gum dsm. as subst. 29, 9

ēage n. *eye* ēagan gs. 66, 22. ēge ds.
199, 43; 200, 44; 200, 45; 200, 46
(twice); 200, 47. ēgan np. 199, 25.
[Related to Lat. oculus *eye.*]

ēaht (ǣht) f. *possessions, property,
estate* ēahta ap. 165, 76

eal adv. *all, entirely* eall 187, 20;
188, 48; 188, 62

eal- see **call** n. and adj.

ēalā interj. *alas!* ēalā 145, 68; 163,
1; 209, 94 etc.

eald adj. *old, ancient* eald npn. 209, 87, ealdra gpn. 126, 34

ealdġewyrht n. *ancient deed, sin* ealdġewyrhtum dp. 189, 100

ealdor m. *lord, prince* Ealdor ns. 189, 90

ealdorbisceop m. *chief bishop* ealdorbisceop ns. 65, 1

ealdormann m. *magistrate, high civil or religious official* ealdormann ns. 65, 13. ealdormannes gs. 111, 9. (Ēadrīċ) ealdormann as. 111, 39. ealdormenn np. 111, 22. ealdormannum dp. 66, 17

eall adj. *all, every* (always declined strong) eall nsm. 208, 74 nsf. 187, 12; 189, 82; 209, 106; nsn. 76, 29; 98, 36; 98, 42; 111, 21; 111, 25; 111, 38; 187, 6; asn. 76, 30; 98, 45; 163, 16; 163, 21; 164, 29; 188, 58; npn. 97, 5; 98, 46; apn. all 199, 23; 199, 27. eal nsn. 127, 75; 127, 85; 209, 110; nsf. 188, 55; 209, 79; 209, 115; asn. 208, 60. ealles gsm. 111, 24; gsn. 163, 3. ealre dsf. 111, 37; 143, 5; eallre 127, 45. ealne asm. 36, 28; 111, 35; 111, 49; 144, 23; ealne weġ *always* 97, 2; 98, 9. mid ealle isn. *entirely* 144, 56; 145, 78; 164, 50; 164, 64; 165, 74; 165, 82. ealle nsf. 87, 17; asf. 86, 11; 98, 29; 98, 47; 127, 75; ealle hwīle *for a long time* 127, 75; 145, 70; npm. 36, 22; 55, 4; 98, 38; 98, 40; 164, 28; 190, 128; np. 87, 17; 111, 30; 126, 43 as subst.; 145, 73; 145, 97; apm. 75, 11; 165, 78; 187, 37; 189, 74; 189, 93; apf. 86, 11; 126, 10 apn. 110, 4; 111, 18. eallra gpm. 165, 73. ealra gpm. 127, 65 as subst; 208, 63; gpf. 190, 125; gp. 145, 65. eallum dpm. 87, 16; 190, 154; dpn. 65, 8; 144, 27; dp. 127, 46; 144, 22. ealla npf. 86, 2; 87, 13 apf. 87, 12

eall n. *all, everything* eall as. 76, 28; 86, 1; eal 144, 52. eal ap. *all (things)* 56, 29

ealles adv. *entirely, altogether*

eallinga adv. *altogether, entirely*

ealne see **eall** adj.

ealneġ (from ealne weġ) adv. *always*

ealo n. *ale* ealo ns. 98, 23. ealað gs. 99, 55

ēalond n. *island* ēalond ns. 44, 1. [Cf. OE ēa *water*.]

eard m. *native place or country, region, land* eard ds. 110, 7; earde 126, 38; 127, 53; 127, 64; 127, 69; 127, 70; 127, 75; 144, 42; 145, 60. eard as. 36, 27; 110, 5; 145, 77; 145, 84. [Cf. Lat. artum *narrow space*.]

eardġeard m. *earth, dwelling-place, habitation* eardġeard as. 209, 85

eardiend m. *dweller, inhabitant* eardiend ap. 199, 19

eardstapa m. *wanderer, land treader* eardstapa ns. 207, 6

earfeþe n. *hardship, tribulation* earfeþa gp. 207, 6

earfoðlīċ adj. *troubled, distressed* earfoðlīċ nsf. 209, 106

earhlīċ adj. *shameful, cowardly* earhlīċe npf. 143, 7

earm adj. *poor, wretched, destitute* earm nsm. 29, 13; 29, 14. earman dsf. 145, 67. earmne asm. 208, 40. earme npm. 126, 37; 165, 72; 188, 68 as subst. earma gp. as subst. 187, 19. earme apm. 164, 57

earmċeariġ adj. *wretched and troubled* earmċeariġ nsm. 207, 20

earmlīċe adv. *wretchedly, miserably*

earnung f. *deserts, merit* earnungan dp. 126, 13; 126, 15

Ēast Centingas pl. *the people of East Kent* n. 111, 30

Ēast Seaxe pl. *the East Saxons* Ēast Seaxum dp. 111, 41. [Cf. MnE Essex.]

ēastan adv. *from the east*

Ēastre f. *Easter* Ēastron dp. 164, 26.

[From the name of a pagan Gmc. goddess, Ēastre, Ēostre.]

ēaðe adv. *easily*

ēaðmōd adj. *humble* ēaðmōd ns. 188, 60

eaxl f. *shoulder* eaxlum dp. 187, 32

eaxlġespann n. *intersection* (of the cross) eaxlġespanne ds. 187, 9

Ebriscġeþīode n. *the Hebrew people* Ebriscġeþīode ds. 86, 9

ēċe adj. *eternal, everlasting* ēċe nsm. 29, 18; 56, 23; 56, 27. ēci 199, 35; 199, 39

ecg f. *edge, point* ecg ns. 30, 20. [Related to Lat. aciēs *keenness, edge.*]

eder m. *building, dwelling* ederas np. 209, 77

ēfen mn. *evening* ēfenne ds. 199, 22. ēfen as. 199, 22; 199, 24

eft adv. *again, a second time, in turn* eft onġēan *back again* 111, 40

efstan (I) *to hasten* efstan inf. 187, 34

ēg- see **ēage**

eġe m. *fear* eġe as. 144, 51

eġelīċ adj. *awful, dreadful, terrible* eġelīċ nsn 126, 4; 127, 77. eġelīċe npf. 127, 85

eġesa m. *fear, awe* eġesa ns. 189, 86

eġeslīċ adj. *dreadful, fearful* eġeslīċ nsf. 189, 74

ehta num. *eight*

ellen n. *strength* mid elne ds. *valiantly* 209, 114. elne micle (mycle) is. *very much* 187, 34; 188, 60; 190, 123

embe see **ymbe**

ende m. *end, district, area, edge* ende ds. 126, 2; 127, 49; 143, 10; 187, 29. ænde 126, 32. [Cf. Lat. antiquus *old.*]

endebyrdnes f. *order, arrangement* endebyrdnes ns. 55, 19. endebyrdnesse as. 55, 4. [Cf. OE byrd *birth, rank.*]

engel m. *angel* engla gp. 36, 27.

englum dp. 190, 153. [From Lat. angelus *messenger.*]

engeldryht f. *host of angels* engeldryhta gp. 187, 9

Engle mpl. *the English* Engle np. 143, 11; 144, 20. Engla gp. 145, 77. Englum dp. 145, 87

Engleland n. *England* Englalande ds. 164, 47; Englelande 164, 26; 164, 37. Engleland as. 163, 8; 163, 18; Englaland 163, 21; 164, 29; Englæland 164, 46

Englisc adj. *English, the English language* Englisc asn. 87, 22; 87, 26; as. 75, 16 (twice); 87, 28; 87, 29; 87, 35

ent m. *giant* enta gp. 209, 87

ēode see **gān**

eom 1s pres. ind. *I am* is 3s pres. ind.; nis 3s pres. ind. neg. 144, 29; 164, 40; 207, 9. sind(on), synd(on), siendon, syndan, syn pl. pres. ind. sīe sg. pres. subj. 65, 2; 66, 17; 76, 20; 87, 42; 189, 112; 198, 6 (twice); 198, 7; 198, 15; sȳ 99, 56; sī 111, 43; 190, 144. sīen pl. pres. subj. 87, 16; 87, 21; 87, 39; 199, 41

eorl m. *warrior, earl* (after 1066) eorl ns. 163, 7; 209, 84; 209, 114. eorle ds. 207, 12. eorlas np. 164, 29. eorla gp. 208, 60. eorlas ap. 164, 32; 209, 99

eorldōm m. *earldom* eorldōm as. 164, 37; 164, 52

eornost f. *earnest* on eornost as. *seriously* 144, 23

eorðe f. *earth* ʹeorðe ns. 44, 8. eorðan gs. 56, 24; 187, 37; 209, 106; 209, 110. eorþan ds. 29, 12; 65, 15; 188, 42; 189, 74; 190, 137; 190, 145; land 199, 18. eorþan as. 36, 27

eorðscræf n. *grave* eorðscræfe ds. 209, 84

eorðweġ m. *earthly-way* eorðweġe ds. 190, 120

ēow d. and a. of **ġē**

ēower 2nd pl. poss. pron. *your* ēowre 200, 48

ēowic a. of ġē

Ēowland the Swedish island *Öland* Ēowland ns. 98, 8

ercanstān m. *pearl* ercanstānas ap. 200, 48

ernian (II) *to earn, deserve* ernian inf. (with gen.) 126, 12

Este *a Baltic people* Estum dp. 98, 12; 98, 24; 98, 25; 99, 50; 99, 53

Estland *the country of the Este* Estland ns. 98, 19. Estlande ds. 98, 15

Estmere m. *the Frisches Haff* Estmere ns. 98, 13. Estmere as. 98, 12; 98, 14; 98, 15

ēðel mn. *country, native land, land* ēðel ns. 190, 156. ēþle ds. 29, 14; dis. 207, 20. ēþel as. 36, 26; 75, 8

Europe *Europe* Europe gs. 44, 3

F

fadian (II) *to arrange, order* fadian inf. 145, 94. fadode 3s pret ind. 127, 57

fæc n. *division, interval, distance, period of time* fæc ns. 66, 22. fæce ds. 66, 23; is. 44, 3

fæder m. *father* fæder ns. 127, 55; 127, 83; 165, 70. fæder ds. 127, 56; Fæder 209, 115

fæġen adj. *glad, jubilant* fæġen nsm. 208, 68

fæġer adj. *beautiful, lovely, fair* fæġer nsm. 189, 73. fæġran dsf. 187, 21. fæġere npm. 187, 8; npf. 187, 10

fæġ(e)re adv. *well, agreeably*

fæġerra adj. *more beautiful* (comp. deg. of fæġer) fæġerra nsm. 45, 15

fǣrcodon see fercian

fǣrlīċe adv. *suddenly*

fæste adv. *fast, firmly*

fæstenbryċe m. *the non-observance of fasts* fæstenbrycas ap. 144, 41

fæstnung f. *security, stability* fæstnung ns. 209, 115

fǣtels m. *vessel* fǣtels ap. 99, 55

fæðm m. *embrace, grasp, bosom* fæðmum dp. 36, 23. [Cf. MnE fathom.]

fāh adj. *guilty, stained; ornamented* fāh nsm. 187, 13; 209, 98

Falster *Falster,* a Danish island Falster ns. 97, 4

fangene see fōn

faran (6) *to go, travel* faran inf. 164, 42; 165, 71. fearu 1s pres. ind. *I shall go* 199, 17

fēa adv. *a little*

feala same as fela

feallan (7) *to fall* feallan inf. 188, 43. fealleþ 3s pres. ind. 208, 63

fealu adj. *dark, dusky* fealwe apm. 208, 46

fearu see faran

fēawe pl. adj. *few* fēawa n. as subst. 75, 14; 76, 18; 76, 27

fēdan (I) *to feed, nourish* fēdan inf. 29, 7. fēdað pl. pres. ind. 36, 17

fela adj. indecl. *many, much*

felafǣcne adj. *very treacherous* felafǣcne asn. 29, 16

fēng see fōn

feoh n. *cattle, money, riches* feoh ns. 209, 108. fēos gs. 98, 34. fēo ds. 98, 40 (twice). feoh as. 98, 32; 98, 43. fēo is. 98, 44. [Cognate with Lat. pecus *cattle.*]

feohġīfre adj. *greedy for wealth* feohġīfre nsm. 208, 68

fēond m. *enemy, foe, adversary* fēond ns. 36, 13. fēonde ds. 36, 13. fēondas np. 187, 30; 187, 33; ap. 187, 38. fēondum dp. 127, 81. [Cf. OE fēon *to hate;* fēond lit. *the one hating.*]

feorgbold n. *body* feorgbold ns. 189, 73

feor adv. *far, far from* feor with dat. 207, 21. feor *from long ago* 209, 90

feorran adv. *from afar*

fēran (I) *to go, come, travel* fērde 3s pret. ind. 111, 21. fērdon pl. pret. ind. 111, 36; 111, 40; 111, 49. fērende prp. nsm. 36, 9

fercian (II) *to bring, convey* fǣrcodon pl. pret. ind. 111, 23

fērende see **fēran**

ferian (I) *to carry, bring* ferode 3s pret. ind. 110, 4; ferede 209, 81

fers nm. *verse* fers ap. 55, 18. [From Lat. uersus *a verse.*]

ferð mn. *soul, heart, mind* ferð ns. *mind(s)* 208, 54. ferðe ds. 209, 90

ferðloca m. *breast, enclosure of the spirit* ferðloca ns. 208, 33. ferðlocan as. 207, 13

fēsan (I) *to drive away* fēseð 3s pres. ind. 144, 13

feter f. *fetter* feterum ip. 207, 21. [Allied to Lat. impedīre *to entangle, hinder.*]

feþer f. *feather* feþra ap. *wings* 208, 47

fīf num. *five* fīfe as subst. 187, 8

fīftēne num. *fifteen*

fīftiġ num. *fifty* fīftegum d. 87, 36

findan (3) *to find* findan inf. 207, 26. findeð 3s pres. ind. 99, 52. funden pp. nsf. *established* 86, 9. [Related to Lat. pons, pontis *bridge;* IE *pent- *go, enter upon, find.*]

fiorm f. *benefit, use* fiorme as. 76, 31. [Also meaning *food, goods* fiorm (feorm) gives MnE farm.]

fīras mp. *men* fīrum dp. 56, 28; 199, 40

first m. *time* oð ðone first ðe as. *until the time when* 87, 22

fiscað m. *fishing* fiscað ns. 98, 21

fiscwylle adj. *filled with fish* fiscwyllum dpn. 44, 9

flēon (2) *to flee* flēoð pl. pres. ind. 45, 20

flēotan (2) *to float* flēotendra prp. gpm. 208, 54

flet n. *floor, hall* flet as. 208, 61

flōd mn. *flood, wave* flōde ds. with ġetenġe 36, 9. flōdas npl. 36, 23

flotman m. *sailor, pirate* flotmen np. 143, 12

fōē(n) see **fōn**

folc n. *folk, people, nation* folc ns. 111, 23; 111, 38; 190, 140. folces gs. 75, 6; 126, 3; 127, 74; 145, 83. folc as. 36, 6

folclagu f. *public law* folclaga np. 126, 33

folde f. *earth, ground* foldan gs. 36, 23; 187, 8; 188, 43; 208, 33. foldan ds. with ġetenġe 36, 9; 190, 132. foldan as. 56, 28; foldu 199, 40. [Cf. OE feld *field, plain.*]

folgian (III) *to follow, observe* (with dat.) flyġean inf. 145, 91; folgian 165, 74. folgade 3rd sg. pret. ind. 163, 24. flyġen pl. pres. subj. 66, 26. [Cf. Ger. folgen *to follow.*]

fōn (7) *to take, seize, grasp* fēng 3s pret. ind. 65, 14; tō rīċe fēng *succeeded to the throne* 76, 19. fōē sg. pres. subj. *may succeed (to)* 198, 4. fōēn pl. pres. subj. 198, 15. fangene pp. np. 44, 10. tō fōnne gerund 111, 38

fōr f. *course, way* fōre as. 111, 28

for prep. *for, because of, before* (with dat., instr., acc.) for *before* 189, 93; for hwan conj. *why* 208, 59. for ðȳ *therefore* 87, 15; 87, 40; 98, 17; 98, 45; for þan *therefore* 189, 84. for þon *for that, therefore* 55, 2; 55, 13; 55, 14; 65, 10; 66, 25; 76, 20; 207, 17; 208, 37; 208, 58; 208, 64; *for* 65, 5; *because* 65, 11. for ðǣm *therefore* 76, 37. for þām *therefore* 126, 11; 127, 63; *because* 126, 13; 126, 31; 127, 46; 127, 52; 144, 29; 144, 48. for ðǣm ðe *because* 76, 32 (twice); 76, 37; 76, 38

forbærnan (I) *to burn, cremate* for-

bærneð 3s pres. ind. 98, 47. forbærnað pl. pres. ind. 98, 31.
forbærnde 3s pret. ind. 111, 19;
127, 70. forbærndon pl. pret. ind.
111, 46. forbærned pp. nsm. 99,
51; nsn. 76, 29

forbēodan (2) *to forbid* forbēad 3rd
sg. pret. ind. *preserved* 165, 68

forceorfan (3) *to cut off* forcorfen
pp. nsn. 199, 21

fordōn (anv.) *to destroy* fordōn inf.
145, 78

fordǽste see **forðrǽstan**

fore prep. *before* (with dat.) fore *on
behalf of* 199, 26

forebegān (anv.) *to intercept* forebegān pp. nsm. 111, 37

foregangan (7) *to precede* foregange
sg. pres. subj. 66, 24

foregenġa m. *predecessor* foregenġa
ns. 163, 15

forespeca m. *sponsor, godparent* forespecan np. 145, 93

forflēon (2) *to avoid, escape from*
forflēon pl. pres. subj. 165, 82

forġeaf see **forġiefan**

forġiefan (5) *to give, grant* forġeaf
3s pret. ind. 190, 147

forġifness f. *forgiveness* forġifenesse
as. 165, 80

forġytan (5) *to forget* tō forġytane
gerund 164, 40

forhealdan (7) *to withhold* forhealdan inf. 126, 21; forehealdað pl.
pres. ind. 126, 22

forhergian (II) *to plunder, devastate,
ravage* forhergod pp. nsn. 76,
29. [Cf. OE *here* *army*.]

forht adj. *afraid, timid* forht nsm.
187, 21; 208, 68

forhtian (II) *to be afraid* forhtiað pl.
pres. ind. *will be afraid* 190, 115

forhwæga adv. *about*

forlǽtan (7) *to abandon, lose* forlǽtan inf. 145, 90. forlēt 3s pret. ind.
left 55, 7. forlēton pl. pret. ind. 86,

7; 111, 22; 188, 61. forlǽten pp.
np. 76, 37

forleġene see **forlicgan**

forlēogan (2) *to lie, perjure oneself*
forlogene pp. np. 128, 87; forlogen
np. 144, 40

forlēosan (2) *to lose, abandon* forlēas
3s pret. ind. 164, 45. forloren pp.
np. 144, 40. [Cf. Ger. *verlieren* *to
lose*.]

forlēt- see **forlǽtan**

forlicgan (5) *to commit adultery, forni-
cate* forleġene pp. npm. *adulter-
ous* 145, 63

forliġer n. *fornication* forliġru ap.
144, 38

forloren see **forlēosan**

forniman (4) *to take away* fornōm
3s pret. ind. 209, 80. fornōmon pl.
pret. ind. 209, 99. fornumene pp.
nsn. 126, 41

fornōm- see **forniman**

fornumene see **forniman**

fornȳdan (I) *to force, compel* fornȳdde ... tō ċeorle pp. npf. *forced
to marry* 126, 36

foroft adv. *very often*

forrǽdan (I) *to betray* forrǽdde 3s
pret. ind. 127, 69. of līfe forrǽde
sg. pres. subj. *should kill treacher-
ously* 127, 67

forsawene see **forsēon**

forsēon (5) *to despise* forsawene pp.
npf. 126, 43

forspendan (I) *to squander* forspendað
pl. pres. ind. 98, 43

forspillan (I) *to kill* forspilde 3s pret.
ind. 127, 71

forst (frost) m. *frost* forst ns. 29, 1.
[Cf. OE frēosan *to freeze*.]

forstandan (6) *to understand* forstōd
1s pret. ind. 87, 34

forstrang adj. *very strong* forstrangne
asm. 36, 13

forswerian (6) *to swear falsely* forsworene pp. np. 128, 87

forsyngian (II) *to sin greatly* forsyngod pp. nsm. *corrupt* 144, 32.
forsyngodan dsf. 145, 68
forð adv. *forth* tō forð *too much* 144,
53. swæ forð *so on* 198, 5
forðēode see **forðgān**
forðgān (anv.) *to go forth* forðēode
3s pret. ind. 188, 54
forðġeseaft see note 10, p. 191. forðġesceaft as. 187, 10
forþolian (II) *to do without, forgo*
forþolian inf. with lārcwidum 208,
38
forðrǣstan (I) *to crush* fordrǣste 3s
pret. ind. 199, 23
forðweġ m. *departure, the way forth*
forðweġe ds. 190, 125; 209, 81
forweorðan (3) *to perish, to come to
nothing, deteriorate* forwurðan
inf. 111, 25. forwurdan pl. pret.
ind. 127, 72; 145, 85. forweorðan
pl. pres. subj. 145, 74. forwurde
sg. pret. subj. 199, 31
forworhtan see **forwyrċan**
forwrēgan (I) *to accuse* forwreġde
3s pret. ind. 111, 9
forwundian (II) *to wound severely*
forwundod pp. nsm. 187, 14; 188,
62
forwurd- see **forweorðan**
forwurðan see **forweorðan**
forwyrċan (I) *to sin, do a wrong*
forworhtan pl. pret. ind. *forfeited*
145, 84. forwyrċan pl. pres. subj.
144, 55
foryrman (I) *to reduce to poverty* foryrmde pp. npf. 126, 36
fōt m. *foot* fōtum ip. 200, 49
fōtmǣl n. *a foot-measure, foot-space*
fōtmǣl ap. 163, 3
fracod adj. *vile, wicked* fracodes gsm.
as subst. 187, 10
frætwe f. pl. *adornments* frætwe np.
36, 6
fram prep. *from, by* (with dat.)
frēa m. *lord* Frēa ns. 56, 28; 199, 40.
Frēan as. 187, 33

frēfran (I) *to comfort* frēfran inf.
207, 28
fremde adj. *foreign, strange, alien*
fremdan asm. as subst. *stranger*
127, 55. fremdan npm. as subst.
99, 49. fremdum dp. as subst. 126,
39; 127, 84
fremsumnes f. *benefit, liberality, kind-
ness* fremsunesse ap. 65, 7. [Cf.
OE fremu *advantage, gain.*]
fremu f. *advantage, benefit* fremum
dp. used adverbially, '*advantage-
ously*' 36, 17
frēo see **frīo**
frēolsbriċe m. *the non-observance of
church festivals* frēolsbricas ap.
144, 40
frēomǣġ m. *(noble) kinsman* frēo-
mǣgum dp. 207, 21
frēond m. *friend* frēond ns. 209, 108.
frēondas np. 189, 76; frynd 29,
14. frēonda gp. 190, 132. frēondum dp. 98, 26. [Cf. OE frēoġan
to love; frēond lit. *the one loving.*]
frēondlēas adj. *friendless* frēond-
lēasne asm. 207, 28
frēondlīċe adv. *in a friendly manner*
frēoriġ adj. *cold, frozen* frēoriġ nsm.
208, 33. [Cf. OE frēosan *to freeze.*]
frēoriht n. *rights of freemen* frēoriht
ns. 126, 41
frēosan (2) *to freeze* frēosan inf. 29,
1. [Lat. cog. prūrīre *to itch,
burn.*]
frīnan (3) *to ask* frīneð 3s pres. ind.
will ask 189, 112
frīo adj. *free* frēo npm. 165, 71.
frīora gpm. 87, 20
frið m. *peace, security* frið ns. 164,
40. friðes gs. 111, 29. frið as. 111,
30. [Cf. OE frīo *free.*]
frōd adj. *wise, experienced* frōd nsm.
209, 90
frōfor f. *comfort, consolation, help*
frōfre as. 209, 115
frumsceaft f. *creation* frumsceaft as.
55, 16

fugel   m.   *bird*   fugel ns. *? ship* 209, 81. fugela gp. 44, 9. [MnE fowl.]

ful   adv.   *full, very, wholly*

fūl   adj.   *foul, vile*   fūlne asm. 145, 83. fūle npm. 145, 63. [Cf. MnE fulsome.]

fūlian   (II)   *to decompose*   fūliað pl. pres. ind. 99, 54. [Cf. MnE foul.]

full   adj.   *full*   be fullan ds. adverbially *'fully, perfectly'* 86, 3. full apm. 99, 55. full with bōsum 164, 42

fullīċe   adv.   *completely*

fulluht   m.   *baptism*   fulluhte ds. 145, 93. fulluht as. 145, 92

fultum   m.   *help*   fultume ds. 87, 18

fultumian   (II)   *to help* (with dat.)   fultumian inf. 65, 10. fultume sg. pres. subj. 198, 10

funden   see   **findan**

fundian   (II)   *to hasten, come*   fundaþ 3s pres. ind. *will come* 189, 103

furðor   same as   **furður**

furðum   adv.   *even*

furður   adv.   *further*

fūs   adj.   *eager*   fūse asn. *shining* 187, 21. fūse np. *the hastening ones* 188, 57

fylġean   see   **folgian**

fylġen   see   **folgian**

fyll   m.   *fall, death*   fyll as. 188, 56

fyllan   (I)   *to fell*   fyllan inf. 189, 73

fȳlþ   f.   *sin, filth*   fȳlþe ds. 127, 80. fȳlþe as. 127, 79

fȳr   n.   *fire*   fȳr ns. 29, 2; 66, 18; as. 45, 20; 126, 18

fyrd   f.   *national army, militia*   fyrd ns. 111, 48. fyrde ds. 111, 37

fyrmest   adj.   *first, foremost* (supl. deg. of forma)   fyrmest nsm. 164, 36

G

gælsa   m.   *pride, wantonness*   gælsan as. 145, 83

gǣst   m.   *spirit*   gǣst ns. 36, 9. gāstes gs. 199, 29. gāst as. 188, 49. gāstas np. 187, 11. gāsta gp. 190, 152. [Cf. Ger. der Geist *spirit*.]

gǣstlīċ   adj.   *ghostly, spectral*   gǣstlīċ nsn. 208, 73

gagātes   m.   *agate, jet*   gagātes ns. 45, 19. [Lat. gagātēs *bitumen*.]

galan   (6)   *to sing*   galan inf. 188, 67. [Cf. OE nihtegale *nightingale*.]

Gallia Bellica   (Lat.)   *Belgic Gaul*

Gallie   *Gaul*   Gallie ds. 44, 2

gān   (anv.)   *to go, come*   ēode 3s pret. ind. 55, 6; 55, 13. gān pl. pres. subj. 165, 83. [For pret. cf. Lat. eo *I go*.]

gang   m.   *flowing*   gange ds. 187, 23

gangan   (7)   *to go, walk*   gongende prp. nsm. 55, 7. [Cf. OE gang *way, path*; MnE gangplank.]

gār   m.   *spear*   gār ns. 30, 20

gārsecg   m.   *sea, ocean*   gārsecges gs. 44, 1

gāst-   see   **gǣst**

ġe   conj.   *and*

ġē   2nd pl. pers. pron. nom.   *you*

ġeǣmetiġian   (II)   *to free, disengage from* (with acc. of person and gen. of thing)   ġeǣmetiġe sg. pres. subj. 76, 22. [Cf. OE and MnE ǣmitiġ, empty.]

ġeǣrnan   (I)   *to gallop (to)*   ġeǣrneð 3s pres. ind. 98, 43

ġealga   m.   *gallows, cross*   ġealga ns. 187, 10. ġealgan as. 188, 40

ġealgtrēo   n.   *gallows-tree, cross*   ġealgtrēowe ds. 190, 146

ġēapscipe   n.   *cunning*   ġēapscipe ds. 164, 46. [Cf. OE ġēap *deceitful, intelligent*.]

ġēar   n.   *year*   ġēare ds. 110, 1; 164, 26. ġēar as. 98, 28. ġēara gp. 126, 6; 127, 53; 144, 30; gēra 199, 18. gēr ap. 199, 27. twā ġēar ap. *(for) two (more) years* 164, 53

ġēara   adv.   *formerly*   iū ġēara *long ago* 44, 1. ġēara iū *long ago* 187, 28; 207, 22 ġēardagas mp. *days of yore, former times* ġēardagum dp. 208, 44

ġeare adv. *clearly, for certain* ġeare clearly, really (what is what) 208, 69; ġearwe *readily* 208, 71

ġearo adj. *ready, prepared* ġearo nsn. 30, 20; ġearu 111, 38. ġearwe npn. 110, 1. [MnE yare.]

ġearu see ġearo

ġearwe see ġeare and ġearo

ġeat n. *gate* ġeatum dp. 45, 22

ġebād see ġebīdan

ġebæd see ġebiddan

ġebēorscip m. *feast, banquet, entertainment* ġebēorscipes gs. 55, 7. ġebēorscipe ds. 55, 3; 55, 13. [Cf. OE bēor *beer.*]

ġebētan (I) *to atone, make amends* ġebētan inf. 99, 52. [Cf. OE bōt *help, atonement.*]

ġebicgan (I) *to buy, pay for* ġebicgan inf. 29, 17. ġebohte 3s pret. ind. 127, 82

ġebīdan (I) *to experience, suffer* ġebīdan inf. 126, 12; *wait* 208, 70. ġebīdeð 3s pres. ind. *experiences* 207, 1. ġebād 3s pret. ind. *felt* 190, 125. ġebiden pp. np. 126, 11; ns. 188, 50; 189, 79

ġebiddan (5) *to pray* ġebiddaþ pl. pres. ind. 189, 83. ġebæd iċ mē 3s pret. ind. *I prayed, worshipped* 190, 122

ġebind n. *fastening, binding* ġebind as. 207, 24; 208, 57

ġebindan (3) *to bind, hold fast* ġebindað pl. pres. ind. 208, 40

ġebohte see ġebicgan

ġebrēowan (2) *to brew* ġebrowen pp. nsn. 98, 24

ġebringan (I) *to bring, produce* ġebringeð 3s pres. ind. 29, 15; 144, 53. ġebringe sg. pres. subj. 190, 139

ġebūgan (2) *to turn, bow* ġebūgan inf. 145, 89

ġebyrian (I) *to pertain to, befit* ġebyriað pl. pres. ind. 144, 46

ġecnāwan (7) *to know, understand* ġecnāwan inf. 87, 17. ġecnāwe sg. pres. subj. 127, 44; 128, 89. ġecnāwað imp. pl. 126, 1

ġecringan (3) *to fall, perish* ġecrong 3s pret. ind. 209, 79

ġecrong see ġecringan

ġecynde adj. *by natural inheritance* ġecynde nsn. 164, 52

ġedǣlan (I) *to divide, share with* ġedǣlde 3s pret. ind. 209, 83

ġedēmed see dēman

gedōē see ġedōn

ġedōn (anv.) *to do, act* ġedōn inf. 87, 18. ġedoð pl. pres. ind. *bring about* 99, 56. gedōē sg. pres. subj. 198, 2; *should bring about* 198, 10. hū ġedōn mann pp. nsm. *what sort of man* 163, 10. geþō imp. sg. *take out* 200, 46

ġedreċċan (I) *to oppress* ġedrehtan pl. pret. ind. 127, 52

ġedrēfed see drēfan

ġedrehtan see ġedreċċan

ġedrēas see ġedrēosan

ġedrēosan (2) *to fail, come to an end* ġedrēas 3s pret. ind. 208, 36

ġedrynċ n. *drinking, carousing* ġedrynċ ns. 98, 30. ġedrynċe ds. 98, 33

ġedwolgod m. *false god* ġedwolgoda gp. 126, 22; 126, 27. ġedwolgodan dp. 126, 24. [Cf. OE dwelian *to deceive.*]

ġeearnian (II) *to earn, deserve, gain* ġeearnian inf. 145, 98. ġeearnaþ 3s pres. ind. *shall have earned* 189, 109. ġeearnedan pl. pret. ind. 126, 14

ġeendian (II) *to end, finish* geendas 2s pres. ind. 199, 22; 199, 24. ġeendod pp. nsf. 111, 26

ġefæstnian (II) *to fasten, make fast* ġefæstnodon pl. pret. ind. 187, 33

ġefaran (6) *to go, travel, fare* ġefōre
sg. pret. subj. 97, 1. ġefaren pp.
nsn. 145, 70

ġefe see ġiefu

ġefeoht n. *fight, battle* ġefeohte ds.
144, 13

ġefeohtan (3) *to fight* ġefuhton pl.
pret. ind. 111, 43

ġefēra m. *comrade, associate* tō ġefēran ds. *as a companion* 207, 30.
tō ġefērum dp. *as companions* 29,
16. [Cf. OE fēran *to go, travel.*]

ġefēran (I) *to go, fare, obtain* ġefērdon pl. pret. ind. 111, 20; 111,
44

ġefetian (II) *to fetch* ġefetiġe sg. pres.
subj. 190, 138

ġefremman (I) *to perform, bring about*
ġefremman inf. 207, 16; 209, 114

ġefrīnan (3) *to hear of, learn by inquiry*
ġefrūnon pl. pret. ind. 189, 76

ġefrūnon see ġefrīnan

ġefuhton see ġefeohtan

ġefyllan (I) *to fell, strike down* ġefyllan inf. 187, 38

ġefyllan (I) *to fill, fill up* (with gen.)
ġefylle 1s pres. ind. 36, 27. ġefyldæ
pp. npf. 76, 30

ġegān (anv.) *to overrun, conquer* ġegān inf. 163, 18. ġeēodon pl. pret.
ind. 111, 29

ġeġearwian (II) *to prepare* ġeġearwod pp. nsm. 145, 99

ġegōdian (II) *to endow* ġegōdade 3s
pret. ind. 163, 19

ġegræmian (II) *to enrage, provoke*
ġegræmedan pl. pret. ind. 145, 77

ġegrētan (I) *to attack, greet* ġegrēteð
3s pres. ind. 144, 50

ġeġyr(w)ed see ġyrwan

ġehadode pl. *ecclesiastics, clerics, those
in holy orders* (the pp. of hādian
to consecrate) ġehadode np. 127,
57

gehaldan see ġehealdan

ġehāten see hātan

ġehealdan (7) *to hold, protect, observe*
ġehealdan inf. 111, 36; gehaldan
198, 7; 198, 9; 198, 15. ġehealdeþ
3s pres. ind. 209, 112. ġehīoldon
pret. pl. ind. 75, 8

gehefeldad adj. *having begun the web*
(pp. of hefeldian *to begin the web*)
gehefeldad asm. 199, 22

ġehīoldon see ġehealdan

ġehola m. *protector* ġeholena gp.
208, 31

ġehwā pron. nom. *each* ġehwā ns.
145, 72. ġehwām ds. 208, 63

ġehwæs gsm. and gsn. of ġehwā ġehwæs 56, 22; gihuæs 199, 34

gehweorfan (3) *to turn* gehwerfæþ
pl. pres. ind. 200, 49

ġehwilċ pron. *each, every* ġehwilcum
ds. 126, 19; ġehwylcum 189, 108.
ġehwylċe ism. 207, 8; is(m.) 190,
136

ġehwylċ see ġehwilċ

ġehȳdan (I) *to hide, bury* ġehȳdde
3s pret. ind. 209, 84

ġehȳġd f. *thought, intention* ġehȳġd
ns. 208, 72

ġehȳnede see hȳnan

ġehȳran (I) *to hear, obey* ġehȳran
inf. 189, 78. ġehȳrde 3s pret. ind.
55, 18; 187, 26. ġehȳrdan pl. pret.
ind. 145, 87

ġelæred adj. *learned* ġelærede npm.
87, 39

ġelæstan (I) *to perform, pay* ġelæstan inf. 145, 92. ġelæste sg. pres.
subj. 126, 20

ġelagian (II) *to ordain, appoint by law*
ġelagod pp. nsn. 126, 21

ġeleornian (II) *to learn* ġeliornode
1s pret. ind. 87, 30. ġeleornade 3s
pret. ind. 55, 2. ġeliornodon pl.
pret. ind. 86, 10; 87, 12. ġeleornad
pp. nsm. 65, 3; ġeliornod 87, 33;
ġeliornod npm. 86, 3

ġelettan (I) *to hinder* ġelet pp. nsn.
111, 39

ġelēwede see lēwian
ġelīċ adj. *alike, like, similar* (with dat.)
bām gelīċ *to both alike* 29, 10.
ġelīċe np. 145, 57. gelicum ipn.
66, 26
ġelīccast adj. *most like* (supl. degree
of ġelīċ; with dat.) ġelīccast nsm.
127, 80
ġelīefan (I) *to believe* ġelīefe 1s pres.
ind. 76, 21. ġelȳfe 3s pres. subj.
127, 76
gelīffestan (I) *to vivify* gelīffestes 2s
pres. ind. 199, 29
ġelimp n. *event, occurrence* ġelimpum
dp. 144, 27
ġelimpan (3) *to happen* ġelimpan inf.
143, 2. ġelimpð 3s pres. ind. 143,
9
ġelimplīċ adj. *fitting, suitable* ġelimplīċe dsf. 55, 9
ġeliornod- see ġeleornian
gelōcian (II) *to look, behold* gelōciu
1s pres. ind. 199, 19. gelōcendu
prp. npn. 199, 25
ġelōgian (II) *to lodge, place* ġelōgode
3s pret. ind. 127, 73
ġelōme adv. *often, frequently*
ġelustfullīcor adv. comp. deg. of
ġelustfullīċe *willingly* [Cf. OE
lust *willing.*]
ġellȳfe see ġelīefan
ġelȳfed adj. *weak, infirm* ġelȳfdre
gsf. 55, 2
ġemæċċa mf. *companion; spouse* tō
ġemæċċan *as a companion* 29, 10.
gemeccan ds. 198, 5
ġemǣne adj. *common, universal* ġemǣne nsm. 127, 44; nsn. 143, 4.
ġemǣnum ċeape ds. *in a joint
purchase* 127, 78. ġemǣne npm.
'commonly' 127, 79; np. 143, 8.
[Cf. Ger. gemein *common.*]
ġemǣtan (I) *to dream* (impersonal
vb.) ġemǣtte 3s pret. ind. 185, 2
ġeman see ġemunan
gemeccan see ġemæċċa

ġemenġan (I) *to mingle, mix* ġemenġed pp. as(m.) 208, 48
ġemet n. *measure, degree, meter* ġemete ds. mid ġemete ryhte *with
due propriety* 36, 16. gemete ds.
199, 42. ġemet as 56, 31; ofer eal
ġemett *beyond all measure* 163,
16
ġemēted see mētan
ġemētte see mētan
ġemon see ġemunan
ġemunan (PP) *to remember, bring to
mind* ġeman 1s pres. ind. 187,
28. ġemon 3s pres. ind. 208, 34;
209, 90. ġemunde 1s pret. ind. 76,
28 (twice); 86, 1; 86, 9; 87, 24.
ġemunde 3s pret. ind. 111, 17
ġemynd f. n. *memory, mind* ġemynd ns. 208, 51. ġemynde ds. 56,
30. ġemynd as. 75, 3
ġemyndiġ adj. *mindful* ġemyndiġ
nsm. 207, 6
ġenām- see ġeniman
ġenāp see ġenīpan
ġeneahhe adv. *frequently, very often*
generian (I) *to save* generedes 2s
pret. ind. 199, 30
ġenihtsum adj. *abundant* ġenihtsume
npm. 45, 13
ġeniman (4) *to take, seize* ġenimeð
3s pres. ind. 29, 16. ġenām 3s pret.
ind. 111, 14. ġenāmon pl. pret. ind.
111, 30; 188, 60; genāman 187,
30. ġenumen pp. nsn. 98, 42.
[Allied to Lat. numerus *number.*]
ġenīpan (1) *to grow dark, vanish*
ġenāp 3s pret. ind. 209, 96
genīwian (II) *to renew* ġenīwad pp.
nsm. 190, 148; nsf. 208, 50; 208,
55
ġenōge see ġenōh
ġenōh adj. *enough* ġenōh nsm. 98,
24. ġenōge npm. 187, 33
ġenumen see ġeniman
ġenyrwde see nyrwan
ġēo same as iū

ġeofen n. *ocean, sea* ġeofen ns. 29, 15

ġeoguð f. *youth, young people* ġioguð ns. 87, 19. ġeoguðe ds. 208, 35. [Cf. Ger. die Jugend *youth.*]

ġeond prep. *throughout* (with acc.)

ġeondhweorfan (3) *to pass through* ġeondhweofeð 3s pres. ind. 208, 51

ġeondscēawian (II) *to look about* ġeondscēawað 3s pres. ind. 208, 52

ġeondþenċan (I) *to contemplate, consider thoroughly* ġeondþenċe 1s pres. ind. 208, 60. ġeondþenċe 3s pres. ind. 209, 89

ġeong adj. *young* ġeong nsm. 188, 39

ġeorn adj. *eager, desirous* (usually with gen.) ġeorn nsm. 29, 6; 208, 69. [Allied to Greek charisma *a grace, favor.*]

ġeorne adv. *eagerly, willingly, well*

ġeornlīcor adv. *more eagerly, ernestly* (comp. deg. of ġeornlīċe)

geornliocar adj. *more eagerly* (comp. deg. of ġeornlīċe) geornliocar nsm. 198, 12

ġeornost adv. *best* (supl. deg. of ġeorne)

ġēr- see ġēar

ġerǣċan (I) *to obtain* ġerǣċan inf. 126, 15

ġeriht see rihtan

ġerihte n. *right, law* ġerihta np. *dues* 126, 32. ġerihta gp. 126, 35. ġerihta ap. *dues* 126, 20; 126, 22

ġerīsan (1) *to rise, stand up* ġerīseð 3s pres. ind. 29, 11

ġerisene n. *what is befitting* ġerisena gp. 126, 35

ġerisenlīcre adv. *more fittingly, more suitably* (comp. deg. of ġerisenlīċe)

Germanie *Germany,* 'Germania' Germanie ds. 44, 2

gerōēfa m. *reeve, official in charge of an estate* gerōēfa ns. 198, 1

ġersum m. *treasure, riches* ġersuman ap. 163, 9

ġerȳman (I) *to open up (a way)* ġerȳmde 1s pret. ind. 189, 89

ġesǣliġlīċe adj. *happy, blessed* ġesǣliġlica npf. 75, 4

ġesǣne see ġesȳne

ġesǣt see ġesittan

ġesǣtt- see ġesettan

ġesamnian (II) *to collect, assemble* ġesamnode pp. npm. 98, 38

ġesāwe see ġesēon

ġesceaft f. *creature, created being; creation* ġesceaft ns. 187, 12; 188, 55; 189, 82; *decree* 209, 107. ġesceafte as. 127, 82

ġescrǣpe adj. *suitable* ġescrǣpe nsn. 44, 7. ġescrǣpe npn. with baðo 45, 17

ġescrīdan (I) *to clothe* ġescrīd pp. nsm. 163, 4

ġeseah see ġesēon

ġeseald- see ġesellan, sellan

ġesēċan (I) *to seek* sceal ġēsēċan inf. *must seek,* or, perhaps, *shall attain* 190, 119

gesees see ġesēon

ġeselda m. *companion* ġeseldan np. 208, 53

ġesellan (I) *to give, yield* ġesealde 3s pret. ind. 127, 75; 127, 83. ġesealdon pl. pret. ind. 111, 31

ġesēlð f. *good fortune* ġesēlða ap. with singular meaning 110, 6. [Cf. OE sēl *good.*]

ġesēne see ġesyne

ġesēon (5) *to see, look* ġesīon inf. 76, 36. gesīo 1s pres. ind. 199, 18. gesihs (tū) 2s pres. ind. 199, 43; gesihst 200, 47. gesees 2s pres. ind. 200, 44. ġesihð 3s pres. ind. 208, 46. ġeseah 1s pret ind. 187, 14; 187, 20; 187, 33; 187, 36; 188, 51; 3s pret. ind. 55, 5; 76, 28.

ġesēo sg. pres. subj. 65, 11. ġesāwe sg. pret. subj. 187, 4. ġesewen pp. nsn. 65, 15. ġesēoh imp. sg. 65, 2

ġeset n. *seat* ġesetu np. 209, 93

ġeseted see settan and ġesettan

ġesettan (I) *to set, place* ġesette 3s pret. ind. 55, 9; ġesætte 163, 19; ġesætt 164, 49. ġesetton pl. pret. ind. 188, 67. ġeseted pp. nsn. *established* 190, 141

ġesewen see ġesēon

ġesib adj. *related;* as subst. *kinsman* ġesib ns. 127, 55. ġesibban as. 127, 55

ġesīene see ġesȳne

gesihst see ġesēon

gesihstū (gesihs tū) see ġesēon

ġesihð see ġesēon

ġesīo (n) see ġesēon

ġesittan (5) *to sit* ġesæt 3s pret. ind. 209, 111

ġestāh see ġestīgan

ġestandan (6) *to stand* ġestōdon pl. pret. ind. 188, 63

ġesteal n. *earthly establishment* ġesteal ns. 209, 110

ġestīgan (1) *to ascend* ġestīgan inf. 187, 34. ġestāh 3s pret. ind. 188, 40

gestillan (I) *to cease, be still* gestilde pp. nsf. 199, 19

ġestōdon see ġestandan

ġestrēon n. *possession, property* ġestrēon np. 98, 46

ġesund adj. *safe, sound* ġesund 111, 44

ġesweorcan (3) *to grow dark, become gloomy* ġesweorce sg. pres. subj. 208, 59. [Cf. OE sweorc *darkness.*]

ġeswīcan (1) *to desert, betray, deceive* (with dat.) ġeswīcaþ pl. pres. ind. 29, 14

ġeswinċ see ġeswincg

ġeswincg n. *effort, oppression* ġeswincg as. 111, 24

ġeswugian (II) *to keep silent* ġeswugedan pl. pret. ind. 145, 87

ġesyhð f. *sight, vision* ġesyhðe ds. 187, 21; 188, 41; 188, 66. ġesyhðe as. 189, 96

ġesȳne adj. *seen, evident* ġesȳne nsn. 145, 67; 128, 88; ġesēne 127, 46; ġesǣne 144, 28. ġesīene npn. 188, 46

ġesynto f. *prosperity* ġesynto as. 65, 8. [Cf. OE sund *sound, healthy.*]

get n. *gate* gete ds. 199, 17

gēt same as ġiet

geteld n. *tent* geteld ns. 199, 20

ġetenġe adj. *near to, resting on* ġetenġe nsm. 36, 8

ġetimbrian (II) *to build* ġetimbrade pp. npf. 45, 23 *built;* ġetymbrad nsn. 163, 20. [Cf. Ger. das Zimmer *room;* MnE timber.]

ġetrēowþ f. *loyalty, truth* ġetrēowþa np. 126, 6; ġetrȳwða 127, 54. ġetrȳwða ap. 145, 95

ġetrȳwlīċe adv. *loyally, truly*

ġetrȳwða see ġetrēow

ġeþafnung f. *assent* ġeþafnunge as. 65, 13. [Cf. OE þafian *to permit.*]

ġeþanc m. *thought, intention* ġeþance ds. 144, 54

ġeþeahtere m. *councilor* ġeþeahteras np. 66, 27. [Cf. OE ġeþeaht *thought.*]

ġeðenċean (I) *to think* ġeðenċean inf. 76, 19; ġeþenċan 208, 58. ġeðenċ imp. sg. 76, 24

ġeþēod- see ġeþīode

ġeðēon (1) *to thrive, prosper, succeed* ġeðīhþ 3s pres. ind. 29, 14. [Cf. Ger. gedeihen *to prosper.*]

ġeþēowede see þēowian

ġeðīhþ see ġeðēon

ġeþīode n. *language, nation, tribe* ġeðēodes gs. *tribe* 99, 51. ġeðīode as. 76, 33; 86, 4; 86, 11; 87, 13; 87, 14; 87, 17. ġeðēoda gp. 86, 8

geþō see ġedōn

ġeþōht m. *thought* ġeþōhte is. 209, 88

** geðrēan** (II) *to rebuke, reprove* geðrēas 2s pres. ind. 199, 29

ġeþyldiġ adj. *patient* ġeþyldiġ nsm. 208, 65

geðynnian (II) *to make thin* geðynnade pp. npn. 199, 25

ġeþwǣre adv. *agreeably*

ġeunnan (PP) *grant, give* ġeūðe 3s pret. ind. 163, 18

ġeūðe see **ġeunnan**

ġewanian (II) *to lessen, curtail* ġewanian inf. 126, 23. ġewanode pp. nsn. 126, 42

ġewarnian (II) *to warn* ġewarnode pl. pret. ind. 111, 47

ġewāt see **ġewītan**

ġeweald m. *power, possession* ġewealde ds. 126, 39; 127, 81; 127, 85; 164, 49. ġeweald as. 189, 107

ġewealdan (7) *to control* ġewealde 3s pret. ind. 164, 50

ġewearð see **ġeweorðan**

ġewelede see **welwan**

ġewelhwǣr adv. *nearly everywhere*

ġewelhwilcan see **ġewelhwylċ**

ġewelhwylċ adj. *nearly every* ġewelhwylcan dsm. 127, 49. ġewelhwilcan 143, 10

ġewendan (I) *to go* ġewende 3s pret. ind. 111, 10. ġewendon pl. pret. ind. 111, 32; 111, 48

ġeweorc n. *a work, construction* ġeweorc np. 209, 87

ġeweorht see **wyrċan**

geweorpan (3) *to cast, throw* gewearpaþ imp. pl. 200, 48

ġeweorðan (3) *to become, happen* ġewearð 3s pret. ind. 111, 8; 127, 83. ġewurdon pl. pret. ind. 110, 1; 110, 3. ġeweorþe sg. pres. subj. 143, 4. ġewurde sg. pret. subj. 144, 17. ġeworden pp. ns. 127, 68; nsn. 127, 76; 144, 46; 145, 79

ġeweorþian (II) *to honor, esteem, distinguish* ġeweorþode 3s pret. ind. 189, 90; 189, 94. ġeweorðad pp. nsn. *distinguished* 45, 21; ġeweorðod *adorned* 187, 15

ġewilnigan (II) *to desire* ġewilniġeð 3s pres. ind. 163, 10

ġewinn n. *struggle, strife, battle* ġewinn ns. 98, 23. ġewinne ds. 188, 65

ġewinnan (3) *to win* ġewunnon pp. nsm. 164, 54

ġewitan (PP) *to know, understand* tō ġewitane gerund 163, 10

ġewītan (1) *to depart, go* ġewāt 3s pret. ind. 55, 14; 188, 71; 209, 95. ġewiton pl. pret. ind. 190, 133. ġewīte sg. pres. subj. 66, 20

ġeworden see **weorðan** and **ġeweorðan**

ġeworhte see **wyrċan**

ġeworhton see **ġewyrċan**

ġewrit n. *writing, record* ġewrit as. 87, 22; 87, 26; (*Domesday Book*) 164, 48

ġewrītan (1) *to write* ġewritene pp. npm. 165, 81

ġewrohte see **ġewyrċan**

ġewuna m. *custom, wont, practice* ġewuna ns. 111, 34. ġewunan ds. 144, 47

ġewunnon see **ġewinnan**

ġewurdon see **ġeweorðan**

ġewurðad see **ġeweorðian**

ġewyrċan (I) *to work, create, produce* ġewyrċan inf. 99, 53. ġewyrċað pl. pres. ind. 145, 100. ġewrohte 3s pret. ind. 164, 50. ġeworhton pl. pret. ind. 187, 31

ġewyrht n. *deed, action* ġewyrhtum dp. 143, 2

ġewyrman (I) *to warm* ġewyrmed pp. nsf. 66, 18

ġeyriġde adj. *disheartened* (pp. of yrgan *to dishearten*) ġeyriġde npm. 143, 11

ġiefstōl m. *gift-seat, the seat or throne at which gifts were dispensed* ġiefstōles gs. 208, 44. [Cf. Ger. der Stuhl *chair*.]

ġiefu f. *gift* ġefe ap. 65, 7. [Cf. OE ġiefan *to give*.]

ġielp m. *boasting* ġielpes gs. 208, 69

ġīet adv. *yet, still*

ġif conj. *if*

ġīferness f. *greed* ġīfernessa ap. 144, 34

gifeðe adj. *granted* gifeðe nsn. 198, 7

gihuæs see **ġehwæs**

ġimm- see **ġym**

ġioguð see **ġeoguð**

ġiond same as **ġeond**

ġiorne same as **ġeorne**

ġirnan (I) *to desire, entreat* ġirndon pl. pret. ind. with tō 111, 30. [Cf. OE ġeorn *eager*.]

ġītsung f. *avarice, covetousness* ġītsunge as. 145, 79; 164, 63. ġītsunga ap. 144, 33

ġiu same as **iū**

glēaw adj. *wise, prudent* glēaw nsm. 208, 73

Glēawċeaster *Gloucester* Glēawċeastre ds. 164, 28

glīwstafas mp. *joy, signs of joy* glīwstafum dp. perhaps adverbially, 'joyfully' 208, 52

gōd adj. *good* gōde nsm. 164, 40. gōdne asm. 144, 17. gōde hwīle asf. *for a long time* 188, 70. gōdan npm. 165, 82. gōdena gpm. 86, 2. gōdum dpm. 163, 16. gōde apm. *good things* 165, 81

god m. *a god, God* God ns. 29, 4; 29, 18; 76, 23; 127, 45; 144, 99; 144, 100; 163, 17; 165, 79; 188, 39; 189, 93; 189, 98; 189, 106; 190, 156; 198, 3; 198, 4; 198, 6. Godes gs. 55, 18; 76, 31; 87, 18; 87, 37; 126, 19; 126, 20; 126, 22; 126, 25 etc.; 143, 1 etc.; 189, 83; 190, 152. Gode ds. 56, 31; 75, 6; 75, 11; 76, 19; 87, 39; 111, 43; 126, 12; 126, 15 etc. God as. 144, 55; 145, 77; 145, 88; 145, 91; 163, 16; 188, 51; 188, 60; 199, 18. godo np. 65, 9. goda gp. 65, 6

godbearn n. *godchild* godbearn ap. 127, 71

godcund adj. *religious, divine* godcundan npm. 75, 10. godcundra gpm. 75, 4. godcundra gpf. 144, 43

gōddǣd f. *good deed* gōddǣdan dp. 144, 48. gōddǣda ap. 144, 49

godfyrht adj. *godfearing* godfyrhte ap. as subst. 144, 49

gōdian (II) *to improve* gōdiende prp. nsn. 126, 16

gōdness f. *goodness* gōdnesse ds. 165, 82

godsib m. *godparent* godsibbas ap. 127, 71. [MnE gossip.]

gold n. *gold* gold ns. 208, 32. goldes gs. 164, 42; 164, 60. golde ds. 163, 4; 187, 7; 187, 16; 189, 77. gold as. 187, 18

goldwine m. *friendly lord* goldwine ns. 208, 35. goldwine as. 207, 22

gongende see **gangan**

Gotland the Swedish island *Gotland* Gotland ns. 98, 8

grǣdinæss f. *greed, avarice* grǣdinæsse as. 164, 64

grēne adj. *green* grēne npm. 36, 24. [Cf. OE grōwan *to grow*.]

grēotan (2) *to weep* grēotende prp. npm. 188, 70

grētan (I) *to greet, hail* grētan inf. 75, 1. grēteð pres. ind. 208, 52. grētte 3s pret. ind. 55, 11

grimlīċ adj. *cruel, terrible* grimlīċ nsn. 126, 4

grimm adj. *fierce, savage* grimme npm. 144, 43. grimmum dpm. 29, 15

grimme adv. *grimly, savagely*

grið n. *sanctuary* griðe ds. 127, 74

griðian (II) *to protect* griðian inf. 126, 30

griðlēas adj. *violated* griðlēase npf. 126, 34

grōwan (7) *to grow* grōwaþ pl. pres. ind. 44, 8

grund m. *ground, bottom, depth* grundum dp. 36, 24

guma m. *man* guma ns. 208, 45. guman gs. 188, 49. gumena gp. 190, 146. [Cog. with Lat. homo *man*.]

gūðbord n. *war-shield* gūðbord ns. 30, 20

ġyldan (3) *to pay, yield* ġylda pl. pres. ind. 144, 24; 144, 25. ġylde sg. pres. subj. 143, 7

ġym m. *gem, precious stone* ġym ns. 45, 19. ġimmas np. 187, 7; 187, 16. ġimmum dp. 163, 4

ġȳman (I) *to observe, respect* ġyme sg. pres. subj. 126, 19

ġynd same as **ġeond**

ġyrwan (I) *to adorn, deck* ġyredon pl. pret. ind. 189, 77. ġeġyred pp. nsn. 187, 16. ġeġyrwed 187, 23

ġȳt(a) same as **ġiet**

H

habban (III) *to have* habban inf. 87, 41; 98, 44; 145, 95; 165, 75; habbon 75, 13. hæbbe 1s pres. ind. 188, 50; 189, 79; 198, 3. hafað 3s pres. ind. 29, 12; 44, 4; 45, 16; 65, 4; 98, 41; hæfð 145, 99. habbað pl. pres. ind. 76, 20; 76, 37; 87, 19; 98, 6; 98, 28; 98, 38; 126, 11; 126, 25; 126, 43; 144, 20; 165, 81. hæfde 1s pret. ind. 87, 33; 3s pret. ind. 56, 30; 111, 11; 163, 11; 164, 31; 164, 37; 164, 48; 188, 49; heafde 111, 37. næfde 3s pret. ind. neg. 163, 2; næfde hē næfre swā myċel yfel ġedōn subj. *however much evil he might have done* 164, 43. hæfdon pl. pret. ind. 65, 4; 65, 9 (twice); 75, 6; 76, 26; 86, 3; 164, 55; 187, 16; 188, 52. næfdon pl. pret. ind. neg. 110, 5. hæbbe

sg. pres. subj. 65, 3; 198, 8. hæbben pl. pres. subj. 87, 20. hæfde sg. pret. subj. 164, 53. tō habbanne gerund 198, 11

habbon see **habban**

habbað see **habban**

hād m. *rank, order, sex* hāde ds. 45, 17 *sex;* 87, 24; 163, 24. hādas np. 75, 10. hāda gp. 75, 4. [Cf. MnE suffix -hood, -head.]

hādbryċe m. *injury to clerics* hādbrycas ap. 144, 37

hæbb- see **habban**

hæfd- see **habban**

hæġl m. *hail* hæġle ds. 208, 48

hæġlfaru f. *hailstorm* hæġlfare as. 209, 105

hǣlan (I) *to save, redeem, heal* hǣlan inf. 189, 85

hǣlend m. *Saviour* Hǣlendes gs. 187, 25

hæle(ð) m. *man, hero, fighter* hæleð ns. 188, 39; hæle 208, 73. hæleð mīn sē lēofa ns. *my dear man* 189, 78; 189, 95. hæleþa gp. 36, 3. hæleþum dp. 209, 105

hǣman (I) *to have intercourse with* hǣmde 3s pret. subj. 164, 44

hǣt see **hātan**

hǣþen adj. *heathen, pagan* hǣþnum dsm. as subst. 29, 19. hǣþene apm. 144, 35; hǣþenum dpf. 126, 20; 126, 23; 126, 28. [Cf. OE hǣþ *heath*.]

Hǣðum *Haddeby* Hǣðum ds. 97, 1

hafað see **habban**

hālettan (I) *to greet, hail* hālette 3s pret. ind. 55, 10. [Cf. OE hāl *hale, whole*.]

half see **healf** (adj.)

hāliġ adj. *holy, sacred* hāliġ nsm. 56, 25; halig 199, 37. hālgum dsm. 29, 19. halig as. as subst. *that which is holy* 200, 48. hāliġe npm. 187, 11; npf. 127, 72. halgum dp. *saints* 190, 143; 190, 154. [Allied to OE hāl *whole*.]

hāliġnes f. *sanctuary* haliġnessa np. 126, 33

hām m. *home* hām as. 190, 148; used adverbially 55, 6; 111, 21

Hamtūnscīr *Hampshire* Hamtūnscīre ds. 111, 33

hand f. *hand* tō handa ds. *within reach* 188, 59. honda ap. 208, 43. hondum ip. 207, 4

hār adj. *gray, hoary* hāra nsm. 209, 82

hara m. *hare* haran dp. 165, 71

hāt adj. *hot* hat apn. 45, 17

hātan (7) *to order, command; be called* hāte 1s pres. ind. 75, 2; 189, 95 *bid;* 198, 1. hātte 1s pres. ind. pass. *am called* 36, 29. hāteþ 3s pres. ind. 44, 5; 75, 1; hǣt 98, 17. hēt 3s pret ind. 111, 34; 163, 6; 163, 7; 163, 8; 164, 35. hātte 3s pret. ind. pass. 145, 75. hēton pl. pret. ind. 111, 27; 187, 31. hāten pp. nsm. *called* 65, 1; nsn. 44, 1; ġehāten nsm. 164, 52; hātene npn. 98, 7

hāten see **hātan**

hāteþ see **hātan**

hātheort adj. *hot-tempered* hātheort nsm. 208, 66

hātte see **hātan**

hē 3rd sg pers. pron. masc. nom. *he* hē '*it*' 45, 16 (twice)

hēa see **hēah**

hēadēor n. *stag, deer* hēadēor ap. ? *wild animals in general* 165, 69

hēafod n. *head* hēafod as. 208, 43. hēafdum dp. with singular meaning 188, 63

hēah adj. *high, tall* hēah nsm. 209, 98. hēa nsf. 36, 4. hēanne asm. 209, 82

hēahfæder m. *the Father* Hēahfædere ds. 190, 134

hēahðungen adj. *of high rank* hēahðungene npm. 98, 27

hēahwita m. *high or chief councillor* hēahwitan np. 111, 22

healdan (7) *to hold, possess, keep* healdan inf. 110, 5; 126, 29; 145, 95. hēoldan pl. pret. ind. 127, 58; hīoldon 76, 34. healde sg. pres. subj. 207, 14

healf adj. *half* healf asn.98, 28; half asn. 198, 11

healf f. *half, side* healfe as. 187, 20. healfum dp. 111, 42. healfe ap. 111, 35; 111, 47

heall f. *hall* heall ns. 66, 18. [Cog. with Lat. cella *cell, room.*]

hēan adj. *abject, despised* hēan nsm. *dejected* 207, 23. hēanan gsm. as subst. 30, 20. hēanne asm. 188, 40; hēanne may also be asm. of hēah *high, lofty*

hēaniss f. *height* hēanis as. 199, 25

hēanne see **hēah**

heard adj. *hard, strong, bold* heardum dsm. 30, 20

heardost adj. *hardest, most severe* (supl. deg. of heard) heardost nsm. 189, 87

hearpe f. *harp* hearpan ds. 55, 4. hearpan as. 55, 5

hēawan (7) *to stab* hēaweþ 3s pres. ind. 127, 62

hebban (6) *to raise up, bear aloft* hebban inf. 187, 31

hefen see **heofon**

hefenrīcæs see **hēofonrīċe**

hefiġ adj. *heavy, grievous* hefian dsn. 188, 61. þȳ hefiġran is. *the more severe* 208, 49

hell f. *hell* helle gs. 145, 98; 199, 17

helle m. *hell* helle as. 36, 25

helm m. *helmet, protection* helm ns. 30, 20. [Cf. OE helan *to conceal, cover.*]

help f. *help, succour* tō helpe ds. *as a help* 189, 102. helpe as. 207, 16

helpan (3) *to help* (with gen.) helpe sg. pres. subj. 145, 100

hēmed n. *marriage* hēmed as. 198, 15. [Related to OE hām *home.*]

hēo the same as hīe *they, them, she*

heofon mf. *sky, heaven, firmament* (often in pl.) heofenes gs. 188, 64. heofon as. 5 6, 25; hefen 199, 37. heofona gp. 188, 45. heofenum dp. 189, 85; 190, 134; heofonum 190, 140; 190, 154; 209, 107; 209, 115. heofonas ap. 36, 25; heofenas 189, 103

heofonlīċ adj. *heavenly* heofonlīcne asm. 190, 148

hēofonrīċe n. *kingdom of heaven* hēofonrīċes gs. 55, 20; 189, 91; hefenrīcæs 199, 32. heofonanrīċe ds. 165, 83

hēold- see **healdan**

heolster m. *darkness* heolster ns. 207, 23

heom same as **him** *them*

heonanforð adv. *henceforth*

heonon adv. *hence, from here*

heora same as **hiera**

heord f. *care, keeping* heord ns. 55, 8. [MnE herd.]

heorde m. *shepherd* heorda gp. 199, 20

heort m. *hart, deer, stag* heort as. 164, 66. heortas ap. 165, 68

heorte f. *heart* heortan gs. 208, 49

hēr adv. *here*

hēran (I) *to obey* (with dat.) hēreð 3s pres. ind. 36, 14. hȳrde 3s pret. ind. 65, 11

here m. *army, armed force, devastation* here ns. 111, 31; 127, 48; 143, 10. here as. 111, 28; 111, 30; 145, 77 (subject of ġewinnan and fordōn)

hereġian see **herian**

herenis f. *praise* herensse ds. 55, 17. [Cf. OE herian *to praise*.]

herga see **herian**

herġian (II) *to harry, ravage, lay waste* herġiað pl. pres. ind. 144, 25. hergode 3s pret. ind. 111, 11. hergodon pl. pret. ind. 111, 34

herian (I) *to praise* herian inf. 29, 4. hereġian 144, 52. herga 199, 32

heriġean see **herian**

hērtōēacan adv. *besides*

hēt- see **hātan**

hete m. *hate, malice* hete ns. 127, 51; 143, 10

hetelīċe adv. *violently*

hetol adj. *hostile, violent, severe* hetole npm. 144, 42

hī same as **hīe** *they, them,* and **hīe** *her*

hīa *she,* the same as **hēo** hīa *herself* 198, 9

hīæ same as **hīe** *they*

hīd f. *a hide of land* hīd ns. 164, 47

hider adv. *hither*

hīe 3rd pl. pers. pron. nom. and acc. *they, them;* also variant in nom. sg. for hēo *she* hīe *'it'* (æ) 86, 10 (twice); 87, 13 (twice); 87, 30; 87, 33 (twice); 87, 34 (twice)

hieder same as **hider**

hiene same as **hine** hiene *'it'* (wīsdōm) 76, 23

hiera g. of hīe *they;* also indeclinable possessive pron. *their*

hierdebōc f. *pastoral book* hierdebōc ns. 87, 29

hierra adj. *higher* (comp. deg. of hēah) hierran dsm. 87, 24

hīersumian (II) *to obey* (with dat.) hīersumedon pl. pret. ind. 75, 6

hiht see **hyht**

hilderinc m. *warrior* hilderincas np. 188, 61. hilderinca gp. 189, 72

him ds. of hē and hit; d. of hīe *him* dsm. used reflexively 29, 12; 29, 16; dpm. 98, 6. him dp. *for their part* 111, 49. him . . . in breostum *in his heart* 190, 118

hind f. *hind, doe* hinde as. 164, 66

hine as. of hē hine *'it'* 45, 20

hīo same as **hīe** *they, them, she* hīo nsf. *'it'* (lār) 75, 14

hīoldon see **healdan**

hiora same as **hiera**

hira same as **hiera**

hire g. and d. of **hēo** *she*

hīrēd m. *household, court* hīrēde ds. 163, 13

his g. of hē and hit; also indeclinable possessive pronoun *his* his dir. obj. of brūce 198, 5

Hispanie *Spain, 'Hispania'* Hispanie ds. 44, 3

hit 3rd sg. pers. pron. neut. nom. and acc. *it* hit ns. *'he'* 198, 4. hit as. (wīsdōm) 76, 24

hīw n. *kind, appearance, species* hīwes. gs. 45, 13

hlāford m. *lord, master* hlāford ns. 144, 18; 163, 2; 163, 11. hlāfordes gs. 127, 66. hlāforde ds. 143, 3. hlāford as. 127, 67. hlāfordum dp. 198, 3. [From OE hlāf-weard *loaf-guardian.*]

hlāfordswica m. *traitor* hlāfordswican np. 127, 65

hlāfordswice m. *treachery, treason* hlāfordswice ns. 127, 65; 127, 67

Hlāmmesse f. *Lammas Day* Hlāmmessan ds. 111, 27. [From OE Hlāfmesse *loaf-mass.*]

hlēoðrian (II) *to make a noise, speak* hlēoðrode 3s pret. ind. 187, 26

hlīfian (II) *to tower* hlīfiġe 1s pres. ind. 189, 85

hlūde adv. *loudly, aloud*

hnāg see hnīgan

hnīgan (1) *to bow (down)* hnāg 1s pret. ind. 188, 59

hōcor n. *derision* hōcore is. 144, 49

hocorwyrde adj. *derisive* hocorwyrde npm. 144, 44

hōl n. *? malice ? envy* hōl ns. 127, 50

holm m. *sea, ocean, water, wave* holm ns. 29, 15. holm as. 209, 82. [Allied to Lat. collis *hill.*]

holt mn. *forest, wood* holtes gs. 187, 29. [Cf. Ger. das Holz *wood, timber.*]

holtwudu m. *a tree of the forest* holtwudu as. 189, 91

hond- see hand

hondwyrm m. *a kind of insect* hondwyrm ns. 36, 21

horn m. *horn* horn as. 198, 14

hopian (II) *to hope* hopode 3s pret. ind. (with tō) 111, 25

hord nm. *hoard, treasure* hord ns. 30, 20

hordcofa m. *treasure chest,* i.e. the breast, where thoughts are contained hordcofan as. 207, 14

hōring m. *fornicator* hōringas np. 145, 63

hors n. *horse* hors as. 98, 41. hors np. 98, 45. hors ap. 98, 38

hrædest adv. *quickest* (supl. deg. of raðe) hrædest is tō cweþenne *to sum up most quickly* 126, 42; 145, 65

hræding f. *haste* hrædinge ds. 145, 69

hrædlīċe adv. *quickly, right away*

hrædwyrde adj. *hasty of speech* hrædwyrde nsm. 208, 66

hræġl n. *garment* hræġl ns. 36, 1. hræġle ds. 98, 47

hrǣw m. *corpse, body* hrǣw ns. 189, 72. hrǣw as. 188, 53

hrēoh adj. *troubled* hrēo nsm. 207, 16, hrēo asf. *fierce* 209, 105

hrēosan (2) *to fall* hrēosan inf. 208, 48. hrēosende prp. nsf. 209, 102

hrēowċeariġ adj. *sorrowful, troubled* hrēowċeariġ nsm. 187, 25

hrēowlīċe adv. *cruelly*

hrēran (I) *to stir (up), move* hrēran inf. 207, 4

hreþer m. *breast, heart* hreþra gp. with singular meaning 208, 72

hrīm m. *rime, hoarfrost* hrīm as. 208, 48. hrīme is. 209, 77

hrīmċeald adj. *frost-cold* hrīmċealde asf. 207, 4

hrīnan (1) *to touch, reach (to)* (with gen. dat. or acc.) hrīne 1s pres. ind. 36, 24. hrinen pp. nsm. 66, 21

hrinen see hrīnan

hrīð f. *snowstorm* hrīð ns. 209, 102
hrōf m. *roof* hrōfe ds. 56, 25; hrōfæ 199, 37
hron m. *whale* hronas np. 44, 10
hrūse f. *ground, earth* hrūsan gs. 207, 23. hrūsan as. 36, 1; 209, 102. [Allied to Lat. crusta *the crust, shell.*]
hryre m. *fall, ruin, death* hryre ? ds. 207, 7
hryðiġ adj. *snow-swept* hryðġe npm. 209, 77
hū adv. *how*
Humber f. *the Humber (river)* Humbre ds. 75, 15; 75, 17
hund m. *dog, hound* hundum dp. 127, 80; 200, 48
hund n. *hundred* hund ns. 44, 4 (twice)
hundeahtatiġ num. *one-hundred and eighty*
hundred n. *a hundred* hundred as. 164, 60
hunger m. *hunger, famine* hunger ns. 127, 48
huniġ n. *honey* huniġ ns. 98, 20
hūru adv. *indeed, certainly, about*
hūs n. *house* hūse ds. 55, 6. hūs as. 55, 7; 66, 19. hūs np. 126, 34. hūsum dp. 98, 29
hūsl n. *Eucharist* hūsl ns. 29, 19
hwā pron. masc. nom. *who, what, anyone, anything* hwā ns. *anyone* 87, 42; 163, 10. swā hwā swā *whosoever* 164, 66
hwænne conj. *when* hwænne *the time when* 190, 136
hwǣr adv. *where, wherever, anywhere*
hwæs g. *of hwā and hwæt*
hwæt nom. and acc. neuter of hwā *who, what, anyone, anything* hwæt ns. 36, 29; 66, 24 (twice); 163, 24; *that which*; 185, 2. hwæt as. 55, 16
hwæt interj. *indeed! what! lo! behold!* hwæt 66, 20; 185, 1

hwæthwugu pron. *something* hwæthwugu as. 55, 12
hwæðre adv. *nevertheless, however*
hwan i. of hwæt for hwan *why* 208, 59
hwelċ see **hwilċ**
hwēorfan (3) *to turn, return, go, move* hwēorfan inf. 29, 11; 208, 72
hwet same as **hwæt**
hwider adv. *where, in what direction*
hwīl f. *while, time* ōðre hwīle ds. *at one time* 165, 13. hwīle as. *for a while* 188, 64; 189, 84; gōde hwile as. *for a long time* 188, 70. ðā hwīle ðe as. *during which time* 87, 21; *for the time that* 198, 6; 198, 8. ealle þā hwīle þe as. *all the while that* 98, 29; lange hwīle as. *for a long time* 187, 24. ealle hwīle as. *for a long time* 127, 75; 145, 70
hwilċ pron. and adj. *which, what, any* hwelċ ns. 65, 2; hwylċ 143, 3 *someone;* hwilċ nsm. 164, 44. hwelċe npm. 75, 3. hwelċ npn. 76, 24
hwīlon same as **hwīlum**
hwīlum adv. *sometimes, from time to time* (dp. of hwīl f. *time, while*)
hwon i. of hwæt for hwon *why* 199, 43
hwylċ see **hwilċ**
hwȳlum same as **hwīlum**
hȳ same as **hīe** *they, them,* and **hīe** *her*
hycgan (III) *to think* hycge sg. pres. subj. 207, 14
hyġe m. *thought, mind, heart, courage* hyġe ns. 30, 20; 207, 16 *mind*
hyht m. *joy* hyht ns. 190, 126; hiht 190, 148 *hope*
hyldan (I) *to bow* hyldan inf. 188, 45
hȳnan (I) *to humiliate, abase* hȳnað pl. pres. ind. 144, 25. ġehȳnede pp. npf. 126, 37
hyra same as **hiera**
hȳran (I) *to hear, obey; belong (to)*

hȳrað pl. pres. ind. 97, 5; 98, 9

hȳrde see hēran

hyrst f. *trappings* hryste np. 36, 4

hyrwan (I) *to abuse, deride* hyrweð 3s pres. ind. 144, 49; 144, 52

hys same as his

hyt same as hit

I

ić 1st sg. pers. pron. nom. *I*

īcan (I) *to increase* īhte 3s pret. ind. 126, 9. [Cf. OE ēac *also*.]

īdel adj. *vain, idle, empty* īdel nsn. 209, 110. īdlu npn. 209, 87. īdelan dpm. 144, 56

ieldra m. *ancestor* ieldran np. 76, 34

īhte see īcan

ilca adj. *same* ilcan dsm. 111, 8; 163, 17. ilċe asn. 56, 30. ylcan ism. 98, 31. [MnE ilk.]

Ilfing *the Elbing* Ilfing ns. 98, 13; 98, 15. Ilfing as. 98, 16

in adv. *in*

in prep. *in, into, upon* (with dat. and acc.)

indryhten adj. *noble, excellent* indryhten nsm. 207, 12

inġeþanc m. *thought, mind, conscience* inġeþanc as. 145, 93

innan prep. *within, in, among* (with dat.)

innanbordes a genitive used adverbially *at home, within borders*

inne adv. *within, inside, at home*

intinga m. *cause, sake, occasion* intinga ns. 55, 3

inwidhlemm m. *wound of malice* inwidhlemmas np. 188, 47

īow same as ēow

is see eom

īsern n. *iron* īsernes gs. 45, 18

iū adv. *once, formerly, of old* iū ġeara *long ago* 44, 1. ġēara iū *long ago* 187, 28; 207, 22

K

kinehelm see cynehelm

kynerīċe n. *kingdom* kynerīċes gs. 87, 28

kyning- see cyning

L

lā interj. *lo! indeed!* lā hwæt *indeed!* 126, 16

lāc n. *offering, gift* tō lācum *as offerings* 126, 25

lǣdan (I) *to lead, take* lǣdan inf. *to extend* 187, 5. lētt 3s pres. ind. 165, 83. lǣdað pl. pres. ind. 144, 26

Lǣden n. *Latin* Lǣdene ds. 75, 16. Lǣden as. 87, 28

Lǣdenġeðīode n. *the Latin language* Lǣdenġeðīodes gs. 87, 25. Lǣdenġeðīode as. 87, 23

Lǣdenware masc. pl. *the Romans* Lǣdenware np. 86, 11

lǣfan (I) *to leave, leave behind* lǣfde 3s pret. ind. 163, 6. lǣfdon pl. pret. ind. 76, 35

lǣġ see licgan

lǣġde see lecgan

Lǣland n. *Laaland, a Danish island* Lǣland ns. 97, 4

lǣn n. *loan* lǣne ds. 87, 41

lǣne adj. *transitory, fleeting* lǣne nsm. 209, 108; 209, 109 (twice); nsn. 209, 108. lǣnum dsn. 189, 109; lǣnan 190, 138 [Related to lǣn.]

lǣran (I) *to teach* lǣran inf. 87, 24. lǣre sg. pres. subj. 87, 23

lǣs *less, fewer* (indeclinable subst.) lǣs 144, 13. þē lǣs *lest* 145, 73

lǣs f. *pasture* lǣswe ds. 44, 7

lǣssa adj. *less, smaller* (comp. deg. of adj. lȳtel) lǣsse nsf. 36, 21. lǣssan dpf. 45, 23

lǣst adj. *least, smallest* (supl. deg. of lȳtel) lǣsta nsm. 98, 37; lǣsste nsn. 66, 22. lǣstan asm. 98, 43

lǣtan (7) *to let* lǣteð 3s pres. ind. 36, 19. lēt 3s pret. ind. 145, 77; lēt wyrċean *he caused to be built* 164, 56; lǣt *considered* 144, 16. lēton pl. pret. ind. 111, 24

lǣwede adj. *lay;* as subst. *layman* lǣwede np. 127, 57. [MnE lewd.]

lāf f. *remainder* tō lāfe bið ds. *is left over* 98, 32. lāfe as. 199, 17

lagu f. *law* tō lage ds. 127, 58 *as law;* lage ds. 144, 46. lage as. 126, 19; 126, 29; 127, 59. laga np. 126, 42; 143, 7. lagum dp. 145, 91. laga ap. 164, 65

lagulād f. *sea, waterway* lagulāde as. 207, 3

lāh see **lēon**

lahbryċe m. *breach of law* lahbrycas ap. 144, 36

lāhlīċe adv. *lawfully*

land n. *land, country; property* land ns. 45, 16; 98, 6; 163, 21; 164, 52; lond 198, 10. landes gs. 163, 2; 163, 3; londes 198, 6. lande ds. 98, 7; 98, 39; 126, 7; 127, 68; 127, 81; 164, 38; 164, 41; londe 86, 8; 198, 4; 198, 13; 198, 16. land as. 111, 18; 165, 75; 198, 7; lond 75, 12; 198, 2. land np. 97, 5; 98, 7; 98, 9. lande gp. 163, 11. land ap. 165, 76

landlēod f. *the people of the country* landlēode ds. 164, 62

lang adj. *long* lang nsn. 44, 4. lang hwīle asf. *for a long time* 187, 24. langan isn. 98, 48

Langaland n. *Langeland ,* a Danish island Langaland ns. 97, 4

lange see **longe**

langunghwīl f. *time of distress* langunghwīla gp. 190, 126

lār f. *doctrine, learning, teaching* lār ns. 65, 2; 66, 25; 86, 6; 87, 25. lāre as. 75, 10; 75, 12; 127, 59. lāra np. 126, 42. [MnE lore.]

lārcwide m. *counsel, precept* lārcwidum dp. 208, 38

lārēow m. *teacher* lārēowa gp. 76, 20. [From lār-þēow *servant of learning.*]

lāst m. *footstep, path* on lāste ds. *behind, after* (with dat.) 209, 97

latian (II) *to delay, hesitate* latiġe sg. pres. subj. 145, 71. [Cf. MnE late.]

lāð adj. *hateful, hated* lāð nsn. 127, 75. lāðe npf. 126, 42. [MnE loath.]

lāðettan (I) *to hate, loathe* lāðet 3s pres. ind. 144, 53

lāðost adj. *most hateful, most hated* (supl. deg. of lāð) lāðost nsm. 189, 88

lēa m. *lion* lēa ns. 199, 23. [Lat. leō *lion.*]

lēad n. *lead* lēades gs. 45, 18

lēanian (II) *to reward, recompense* (with dat.) lēanað 3s pres. ind. 36, 18. [Cf. OE lēan *loan, gift.*]

lēas adj. *vain, false, deceitful; lacking, deprived of* lēas nsm. 163, 1. lēase npn. 209, 86

lēasung f. *falsehood, lying* lēasunga ap. 144, 40

lecgan (I) *to establish, lay* læġde 3s pret. ind. 164, 65. lecge sg. pres. subj. 208, 42

lēfdon see **līefan**

leġer n. *lying (unburied)* leġere is. 98, 48

lehtrian (II) *to blame, revile* lehtreð 3s pres. ind. 144, 49

lencg see **lenġ**

lencten m. *spring, Lent* lencten as. 111, 49

lenġ adv. *longer* (comp. deg. of longe)

lēod f. *people, nation* lēode gs. 145, 80. lēodum dp. 126, 28; 189, 88. [Allied to Lat. līber *of free birth.*]

lēodbiscop m. *a suffragan bishop* lēodbiscopas np. 164, 29

lēodhata m. *tyrant, persecutor* lēodhatan np. 144, 42

lēof adj. *dear, beloved* lēofa nsm. 189, 78; 189, 95. lēofes gsm. 208, 38. lēofre dsf. 209, 97. lēofan npm. 126, 1. lēofra gpm. 208, 31

leofodan see **libban**

lēoht adj. *light, bright* lēohtre nsf. (comp. deg.) 36, 21

lēoht n. *light, daylight, brightness* lēohte ds. 29, 11; is. 187, 5. [Related to Lat. lux *light,* Greek leukos *white.*]

lēohtlīċe adv. *slightly, inconsiderately*

leomu see **lim**

lēon (I) *to lend, grant* lāh 3s pret. ind. 198, 3

leornere m. *learner, scholar* leornere ds. 29, 19

lēoð n. *song, poem* lēoð as. 55, 2. [Cf. Ger. das Lied *song.*]

lēt- see **lǣtan**

lētt see **lǣdan**

lēw f. *blemish, imperfection* lēwe ds. 145, 58

lēwian (II) *to blemish, injure* ġelēwede pp. np. 145, 59

libban (III) *to live* libban inf. 29, 13; 164, 53; 165, 75. lifiaþ pl. pres. ind. 190, 134. lifedon pl. pret. ind. 111, 41; leofodan 163, 22. lifiendne prp. asm. 127, 68. lifgendra prp. gp. as subst. 199, 18. bið lifd pp. ns. *it is lived* 199, 28

līċ n. *body, corpse* līċ ns. 98, 30. līċes gs. 188, 63

līcettere m. *hypocrite* līcettere ns. 200, 46

licgan (5) *to lie; run, extend, go* licgan inf. 110, 5. līð 3s pres. ind. 98, 12 (twice); 98, 25; 98, 37. liġeð *flows* 98, 17. licgað pl. pres. ind. 98, 29; 99, 54; 209, 78 *lie dead.* læġ 3s pret. ind. 163, 4. licge sg. pres. subj. *would lie dead* 143, 5. [Allied to Greek lechos, Lat. lectus *bed.*]

lida m. *sailor* lida ns. 29, 3. [Allied to Lat. litus, *coast;* cf. OE līðan *to travel, sail.*]

līefan (I) *to allow, grant, permit* lēfdon pl. pret. ind. 76, 25

līf n. *life, existence* līf ns. 65, 15; 66, 23; 199, 21; 199, 29. līfes gs. 189, 88; 190, 126. līfe ds. 127, 67; 189, 109; 190, 138; līfe on *in life* 36, 18. līf as. 127, 56; 190, 147; 208, 60; 209, 89. līf ap. 163, 22

lifd see **libban**

lifedon see **libban**

lifgendra see **libban**

lifiaþ see **libban**

lifiendne see **libban**

liġeð see **licgan**

lim n. *limb, member, part* leomu ap. 55, 9; limu 164, 45

limweriġ adj. *weary in limb* limweriġne asm. 188, 63

līofre adj. *preferable* (comp. deg. of lēof) līofre a predicate adj. modifying the subject-phrase ōðer hēmed tō nīomanne 198, 15

liornung f. *learning* liornunga ds. 87, 21. liornunga as. 75, 11

liss f. *joy* lissum dp. used adverbially *'joyfully'* 36, 18

litle see **lȳtel**

līð see **licgan**

loc n. *lock* locum dp. 45, 23

lōc hū adv. *however*

lōcian (II) *to look* lōcað 3s pres. ind. 144, 16. lōcodan pl. pret. ind. 163, 13

lof m. *praise, glory* lof ns. 111, 43

lond see **land**

longe (**lange**) adv. *long, a long time*

lufian (II) *to love* lufian inf. 144, 53; 145, 91. lufiað pl. pres. ind. 144, 51. lufode 3s pret. ind. 164, 64; 165, 69. lufedon pl. pret. ind. 76, 25; 163, 16; lufodon 76, 34

lūflīċe adv. *lovingly*

Lunden f. *London* Lundene gs. 111, 43. Lundene ds. 111, 24; 111, 48

lust m. *desire, pleasure, lust* lust as. 127, 58

lyft f. *air, sky, clouds* lyft ns. 36, 4. on lyft lǣdan as. *to extend into the air* 187, 5. [Cf. Ger. die Luft *air.*]

lȳsan (I) *to redeem* lȳsan inf. 188, 41

lȳt *few* (indeclinable subst.) lȳt as. 208, 31

lȳtel adj. *little, small* littelre dsf. 164, 62. lȳtelre ds. *petty* 126, 40. lȳtle asf. 76, 31. lȳtel as. as subst. 126, 21. litle is. used adverbially 111, 8. lȳtle npf. *few* 126, 6

lȳðre adj. *wicked, base* lȳðre asf. 145, 81

M

mā *more* (indeclinable subst.) mā 86, 8; 98, 33; 144, 13; 144, 40

mā comp. adv. *more* þē mā þe *any more than* 110, 7; 127, 55

macian (II) *to make* macode 3s pret. ind. 164, 41

māē (mǣ) same as **mā** (adv.)

mæcgas see **mago**

mæǵ- (vb.) see **magan**

mǣǵ m. *kinsman* mǣǵ ns. 209, 109. mēgas np. 198, 16. māga gp. 208, 51. māgum dp. 98, 26

mæǵen m. *stomach* mæǵen as. 29, 7

mæǵen n. *strength, power, virtue* mæǵenes gs. 65, 4

mæǵester m. *master, ruler* mæǵester ns. 164, 38

mæǵeð f. *girl, woman* mæǵeð ns. with pl. meaning 36, 16

mǣǵrǣs m. *attack on kinsmen* mǣǵrǣsas ap. 144, 36

mǣǵslaga m. *slayer of a kinsman* mǣǵslagan np. 145, 60

mǣǵð f. *nation, tribe, family* mǣǵð ns. 99, 53. mǣǵðe ds. 143, 6. mǣǵþe as. 44, 5. [Cf. OE mǣǵ *kinsman*.]

mǣnan (I) *to lament, complain of* mǣndon pl. pret. ind. 165, 72

mæneǵe see **maniǵ**

mæniǵfeald see **maniǵfeald**

mæniǵfealdre adj. *more various* (comp. deg. of maniǵfeald) mæniǵfealdre ns. 127, 86

mæniǵo f. *multitude* mæniǵe ds. 189, 112; maniǵeo ds. 190, 151

mænn see **mann**

mǣre adj. *glorious, splendid, great, famed* mǣre nsn. 163, 20; nsf. 187, 12; 189, 82; 209, 100. mǣran dsm. 188, 69. mǣre asn. 163, 18

mǣrþ f. *glory* mǣrþa as. 145, 98

mæssepriost m. *(mass) priest* mæsseprioste ds. 87, 32; mæssepreoste 87, 33

mæsserbana m. *slayer of a priest* mæsserbanan np. 145, 61

mǣst adj. *most, greatest* (supl. deg. of miċel) mǣst nsm. 127, 65; mǣst ælċ ns. *almost everyone* 127, 60; 127, 62. mǣstan asm. 98, 35; mǣstan (dǣl) 98, 42. mǣstum dpm. 44, 3

mǣte adj. *small, limited* mǣte dsn. *with limited company*, i.e. himself only, therefore, *alone* 188, 69; 190, 124

mǣþ f. *honor, respect* mǣþe gs. 126, 26. mǣþe as. 127, 74

māg- see **mǣǵ**

magan (PP) *may, be able, can* mæǵ 1s pres. ind. 76, 18; 189, 85; 208, 58; 3s pres. ind. 29, 9; 76, 36; 127, 53; 143, 1; 144, 32; 145, 59; 189, 110; 207, 15; 208, 64. meaht 2s pres. ind. 55, 15; miht 189, 78. magon pl. pres. ind. 87, 18; 99, 53; magan 145, 58; 145, 68; 145, 73. meahte 3s pret. ind. 187, 18. meahton pl. pret. ind. 76, 32. mæǵe sg. pres. subj. 76, 22; 76, 23; 127, 63; mege 198, 8. mæǵen pl. pres. subj. 87, 17; 87, 21; 87, 22. meahte sg. pret. subj. 87, 34; 207, 26; mehte 145, 69; mihte 111, 13; 164, 42; 187, 37

mago m. *young man, warrior* mago ns. 209, 92. mæcgas np. 36, 16

maguþeǵn m. *(young) retainer* maguþeǵnas np. 208, 62

man indef. pron. *one, they, people*

(used in the nom. sg.; a form of mann) mann 111, 13; 111, 35

mān n. *crime, evil deed* māna gp. 145, 65

mancus m. *mancus, a coin worth one-eighth of a pound* mancessa gp. 87, 36

māndǣd f. *crime* māndǣda ap. 144, 33

maneġ- see **maniġ**

maniġ adj. *many, many a* maniġ nsf. 98, 19; maniġ ōðer nsn. *many another* 163, 20. maniġes gsn. 163, 2. maniġ asn. 164, 59; moniġ 56, 30. moniġe npm. 29, 12; as subst. 75, 17; 87, 26; maneġe 127, 65; 127, 77; 144, 43; 145, 63; 145, 68. maneġe npf. 126, 39; mæneġe 127, 72. mæniġe np. 128, 87. maniġra gp. 188, 41. manegum dpf. 189, 99. maniġe apm. 164, 55; maneġe apn. 126, 10; ap. 144, 54. [Cf. OE meniġu f. *crowd.*]

maniġeo see **mæniġo**

maniġfeald adj. *manifold, various* maniġfealdum dpf. 87, 27. mæniġfealde apf. 144, 32; 145, 84

man(n) m. *man* man ns. 98, 37; 98, 41; 99, 51; 145, 69 (? Wulfstan); 163, 14; 163, 23; 164, 41; 164, 43; 165, 77; 189, 112; mann 111, 17; hū ġedōn mann *what sort of man* 163, 10; mon 209, 109. mannes gs. 98, 48. men ds. 29, 19; 30, 20. man as. 164, 43; mon 199, 19. men np. 29, 5; 29, 12; 98, 21; 98, 27; 99, 54; 126, 1; 126, 37; 164, 28; 164, 55; 165, 72 (twice); 165, 82; 187, 12; 190, 128; menn 86, 5; 98, 38; mænn 144, 30. manna gp. 65, 15; 126, 8; 126, 19; 127, 59; 144, 21; 164, 36; monna 66, 23; 87, 20. mannum dp. 126, 7; 127, 54; 143, 1; 163, 16; 163, 17; 189, 96; 189, 102; monnum 76, 25; 87, 16. men ap. 127, 73; 164,

57; 165, 78; menn 189, 93; man 164, 59

manncynn n. *mankind, people* mancynnes gs. 187, 33; 189, 99. monncynnes 56, 26; moncynnæs 199, 38. manncynn as. 164, 50; mancyn 188, 41; mancynn 189, 104

mannslaga m. *man-slayer* mannslagan np. 145, 60

mannsylen f. *the selling of men* (into slavery) mannsylena ap. 144, 34

Mans *Maine* Mans ns. 164, 52

manslyht m. *manslaughter* manslyhtas ap. 144, 37

mānswora m. *perjurer* mānsworan np. 145, 61

māra adj. *more, greater* (comp. deg. of miċel) māra nsm. 86, 7. māre nsf. 36, 20; 143, 1; māre ns. 127, 86; māre as. as a subst. 127, 62. māran asf. 65, 8; 98, 28. māran apm. and f. 65, 7

marc n. *a mark, half a pound* marc as. 164, 59

margen (morgen) m. *morning* marne ds. 199, 22; 199, 23. margen as. 199, 23

Maria f. *the Virgin Mary* Marian as. 189, 92

marn see **margen**

māðum m. *treasure, gift* māðma gp. 76, 30

māþþumġyfa m. *giver of treasure* māþþumġyfa ns. 209, 92

mē dat. of **iċ** (also acc.)

meaht- (vb.) see **magan**

meaht f. *power, might* mihte ds. 189, 102. meahte ap. 55, 21; mehti 199, 33; mihte 65, 9. [Cf. OE magan *be able.*]

mearg m. *horse, steed* mearg ns. 209, 92. [MnE mare.]

mec acc. of **iċ**

medmiċel adj. *moderate-sized, limited* medmiclum dsn. 66, 23

medo m. *mead* medo ns. 98, 24. medo as. 98, 22

mēgas see **mǣġ**

mege see **magan**

mehte see **magan**

meltan (3) *to melt, burn up* meltan inf. 29, 2. [Allied to Lat. adj. mollis *soft, tender, pliant*.]

menġeo see **meniġu**

meniġu f. *multitude* menġeo ns. 76, 31. [Cf. Ger. die Menge *crowd*.]

menn see **mann**

meoduheall f. *meadhall* meoduhealle ds. 207, 27

meolc f. *milk* meolc as. 98, 22

Mēore the Swedish district of *Möre* ns. 98, 8

Meotod m. *Lord, Creator* Meotodes gs. 55, 21; Metudes 207, 2. Metudǣs 199, 33

mere m. *lake, sea* mere ds. 98, 14; 98, 17. [Cf. Lat. mare *sea*.]

meregrota m. *pearl* meregrotan np. 45, 13

merestrēam m. *ocean stream* mere- strēamas ap. 36, 28

mereswȳn n. *porpoise, dolphin* mere- swȳn np. 44, 11

messe f. *mass, feast day* messan ds. 111, 40

metan (5) *to measure* metaþ pl. pres. ind. 199, 42. meten pp. np. 199, 43

mētan (I) *to meet, find* ġemēted pp. nsm. *found* 45, 19. ġemētte npm. 44, 12. [Cf. OE mōt *assembly*.]

mete m. *meat, food* mete ds. 29, 7

Metudǣs see **Meotod**

mēðe adj. *weary, exhausted, tired* mēðe nsm. 188, 65. mēðe npm. 188, 69

miċel (myċel) adj. *great, many, much* miċel nsm. 127, 66; myċel 190, 130. miċel nsf. 76, 31; 126, 17; 126, 18 ; 145, 88; myċel 98, 10; 190, 139. myċel nsn. 98, 19; 98, 20; 98, 23. myċeles wordes gsn. *a*

great reputation 111, 15. miclan dsm. 126, 17 (twice); dsf. 189, 102; dsn. 188, 65; myċelan dsn. 164, 61. miclan asm. 145, 97. miċel asn, as subst. 126, 21; 145, 68; myċel 164, 43; 164, 65. myċele isf. 164, 51. micle isn. 187, 34; mycle 188, 60; 190, 123; myccele 44, 3. micle npf. 127, 63; 127, 85. miclan dpf. 126, 13; miċelan 126, 14. miclum dp. *greatly* 99, 52. [Allied to Lat. magnus *large, great;* cf. the Eng. proper name Mitchell.]

micle adv. *much, greatly* swā micle lencg swā *just so much longer as* 98, 27

mid prep. *with, by, among* (with dat. and instr.) mid ealle *entirely* 144, 56; 144, 78; 164, 50; 164, 64; 165, 74; 165, 82. mid as adverb, *at the same time* 189, 106. mit te (mid þe) *while* 199, 21. [Cf. Greek meta *with, among, after*.]

midd adj. *mid* tō midre nihte dsf. *at midnight* 185, 2

middaneardes see **middanġeard**

middanġeard m. *world, earth, globe* middanġeard ns. 36, 20; 208, 62. middaneardes gs. 163, 1. mid- danġeard as. 36, 28; 56, 26; 189, 104; 209, 75; middingard 199, 38

middanwinter m. *mid-winter, Christ- mas* middanwintra ds. 111, 45

midde adj. *the middle of* midum ds. as subst. 199, 17

middingard see **middanġeard**

midewinter m. *mid-winter, Christmas* midewintre ds. 164, 27

mihte (n.) see **meaht**

mihte (vb.) see **magan**

mihtiġ adj. *mighty, powerful* mihtiġ nsm. 190, 151

mīl f. *mile* mīle ds. 98, 35; 98, 36. mīla gp. 44, 4 (twice); 98, 13. mīlum dp. 98, 39 (twice). [From the Latin phrase mille passuum *a thousand of paces*.]

milde adj. *gentle, mild* milde nsm. 163, 15

milts f. *mercy* miltse as. 207, 2

mīn 1st. pers. sg. poss. pron. *mine* (declined strong); also g. of **iċ** mīn nsm. 189, 78; 189, 95; 198, 1; 198, 3; 198, 8; 198, 9; nsf. 199, 19; nsn. 36, 1; 198, 5; 198, 8; 198, 14; 199, 21. mīnes gsm. 199, 29. mīnre gsf. 199, 28. mīnum dsm. 87, 31 (twice); 87, 32 (twice); 187, 30; 198, 2; dsn. 87, 35. mīnne asm. 207, 10; 207, 19; 207, 22. mīne asf. 207, 9; 199, 30. mīn asn. 198, 2 (twice). mīne npm. 198, 16; npf. 36, 4; 36, 6. mīnra gpm. 199, 17; gpn. 199, 18; mīnum dpm. 198, 3. mīn apn. 199, 23; 199, 27. mīn *of me,* i.e. *my* 207, 27.

mine m. *thought, affection* mine as. 207, 27

misbēodan (2) *to injure, ill -use* (with dat.) misbēodan inf. 126, 27

misdǣd f. *misdeed, sin* misdǣdan dp. 144, 48; misdǣdum 145, 76. misdǣda gp. 144, 65. misdǣda ap. 144, 33; 145, 57

mislīċ adj. *various* mislīcum dpf. 87, 27

mislimpan (3) *to go wrong* (impersonal verb with dat.) mislimpe sg. pres. subj. 144, 29

missenlīċ adj. *various, diverse* missenlīcra gpm. and f. 44, 9; gpn. 44, 6; 44, 11

missenlīċe adv. *variously, here and there*

mistlīċ adj. *various* mistlīċe apf. 127, 64; 144, 39. mistlīċe apn. 144, 38

mit see **mid**

mōd n. *heart, spirit, mood* mōde ds. 29, 8; 76, 38; 190, 122; 190, 130; 208, 41; 209, 111. mōd as. 208, 51

mōdċeariġ adj. *sad, troubled in heart* mōdċeariġ nsm. 207, 2

mōdġeþanc m. *thought, mind, intent* *of mind* mōdġeþanc as. 55, 21; mōdgithanc 199, 33. mōdġeþancas np. 29, 12

mōdiġ adj. *brave, courageous* mōdiġ nsm. 188, 41. mōdġe npm. 208, 62. [MnE moody.]

mōdigan (I) *to become proud* mōdigan inf. 165, 77

mōdor f. *mother* mōdor as. 127, 84; 189, 92

mōdsefa m. *spirit, mind, innermost thoughts* mōdsefa ns. 190, 124; 208, 59. mōdsefan as. 207, 10; 207, 19

molde f. *earth* moldan ds. 163, 5. moldan as. 187, 12; 189, 82. [MnE mould.]

moldern n. *tomb, sepulchre* moldern as. 188, 65

mon see **man**

mōna m. *moon* mōna ns. 36, 21. [Cf. OE mōnað *month.*]

mōnað m. *month* mōnað as. *for a month* 98, 26

mondryhten m. *liege lord* mondryhten as. 208, 41

moniġ- see **maniġ**

mon(n)- see **mann**

mon(n)cynn- see **manncynn**

morðdǣd f. *murder* morðdǣda ap. 144, 33

morþorwyrhta m. *murderer* morþorwyrhtan np. 145, 62

mōst- see **mōtan**

mōtan (PP) *be permitted, must, may* mōtan inf. 98, 44. mōt 1s pres. ind. 190, 142. mōte (for mōton) pl. pres. ind. 126, 12; mōtan 126, 15. mōston pl. pret. ind. 165, 74. mōte sg. pres. subj. 190, 127. mōste sg. pret. subj. 163, 18; 164, 53. mōsten pl. pret. subj. 165, 74

mund f. *security, protection* munde gs. 126, 26. [Allied to Lat. manus *hand.*]

mundbyrd f. *protection, help* mundbyrd ns. 190, 130

munec m. *monk* munecan dp. 163, 22. munecas ap. 163, 19

muscule [muskule] f. *mussel* musculan np. 44, 12. [From Lat. musculus *sea-mussel,* originally *little mouse.*]

myccle see **miċel**

myċel- see **miċel**

myltestre f. *prostitute* myltestran np. 145, 62. [Lat. meretrīx *prostitute,* from merēre *to earn.*]

mynster n. *monastery, church* mynster ns. 163, 20. mynstre ds. 87, 38. mynster as. 163, 18. [From Lat. monastērium.]

mynsterhata m. *persecutor of monasteries* mynsterhatan np. 145, 61

mȳre f. *mare* mȳran gs. 98, 21

myrhð f. *mirth, joy* myrhða as. 145, 99

N

nā adv. *not, never*

næfd- (from ne hæfd-) see **habban**

næfre adv. *never*

næġl m. *nail* næġlum ip. 188, 46

næniġ (from ne æniġ) pron. *no one, none* (used as subst. and adj.) næniġ nsm. 65, 5; nsn. 98, 23. næniġ asn. 55, 2

nænne see **nān**

næren (from ne wæren) *were not;* see **wesan**

næron (from ne wæron) see **wesan**

næs (from ne wæs) *was not;* see **wesan**

nāh see **āgan**

nāht (from nā-wiht) n. *nothing* nāht as. 55, 14; nōht 55, 12. nōht used adverbially *not* 75, 17. nōht þon læs *nevertheless* 65, 6

nalæs same as **nales**

nales adv. *not at all*

nām- see **niman**

nama m. *name* naman gs. 98, 16. naman ds. 87, 37; 145, 72; 189, 113 'sake; noman 55, 11. naman

as. 76, 26. [Cog. with Lat. nōmen *name.*]

nān pron. and adj. *none, not one* nān nsm. 87, 37; 111, 17; 164, 43; 207, 9; nsn. 144, 29. nānes gsm. 110, 3. nānre dsf. 87, 21. nænne asm. 86, 3. nān asn. 164, 31

nānwuht n. *nothing* nānwuht as. 76, 32

nāþor . . . ne conj. *neither . . . nor* nāþor . . . ne 127, 58

nāwiht n. *nothing* nāwiht as. 65, 3

ne adv. *no, not;* conj. *neither, nor*

nē conj. *nor*

nēah adv. *near*

neahte see **niht**

nēaleċan (I) *to approach, draw near* nēaleċan inf. 55, 5. nēalæċð 3s pres. ind. 126, 2

nēat n. *animal, beast* nēata gp. *cattle* 44, 7; 55, 8

nēd see **nēod**

nēddre f. *snake, serpent, adder* nēddran np. 45, 20

nellað (from ne willað) see **willan**

nemman (I) *to name* nemnde 3s pret. ind. 55, 11. ġenemned pp. nsf. 87, 28

nemþe conj. *unless*

nēod f. *need, necessity* nēod ns. 145, 72; nēd 199, 26. nēode ds. 164, 62

nēodlīcor adv. comp. deg. of nēodlīċe *zealously* [Cf. OE nēod *desire, earnestness.*]

nēxtan see **nyhst**

nīedbeðearfost adj. *most necessary* nīedbeðearfosta npf. 87, 16. [Cf. Ger. bedürfen *to need.*]

niht f. *night* neahte ds. 55, 8; tō midre nihte ds. *at midnight* 185, 2. nihtum dp. 97, 2. [Allied to Lat. nox (n.), noctis (g.) *night.*]

nihthelm m. *cover of night* nihthelm as. 209, 96

nihtscua m. *the shadow of night* nihtscua ns. 209, 104

niman (4) *to take, seize, capture* ni-

man inf. 29, 9. nimð 3s pres. ind.
98, 43. nimað pl. pres. ind. 99, 50.
nam 3s pret. ind. 164, 61. nāmon
pl. pret. ind. 111, 41; 111, 45; 111,
46. niman æfter pl. pres. subj.
may imitate 165, 82. numene pp.
npf. *taken* 44, 11. tō nīomanne
gerund 198, 15. [MnE numb derives from the pp.]

nīomanne   see **niman**

nīpan   (1)   *to grow dark*   nīpeð 3s pres.
ind. 209, 104

nis (from ne is)   see **eom**

nīð m.   *enmity, rancor*   nīð as. 165, 73

nīwan adv.   *recently, newly*

nō   same as **nā**

nōht   see **nāht**

nōhwæðer conj.   *neither*   nōhwæðer
. . . ne *neither* . . . *nor* 76, 25

noldon (from ne woldon)   see **willan**

noman   see **nama**

Normandīġ   *Normandy*   Normandīġe
gs. 164, 51. Normandīġe ds. 163,
7; 164, 35; 164, 38

norð adv.   *north, northwards*

norðan adv.   *from the north*

norðdæl m.   *north*   norðdæle ds. 44, 2

notu f.   *employment, office*   note ds.
87, 22

nū adv.   *now*

numene   see **niman**

nȳde adv.   *necessarily*

nȳdġyld n.   *tribute*   nȳdġyld np. 143,
7

nȳdmāge f.   *near kinswoman*   nȳdma-
gan as. 144, 16

nȳdþearf f.   *need, necessity*   nȳdþearf
ns. 126, 19

nyhst adv. and prep.   *next, closest to*
(with dat.) (supl. deg. of nēah)
æt nȳhstan *at length* 145, 77; æt
nēxtan 164, 34

nyrwan   (I)   *to narrow, restrict*   gen-
yrwde pp. nsn. 126, 41

nyste (from ne wiste)   see **witan**

nytt adj.   *useful, profitable*   nytt nsn.
198, 10

nytt f.   *use, advantage*   nytt ns. 110,
6. nytte ds. 36, 11. [Cf. OE nēotan
to use, enjoy.]

nyttnes f.   *use, utility*   nyttnesse gs.
65, 4

nyxt   same as **nyhst**

O

of prep.   *of, from, out of* (with dat.)

ofdōn (anv.)   *to take out*   ofdō 1s pres.
ind. 200, 45

ofer adv.   *over, across*

ofer prep.   *over, beyond, upon, in* (with
dat. and acc.)   ofer ealle men
above all men 165, 78. ofer Dryhtnes word *contrary to the word of
the Lord* 187, 35. [Related to the
Lat. prep. super *over, above.*]

oferfrēosan   (2)   *to freeze over*   oferfroren pp. nsm. 99, 56

oferfroren   see **oferfrēosan**

oferfyllu f.   *gluttony*   oferfylla as. 145,
84

oferhoga m.   *despiser*   oferhogan np.
144, 43

oferlīċe adv.   *excessively*

oferstīgan   (1)   *to surmount*   oferstīġe
1s pres. ind. 36, 25

oferwrēon   (1, 2)   *to cover over*   oferwrogen pp. nsm. 163, 4

ofġēafon   see **ofġiefan**

ofġiefan   (5)   *to leave, relinquish*   ofġēafon pl. pret. ind. 208, 61

ofst f.   *haste*   ofste ds. 126, 1

oft adv.   *often, frequently*

oftor adv.   *more often* (comp. deg. of
oft)

oftost adv.   *most often* (supl. deg. of
oft)

oll n.   *contempt, scorn*   olle is. 144, 50

on prep.   *on, upon, in* (with dat., acc.,
instr.)

onǣlan   (I)   *to kindle*   onǣled pp. nsn.
66, 18. [Cf. OE ǣlan *to burn,* āl
fire.]

onbyriġan   (I)   *to taste*   onbyriġan inf.
190, 114

ond (and) conj. *and*

ondswarian (II) *to answer* ondsweorað 3s pres. ind. *will answer* 199, 27. ondswarede 3s pret. ind. 55, 12; ondswarode 65, 1. ondsweora imp. sg. 199, 26

ondsweorian see ondswarian

onfēng(on) see onfōn

onfōn (7) *to receive* (with dat.) onfēng 3s pret. ind. 55, 17. onfēngon pl. pret. ind. 65, 8. onfōn 1p pres. subj. 65, 12

ongan see onġinnan

onġēan adv. *opposite, back* eft onġēan *back again* 111, 40

onġēan prep. *towards, against, opposite* (with dat. and acc.)

onġeġen see onġēan (prep.)

onġemang prep. *among* (with dat.)

onġietan (5) *to perceive, understand* onġiotan inf. 76, 32; onġytan 187, 18. onġietan 208, 73

onġinnan (3) *to begin* ongan 3s pret. ind. 87, 26; 187, 19; 187, 27; 189, 73; ongon 55, 17. ongunnon pl. pret. ind. 188, 65; 188, 67. onġinnen pl. pres. subj. 190, 116

onġiotan see onġietan

ongon see onġinnan

ongunnon see onġinnan

onġyrwan (I) *to disrobe* onġyrede 3s pret. ind. 188, 39

onġytan see onġietan

onlūtan (2) *to incline, bend down* onlūtan inf. 76, 39. [Cf. MnE lout.]

onlȳsan (I) *to redeem, liberate* onlȳsde 3s pret. ind. 190, 147

onsǣġe adj. *attacking, assailing* onsǣġe ns. as subst. 127, 53

onscyte m. *attack, assault* onscytan dp. 127, 62; *attacks (in words)* 144, 56

onsendan (I) *to send* onsendan inf. 87, 36. onsended pp. nsm. 188, 49

onslǣpan (7) *to fall asleep, sleep* onslēpte 3s pret. ind. 55, 10

onstāl m. *supply* onstāl as. 76, 20

onstellan (I) *to create, establish* onstealde 3s pret. ind. 56, 23; āstelidæ 199, 35

onwæcnan (6) *to wake up* onwæcneð 3s pres. ind. 208, 45

onwald same as anweald

onweald same as anweald

onweġ adv. *away*

onwendan (I) *to change* onwendeð 3s pres. ind. 209, 107

onwrēon (1) *to reveal, disclose* onwrēoh imp. sg. 189, 97

open adj. *open* opene npm. 188, 47

ōr n. *beginning* ōr as. 56, 23; 199, 35. [Cf. OE ord *point, spear-point.*]

ōra m. *ore* ōrum dp. 45, 18

ord m. *point, spear-point, spear* ord ns. 30, 20

orfcwealm m. *cattle-plague* orfcwealm ns. 127, 50

ot same as oð

oð prep. *until, up to* (with acc.) oð þet *until* 111, 32; oð ðæt 187, 26; 187, 32; 208, 71; *to the point that* 209, 86

oþberan (4) *to carry off* oþbær 3s pret. ind. 209, 81

ōþer adj. and pron. *other* ōþer nsm. 65, 13; 99, 56 both?; 163, 7; (æniġ) ōðer *anything else* 144, 27; maniġ ōðer ns. *many another* 163, 20. ōðrum dsm. 98, 42; 127, 56; 127, 61; 127, 80; 144, 14; dsn. 126, 9. ōðerre dsf. 87, 21; ōðre hwīle dsf. *at one time* 163, 13. ōþerne asm. 127, 60; 127, 62; 127, 84; 164, 43; 164, 44; ōðerne (dǣl) 98, 35. ōðre asf. 66, 20 (twice) 86, 11; 87, 42. ōðer asn. *another, a second* 198, 15. ōðre npm. 66, 26; 98, 27; 111, 20. ōðra npf. 87, 13. ōðrum dpm. 76, 25; dpf. 45, 23; 87, 27; dpn. 111, 20; 164, 40

oðfæstan (I) *to set (to a task)* oðfæste pp. npm. 87, 21

oðfeallan (7) *to fall off, decline, decay*

oðfeallan inf. 86, 6. oðfeallenu pp. nsf. 75, 14

oðða same as **oððe**

oððe conj. *or*

oððon conj. *or*

owiht pron. *anything* owiht as. 66, 25

oxa m. *ox* oxan ap. 198, 13

Oxneford *Oxford* Oxneforda ds. 111, 46

P

Pentecosten m. *Pentecost* Pentecosten ds. 164, 27

plega m. *play, sport* plega ns. 98, 30. plegan ds. 98, 33

plegian (II) *to play* pleagode 3s pret. ind. 164, 45

prȳte f. *pride* prȳtan ds. 145, 58

pund n. *a pound* punda gp. 111, 31; 164, 60. [From Lat. pondo *heavy, a pound in weight.*]

R

rǣċan (I) *to stretch out, reach out* rǣċe 1s pres. ind. 36, 26

rǣdlēas adj. *helpless* rǣdlēas nsn. 111, 21

rǣran (I) *to create, commit* rǣrde 3s pret. ind. 126, 9

ræst see **rest**

rǣðe adj. *violent, fierce* rǣðe nsm. 164, 30. [Cf. OE hrǣðe *quick.*]

ranc adj. *proud, brave, important* rancne asm. 144, 16

raðe adv. *soon, quickly*

raðor adv. *sooner, more quickly* (comp. deg. of raðe) þē raðor *the sooner* 111, 29

rēafere m. *robber, plunderer* rēafere ds. 29, 19. rēaferas np. 145, 64. [Cf. OE rēaf *plunder, booty.*]

rēafian (II) *to rob, plunder* rēafiað pl. pres. ind. 144, 26

rēaflac m. *robbery, spoliation* rēaflac ns. 127, 51. rēaflac as. 145, 79

reċċan (I) *to care* rōhte 3s pret. ind. 165, 73. rōhtan pl. pret. ind. 144, 30

reċċlēas adj. *reckless, careless* reċċlēase npm. 86, 6

reġn m. *rain* reġn ns. 45, 15

regollīċe adv. *according to religious rule*

regul m. *rule, monastic rule* regule ds. 163, 23

reordberend m. *man, person* reordberend np. 187, 3. reordberendum dp. 189, 89. [Cf. OE reord *speech*, beran *to bear.*]

rest f. *rest* ræste ds. 55, 9; reste *at rest*, or ap. beds if dir. obj. of wunedon 187, 3

restan (I) *to rest* reste 3s pret. ind. 188, 64; 188, 69

rīċe adj. *rich, strong, powerful* rīċe nsm. 163, 2; 163, 14; 164, 35. rīcne asm. 144, 17; 188, 44. rīċe npm. 164, 28; 165, 72. rīcra gpm. 190, 131; gp. as subst. 145, 79

rīċe n. *kingdom, sovereignty* rīċe ns. 209, 106. rīċe ds. 76, 19; 87, 35. rīċe as. 164, 42; 190, 119; 190, 152. [Cf. MnE bishopric.]

rīcost adj. *most powerful, having the highest rank and authority, richest* (supl. deg. of rīċe *powerful*) rīcostan npm. 98, 21

rīcsian (II) *to prevail, rule, reign* rīcsōde 3s pret. ind. 126, 7; rīxade 164, 46; 164, 53

rīdan (1) *to ride* rīdeð 3s pres. ind. 98, 44

riht adj. *right, proper* rihtne asm. 189, 89

riht n. *right, justice* rihte ds. 145, 89. mid rihte ds. *properly* 126, 20; 144, 46. riht as. 144, 51. [Allied to Lat. rectus *straight, right.*]

rihtan (I) *to direct* ġeriht pp. nsf. 190, 131

rihte adv. *rightly, justly*

rihtlagu f. *just law* rihtlaga gp. 144, 43

rihtlīċe adv. *rightly*

rīnan (1 and I) *to rain* rīne 3s pres. subj. 66, 18

rīxade see **rīcsian**

rōd f. *cross, rood* rōd ns. 188, 44; 190, 136. rōde ds. 188, 56; 190, 131. rōde as. 190, 119

rōht- see **reċċan**

rūn f. *private meditation, counsel* rūne ds. 209, 111

rycene adv. *quickly*

ryhte adv. *right, rightly, duly*

rȳman (I) *to extend, enlarge* rȳmdon pl. pret. ind. 75, 8. [Cf. OE rūm *room*.]

rȳpan (I) *to rob, plunder* rȳpað pl. pres. ind. 144, 26

rȳpere m. *plunderer, robber* rȳperas np. 145, 64. rȳpera gp. 127, 51

S

sǣ mf. *sea* sǣs gs. 36, 22. sǣ ds. 144, 21 (twice). sǣ as. 98, 17; 207, 4

sǣl mf. *time, season* sǣl ns. 189, 80. sǣlum dp. 29, 15

sǣlan (I) *to fasten, bind* sǣlan inf. 207, 21. [Cf. OE sāl *rope*.]

sǣtte see **settan**

saga see **secgan**

sǣd- see **secgan**

sǣman m. *seaman, pirate* sǣmen np. 144, 20

sǣwiht f. *sea-animal* sǣwihta gp. 44, 9

sam conj. *whether, or*

samod adv. *together*

Sanctus Benedictus *Saint Benedict*

Sandwīċ *Sandwich* Sanwīċ ds. 110, 4; 111, 28

sār adj. *sore, grievous* sāre æfter npf. *sore with longing for* 208, 50. sārra apf. 189, 80

sāre adv. *sorely, grievously*

sāule see **sāwol**

sāwol f. *soul* sāwl ns. 190, 120. sāwle gs. 199, 28. sāule ds. 165, 79. sāule

as. 127, 66; sāwle 199, 30. sāwlum dp. 29, 5

scamian (II) *to be ashamed* scami-ande prp. nsm. 29, 11. scamað pl. pres. ind. 144, 47; 144, 55; 144, 56; 145, 66 (twice)

scamu f. *shame, dishonor* scamu ns. 143, 1

scandlīċ adj. *shameful* scandlīċ nsn. 127, 76. scandlīċe npn. 143, 7. sceandlīcan dpm. 127, 62

sceadu f. *shade, shadow, darkness* sceadu ns. 188, 54. sceade ds. 29, 11

sceaft m. *spear-shaft, spear* sceaft ns. 29, 19. sceafte ds. 30, 20. [Cf. Lat. scāpus *shaft, stem*.]

sceal see **sculan**

sceandlīcan see **scandlīċ**

scēap n. *sheep* scēapa gp. 44, 7. scēpa ap. 198, 13

scēat m. *surface, 'corner'* scēatum dp. 187, 8; 188, 43; scēatas ap. 187, 37. [MnE sheet.]

sēaþ m. *pit* sēaþe as. 189, 75

scēawian (II) *to see, behold* scēawode 3s pret. ind. 190, 137

scendan (I) *to insult, corrupt* scendað pl. pres. ind. 144, 15; 144, 24

sceold- see **sculan**

sceop see **scieppan**

scēotan (2) *to pay, contribute* scēotað pl. pres. ind. 127, 78

scēpa see **scēap**

Sceppend see **scyppend**

sceððan (6) *to injure* (with dat.) sce-ððan inf. 188, 47. [MnE scathe.]

scieppan (6) *to create* scēop 3s pret. ind. 56, 24; scōp 199, 36

scilun see **sculan**

scīma m. *radiance, splendor* scīman as. 188, 54

scīnan (1) *to shine* scīnan inf. 187, 15

scip n. *ship* scip ns. 97, 2. scipe ds. 111, 23; 144, 26. scipu np. 110, 1. scipa gp. 111, 11; 111, 14. scipon dp. 111, 20; scipan 111, 38; 111, 47. scipo ap. 111, 18; 111, 19; 111, 22; 111, 23; scipa 111, 50

scipen n. *stall, cattle-shed* scipene ds. 55, 8

scipfyrd f. *naval force or expedition* scipfyrd ns. 110, 6; 111, 26. scipfyrde ds. 111, 13. [Cf. OE fyrd *national levy.*]

scīr adj. *bright, gleaming, pure* scīr nsm. as subst. 29, 11. scīrne asm. 188, 54

scīr f. *shire, district* scīrum dp. 111, 42

scold- see **sculan**

scomu f. *shame* scome ds. 55, 5

Scōnēġ f. *Skåne,* southwestern area of Sweden Scōnēġ ns. 97, 4

scōp see **scieppan**

Scotland n. *Scotland* Scotland as. 164, 50

scrīfan (I) *to have regard for, care about* scrīfað pl. pres. ind. 127, 80

sculan (PP) *shall, ought, be necessary, be destined* sceal 3s pres. ind. sculon pl. pres. ind. 55, 20; 145, 97; sceolon 98, 38; sceolan 99, 52; scilun 199, 31. sceolde 1s pret. ind. 188, 43; 207, 8; 207, 19. scoldon pl. pret. ind. 75, 11. scylan pl. pres. subj. 126, 12. sceolde sg. pret. subj. 111, 15; 111, 16; 111, 36; 127, 57; 165, 67; 165, 77; 207, 3; scolde 126, 9; 127, 60; 127, 73; 144, 40; 144, 52; 144, 53. sceolden pl. pret. subj. 55, 4; 86, 5; scoldan 126, 29; 127, 59; 145, 83; sceoldon 75, 13 (twice); sceoldan 110, 4

sculon see **sculan**

scylan see **sculan**

scyld m. *shield* scyld ns. 29, 19

scyppend m. *creator, God* Scyppend ns. 56, 25; 209, 85. Sceppend 199, 37. Scyppendes gs. 55, 18

sē m., **sēo** f., **þæt** n., def. art., dem. and rel. pron. nom. (þæt also acc.) the, the one, he, she, it   sē þe ns. *he who, the one who* 29, 13. sē *which* 127, 65. wāt sē þe sceal *he knows who must* 208, 37. sē *the wanderer* 209, 88

sealde see **sellan**

sealtsēað m. *salt spring* sealtsēaðas ap. 45, 16

searacræft m. *fraud* searacræftas ap. 144, 35

sēċan (I) *to seek, strive for* sēċan inf. 189, 104; 190, 127. sēċeð 3s pres. ind. 209, 114. sōhte 1s pret. ind. 207, 25; 199, 17; 3s 75, 12. sōhton pl. pret. ind. 190, 133

secg m. *man* secga gp. 208, 53. secgum dp. 188, 59. [Cog. with Lat. sequor *I follow,* socius *companion.*]

secgan (III) *to say, tell* secgan inf. 185, 1. secge 1s pres. ind. 126, 31; 145, 86. secgað pl. pres. ind. 110, 3. sǣde 3s pret. ind. 97, 1; 145, 79. secge sg. pres. subj. 189, 96. saga imp. sg. 36, 29

sefa m. *mind, spirit, heart* sefan as. 208, 57

seġel m. *sail* seġl ds. 97, 3

seht f. *friendship, favor, peace* his sehta ap. *his favor, peace with him* 165, 76

sehðe interj. *behold!*

sele m. *hall, meadhall* sele as. 207, 25

seledrēam m. *hall-joy, festivity, revelry* seledrēamas np. 209, 93

selesecg m. *hall-retainer, hall-warrior* selesecgas ap. 208, 34

sēlest adj. *best* (supl. deg. of sēl *good*) sēlesta nsm. 187, 27. sēlest as(n.) 190, 118

self- see **sylf**

sellan (I) *to give, sell* syllan inf. 29, 9; wið weorðe syllan *to sell* 127, 81. sealde 3s pret. ind. 65, 14; 76, 23; 127, 84. selle sg. pres. subj. 198, 11; 198, 13. ġesealde pp. npm.

126, 38. sellað imp. pl. 200, 48. [Cf. Lat. consilium *advice*.]

sendan (I) *to send* sendan inf. 208, 56

seofon num. *seven* syfan 97, 2

seo[l]fa see **sylf**

seolfor n. *silver* seolfres gs. 45, 19; 164, 60. seolfre ds. 189, 77

seolh m. *seal* sēolas np. 44, 10

sēon (5) *to look, see* sis 2s pres. ind. *will see* 200, 44

setl n. *seat, residence, quarters* settl as 111, 41

settan (I) *to set, lay, put, to make to sit* sætte 3s pret. ind. *deposed* 164, 33; *put* 164, 39; *established* 164, 65; 165, 71. ġeseted pp. nsm. 55, 1; nsf. *set* 44, 2. [Causative derived from PGmc *setjanan *to sit*.]

sibb f. *peace, friendship, relationship* sibbe ds. *peace* 199, 29. sibbe as. 75, 7. [Cf. MnE gossip from ME godsib, gossib *related in God*, hence formerly a sponsor in baptism.]

sibleġer n. *incest* sibleġeru ap. 144, 37

sīde adv. *amply, widely, extensively*

sīde f. *side* sīdan ds. 188, 49

sī(e) (n) (don) see **eom**

siġe m. *victory, success* siġe ns. 111, 25

siġebēam m. *(victorious) cross* siġe-bēam ns. 187, 13 siġebēam as. 190, 127

siġelēas adj. *without victory, defeated* siġelēase npm. 143, 11

sigor m. *victory* sigora gp. 188, 67

sigorfæst adj. *triumphant, victorious* sigorfæst nsm. 190, 150

sihþe same as **sehðe**

sinc n. *treasure* sinces gs. 207, 25. since ds. 187, 23

sincþegu f. *receiving of treasure* sinc-þeġe as. 208, 34

sind see **eom**

singal adj. *perpetual, everlasting* sin-gal nsf. 190, 141

singallīċe adv. *continually, incessantly*

singan (3) *to sing, compose in verse* singan inf. 55, 4; 55, 13; 55, 15; 55, 16; 55, 17. song 3s pret. ind. 56, 29. sing imp. sg. 55, 11; 55, 16

sīo same as **sēo**

siodu m. *custom, morality* siodu as. or ap. 75, 7. [Cf. Ger. die Sitte *custom*.]

sioððan same as **syððan**

sis see **sēon**

sittan (5) *to sit* sit 3s pres. ind. 128, 89. sittað pl. pres. ind. 126, 14. sitte sg. pres. subj. 66, 17. [Allied to Lat. sedēre *to sit*.]

sīþ m. *journey, time, occasion* sīþe ds. 29, 3. sum sīðe is. *on a certain occasion* 111, 37

sīðfæt m. *expedition* sīðfate ds. 190, 150

sīðian (II) *to depart, go, journey* siðian inf. 188, 68

siðð̄an same as **syððan**

six num. *six*

slǣp m. *sleep* slǣp ns. 208, 39. slǣpe ds. 56, 29

slǣpan (7) *to sleep* slǣpende prp. nsm. 56, 29

slēan (6) *to strike, slay* slēan inf. 164, 43. slōge sg. pret. subj. 164, 66

slīþen adj. *cruel, dire* slīþen nsf. 207, 30

slōge see **slēan**

smēagan (II) *to think, meditate, examine* smēgu 1s pres. ind. 199, 24. smēade 3s pret. ind. 126, 8. smēage sg. pres. subj. 145, 71

smēgu see **smēagan**

snāw m. *snow* snāw as. 208, 48

snīwan (I) *to snow* snīwe sg. pres. subj. 66, 18

snot(t)or adj. *wise, clever* snottor ns. as subst. 209, 111. snotre np. 29, 5

sōht- see **sēċan**

somod same as **samod**

sōna adv. *immediately, right away*

song (vb.) see **singan**

song mn. *song, poem* songes gs. 56, 31

sorg f. *sorrow, trouble* sorg ns. 207, 30; 208, 39; 208, 50. sorga ap. 189, 80. sorgum ip. 187, 20; 188, 59. [Cf. Ger. die Sorge *care, sorrow.*]

sorhlēoð n. *dirge, lament* sorhlēoð as. 188, 67

sōð n. *truth* sōð ns. 126, 1; 126, 31; 145, 86. sōþes gs. with ġeswugedan 145, 82. tō sōþe ds. *truly, indeed* 207, 11. [Cf. MnE forsooth.]

sōðlīċe adv. *truly, indeed*

sparian (II) *to spare* sparode 3s pret. ind. 164, 34

spearwa m. *sparrow* spearwa ns. 66, 19

specan (5) *to speak* specað pl. pres. ind. 163, 14. spǣcan pl. pret. ind. 126, 7. tō specenne gerund 127, 76

spēd f. *riches, power, speed* spēda as. 87, 20; 98, 28; 98, 48

spēdiġ adj. *successful* spēdiġ nsm. 190, 151

spere n. *spear, lance, javelin* spere ds. 30, 20

spor n. *track, footprint* spore ds. 76, 38

spōwan (7) *to succeed* (impersonal verb with dat.) spēow 3s pret. ind. 75, 9

sprecan (5) *to speak* sprecan inf. 187, 27. spriċeð 3s pres. ind. 208, 70. sprǣcon pl. pret. ind. 110, 2; sprǣcan 66, 27. sprecende prp. nsm. 55, 15. [Cf. Ger. sprechen *to speak.*]

sprǣċ f. *speech, conversation, discourse* sprǣċe ds. 65, 14

spriċeð see **sprecan**

spyriġean (II) *to follow, pursue* spyriġean inf. 76, 36

stæð n. *shore* staðe ds. 98, 14. [Allied to Lat. status *standing, position.*]

stalu f. *stealing, theft* stalu ns. 127, 50. stala ap. 144, 34

stān m. *stone* stān ns. 45, 19. stāne ds. 188, 66

Stān *Staines* Stāne ds. 111, 48

standan (6) *to stand* standan inf. 188, 43; 188, 62. standeð 3s pres. ind. 98, 14; stondeð 208, 74; 209, 115; stent 111, 44; stondeð nu on lāste *survives* 209, 97. stondaþ pl. pres. ind. 209, 76. stōd 1s pret. ind. 187, 38; 3s 55, 10. stōdon pl. pret. ind. 76, 30; 187, 7; 188, 71; 209, 87. [Related to Lat. stāre *to stand.*]

stānhliþ n. *stone cliff* stānhleoþu ap. *the walls of stone buildings* 209, 101

staðe see **stæð**

staðol m. *position* staðole ds. 188, 71

stēam m. *moisture* stēame is. 188, 62. [MnE steam.]

stearc adj. *stern* stearc nsm. 163, 16; 164, 30; 164, 58. [MnE stark.]

stede m. *place* steode ds. 163, 17

stefn f. *voice* stefn ns. 188, 71

stefn m. *root, stem* stefne ds. 187, 30

stent see **standan**

stēorbord n. *starboard, right side of a ship* stēorbord as. 97, 3; 98, 10

steorfa m. *pestilence* steorfa ns. 127, 50

stēpan (I) *to enrich, support* stēpeð 3s pres. ind. 36, 17

stilnes f. *stillness, tranquillity* stilnesse as. 87, 19

stīð adj. *fierce, inexorable* stīð nsm. 165, 73

stīðmōd adj. *resolute* stīðmōd nsm. 188, 40

stōd- see **standan**

stond- see **standan**

storm m. *storm* storm as. 29, 15. storme is. 66, 21. stormas np. 209, 101. [Cf. OE styrian *to stir*.]

stōw f. *place* stōwe ds. 87, 40. stōwe as. 45, 17. stōwa np. 127, 72. stōwum dp. 44, 8. stōwa ap. 76, 34

strǣl fm. *arrow* strǣle ds. *for the arrow* 29, 10. strǣlum ip. *nails* 188, 62

strang adj. *strong, powerful, firm* strang nsm. 188, 40. strangum ds. 29, 8. strange npm. 143, 12; 187, 30

strangra (strengŕa) adj. *stronger, more powerful* (comp. deg. of strang) strenģere nsm. 163, 15. strangran apn. 65, 12

strenģere see **strangra**

strenģu f. *strength, power, vigor* strenģu ns. 36, 5

strengþ f. (military) *strength* strengþe isf. 164, 51

strēu n. *straw* strēu as. 199, 43; 200, 45; 200, 47

strīċ n. *? sedition, ? plague* strīċ ns. 127, 50

strūdung f. *spoilation, robbery* strūdunga ap. 144, 34

stȳran (I) *to rule, guide* stȳran inf. 29, 8

styrman (I) *to storm* styrme sg. pres. subj. 66, 19

suē same as **swā**

sum adj. and pron. *some, a certain (one)* sumre dsf. 55, 6. sumne asm. 87, 14; 209, 81; 209, 82; 209, 83. sum (for sume) is. 111, 37. sumum dpf. 44, 8. sume apm. 127, 73; 209, 80. suma apf. 87, 15; sume 145, 95

sumor m. *summer* sumor ns. 99, 56

sundor adv. *separately, apart* him sundor *by himself* 209, 111

sundorsefa m. *special (separate) mind* sundorsefan as. 29, 12

sunne f. *sun* sunne ns. 36, 22; 45, 14

sunu m. *son* Sunu ns. 190, 150. sunan ap. 163, 6

sūðan adv. *from the south* be sūðan *south of* (with dat.) 76, 19

sūðdǣl m. *south, southern part* sūðdǣle ds. 44, 5

sūðrima m. *the south coast* sūðriman ds. 111, 12. [Cf. MnE rim.]

Sūðseaxe pl. *the South Saxons* Sūðseaxum dp. 111, 33. [Cf. MnE Sussex.]

Sūðseaxisc *South Saxon* Sūðseaxscian (a misspelling) asm. 111, 10

swā adv. and conj. *so, as* swā...swā *as . . . so* 29, 12. swǣ swǣ *just as* 87, 30

swǣ same as **swā** swǣ forð *so on* 198, 5

swǣs adj. *dear, beloved* swǣsne asm. as subst. 208, 50

swǣsendu n. pl. *banquet, meal* swǣsendum dp. 65, 16

swǣtan (I) *to bleed* swǣtan inf. 187, 20

swæð n. *track, vestige, trace* swæð as. 76, 36

swalwe f. *swallow* swalwan as. 199, 24

swāt m. *blood* swātes gs. 187, 23. [MnE sweat.]

swē same as **swā** swē swē . . . swē *just as . . . thus* 199, 24

swefn n. *dream, sleep* swefn as. 55, 10. swefna gp. 185, 1. [Cog. with Lat. sommnus *sleep*.]

swelċe same as **swylċe**

swenċean (I) *to oppress* swenċean inf. *to be oppressed* 164, 57

Swēom dp. *the Swedes* 98, 9

sweord n. *sword* sweorde ds. 30, 20

sweotule adv. *clearly*

swicdōm m. *betrayal, treason, fraud* swicdōmas ap. 144, 35

swician (II) *to deceive* (with dat.) swicode 3s pret. ind. 127, 61

swift adj. *swift, quick* swiftre nsf.

comp. deg. 36, 22. swiftan npn. 98, 45

swiftoste see **swyftost**

swīgian (II) *to be silent, noiseless* swīgað 3s pres. ind. 36, 1. [Cf. Ger. schweigen *to be silent.*]

swilċ- see **swylċ, swylċe**

swimman (3) *to swim* swimmað pl. pres. ind. 208, 53

swīn n. *hog, pig* swīnum dp. 200, 49

swinsian (II) *to sound melodiously* swinsiað pl. pres. ind. 36, 7. [Cf. OE swinn *music, song.*]

swīðe same as **swȳðe**

swīðost see **swȳðost**

swīðra adj. *stronger, right side* (comp. deg. of swīð) swīðran asf. 187, 20

swōgan (7) *to sound, rustle, whistle* swōgað pl. pres. ind. 36, 7

swulung n. *a ploughland, a Kentish measure of land corresponding to the hide* swulung as. 198, 11

swutol adj. *clear, evident* swutol nsn. 127, 46; 144, 28

swyftost adj. *fastest* (supl. degree of swift) swiftoste asn. 98, 41. swyftoste apn. 98, 38

swylċ pron. and adj. nom. *such (a)* swylċ swā *just as* 65, 16. swilċ nsm. 111, 17; 163, 23. be swilcan dp. *from such things* 145, 86

swylċe adv. *likewise, as* swilċ *as if* 111, 21

swȳðe adv. *very (much), exceedingly* swīðe swīðe *very much* 86, 1

swȳðor adv. *more* (comp. deg. of swȳðe)

swȳðost adv. *most, especially* (supl. deg. of swȳðe) swīðost *almost* 98, 47

sȳ same as **sīe;** see **eom**

syfan see **seofon**

sylf pron. and adj. *self, selfsame* sylfa nsm. 189, 105; seolfa 199, 27. mē sylfum dsm. *myself* 36, 29; mē selfum *to myself* 86, 4; him

sylf 164, 41. selfe dsn. *for itself* 76, 25. sylfne asm. 65, 6; 144, 16; 144, 55; 145, 71; 145, 88; hine sylf 165, 78. sylfe asf. 189, 92. sylfe npm. 98, 6; selfe 145, 85. sylfum dp. 145, 73

syllan see **sellan**

syllīċ adj. *marvelous, wondrous* syllīċ nsm. 187, 13. syllīċre asn. an absolute comparative 187, 4

symbel n. *feast, banquet* symble ds. 55, 6; symle 190, 141. symbla gp. 209, 93

symle see **symbel**

syn(d)- see **eom**

syngian (II) *to sin* syngian pl. pres. subj. 144, 55

synlēaw f. *stain or injury of sin* synlēawa ap. 145, 59

synn f. *sin, guilt, crime* synne np. 29, 19. synna gp. 165, 80. synnan dp. 126, 3; synnum 144, 14; 145, 76; 189, 99; 190, 146. synna ap. 144, 32; 145, 84. synnum ip. 187, 13

syððan adv. and conj. *after, since*

syx same as **six**

T

tǣċan (I) *to teach, prescribe* tǣċan pl. pres. subj. 145, 57; 145, 67

tǣlan (I) *to blame, reproach* tǣleð 3s pres. ind. 144, 50

tælhġ m. *dye* tælhġ ns. 45, 14. [MnE tallow.]

tealt adj. *unstable, wavering* tealte npf. 127, 54

tellan (I) *to reckon* tellan inf. 165, 78

Temes f. *the Thames* Temese gs. 111, 43; 111, 47. Temese ds. 76, 19; Temesan 111, 41

tēode see **tēogan**

tēogan (tēon) (II) *to create* tēode 3s pret. ind. 56, 27; tīadæ 199, 39

tēon m. *injury, enmity* tēon ds. 36, 12. tēonan ap. 164, 55 tīadæ   see **tēogan**

tīd   f.   *time, hour, tide*   tīde ds. 55, 1; 55, 6; 55, 9. tīd as. 66, 20. tīda np. 75, 4. tīdum dp. 145, 75. [Cf. Ger. die Zeit *time*.]

til   adj.   *good, commendable*   til nsm. 209, 112

tīma   m.   *time*   tīman ds. 111, 8; 164, 55

tō   adv.   *too, overly*

tō   prep.   *to, at, for* (with dat., instr.)

tōbēatan   (7)   *to beat severely, beat into pieces*   tōbēot 3s pret. ind. 111, 18

tōbrecan   (4)   *to break, violate*   tōbrocene pp. npn. 128, 88

tōcyme   m.   *coming*   tōcyme ds. 126, 3

tōdǣlan   (I)   *to separate, divide*   tōdǣlað pl. pres. ind. 98, 32. tōdǣlede pp. as. *separated* 45, 17ᶜ

tōgædere   adv.   *together*

tōġeþēodan   (I)   *to join*   tōġeþēodde 3s pret. ind. 56, 31

tōlicgan   (5)   *to separate*   tōlīð 3s pres. ind. 98, 11

tōlīð   see **tōlicgan**

torht   adj.   *bright, gleaming*   torht ns. 36, 12

torn   n.   *passion, anger, resentment*   torn as. 209, 112

torr   m.   *tower*   torrum dp. 45, 22. [From Lat. turris *tower*.]

tōslītan   (1)   *to tear to pieces*   tōslīte inf. 200, 49

tōþrescan   (3)   *to dash into pieces*   tōþræsc 3s pret. ind. 111, 18

toweard   prep.   *toward* (with dat.)

tredan   (5)   *to step, pass over*   tredan inf. *trample* 200, 49. trede 1s pres. ind. 36, 1

trēow   f.   *good faith, trust*   trēowe as. 209, 112

trēow   n.   *tree, wood, timber; cross, rood*   trēow as. 187, 4; 187, 14; 187, 17; 187, 25. trēowum dp. 44, 6

trum   adj.   *strong*

trumest   adj.   *strongest* (supl. deg. of trum)   trumestum dpn. 45, 23. [Allied to Lat. dūrus *hard*.]

Trūsō   a lost, ancient town on the Drausen Sea   Trūsō ns. 98, 14. Trūsō as. 97, 2

tū   see **tweġen**

tūn   m.   *town, homestead*   tūne ds. 98, 35; 98, 37; 98, 43. [Cf. OE tȳnan *to enclose*.]

twā(m)   see **tweġen**

tweġen   num.   *two, (both)*   tweġen nom. masc. 144, 20. tū nom. neut. 44, 4. twǣm dat. neut. 36, 11; dat. fem. 111, 42. tweġen acc. masc. 98, 26; 98, 55. twā acc. fem. 111, 46. twā ġēar acc. neut. *(for) two (more) years* 164, 53

twelfe   num.   *twelve*

tȳne   num.   *ten*

þ

thā   adv.   *then*

þā   adv. and conj.   *then, when*   þā he . . . þā *when he . . . then* 55, 6. ðā ðā *when then* 76, 19. ðāðā *since* 76, 24

þā   asf. and nap. of **sē**   ðā þe *those which* 45, 22. þā *which* (with eal) 56, 29. þā þe *those who* 65, 7; 76, 34. ðā *they* 76, 31; ðā *them* 200, 49. ðā ðe *those whom* 87, 23

þǣm   same as **þām**

þæne   same as **þone**

þænne   same as **þonne**

þǣr   adv.   *there, where*   þǣr þǣr *there where* 76, 23

þǣra   same as **þāra**

þǣre   gs. and ds.   of **sēo** (see **sē**)   þǣre dsf. *'it'* 66, 26

þǣron   adv.   *thereon, therein*

þǣrwið   adv.   *therewith*

þæs   adv.   *to that degree, to such an extent, therefore*

þæs   gs. masc. and neut. of **sē**   þæs þe *of that which* 99, 49; 126, 21. þes þe *according to what* 110, 2.

þæs *of that* 145, 66; 145, 71. þæs þe *according as* 145, 79

þæt conj. *that, so that*

þæt n. and a. neut. of **sē** ðæt ns. *it* 44, 1; 44, 3. þæt þæt as. *that which* 145, 92

þætte (from þæt þe) conj. *that, so that*

þafung f. *consent, permission* þafunge as. 143, 12

þām (þǣm) ds. masc. and neuter of **sē**; dp. of **þā (sē)** þām þe *the one who* 36, 17; *by which means* 144, 24; *for those who* 145, 99; 190, 149; *for the one who* 208, 31; 208, 56. tō ðǣm *to such an extent* 76, 22. ðǣm dp. *themselves* 87, 20. tō ðām *for that* 190, 129. þām þe *to those who* 190, 154. þām þe *for that one who for himself* 209, 114

þan same as **þȳ, þām** wið ðan ðe ds. *with which* 198, 12

þāra gp. of **sē** and **þæt**

þās dem. pron. np. and ap. *these;* also as. of **þēos**

þe rel. particle (not declined) *who, which* sē þe ns. *he who, the one who* 29, 13. þe . . . tō *for which* 111, 25. þe *a person, someone* 198, 6

þē dat. (also acc.) of **þū**

þē is. of **sē** and **þæt** þē mā þe *any more than* 110, 7; 127, 55. þē lǣs *lest* 145, 73

þēah conj. and adv. *though, although, however* þēah þe *although* 207, 2

þēahhweðere conj. *however, nevertheless*

þeara same as **þāra** ðeara *of them* 198, 6

þearf f. *need, necessity* þearf ns. 126, 31; 145, 85; 145, 88; 145, 89. þearfa ap. 198, 12

þearf (vb.) see **þurfan**

þearle adv. *severely*

þēaw m. *custom, habit, practice* ðēaw ns. 98, 25; 99, 50; 207, 12. þēawa gp. 144, 44. ðēawas ap. *virtues, morals* 76, 27

þeġn m. *retainer, warrior, thane, servant* þeġen ns. 143, 6. þeġenes gs. 144, 15. þeġene ds. 143, 4. þeġen as. 143, 5; 144, 17. þeġnas np. 164, 30; 189, 75. þeġna gp. 65, 5. þeġnum dp. 66, 17; þēnan 126, 27

þeġenġylde n. *the compensation ('wergild') for a thane* þeġenġylde as. 143, 7

þeġnian (II) *to serve, wait on* (with dat.) þeġniað pl. pres. ind. 36, 15. [Cf. OE þeġn *servant, retainer.*]

þēh same as **þēah**

þēm same as **þām** tō ðēm londe *along with the land* 198, 13

þēnan see **þeġn**

þenċan (I) *to think, consider* ðencu 1s pres. ind. 199, 27. þenċeð 3s pres. ind. 190, 121. þenċaþ pl. pres. ind. *will think* 190, 115. þōhte 3s pret. ind. 111, 14; *intended* 127, 60

þenian (I) *to stretch out* þenian inf. 188, 52

þēning f. *service, office* ðēninga ap. *mass books* 75, 15

þēod f. *people, nation* þēode ds. 126, 32; 127, 45; 127, 47; 128, 87; 128, 89; 143, 9; 144, 44; 145, 68. þēode as. 126, 5; 126, 10; 126, 40; 127, 71; 144, 22; 144, 28; 145, 70. ðīode np. 87, 14. þēodum dp. 126, 20; 126, 23. [Cog. with Lat. totus *all,* also with ger. deutsch *German.*]

þēodde see **þēowian**

þēoden m. *chief, prince, lord* þēodnes gs. 209, 95. þēodne ds. 188, 69

þēodscipe m. *people, population* þēodscipe ns. 144, 31. ðēodscipes gs. 111, 24. þēodscipe as. 111, 35

þēodwita m. *learned man* þēodwita ns. 145, 75

þeora g. and d. of **sēo**

þēos f. dem. pron. nom. *this* þēos ns. 36, 4; 44, 8; 65, 2; 66, 25

þeossum dp. of **þēs** þeossum ds. Anglian for WS þissum 55, 13 þēow m. *servant* þēowas np. 126, 26. ðīowa gp. 76, 31. þēowum dp. 126, 28. þēowas ap. 126, 30

þēowa m. *servant* þēowan np. 28, 22

þēowian (II) *to serve* (with dat.) þēowaþ 3s pres. ind. 36, 15. þēodde 3s pret. ind. 65, 10. ġeþēowede pp. nsn. *enslaved* 126, 39. [Cf. OE þēow *servant, slave*.]

þes see þæs (gs. of sē and þæt)

þēs masc. dem. pron. nom. *this*

þet same as þæt þet for sē 164, 40

þīn 2nd pers. sg. poss. pron. (declined strong); also g. of þū þīn nsf. 66, 18. þīnes gsm. 200, 47; þīne[s] 199, 43. þīnum dsm. 200, 45; dsn. 200, 44; 200, 45; 200, 46 (twice). þīnra gpm. 65, 5. þīnum dpm. 66, 17

þinċ- see þynċan

þing n. *thing* þing as. 164, 31. þinga gp. 126, 24. þingum dp. 65, 8; 164, 40. þing ap. 65, 11; 144, 45 (twice); 165, 81

þingian (II) *to intercede* þingian pl. pres. subj. 145, 88

þīode see þēod

þīow see þēow

þīowotdōm m. *service* ðīowotdōmas ap. 75, 11

þis neut. dem. pron. n. and a. *this* ðissum ds. 87, 25

þisan d. of þēs, þīs, and þās

þisne a. of þēs

þissa g. of þās

þisse g. and d. of þēos

þisses gs. of þēs and þis

þis(s)um d. of þēs, þis, and þās

þōhte see þenċan

þolian (II) *to suffer, endure* þoliað pl. pres. ind. 144, 24. þolodan pl. pret. ind. 190, 149

þon is. of sē and þæt

þonan adv. *thence*

þonc m. *thanks* ðonc ns. 76, 20; 87, 39

þone asm. of sē þone *(the one)* *which* 36, 12. ðone *'it* (wīsdōm) 76, 35

þonne adv. and conj. *then, when, than*

þræl m. *slave* þræl ns. 143, 5; 144, 17. þræle ds. 143, 5; 144, 18. þræl as. 143, 6. þræla gp. 143, 2. [Cf. MnE enthralled.]

þrælriht n. *the rights of a slave* þrælriht ns. 126, 41

þrāg f. *(period of) time* þrāg ns. 209, 95

þrēo see þrīe

þridda num. and adj. *third* þridda nsm. 163, 8. þriddan (dǣl) asm. 98, 36

þrīe num. *three* þrȳ nom. masc. 144, 20. þrēo acc. masc. 163, 6

þrīttiġ num. *thirty* þrīttigum dp. 45, 22

þriwa num. adv. *three times, thrice*

þrōwian (II) *to suffer* ðrōwiu 1s pres. ind. 199, 26. þrōwode 3s pret. ind. 189, 84; 189, 98; 190, 145

þrȳ see þrīe

þrym m. *glory, majesty* þrym ns. 209, 95

þrymfæst adj. *glorious* þrymfæst nsm. 189, 84

þrȳþ f. *strength, power* þrȳþe np. 209, 99

þȳfþ f. *theft* þȳfþe ds. 126, 40

þū 2nd sg. pers. pron. nom. *you*

þūhte see þynċan

þurh prep. *through, by* (with acc.) þurh þæt þe *because* 127, 72; 144, 51

þurhdrīfan (1) *to pierce, drive through* þurhdrifan pl. pret. ind. 188, 46

þurhflēon (2) *to fly* þurhflēo sg. pres. subj. 66, 19

þurhsmēagan (II) *to investigate* þurhsmēade 3s pret. ind. 164, 47

þurfan (PP) *need* þearf 3s pres. ind. 190, 117

þus adv. *thus*

þūsend num. *one thousand*

þȳ adv. *therefore* þȳ 126, 2; 127, 47; 145, 87; 198, 12

þȳ is. of **sē** and **þæt**

þyderweard adv. *thither*

þȳles (þȳ lǣs) conj. *lest*

þynċan (I) *to seem, appear* þinċan inf. 127, 53; 144, 31; 145, 59. þynċeð 3s pres. ind. impersonal 65, 11; þinċeð 208, 41; ðynċð 87, 15 (twice). þūhte 3s pret. ind. impersonal 187, 4

þysan dsn. of **þēs** and **þis**

þyslīċ pron. and adj. *such* þyslīċ nsn. 65, 14

þysne a. of **þēs**

þysse g. and d. of **þēos**

þysses g. of **þēs** and **þis**

þysson d. of **þēs, þis,** and **þās**

þyssum d. of **þēs, þis,** and **þās**

þȳstro n. *darkness* þȳstro np. with singular meaning 188, 52

U

uard see **weord**

uerc see **weorc**

ūhta m. *dawn, period before daylight* ūhtna gp. 207, 8

unāteallendlīċe adv. *incalculable, untold*

unc *us two;* d. and a. of **wit** *we two* unc būtū a. *both of us* 188, 48

uncoþu f. *disease, plague* uncoþu ns. 127, 50

uncræft m. *deceit* uncræftan dp. 145, 96

uncūð adj. *unknown, uncertain* uncūð nsf. (with tīde) 65, 16; ns(n). 87, 38. [MnE uncouth.]

undǣd f. *crime, wicked deed* undǣde ds. 144, 54

under prep. *under* (with dat. and acc.)

underfēngan see **underfōn**

underfōn (anv.) *to receive* underfēngan pl. pret. ind. 145, 92

underhnīgan (1) *to sink under* underhnīġe 1s pres. ind. 36, 25

understand- see **understondan**

understondan (6) *to understand* understondan inf. 75, 15; understandan 144, 23; 145, 96. understande sg. pres. subj. 127, 85; 143, 8. understandað imp. pl. 126, 5

underþǣdde see **underþēodan**

underþēod adj. *subjected, subject* underþēoddan apm. 164, 59

underþēodan (I) *to subject to* (with reflexive in dat. or acc.) underþēodde 3s pret. ind. 65, 6; underþǣdde 164, 51

unforbærned adj. *unburned, uncremated* (pp. of unforbærnan) unforbærned nsm. 98, 25; nsn. 99, 52; npm. 98, 28

unforht adj. *unafraid* unforht nsm. 189, 110

unforworht adj. *innocent* unforworhte npm. as subst. 126, 39

unfriðhere m. *hostile force or army* unfriðhere ns. 111, 27

unġefoge adv. *exceedingly*

unġelimp m. *misfortune* unġelimpa gp. 143, 9

unġemetlīċ adj. *immense* unġemetlica nsm. 111, 27

unġederad adj. *uninjured, unmolested* (a pp.) unġederad nsm. 164, 42. [Cf. OE derian *to injure.*]

unġerim n. *a countless number* unġerim ns. 145, 65

unġetrȳwþ f. *disloyalty, treachery* unġetrȳwþa np. 127, 63

unġinnost adj. supl. deg. of **unġinne** *not great* unġinnost nsn. 30, 20

unġylde n. *excessive tax* unġylda np. 127, 51

unlagu f. *injustice, violation of law* unlaga gp. 126, 10. unlaga ap. 126, 40; 145, 80

unlȳtel adj. *much, great* unlȳtel nsn. 126, 18

unnan (PP) *grant* (with gen.) unnan inf. 198, 4

unriht n. *wrong, injustice* unriht as. 126, 9; 145, 90; on unriht as. *'wrongfully'* 126, 36. unrihte ds. 164, 61. unrihta gp. 126, 7; 127, 53

unrihtlīċe adv. *unrightly, wrongly*

unrīm n. *a countless number* unrīm ns. 45, 23. [Cf. OE rīm *number, reckoning.*]

unsidu m. *vice, abuse* unsida ap. 144, 35

unsnotorness f. *folly* unsnotornesse as. 145, 81

unspēdiġ adj. *poor* unspēdigan npm. as subst. 98, 22

unðanc m. *dislike, displeasure* hire unðances gs. *against her will* 164, 45

unwæstm m. *crop failure* unwæstma gp. 127, 52

unweder n. *storm, bad season* unwedera np. 127, 52

unwrēst adj. *unsteady, untrustworthy* unrēst nsm. 163, 1

ūpgang m. *incursion* ūpgang as. 111, 45

ūpp adv. *up*

uppe adv. *up, above*

ūre 1st pers. pl. poss. pron. *our* (declined strong); also g. of **wē** ūre asm. 145, 94. ūre npm. 65, 9; 145, 93. ūra gpm. 65, 6. ūrum dpf. 144, 14. ūre *of us* 127, 56; *us* (with helpe) 145, 100

ūs d. (and a.) of **wē**

ūt adv. *out*

utan *let us* (1st pers. pl. pres. subj. of wītan *to go*) utan 145, 72; 145, 89; 145, 91; 145, 93; 145, 96. wutan 145, 85

ūtanbordes genitive used adverbially *abroad*

ūte adv. *out, outside, abroad*

ūthere m. *foreign force* ūthere as. 110, 5

Uuldurfader see **Wuldorfæder**

uundra see **wundor**

W

wāc adj. *weak* wāc wiga nsm. *weak in battles* 208, 67

wadan (6) *to traverse* wadan inf. 207, 5. wōd 1s pret. ind. 207, 24. [MnE wade.]

wado see **wæd**

wæd n. *water, sea* wado ap. 36, 2. [Cf. OE wadan *to go, move, wade.*]

wǣd f. *garment* wǣdum ip. ? *banners* 187, 15; 187, 22. [Cf. the expression widow's weeds.]

wæfersȳn f. *spectacle* wæfersȳne ds. 187, 31

wælcyrie f. *walkyrie, sorceress* wælcyrian np. 145, 64

wælġīfre adj. *greedy for slaughter* wælġīfru npm. 209, 100

wælhrēow adj. *savage, cruel* wælhrēowe apf. 126, 40

wæll same as **wel**

wælsleaht n. *bloody battle, deadly combat* wælsleahta gp. 207, 7; 209, 91

wǣpen n. *weapon* wǣpen np. 209, 100. wǣpnum dp. 98, 47; wǣpnon 164, 54

wǣpnġewrixl n. *exchange of weapons, hostile encounter* wǣpnġewrixl ns. 143, 4

wǣr- see **wesan**

wǣrlīċe adv. *carefully*

wǣs see **wesan**

wæstm m. *produce, plant, fruit* wæstmum dp. 44, 6

wǣta m. *moisture* wǣtan ds. 187, 22

wæter n. *water* wæter ns. 126, 17. wæteres gs. 99, 56. wæterum dp. 44, 9. wæter ap. 45, 16

wala interj. *alas!*

wālāwā interj. *alas!*

waldend see **wealdend**

wana adj. *wanting, less* (indeclinable)

wanhȳdiġ adj. *heedless, imprudent* wanhȳdiġ nsm. 208, 67

wanian (II) *to lessen, dwindle, wane* wanedan pl. pret. ind. 126, 32

wann adj. *dark, black* won nsm. 209, 103. wann nsf. 188, 55

wansǣliġ adj. *unhappy* wansǣliġ nsm. 29, 16

warian (II) *to guard, attend* warað 3s pres. ind. 208, 32

warnian (II) *to take warning* warnian ūs inf. *to take warning for ourselves* 145, 85

wāt see witan

waþum m. *wave* waþema gp. 207, 24; 208, 57

wē 1st pl. poss. pron. nom. *we*

wealdan (7) *to cause, bring about* (with gen.) wēoldan pl. pret. ind. 127, 52

wealdend m. *Lord, ruler* Wealdend ns. 189, 111; 190, 155. Wealdendes gs. 187, 17; 187, 53. Wealdende ds. 190, 121. Wealdend as. 188, 67. waldend np. 209, 78

wealhstōd m. *translator* wealhstōd-as ap. 87, 13

weall m. *wall* weal ns. 209, 98. wealle ds. 209, 80. weallas np. 209, 76. weallum dp. 45, 22. [From Lat. uallum *wall, fortification.*]

weallan (7) *to surge, boil* weallendan prp. asm. 145, 98

wealsteal m. *site of a wall, foundation* wealsteal as. 209, 88

weard adv. *towards*

weard (n.) see weord

wearp see weorpan

wearð see weorþan

wecg m. *mass or lump of metal* wecga gp. 45, 18. [MnE wedge.]

wed n. *pledge* wed as. 145, 95. wed np. 128, 88

wedbryċe m. *the breaking of a pledge* wedbrycas ap. 144, 39

weġ m. *way* weġes gs. 98, 44. weġ as. 165, 83; 189, 88; ealne weġ *always* 97, 2; 98, 9; on weġ *away* 208, 53. wegum dp. 99, 49

wēġ m. *wave* wēgas ap. 208, 46

wel adv. *well*

wela m. *riches, prosperity* wela ns. 163, 1; 208, 74. welan as. 76, 35; 76, 37

welhwǣr adv. *nearly everywhere*

weliġ adj. *rich, wealthy* weliġ nsn. 44, 6

welwan (I) *to roll, huddle together* ġewelwede pp. nsf. (with drāfe) 144, 22

wēman (I) *to entertain* wēman inf. 207, 29

wēnan (I) *to hope, expect, believe, imagine* wēne 1s pres. ind. 75, 17; with reflexive mē 190, 135. wēndon pl. pret. ind. 86, 5. wēne sg. pres. subj. 127, 45

wendan (I) *to turn, go, change; translate* wendan inf. 86, 4; 87, 28; 187, 22. wendaþ pl. pres. ind. 29, 18. wendon pl. pret. ind. 86, 10; 87, 13; 87, 14; 111, 28. wenden pl. pres. subj. 87, 17

wenian (I) *to accustom* wenede 3s pret. ind. 208, 36. [Related to OE wunian *to dwell.*]

Wenoðland same as Weonodland

weofan (5) *to weave* weofendan prp. ds. as subst. 199, 21

weolcscyll f. *shellfish* weolcscylle np. 44, 12

wēold- see wealdan

weoler m. *lip* weolerum dp. 199, 28; weolerum makes no sense in context, and presumably represents a misreading of MS. talibus (*in such things*) as labiīs the dat. pl. of labia *lip.*

weoloc m. *cockle* weolocas np. 45, 13

weolocrēad adj. *scarlet, purple* weolocrēada nsm. 45, 14

Weonodland *the country of the Wends*

Wenoðland ns. 97, 3; Weonodland 98, 9. Weonodlande ds. 98, 12; Winodlande 98, 16. Weonodland as. 98, 11

wēop see **wēpan**

weorc n. *word, deed, action* weorc as. 56, 22; uerc 199, 34. weorc ap. 145, 94; 189, 79

weord m. *guardian, keeper* Weard ns. 56, 26; 189, 91; Uard 199, 38. Weord as. 55, 20; Uard 199, 32

weorod n. *host* weorode ds. 188, 69; 190, 152; werede 190, 124. weruda gp. 188, 51

weorpan (3) *to throw, cast* wearp 3s pret. ind. 111, 18

weorð n. *worth, price* wurð ns. 164, 48. wið weorðe ds. *for a price* 127, 81; 127, 83

weorðe adj. *worthy* weorðe nsm. 198, 6; ns(n). 66, 26. wyrðes gsm. 56, 31

weorþan (3) *to become* weorþan inf. 36, 19; 86, 6; 126, 16; 208, 64. weorþeð 3s pres. ind. 209, 110; wyrð *will become* 126, 4; 127, 44. wearð 3s pret. ind. 144, 31. weorþe sg. pres. subj. 143, 3 *should turn;* 143, 4. ġeworden pp. nsm. 189, 87. [Related to Lat. uertere *to turn;* cf. OE wyrd *fate.*]

weorþian (II) *to worship, esteem, venerate* weorþian inf. 190, 129. weorðiað pl. pret. ind. 189, 81

weorðlīċe adv. *splendidly, magnificently*

weorðscipe m. *honor, dignity, worth* weorðscipe ds. 144, 24. wurðscipe as. 110, 6; 163, 11

weorðung f. *worship* weorðunge ds. 126, 22

weoruld see **woruld**

weoruldhād m. *secular life* weoruldhāde ds. 55, 1

wēpan (7) *to weep* wēop 3s pret. ind. 188, 55

wer m. *man* wer ns. 208, 64. [Cog. with Lat. uir *man;* cf. MnE werewolf.]

werede see **weorod**

werg m. *criminal* wergas ap. 187, 31

weriġ adj. *weary, exhausted* weriġne asm. 208, 57

weriġmōd adj. *weary in spirit, dejected* weriġmōd nsm. as subst. 207, 15

werscipe n. *prudence, cunning* werscipe is. 164, 54. (Cf. MnE wary.]

weruda see **weorod**

wesan (anv.) *to be* wesan inf. 189, 110; 190, 117. wæs 1s and 3s pret. ind. næs 3s pret. ind. neg. 111, 25; 164, 47. wǣron pl. pret. ind.; wǣran 126, 6; 145, 93. nǣron pl. pret. ind. neg. 76, 33. wǣre sg. pret. subj. wǣren pl. pret. subj. nǣren pl. pret. subj. neg. 76, 18

west adv. *west, westwards*

westdǣl m. *west* westdǣle ds. 44, 2

wēste adj. *waste, desolate* wēste nsm. 208, 74

Westmynster *Westminster* Westmynster ds. 164, 27

wīċ nf. *dwelling-place* wīċ ap. 36, 2

wiċċa m. *wizard,* or **wiċċe** f. *witch* wiċċan np. *wizards,* or *witches* 145, 63

wīċing m. *viking* wīċinge ds. 143, 3

wīde adv. *widely, far and wide*

wīf n. *woman, wife* wīf ns. 36, 14; wiif 198, 8; 198, 14. wīfa gp. 189, 94

wīġ m. *war, battle* wiġ ns. 209, 80. wīġe ds. 75, 9. wīga gp. 208, 67

wiga m. *fighter, warrior* wiga ns. 36, 10

wīgan (1) *to fight, make war* wīġeð 3s pres. ind. *makes war with* 36, 12. [Allied to Latin uincere *to conquer.*]

wiht fn. *anything, something* wiht ns. 29, 18

wiht f. *weight, weighing* wihte ds. 164, 61

Wihtland *the Isle of Wight* Wihtlande
ds. 111, 32
will n. *will, pleasure* wille ds. 165,
74
willa m. *will, pleasure, desire* willa
ns. 198, 1; 198, 3; 198, 8. mē is
willa *my desire is* 190, 129. willan
as. 145, 99; 163, 17; 164, 31; 164,
32
willan (anv.) *will, be willing, wish*
wille 1s pres. ind. 87, 35; wylle
185, 1. wile 3s pres. ind. 189, 107;
198, 9. wyllað pl. pres. ind. 98, 32;
wille 163, 12. nellað pl. pres. ind.
neg. 145, 58. wolde 3s pret. ind.
127, 74; 187, 34; 188, 41. woldon
pl. pret. ind. 86, 7; 111, 36; 111,
38; 165, 75; 188, 68; woldan 65,
10. noldon pl. pret. ind. neg. 76,
38; 86, 3. wille sg. pres. subj. 76,
21; 87, 24 (twice); 87, 41; 127, 76;
127, 86; 207, 14; 208, 72; 198, 4;
198, 6. nylle sg. pres. subj. neg.
198, 14. willan pl. pres. subj. 145,
58. wolde sg. pret. subj. 87, 40;
111, 14; 163, 24; 189, 113; 207,
28
wilnung f. *wish, desire* wilnunga ds.
86, 7
wīmman (from wīfman) m. *woman*
wīmman as. 164, 45
Winċeaster *Winchester* Winċeastre
ds. 164, 27
wind m. *wind* wind ns. 111, 17.
winde is. 209, 76
winedryhten m. *lord and patron* winedryhtnes gs. 208, 37
winelēas adj. *friendless, bereft of
friends* winelēas nsm. 29, 13; 29,
16; 208, 45
winemǣġ m. *beloved kinsman* winemǣga gp. 207, 7
wīneġeard m. *vineyard* wineġeardas
np. 44, 8
Winodland- same as *Weonodland*
wīnsæl n. *wine-hall* wīnsalo np. 209,
78

winter m. *winter, year* winter ns. 99,
57. wintres gs. 66, 21; 209, 103.
wintra ds. 66, 22. winter as. 66,
22; *for the winter* 111, 41; 111, 49.
wintra gp. 208, 65
winterċeariġ adj. *desolate as winter*
winterċeariġ nsm. 207, 24
wintertīd f. *winter-time* wintertīde
ds. 66, 17
wiot- see **wita, witan**
wiotudlīċe adv. *truly, certainly*
wirċean see **wyrċan**
wīs adj. *wise* wīs nsm. 163, 14; 208,
64. wīse apm. 87, 13. wīse ism.
209, 88
wīsdōm m. *learning, scholarship, wisdom* wīsdōm ns. 86, 7. wīsdōme
ds. 75, 9. wīsdōm as. 75, 12; 76,
23; 76, 35; 76, 38
wīse f. *way, manner* wīsan as. 126,
28. wīsan ap. 127, 64
Wīsle f. *the Vistula* Wīsle ns. 98, 10;
98, 12; 98, 15; 98, 16
Wīslemūða m. *the mouth of the Vistula*
Wīslemūða ns. 98, 18. Wīslemūð-
an as. 98, 10
wīslīċ adj. *wise* wīslīċ nsn. 65, 11
wisse see **witan**
wist f. *feast* wiste ds. 208, 36
wiston see **witan**
wita m. *councilor, wise man* wita ns.
65, 13; 208, 65. wiotan np. 75, 3.
wiotena gp. 86, 2. [Cf. OE witan
know.]
witan (PP) *know* witan inf. 126, 16;
127, 74 *to show;* 127, 82; 144, 29.
wāt 1s pres. ind. 65, 9; 207, 11; 3s
207, 29; 208, 37. witan pl. pres.
ind. 145, 86. nyste 3s pret. ind.
neg. 164, 47. wiston pl. pret. ind.
76, 32. wisse sg. pret. subj. *might
know* 207, 27. tō wiotonne gerund
87, 16; tō witanne 127, 77. [Cog.
with Lat. uidēre *to see*.]
wīte n. *punishment, injury, torment*
wīte ds. 188, 61. wītu np. 76, 24.
wīta gp. 189, 87

Wītland *the region east of the Vistula* Wītland ns. 98, 11; as. 98, 11

witodlīċe adv. *truly, certainly*

wið prep. *with, against* (with dat. and acc.) wið ðan ðe *with which* 198, 12

wiðcweðan (5) *to oppose* wiðcwæd-on pl. pret. ind. 163, 17

wiðlǣdan (I) *to take away* wiðlāēded pp. nsf. 199, 20

wiðmetenes f. *comparison* wiðmet-enesse ds. 65, 16. [Cf. OE metan *to measure.*]

wiðstondan (6) *to withstand* (with dat.) wiðstondan inf. 207, 15

wiðūtan prep. *without* (with dat.)

wlonc adj. *proud, arrogant, bold* wlonc nsf. 209, 80. wloncne asm. 36, 19

wōd see **wadan**

wōhdōm m. *unjust sentence* wōh-dōmas ap. 145, 80

wōhġestrēon n. *ill-gotten gains* wōh-ġestrēona gp. 145, 80

wolcen nm. *cloud* wolcna gp. 36, 5. wolcnum dp. 188, 55; ip. 188, 53. [Cf. Ger. die Wolke *cloud.*]

wold- see **willan**

wōma m. *tumult* wōma ns. 209, 103

womm m. *defilement, sin* wommum ip. 187, 14

won see **wann**

wong m. *plain, field* wongas np. 36, 24

word n. *word* wordes gs. *by word* 127, 61; 144, 31; myċeles wordes *a great reputation* 111, 15. worde ds. 87, 29; 189, 111. word as. 87, 29, ofer Dryhtnes word *contrary to the word of the Lord* 187, 35. wordum dp. 56, 30; 65, 13. word ap. 55, 18; 145, 94; 187, 27; 209, 91. wordum ip. 66, 26; 75, 1; 189, 97

worhtan see **wyrċan**

wōrian (II) *to wander, go astray* wō-riað pl. pres. ind. *crumble, fall into ruin* 209, 78

worn m. *a great number* worn as. 209, 91

worold see **woruld**

woroldscamu f. *public disgrace* wor-oldscame ds. 144, 19; 144, 22

worolstrūdere . m. *robber* worol-strūderas np. 145, 64

woruld f. *world* worold ns. 126, 1. worulde gs. 190, 133; 208, 74. worolde ds. 126, 2; 126, 5; 127, 64; 127, 66; 127, 67; 145, 99; worulde 76, 24. woruld as. 208, 58; weoruld 209, 107

woruldcund adj. *secular* woruldcund-ra gpm. 75, 4

woruldrīċe n. *kingdom of the world* woruldrīċe ds. 208, 65

woruldðing n. *worldly thing* woruld-ðinga gp. 76, 22

wræclāst m. *path of exile* wræclāst ns. 208, 32. wræclāstas ap. 207, 5

wrāð adj. *cruel, hostile* wrāðra gpf. 188, 51; gpn. 207, 7

wrītan (1) *to write* wrītan inf. *to be written* 198, 1. bī wrīte sg. pret. subj. *copy* 87, 42

wrīðan (1) *to bind, fetter* wrīð 3s pres. ind. 36, 14

wudu m. *wood, piece of wood* wudu ns. 187, 27. wudu as. 29, 2

wuldor n. *glory, splendor, honor* wul-dres gs. 36, 26; 187, 14; 189, 90; 189, 97; 190, 133. wuldre ds. 190, 135; 190, 143; 190, 155

Wuldorfæder m. *heavenly Father* Wuldorfæder gs. 56, 22; Uuldur-fader gs. 199, 34

wulf m. *wolf* wulf ns. 209, 82. wul-fas ap. 29, 16

wunden adj. *twisted* (pp. of windan *to wind*) wunden nsn. 208, 32

wundor n. *wonder, miracle* wundor ns. 144, 29. wundra gp. 56, 22; uundra 199, 34. wundrum dp.

used adverbially, '*wondrously*' 36, 10; 209, 98

wundrian (II) *to wonder at a thing* (with gen.) wundrade 1s pret. ind. 86, 1

wunian (II) *to dwell, remain, live* wunian inf. 29, 13; 190, 121; 190, 143. wuniaþ pl. pres. ind. 190, 135; wunedon pl. pret. ind. 163, 13; 187, 3 *were at rest,* or *occupied (their) beds;* 190, 155 *dwelled.* [Cf. OE wuna m. *habit, custom.*]

wurð see **weorð**

wurðful adj. *honorable, worshipful* wurðful nsm. 163, 25. wurðfulre comp. deg. nsm. 163, 14

wurðscipe see **weorðscipe**

wutan same as **utan**

wyduwe f. *widow* wydewan np. 126, 35

wyllað see **willan**

wylle see **willan**

wyllġespryng n. *spring* willġe-spryngum dp. 44, 10

wynn f. *joy* wyn ns. 208, 36. wyn-num dp. as adv. '*beautifully*' 187, 15. wynnum ip. 207, 29

wyrċan (I) *to make, work* wyrċan inf. 188, 65; wirċean 111, 15; lēt wyrċean *he caused to be built* 164, 56. wyrcð 3s pres. ind. 144, 18. wyrċað pl. pres. ind. 99, 54. worht-an pl. pret. ind. 144, 31; (wē) worhtan 127, 58; wrohton 111, 12. ġeweorht pp. nsm. 45, 14; ġeworhte np. 144, 41

wyrd f. *fate, chance, destiny* wyrd ns. 189, 74 *experience; fate* 207, 5; 209, 100. wyrde ds. 207, 15. wyrda np. 29, 18. wyrda gp. 188, 51 *ex-periences;* 209, 107 *fates.* [MnE weird; cf. OE weorþan *to be-come.*]

wyrdan (I) *to injure, damage* wyrd-an inf. 45, 15

wyrmlīca m. *serpentine form* wyrm-līcum ip. 209, 98

wryse adj. *worse* (comp. deg. of yfel) wyrsan apf. 145, 86

wyrse adv. *worse* (comp. deg. of yfele)

wyrsian (II) *to deteriorate, grow worse* wyrsedan pl. pret. ind. 126, 33

wyrð see **weorþan**

wyrðes see **weorðe**

Y

yfel adj. *evil, wicked* yfelan dsm. 144, 47; 144, 54. yfele apm. *evil things* 165, 81

yfel n. *evil, damage* yfel as. 111, 12; 111, 44; 126, 9; 164, 44

yfelian (II) *to grow worse* yfelian inf. 126, 4

yfelness f. *evilness, wickedness* yfel-nesse as. 165, 83

ylca see **ilca**

yldest adj. *oldest* (supl. deg. of eald) yldesta nsm. 163, 6

yldo f. *age, old age* yldo ns. 29, 18. ylde gs. 55, 2. yldo ds. 45, 17. [Cf. OE eald *old, aged.*]

yldra adj. *older* (comp. deg. of eald) yldra nsm. 45, 15

ymb(e) prep. *around, about* (with acc.) embe with þe 163, 14. ymbe bēon *to set about (a thing)* 111, 13

ymbclyppan (I) *to embrace* ymb-clyppte 3s pret. ind. 188, 42

yrhðu f. *slackness, cowardice* yrhðe as. 145, 81

Ȳrland n. *Ireland* Ȳrlande as. 164, 53

yrmð(u) f. *misery, crime* yrmð ns. 127, 83. yrmðe ds. 144, 19. yrmþe as. 127, 78. yrmða ap. 126, 14

yrnan (3) *to run* yrnende prp. nsm. 97, 3

yrre n. *anger, wrath* yrre ns. 128, 89; 144, 27. yrre as. 126, 43; 143, 1; 143, 8; 143, 12; 144, 19; 144, 20. [MnE ire.]

ȳþan (I) *to lay waste, destroy* ȳþde 3s pret. ind. 209, 85

Index

(*References are to page numbers.*)